PRESENCE-SOLIDARITY

*The Significance of Jesus Christ for India Today
in the Writings of Samuel Rayan SJ
and Elisabeth Schüssler Fiorenza*

PRESENCE-SOLIDARITY

*The Significance of Jesus Christ for India Today
in the Writings of Samuel Rayan SJ
and Elisabeth Schüssler Fiorenza*

Flossy Molly Lobo (Sr M Surekha BS)

Foreword by Prof. Dr Mohan Doss, SVD

2021

Presence-Solidarity: The Significance of Jesus Christ for India Today in the Writings of Samuel Rayan SJ and Elisabeth Schüssler Fiorenza - Published by the Indian Society for Promoting Christian Knowledge (ISPCK), Post Box 1585, Kashmere Gate, Delhi-110006.

Online order: http://ispck.org.in/book.php

Also available on amazon.in

ISBN: 978-93-90569-62-5

Cover Page: The imagery of ripples on the cover page illustrates an integral unity that does justice – justice to oneself, justice to others, especially to those on the periphery of society and to the environment. Ripples inherently generate and effect a kind of wholeness that in turn leads to harmony and hope – an integral wholeness.

Laser typeset by

ISPCK, Post Box 1585, 1654, Madarsa Road, Kashmere Gate, Delhi-110006 • *Tel:* 23866323

e-mail: ashish@ispck.org.in • ella@ispck.org.in
website: www.ispck.org.in

Dedicated to

The loving memory of my parents,

Late Mr Charles Lobo & Late Mrs Emmy Lobo

and their love and commitment to Jesus Christ

&

The Congregation of the Sisters of the Little Flower of Bethany (BS),
Mangalore

On the occasion of 100th anniversary of its Foundation

(1921-2021)

Contents

Dedication ... v
Acknowledgements ... xi
Foreword ... xv
Abbreviations ... xxi
Introduction ... xxv

Chapter 1
The Context of India Today: Challenges For The Church ... 1
Introduction ... 1
1. The Indian Contemporary Scenario ... 2
2. Identifying the Issues ... 9
3. The Church in the Contemporary India ... 32
4. Identifying the Concerns of Women in the Church ... 38
Conclusion ... 44
Endnotes ... 45

Chapter 2
Samuel Rayan's Interpretation of Jesus ... 65
Introduction ... 65
1. Biographical Sketch of Samuel Rayan ... 66
2. Theological Framework of Samuel Rayan ... 69
   2.1 Theological Method ... 70
   2.2 Reasons and Influences for the Choice of Method ... 77
   2.3 Need for a New and Appropriate Language ... 84
3. Rayan's Interpretation of God and Jesus Christ ... 92

3.1 The God of Samuel Rayan ... 92
3.2 The Jesus of Samuel Rayan ... 94
4. Implications of Rayan's Christology ... 106
Conclusion ... 109
Endnotes ... 110

Chapter 3
Elisabeth Schüssler Fiorenza's Interpretation of Jesus ... 124
Introduction ... 124
1. Biographical Sketch of Schüssler Fiorenza ... 125
2. The Theological Framework of Fiorenza ... 128
2.1 Theological Method ... 130
2.2 Reasons and Influences for the Choice of Method ... 136
2.3 Need for a New and Appropriate Language ... 144
3. Fiorenza's Interpretation of God in Jesus Christ ... 151
3.1 The Jesus of Fiorenza ... 152
4. Implications of Fiorenza's Christology ... 163
Conclusion ... 164
Endnotes ... 166

Chapter 4
Horizons for an Emerging Christology: Convergences, Divergences and Synthesis ... 186
Introduction ... 186
1. Basic Theological Elements of Convergence and Divergence ... 186
2. Converging Themes in Relation to the Theological Vision ... 188
2.1 Socio-Political Oppressive Ptriarchal System ... 189
2.2 Religio-Theological Influence ... 191
2.3 Praxis of Solidarity and Identification ... 194
2.4 Inadequacy of the Hermeneutics of the Bible ... 198
2.5 All-inclusive Integral Approach ... 200
3. Diverging Themes in Relation to the Theological Vision ... 203
The Conversation Partner ... 203
Jesus' Death on the Cross ... 205
The Resurrection ... 208

4. A Critical Appraisal of Rayan and Fiorenza's Theological
   Avenues   ... 210
   Complementary Horizons   ... 211
   Differing Perspectives   ... 213
   Christological Unity   ... 215
5. Critique of Fiorenza's Christology   ... 217
   Theology of the Cross   ... 217
   Empty Tomb   ... 220
   Wisdom's Messenger   ... 222
   Christian Women around Jesus   ... 222
6. An Emerging Christology for 21st Century India   ... 224
   6.1 Key Questions   ... 226
   6.2 A Christology of Presence-Solidarity   ... 228
       Jesus: The Love Incarnate   ... 230
       Jesus: The Supreme Symbol of the Spirit   ... 231
       Jesus: The Inclusive House   ... 233
       Jesus: The Initiator of a New Social Order   ... 234
       Jesus: The Epitome of Freedom   ... 235
       Jesus: The Very Presence of God   ... 238
       Jesus: The Self-emptying of God   ... 239
       Jesus: The Power of Empowerment   ... 241
       Jesus: The Presence-Solidarity with Us   ... 242
Conclusion   ... 245
Endnotes   ... 247

Chapter 5
Presence-Solidarity: A Paradigm for a *Kenotic* Mission   ... 258
Introduction   ... 258
1. The Vocation of the Church   ... 259
       1.1 *Imago Dei* Based Approach   ... 259
       1.2 Preferential Option for the Poor   ... 260
       1.3 A Church of the Poor   ... 262
       1.4 Dignity of Labour and of the Labourer   ... 264
       1.5 Inclusive Approach to Humanity   ... 265

1.6 Communion of Communities ... 266
1.7 Gender Sensitive Approach ... 267
2. Presence-Solidarity as a Paradigm for Mission Today ... 269
2.1 Review of Today's Key Challenges ... 269
2.2 Presence–Solidarity ... 271
2.3 Partners of Mission Today ... 272
3. The Implications of the Presence–Solidarity for Mission Today ... 274
3.1 Presence-Solidarity that Responds to Intra-Church Concerns ... 275
Partnership – A Challenge to Clericalism ... 275
Engendering Emancipation of Women ... 280
Renewed Passion for Missionary Outreach ... 283
3.2 Presence-Solidarity that Renews a Mission to Indian Society ... 286
Church that Walks on the Periphery ... 286
A Liberative Leadership ... 290
Participative Presence-Solidarity ... 291
Conversion of Minds for a Societal Transformation ... 294
3.3 Presence-Solidarity that Renews a Multi-Religio-Cultural Society ... 295
Integral Unity in Diversity ... 296
Mediating God-Consciousness ... 298
Presence-Solidarity as *Shalom* ... 300
Conclusion ... 303
Endnotes ... 305
Conclusion ... 315
Glossary ... 327
Bibliography ... 330

Acknowledgements

It gives me immense pleasure to express my deep, heartfelt gratitude, to those persons who have contributed their share in the completion of my doctoral dissertation. I am indebted to many people who envisioned my journey, prepared the way and accompanied me all along with support and provisions. My journey was beset with numerous blessings. I am happy to mention their names, though the list ever remains incomplete.

First and foremost I thank God for every blessing I have received and for accompanying me all through my life. I gratefully acknowledge God's intervention in and through the experiences and persons I encountered during the course of my studies at the portals of *Jnana-Deepa Vidyapeeth* (JDV), Pune. The study has certainly enriched my insights, strengthened my convictions, challenged my commitment, and most importantly, deepened my faith.

In a very special way I would like to thank Sr M Wilberta BS my former Superior General and her Councillors and Sr M Rose Celine BS the present Superior General, Sr M Lillis BS the Assistant Superior General and her General Councillors (Sr M. Shanti Priya BS, Sr M Mariette BS and Sr M Lilitta BS), Sr M Joy Monteiro BS the former Provincial Superior of North east Province and her Councillors, Sr M Lucious BS the present Provincial Superior of Bethany Silchar Province and her Councillors and every Sister of the Congregation of the Sisters of the Little Flower of Bethany, Mangalore, for their blessings in my endeavours. I sincerely thank

Sr Rose Celine BS, the Superior General and Sr Joy BS, the Former Provincial of North East Province for providing me with an opportunity to study at the portals of Jnana Deepa Vidyapeeth (JDV), Pune. I remain ever grateful to them for the privilege given to me to spend some time exclusively for research and study on the significance of Jesus for India today. My research has been an additional blessing to my personal experience of God in Jesus.

My heartfelt thanks to my research guide Prof. Dr Mohan Doss SVD, who accepted my request to be my guide and gave me his scholarly direction, valuable suggestions and his eye for every detail. The respect and understanding with which he accompanied me provided me with a lot of freedom and motivation to complete this serious work. His humble and serene personality coupled with his academic excellence has been truly a role model for me. I truly appreciate the trust and confidence with which he allowed me to progress in my work.

My deepest thanks go to Prof. Dr Mohan Doss SVD and Prof. Dr Konrad Noronha SJ who have read through the entire draft of this dissertation, correcting and editing and bringing the same to the final shape.

I am sincerely grateful to JDV Pontifical Athenaeum of Philosophy and Religion, former Provincial of South Asia (POSA) Prof. Dr George Pattery SJ and the former President of JDV, Prof. Dr Selva Rathinam SJ, for having played a vital role during my stay in JDV. I express my deepest thanks to the professors at the Institute for sharing their spiritual wealth especially through the orientation programme and thus enhancing my intellectual formation. I thank the Deans of Theology, the Registrars, the Chairpersons of Doctoral Committee, and the Doctoral Committee members present and past – Dr Thomas Kuriacose SJ, Prof. Dr Mohan Doss SVD, Fr Vincent Crasta SJ and Prof. Dr Jose Thayil SJ who played their significant part in seeing me through this phase of my life and work. A special thanks to Prof. Dr Francis Gonsalves SJ, the former Dean of Theology, Dr M. Paul Raj, the Chairperson of

Doctoral Committee and the members of the Doctoral Committee for their guidance and encouragement. A special thanks to to Dr Konrad Noronha SJ, the Director MPM, Prof. Dr Jose Thayil SJ the Registrar, Fr Biju Vadakkumchery, SJ, the Librarian, and the library staff for their generous services. Besides JDV library, I am also indebted to other libraries like Ishvani Kendra, Pune, Dharmaram College, Bangalore, Vidyajyoti College, Delhi and United Theological College, Bangalore and Mangalore respectively. The JDV staff (teaching and non-teaching) and student companions have been so good to me all through my stay and work in JDV.

I am indeed grateful to Fr Richard Sequeira SJ, for painstakingly going through the script and doing the proof reading of the text since the inception of my doctoral studies. I remain grateful to Late Prof. Dr Kurien Kunnumpuram SJ, Dr Joseph Lobo SJ, Dr Joseph Martis, Dr Joseph Xavier SJ, Prof. Dr Scaria Kuthirakkattel SVD, Prof. Dr Gertraud Ladner, Dr Joe Arun SJ, Dr Dinesh Braganza SJ, Dr Arjen Tete SJ, Fr Naveen Rebello SVD, Fr Jeyaraj Vellusamy SJ, Dr Sashikala Gurpur, Dr Dona Sanctis BS, Sr Kasper OSM, Fr B.L. Matthai, Dr Edward Frank, Fr Kevin Ward and Fr Derek Coutinho for their valuable and timely help and guidance. Thanks to Fr Raju Felix Crasta, Joby Joseph OP, and Fr Sijo for their technical help in setting the pages. I thank Late Prof. Dr Kurien Kunnumpuram SJ and Fr Vincent Crasta SJ for their spiritual guidance during my stay in JDV, Pune. I am indeed grateful to *Jesuit Source* for funding my studies partially.

I am indeed indebted to Fr Edward Mudavassery SJ, The Rector of De Nobili College, Pune and Prof. Dr George Pattery SJ, The then POSA, for providing me with accommodation during my three year stay at the PG Block Community. I thank Dr Francis Ezhakunnel SJ, Fr Vincent Crasta SJ the then moderators of PG Block, and Fr Alex G. SJ the Administrator and the entire PG Block Community for their scholarly sharing, and companionship. It was Prof. Dr Jose Thayil SJ, who continued to sustain that cordial relationship when I was appointed as the moderator of *Centre for Women Studies* (CWS) at a later stage.

I place on record my deep appreciation and gratitude for the daring step taken to have a *Centre for Women Studies* in the Campus. Indeed, the first of this kind in the history of Jnana-Deepa Vidyapeeth. *Kudos* to JDV administration!

I gratefully remember and thank my family. My parents late Mr Charles and Mrs Emmy Lobo, my loving sister and brothers Ida, James and Roody, brother-in-law Vincent Lasrado, sisters-in-law Della and Savita, uncle Felix Lobo and my loving nephews and nieces: Vikas, Vilas, Jeshal, Jencil and Reuelle for their love and encouragement. A special thanks to my cousin Dr Jerome Stanislaus D'Souza SJ, Provincial of South Asia (POSA) and the former Provincial of Karnataka Province, for his constant support and timely response to all my cares and concerns. Thanks to all my friends in Pune and elsewhere who have been a source of joy and support to me in varied ways. I thank them for their share of contribution in providing me with study materials, and good wishes. May every gesture of love be abundantly blessed by God in Jesus who, ever continues to challenge us to a Radical commitment to God's people.

Foreword

Jesus' life on this earth was short. His public life was very brief. The geographical area of his activities was limited. He died very young. But his impact was immense and incredible. The impact of Jesus on his disciples with whom he walked and worked, taught in words and deeds, for whom he cared for and with whom he shared his life and love was a life-defining experience for them. He touched the core of their lives and he became the very defining point of their identity. Jesus' disciples were greatly influenced by his personal and incredible concern for the poor and needy, by his indomitable courage to stand for the dignity of people, by the authoritative style of his teaching, his power over the forces of evil spirits and nature, by his unbelievable intimacy with God, whom he called *Abba* and the incomprehensible way he surrendered his life.

Jesus' disciples were christified by their Master's life, death, and resurrection. They were left with no choice but follow the Christopraxis, the way of their Master and Lord. In their life of Christopraxis, they imbibed the spirit of their Master, the Incarnate-Word, who became human to share His Father's love with all. They realized that they need to communicate the Good news with others in the manner others would understand; speak about their Master, Jesus Christ, and interpret his significance to humanity in the language of the people with whom they wanted to share the gift that they were privileged to receive in God's plan. They also realized that like their Master, they needed the presence and power of the Spirit to carry on their life of love and service to others. In the process of following their Lord, they became Christophanies to others.

Jesus' disciples shared with others what they had seen with their eyes, heard with their ears, and touched with their hands. They believed that they were called to be witnesses to the revelation of life in Jesus, the word of life. They lived for him and shared his life with others. The articulation of their faith experience of Christ, the New Testament, is the work of the Spirit, who led them into the very Christ-Event and enabled them to proclaim the revelation of God's presence and love in Jesus. Their articulation of the Christ-Event responded to the needs of the believing community, and following the principle of incarnation, wrapped the core message of salvation in the culture and language of the given time. Their experience of Jesus' life and ministry narrated in the New Testament continues to inspire people down the centuries.

Needless to mention that much has been written on Christology for India in recent times, that it is simply impossible to summarize all in a preface and do it justice. The pages of this book will survey and engage in highlighting key Christological contributions of two theologians of our time, who come from different contexts: Samuel Rayan, an Indian Jesuit liberation theologian, and Elisabeth Schüssler Fiorenza, a biblical, feminist, and Western theologian. This work has been stimulated by a deeper conviction of the author that these two theologians have made significant contributions towards understanding the person and message of Jesus Christ for the India of today. It seeks not only to engage with the Christological scholarship of these two theologians, but also to portray a convincing portrait of Jesus based on their scholarship and in response to the contextual concerns and issues of the contemporary Indian situation.

One of the factors that brings these two theologians—Samuel Rayan and Elisabeth Schüssler Fiorenza—together, despite their cultural and contextual variations, is their understanding of the faith. Their interpretation of Jesus underscores the deeper sense of what

Pope Francis in his Encyclical, *Lumen Fidei: The Light of Faith* (2013) emphasizes on faith. "Faith does not merely gaze at Jesus but sees things as Jesus himself sees them, […] it is a participation in his way of seeing" (#18). Responding to the revelation in Jesus is accepting the amazing love of God manifested in and through Jesus, and sharing in his way of seeing things, persons, and events and thus become a new creation. Consequently, these two—Rayan and Fiorenza—theologians' interpretation of Jesus emphasizes solidarity with the last, least, and the lost of society, with those who are on the margins and considered as disposables by the power structures of our contemporary times. They strongly believe that the economically and socially poor, the victims of exploitative structures—political, social, and religious— are the privileged locus of God's encounter today. They advocate more participatory structures in society and the Church. This springs from their respect for the inalienable value of the dignity of the human person and their passion for Jesus' all-inclusive vision and his prophetic spirit.

The author of this work, Sr Surekha, admires the Jesus of Rayan, who is the compassionate love of the Father, the high-point of God's self-manifestation, the unique symbol of the Spirit and God's very presence and solidarity with humanity. She affirms Fiorenza's emphasis on the *basileia* vision of Jesus, and her clarion call for an all-inclusive approach that incorporates inclusiveness, participation, wholeness, and well-being. However, the author's appreciation of Fiorenza's creative and provocative approaches is also punctuated with pertinent critical notes. The author unearths from the writings of Rayan and Fiorenza an apt paradigm for a kenotic mission in the twenty-first-century of India by bringing together their Christologies. She sketches a Christology of Presence-Solidarity for India of today. The hyphenated phrase "Presence-Solidarity" is taken from the writings of Rayan and is brought to focus in this volume. She argues further that this foundational perspective in interpreting Jesus aptly includes the Christological thrust of Fiorenza also. The author presents the Christology of Presence-Solidarity as praxis and a pathway and rightly acknowledges that the Church in her teachings and life has continually witnessed to the Lord who emptied himself totally to be one with humanity. However, the author candidly admits that "much remains to be done" (*Centesimus Annus* #58) to affirm the equality of all and the full discipleship of women, particularly in the context of contemporary India.

In a research project like the present one, an individual scholar interacts with the scholarly community through the literature that has been published already, trying to see a little further standing on the shoulders of significant theologians of stature and depth. Every research scholar seeks to throw light on an area that has gone greatly unnoticed till now or break new ground or come up with new ideas and interpretations or read the literature anew to make a renewed emphasis on an area of contextual significance. On this score, the present volume provides an insightful reading of the two theologians' writings understudy and offers the possibility of application in relevant areas.

On the pages that follow one finds the first-ever academic attempt to compare the two theologians Samuel Rayan S.J., and Elisabeth Schüssler Fiorenza who belong to different streams of theology (Systematic and Scriptural), different contexts (Eastern and Western), have differing perspectives but emphasize subaltern perspectives (an Indian liberation theological thrust and a Western Feminist biblical thrust). Sr Surekha, the author of this book has unearthed from the writings of Rayan and Fiorenza an apt paradigm for a kenotic mission in 21st century India, i.e., 'Presence-Solidarity Christology' by bringing together their Christologies. Indeed, it is a commendable accomplishment in exploring their original writings as well as the secondary sources.

The present work reaffirms the necessity of an on-going dialogue between the context and text. The context of the present work is the contemporary Indian context and the text is the Christological reflections of Rayan and Fiorenza. The assumption of the author, namely, contextual theologies must engage in a constructive dialogue to overcome their limited perspectives and be open to being confronted and complemented by each other, becomes illustrative in the pages that follow. One will certainly find an on-going dialogue between two contextual Christologies and how each perspective enriches the other and offers insights and challenges calling the followers of Jesus to follow the footprints of their Lord and Liberator.

The first chapter makes nearly a comprehensive presentation of the contemporary context of India in the pre-coronavirus pandemic and highlights most issues that need a response from faith communities, especially from the Church in India today. The issues include poverty, inequality, discrimination, and fundamentalism in the society, and the concerns of women – patriarchal ideology, domination, and subordination – in the Church. The presentation of Christology of Rayan and Fiorenza in Chapters 2 and 3 respectively is well organized and gives a clear understanding of their respective views to readers. In chapter four, the researcher has made a commendable effort in bringing the two theologians together, to see the convergences and divergences. In particular, this chapter deserves much appreciation, as it demonstrates the author's original work and as well the immense efforts that have gone into it. The final chapter presents the implications of the dialogue between the context of India and the Christological reflections of the two theologians for whom Jesus is the liberator, the empowering person, the protester against all oppressive structures – the resurrection of Jesus is, among other significance, the loudest protest of God against all exploitations –, and God's presence-solidarity with humanity.

In the final chapter, the author spells out various dimensions of the kenotic mission of the Church in India today. She advocates the need for partnership in the place of clericalism in the Church; emancipation of women, and calls for a renewed passion to re-orient the mission of the Church according to the vision of Vatican II. Further, inspired by the example of Pope Francis, she pleads the Church to walk with the oppressed, empower women to mould the Church as a participative community, and longs for a liberative model of leadership that would guide towards the conversion of minds for a societal transformation. The author acknowledges that the multi-religio-cultural society of India is an opportunity and a challenge for the Church. It is an opportunity to collaborate with the people of other religions, to discern the movements of the Spirit together with them and face the challenges of building a humane, harmonious, and peaceful society. The Church is a fellow pilgrim with other religions journeying towards the Ultimate destiny. In this common pilgrimage that is led by the Spirit, the author hopes, every pilgrim community can become aware of the Ultimate source of life, experience integral unity in diversity, social and cosmic harmony, communion and fellowship leading to an intercultural society where every religion is recognized, respected, and accepted in love and service.

Sr Surekha, the author of the book, has illustrated her arguments with the documents of the Church and the insightful and praxis-oriented teachings of Pope Francis. She has succeeded, based on the insights and challenges gleaned from the writings of Rayan and Fiorenza, in presenting to the readers a renewed mission of the Church in India today. The author gives a clarion call to the leaders of the Church today, particularly in India, to take seriously the dialogical and participative approaches God used to bring about human collaboration in accomplishing His project of liberation and salvation, and to work together collaboratively with people of all faiths and ideologies, to provide grounds for hope and new life to people who experience injustice, poverty, violence, and all forms of oppression. This book illustrates the conviction of the author that all are called to reciprocity and mutuality, and to work together as partners in the project of the reign of God amidst us today.

Prof. Dr Mohan Doss, SVD
Faculty of Theology
Jnana-Deepa Vidyapeeth
Pune 411014.

Abbreviations

SCRIPTURE
NRSV New Revised Standard Version

CHURCH DOCUMENTS

CA	*Centesimus Annus*
	Encyclical commemorating the hundredth year of *Rerum Novarum*.
CCC	Catechism of the Catholic Church
CL	*Christifideles Laici*
	Post-Synodal Apostolic Exhortation on the Vocation and Mission of the Laity in the Church and in the world.
CSDC	The Compendium of the Social Doctrine of the Church
EA	*Ecclesia in Asia*
	Post-Synodal Apostolic Exhortation on Mission in Asia
EG	*Evangelii Gaudium*
	Apostolic Exhortation on the Joy of the Gospel.
GS	*Gaudium et Spes*
	Pastoral Constitution of the Church in the Modern World – Vatican II
LG	*Lumen Gentium*
	Dogmatic Constitution on the Church – Vatican II
NA	*Nostra Aetate*
	Declaration on the Relationship of the Church to Non-

	Christian Religions – Vatican II
MM	*Mater et Magistra*
	Encyclical on the Role of the Church as Mother and Teacher.
PP	*Populorum Progressio.*
	Encyclical on the Development of Peoples.
PT	*Pacem in Terris.*
	Encyclical on Establishing Universal Peace on Earth.
QA	*Quadragesimo Anno.*
	Encyclical on the 40th year of *Rerum Novarum.*
RH	*Redemptor Hominis.*
	Encyclical on the Human Person and Christ's Redemption.
RM	*Redemptoris Missio*
	Encyclical on the Church's Missionary Mandate.
RN	*Rerum Novarum*
	Encyclical on the Rights and Duties of Capital and Labour.
SRS	*Sollicitudo Rei Socialis*
	Encyclical on the Twentieth Anniversary of *Populorum Progressio.*
TMA	*Tertio Millennio Adveniente*
	Apostolic Letter for the Church's Preparation for the Jubilee Year 2000.
TMI	*Tertio Millennio Ineunte*
	Apostolic Letter with a Pastoral Plan for the Church in the New Millennium.
UR	*Unitatis Redintegratio*
	Decree on Ecumenism – Vatican II

OTHER ABBREVIATIONS

AJT	Asian Journal of Theology
AMRAT	Asian Movement of Women Religious against Trafficking
ATC	Asian Trading Corporation
BB	Bible Bhashyam
BLS	Bureau of Labour Statistics
CACT	Campaign against Child Trafficking
CBCI	Catholic Bishops' Conference of India
CLTS	Community-Led Total Sanitation

CM	Clergy Monthly
CONCIL	Concilium
CTQ	Concordia Theological Quarterly
EPW	Economic and Political Weekly
ETL	Ephemerides Theologicae Lovanienses: Louvain Journal of Theology and Canon Law.
EWA	Ecclesia of Women of Asia
FABC	Federation of Asian Bishops' Conferences
GDP	Gross Domestic Product
GLTCRI	Gurukul Lutheran Theological College and Research Institute
HORIZO	Horizons
IDS	Institute of Development Studies
IJCS	Indian Journal of Christian Studies
IOS	Institute of Objective Studies
IRM	International Review of Mission
ITA	Indian Theological Association
IWIT	Indian Women in Theology
IWTF	Indian Women Theologians' Forum
JARS	Journal of the Adventist Theological Society
JATS	Journal Article Tag Suite
JCSA	Jesuit Conference of South Asia
JD	Jeevadhara: A Journal of Christian Interpretation
JDV	Jnana-Deepa Vidyapeeth, Pune
JIT	Journal of Indian Theology
JOSR	Journal of Research & Method in Education
JPJRS	Jnanadeepa: Pune Journal of Religious Studies
KCBC	Kerala Catholic Bishops' Council
MDI	Multi-Dimensional Poverty Index
NCCI	National Council of Churches in India
NCDC	National Council of Dalit Christians
NCRB	National Crime Records Bureau
PPP	Purchasing Power Parity
PTI	Press Trust of India
RV	Radio Vatican
SCM	Student Christian Movement

SMBS	Syro-Malabar Bishops' Synod
SPCK	Society for Promoting Christian Knowledge
TMILL	Third Millennium
UNDP	United Nations Development Programme
UNFPA	United Nations Population Fund (formerly the United Nations Fund for Population Activities)
VJTR	Vidyajyoti Journal of Theological Reflections
WCC	World Council of Churches
WDI	World Development Indicators
WTF	Women Theologians Forum
WW	Word and Worship

Introduction

Walking the walk of the periphery with the people of the periphery and go beyond the comfort zone and embrace the periphery are some of the catchy phrases used in the twenty-first century to create an alert for the Church to move from inward looking to outward looking. Since the beginning of his papacy in 2013, Pope Francis has used the concept of periphery as a metaphor of social marginality.[1]

The Church's immense contribution envisions God's presence in Jesus for the vulnerable and in the pursuit of human solidarity. There still exists in the Church[2] and in India widening inequalities between men and women and within the different subgroups of caste, creed, colour, and gender.[3] The darker side of the Indian reality makes one reflect deeper on the various manifestations of similar realities in our time. The leaders of the Church in India today need to take seriously the dialogical and participative methods God used in dealing with humanity in His project of liberation and salvation as exemplified in the relationship that grew between God and Jesus.

As a member of a religious Congregation whose charism is deeply incarnational, rooted in the humanity of Jesus, this seems so obvious to me, that there is nothing more important than venturing into a deeper understanding of Jesus Christ and the compelling significance of his message for the 21st century India. In the ultimate analysis the option one makes for the periphery must always integrate the reign of God values into one's strategies and struggles for the liberation of the oppressed. The book is significant because in one's option for the periphery one encounters God in Jesus. This God experience moves one towards empowering the powerless which is meant to make for an equitable distribution of power in our society. Therefore, this book begins by analysing the context of India today.[4]

Presence-Solidarity is a REWORK of my doctoral thesis now published as a book. It envisions a renewed understanding of Jesus' *Presence-Solidarity* which is not limited to Christianity but goes beyond the boundaries of caste creed and gender. Jesus' *Presence-Solidarity* is an assurance of God's dynamic presence, which involves active solidarity - *Immanuel* or God-with-us. The conclusion gives a summary of the book and the contextual concerns in the light of the deliberations in the chapters. Reflecting again on the *kenotic* dynamics already considered in the book, the last section would be a fruit-gathering of the attempt done on the theme along with some challenges for the immediate action: One of the most essential steps for a *kenotic* mission is the need for a renewed understanding of the nature and mission of the Church in India today. Keeping this in mind, this book basing itself on the writings of Samuel Rayan SJ, an Indian theologian, and Elisabeth Schüssler Fiorenza, a biblical, feminist and Western theologian, attempts to unearth their Christological legacy for India today.

This present book acknowledges that the valuable contribution made by Rayan especially his theological framework revolves around human dignity and equality. Fiorenza has been instrumental in the development of the field of reformist feminist theology. It is also of the view that though the scholarly attempts referred above focuses on Fiorenza's views concerning structures of oppression and hermeneutical methods, they do not adequately reflect her emphasis on the *basileia* vision of Jesus. This book chips in that dimension to highlight Fiorenza's theological perspective of an egalitarian vision of the Church that affirms the equality of all baptized based on her understanding of Jesus from the situations of domination and oppression. The focus of this study will be to explore and undertake the significance of Rayan's interpretation of Jesus as "the *presence-solidarity*",[5] and argue that Fiorenza's Christological interpretation also finds a symphony along with Rayan's passion for liberation, although from a different cultural context..

Although Rayan and Fiorenza hail from different milieus, they bring in deep Christological insights into significance to human life as a whole. The commonality of their foundational emphasis on the dignity of human person, coupled with the all-inclusive vision they hold provides a relevant understanding of Jesus Christ as "the presence-solidarity" for India today. The prophetic spirit of these two eminent theologians could help us imagine and realize a societal transformation. A critical collaboration and coordination of the two minds – Rayan and Fiorenza – has much to offer to the 21st century society and the Church in India. Living as we are in the second decade of the third Millenium, the need to search for alternative articulations of Christology is an urgent one.

The book is coloured by the experiences of oppression and poverty, especially of those on the edges of society of their respective contexts. Hence, we intend to investigate the Christological writings of Rayan in relationship to the Mission of the Church within the socio-economic and religio-cultural diversity of the 21st century India today. However, the focus of the book will be on Jesus the *Presence-Solidarity*, a relevant Christology that emerges primarily from the theological pursuits of Rayan and Fiorenza. The book begins with an introduction basically examines as to what this book is attempting to convey and why I have chosen this particular topic.

The **First Chapter** presents the setting of the theological investigation of our research concern in the context of the socio-economic and cultural diversity in India. Within this context, we look from the view point of the marginalized, namely the dehumanizing issues. Hence, this chapter has twofold objectives. First is to present the context of India today followed by a critical analysis of the socio-economic and cultural factors as well as an analysis of the issues that disfigure human beings on the periphery of society. The second objective is to identify the Church's fundamental challenges in relation to Christian women in India.

The Second and the Third Chapters are an elaborate research into the contextual theological-liberationist methods within the confluence of ecclesiology and Christology in particular. While differing in focus and context for whom they are promoting, these theologians' interpretation of Jesus share in common an emphasis on solidarity with the marginalized and the dehumanized; a preferential option for the poor and the marginalized; and an advocacy toward more participatory structures in society and the Church. Accordingly an attempt is made to reflect on how, although belonging to different milieus, Rayan and Fiorenza brought in aspects of their theological method and factors that have influenced their theological horizon that would contribute to the development of their Christological reflections.

The Fourth Chapter makes a comparative study of Rayan and Fiorenza approaches and Christological thrusts to set the way towards the final chapter. The chapter concentrates on the areas of convergence and divergence of their theological horizons leading to sketch out a Christology that emerges primarily from their theological pursuits, a Christology of *Presence-Solidarity* for today's milieu.

The Fifth Chapter focuses on the correlation between the Christology of *Presence-Solidarity* and the polarized Indian society of today. This chapter reflects on how Jesus' *Presence-Solidarity* is carried forward by the Church. The effort here is to enhance, adhere and deepen insights into the rich heritage of the Church's teachings founded on the Gospel values. This chapter is a lively interaction between the findings of chapters one and four to seek a relevant paradigm shift in the way we understand Jesus with reference to the 21st century Indian context.

This book enables us Christians, engaged in mission and proclamation especially in India, to understand better both in theory and practice the relevance of Jesus Christ, in keeping with the spirit of Vatican II and of Pope Francis in particular. A Christology that emerges from the encounter with reality resists death dealing forces. That is to say, it would bring about new life and hope to people who experience injustice, poverty, violence and all forms of oppression.

Finally, this book draws insights and inspiration for praxis from the works of the two theologians – liberationist and feminist – of our own times. There has to be bold statements made at the level of theological parlance in the context of a growing sense of insecurity the Church of today feels while facing the multi-faceted challenges. This book proposes also to read the Scriptures in the light of people's struggles and problems and this text-context dialogical dynamic will enable and enhance the liberative praxis that the two theologians finally aim at.

Endnotes

[1] Pasquale Ferrara, "The Concept of Periphery in Pope Francis' Discourse: A Religious Alternative to Globalization?" *Academic Journal* 6/1 (March 2015): 42.

[2] The term 'Church' refers to the Catholic Church.

[3] George M. Soares-Prabhu aptly summarizes the Indian context, as a "cry-for-life" situation. Such a "cry" has three dimensions: "The cry for survival," which arises from the massive economic deprivation, "the cry for dignity and affirmation," which is the result of caste and sexist discrimination, and "the cry for meaning," which represents the religious quest of the Indian people. George M. Soares-Prabhu, "The *Jesus of Faith*: A Christological Contribution to an Ecumenical Third World Spirituality," in *Collected Writings of George M. Soares-Prabhu: Theology of Liberation: An Indian Biblical Perspective, vol. IV*, ed. Francis X. D'Sa (Pune: Jnana-Deepa Vidyapeeth, 2001), 276.

[4] In this thesis, by the word "today" we mean 21st century which is marked by polarizations that will be dealt with in chapter one.

[5] Samuel Rayan, "With Us-With Whom?-Is God?" In *The Dharma of Jesus, Interdisciplinary Essays in Memory of George M. Soares-Prabhu*, ed. Francis X D'Sa (Pune: Institute for the Study of Religion, Anand: Gujarat Sahitya Prakash, 1997), 37-83.

Chapter 1

The Context of India Today: Challenges For The Church

Introduction

This chapter offers the backdrop to the theological investigation in the context of the socio-economic and religio-cultural diversity in India. Within this context, this chapter looks from the view point of the marginalized, namely the dehumanizing issues. Hence the objectives of this chapter are twofold: first, to situate the context of India today followed by a critical analysis of the socio-economic and religio-cultural factors as well as an analysis of the issues that disturb the very core of human existence; second, to situate the Church in India in relation to women.

The first part of this chapter takes up the analysis of the socio-economic and cultural context of the present day India with particular reference to the issues related to globalization. The multi-religious and multi-socio-cultural Indian context is analyzed under four aspects: i) growing economic might, ii) political influence, iii) social dynamics, and iv) religio-cultural diversity. This is followed by a brief look into the fundamental concerns related to equality and dignity of the human person. These concerns are identified in four broad categories: i) Increase in poverty amidst plenty, ii) disparity despite unity, iii) discrimination despite gender[1] equity, and iv) religious fundamentalism despite pluralism. In this section, the analysis is limited to the perspective of those who are on the periphery.

The second part of this chapter provides an overview of the Church in India with an emphasis on women in the Church. Though science and technology have made rapid progress and life at large has become easier and more comfortable, women still continue to be the victims of discrimination in all spheres of life. Hence the Indian Christian women become the protagonist of this part of the chapter. Accordingly, the socio-political-historical context of the contemporary Church is analyzed from a feminist perspective. The identified concerns related to women in the Church are grouped under three significant factors: i) patriarchal ideology despite gender sensitivity ii) domination iii) submission. The final chapter of this analyses each of these issues in the light of the Christological insights of two contemporary theologians: Samuel Rayan and Elisabeth Schüssler Fiorenza. Through the analysis of the present day Indian context and its impact on the marginalized in the Church as well as society, this study will present the contemporary context of India with its dehumanizing structures[2] with a view to find a response from the Church in India today.

1. The Indian Contemporary Scenario

With growing economic might, new political influence, and changing social dynamics, India has emerged as a major world power in the twenty-first century.[3] India has come a long way since its independence 70 years ago. Since independence in 1947, India has made enormous strides towards the progress of the nation. From a population of 360 million in 1951, "India's 2019 population is estimated at 1.37 billion based on the most recent UN data. India is the world's 7th largest country by area and the 2nd most populous country with more than 1.3 billion residents."[4] The economy of the United States is the largest in the world. At $18 trillion, it represents a quarter share of the global economy (24.3%), according to the latest World Bank figures. India is in the seventh place with $2 trillion, and Italy in the eighth with an economy of over $1.8 trillion.[5]

> It [India] is the second largest reservoir of scientific and technical human power, has the third largest army, is the sixth member of the nuclear club, the sixth member in the race for space, and the tenth largest industrial power. From being a net food grains importing country, India is now a leading exporter of food commodities. The journey so far has been eventful, sometimes painful, but most of the times, exhilarating.[6]

India is certainly an emerging superpower and has a huge potential for growth. Today we are at the crossroads and our nation is very much influenced by globalization. Globalization in contemporary times has drawn our attention primarily because of the exceptional and stupendous pace involving and affecting humanity. By keeping pace with it, India has got a global recognition and has become a major economic and political super power. It has integrated people, markets and work, and the digital revolution has changed human lives obviously. Globalization refers to the world being experienced as a "global village."[7] Increased trade, new technologies, foreign investments, expanding media and Internet connections are fuelling economic growth and human advancement. It is one of such phenomena which is opening many opportunities for millions of people around the world.

Nonetheless, it is important to note that globalization has led to a further development called "a universal homogenous culture of consumerism and love for money." What is being propagated is: "a materialistic outlook on life and reality, a spirit of individualism and competition, an attitude of consumerism."[8] However, the truth is most often the reverse. The problem with globalization is a hierarchy of supremacy.[9] Terms of functioning are dictated by those who have the technical advantage. The 2016 Human Development Report of the United Nations highlights the staggering fact of how globalization has failed to address poverty. It brings to the fore not the concern of poverty alone but the multidimensionality[10] linked with the plight. According to the Multi-Dimensional Poverty Index for 2016,[11] India has the highest multi-dimensional poverty after Afghanistan in South Asia. Nearly 54% of the Indian population is multidimensionally poor compared to 66% in Afghanistan. The poorest region in South Asia is Bihar, followed by

'South' Afghanistan. There are more 'Multidimensional poor people (421 million) in the eight poorest Indian states (Bihar, Chhattisgarh, Jharkhand, Madhya Pradesh, Orissa, Rajasthan, Uttar Pradesh, and West Bengal) than in 26 poorest African countries combined.[12]

If economic prosperity does not ensure justice to all, it will not lead to long-lasting peace and development. India completed 71 years of political freedom but has it become more democratic or hierarchical? Indeed, India remains a deeply hierarchical society. Our democracy is disfigured by the persistence of inhumane practice such as manual scavenging etc. However, while hierarchy remains, the form and substance of this hierarchy is being increasingly challenged. The modern day women have begun to claim their rightful place in society and in the Church as well. Over the years, we see *Dalits* across India getting educated and organizing themselves socially and politically.

The rising self-consciousness and self-assertion of these two historically disadvantaged groups have provoked an upper caste and patriarchal ramification, with a wave of attacks on *Dalits* in villages and on women in villages as well as in towns. Yet this ramification itself demonstrates the steady undermining of social hierarchies in the 21st century India.[13] The dehumanizing problems and issues infuse a feeling of upheaval among humans which thwarts peace to linger in this beautiful land.[14] However, a paradox emerges in that, on the one hand, a distinctive feature of 21st century Indian society is the awakening of peoples' movements, which is the result of the heightened consciousness of peoples over perceived injustice or deprivation of their rights,[15] and on the other, *Dalits* and women are still exploited and suppressed. Speaking in the context of social movements Jacob Parappally notes, "a social movement engages in resistance against the threat or the perceived threat to the groups' rights and means of existence. Some of the major movements of India are Peasant Movements, Tribal (Adivasi/ Indigenous) Movement, *Dalit* Movements, Women's movements, and Environmental Movements."[16] When the social Movements aim at changes in the religious beliefs they turn out to be religious movements.

According to Prasad Lankapalli, Religious Movements are of two types: alternative and reformative. The alternative type is for example, a new identity for *Dalits* based on dignity, equality and community, whereas the reformative one advocated modifications and changes in Hinduism as *Bhakti* and Neo-Vedantic Movements.[17]

Besides, in his 8.00 pm address to the nation, on 8 November, 2016, Prime Minister announced the government's decision to demonetize the currency notes of Rs. 500 and Rs.1000, assuring billions of Indian citizens that demonetization and digitalization are a panacea for the country's growth challenges and a solution to its core economic problems that require constructing a new moral economy, and a "different" imaging of India in the minds of the people.[18] However, a cursory glance into the grass-root strata of Indian society would disclose India as a nation of teeming paradoxes.

Growing Economic Might

The foundation of an economy is built on the four factors of production: land, labor, capital and entrepreneurship. Economy is one of the basic factors that determine the destiny of a nation. The economy of India is the seventh-largest in the world as measured by nominal Gross Domestic Product (GDP) and the third-largest by purchasing power parity (PPP). India is one of the fastest growing economies in the world. India is moving ahead of Japan to become the world's third biggest economy in terms of PPP, according to a World Bank Report released on Tuesday the 28 April, 2017.[19] As per the 'First Advance Estimates of National Income, 2016-'17 released by the Central Statistics Office (CSO), the per capita net national income during 2016-'17 is "estimated to be Rs 103,007" at current prices. This is higher by 10.4 percent as compared to Rs 93,293 during 2015-'16.[20] India's ranking in terms of per capita income is 129th among all the nations of the world.[21] Despite recession and its aftermath, the country was classified as a newly industrialized country, and one of the G-20 major economies, with an average growth rate of approximately 7 percent over the last two decades.[22] However, 32.9 percent of the world's poor live in India. One third of the world's 1.2

billion poorest people live in India, according to the latest Millennium Development Goals report by the U.N.[23]

The Gross National Product (GNP) has grown and foreign investment has been flowing into the country. There is a sense of comfort and luxury in a section of Indians. But the progress and the benefits of globalization are not universal. It's the philosophy of a neo-liberal[24] paradigm of development that speaks more of growth rather than of development. The ambit of social life is more than the realm of economics. A paradox that we find here is that India with its ample natural resources, human and financial resources, has been unable to achieve economic growth and distributive justice. Although, India has enhanced its economic position in recent years, poverty continues to be the main challenge of our time. The dichotomy between economic growth and poverty reveals that the resources available to a society are used to satisfy the wants of a few while a vast majority do not have even their basic needs met.[25]

As a result, a few affluent individuals who are at the apex of the pyramidal structure always try to maintain the status quo, which they succeed in doing, as the political power too is virtually in their hands. The unequal distribution of land and other material resources is another factor that leads to the exploitation of workers, bonded labour, child labour, exploitation of migrant labour and exploitation of cheap labour by contractors; such are some of the manifestations of an unjust economic system and of structural violence. These are some of the data revealing the unjust reality of our country.

Political Influence

India is a sovereign, socialist, secular, democratic republic with a parliamentary form of government and a system of universal adult franchise. As a secular country India has enshrined the right to freedom of religion in its Constitution, granting 'equality before the law' for 'all persons'. India's secular cultural heritage is something that we could be proud of. In the Indian context the term 'secular' denotes a way of life neutrality which is both pluralistic and dialogical. This secularism has been hailed as one of the basic features of the Constitution consisting of the basic structure itself. This is uniquely Indian which has been inbuilt in the ethos and tradition of India from its early days.[26] The Constitution of India firmly affirms this secular ethos of justice (social, political and economic). Liberty of thought, expression, belief, faith and worship, freedom of religion and non-interference by state *vis-à-vis* religion and its institutions were guaranteed. "India is a country where religion is caught up in a treacherous mix of caste, race, ethnicity, politics, class, and economics."[27]

Although all religions generally live in harmony, communal violence, riots and programs targeting religious minorities are on the rise data. As a result, the economically rich become politically powerful and the economically deprived become politically powerless. The unjust divide of political power deprives the illiterate, the landless, the unorganized workers and slum dwellers of their rights and freedom in their own country.

Social Dynamics

To understand India, one must understand its diversity. There are 22 official languages and over 1600 dialects spoken. Keeping this cultural diversity alive is part of the challenge ahead, especially given the ever-increasing lure of Westernization and Hindization. The most important factor that has affected the social context of India is the caste system which determines one's social status. It has a very strong religious support, on account of which it is an all-pervasive reality in India.

> The caste system divides the whole society into a large number of hereditary groups, distinguished from one another and connected together by three characteristics: separation in matters of marriage and contact, whether direct or indirect; division of labour: each group having, in theory or by tradition, a profession from which their members can depart only within certain limits; and finally hierarchy, which ranks the groups as relatively superior or inferior to one another.[28]

The origins of caste[29] are deeply rooted in India's ancient past. The Aryans invaded India in 1500 BC and introduced the caste system. The Rig-Veda also speaks of the caste system.[30] Caste is a stratified system in which each segment has its own identity with a common name, origin and strictly specified inter-group relations. Caste system and exploitation of *Dalits* are realities that are closely interconnected and one cannot be understood without the other. Centuries of discrimination and exploitation shape the conscience of the people so much so, that the oppressed themselves have been forced to accept their misery passively as their destiny.

Religio-Cultural Diversity

Religion and culture are intimately intertwined in the Indian context. The uniqueness of India is said to be its religious plurality and cultural diversity. One of the significant and characteristic features of the people of India is their faith in religion. Religion is the nucleus of the social life of men and women in India. The country has a long history spanning over 5,000 years of human habitation and a rich cultural heritage handed down by the native Dravidian, Aryan and invading civilizations. The world religions such as Hinduism, Buddhism, Jainism, Christianity and Islam existed in India for millennia and they co-exist side by side with a spirit of not mere tolerance, but of mutual acceptance, harmony and collaboration. According to World Population Review of the 2011 census, Hinduism is the most common religion in India, accounting for about 80% of the population. Islam is the second-largest religion accounting for 13% of the population. Other religious groups in India are Christians (2.3%), Sikhs (1.9%), Buddhists (0.8%) and Jains (0.4%).[31] Having a distinct religious and cultural tradition of its own, rich and profound as they are, they have scope for interaction, dialogue, experimentation and experience on the one hand and an air of suspicion and scepticism on the other. What we witness today is suspicion, deficit of trust and reactionary responses rather than peaceful co-existence. The religio-cultural reality of India exerts its influence in almost every other sphere of life in India. It permeates into the decision making process at the micro level as well as at the macro level. India is a secular nation and secularism is the heart and soul of India.[32] However, India, the proud mother of many great religions is terribly wounded today; mainly because of religious fundamentalism,[33] religion seems to have become a disintegrating force. Under the guise of a socio-political movement Hinduism asserts an ideology and programme of Hindu-Rashtra, Hindu Nation, based on a mythologized version of Hindu Indian past and all its traditions, as a "golden age" which must be revived. The reconstruction of a Hindu India is an exclusionary process that leaves out vast numbers of backward castes, *Dalits* and minorities, and assigns to them a subordinate role in the socio-political life. It does not believe that there is an exchange between cultures inspired by different faiths and religions to create a richer, non-sectarian culture. Paradoxically, the Indian Constitution claims India to be a sovereign, democratic republic, assuring its citizens justice, equality and liberty and promoting fraternity among them all. By a constitutional amendment in 1976, the concepts of socialist and secular ideals were added to promote and keep the real spirit of democracy and freedom of religions among all citizens.[34]

The various factors analyzed above give a brief overview of 21st century Indian reality. The Indian society is in a process of change which can be described in various ways: it is a pluralistic, multicultural, post-modern, digital, and globalized society adorned by market economy, modern information and communication technology.[35] India is and always has been a country of contrasts and diversities, union of cultures and a strange combination of continuity and modernity. Though India is a fast developing country in terms of world economy, science and technology, there still remains a big chasm between the haves and have-nots, the rich and the poor, the centre and the periphery. These factors are dialectical, interrelated and influence each other.

2. Identifying the Issues

An analysis of the totality of the Indian reality would be incomplete without a brief look into the factors that affect the very human existence. Obviously there are many aspects leading to such a situation. Hence, this part of the chapter utilizes a broad brush to paint a quick picture of the fundamental phenomenon faced by those on the periphery of today. The primary focus of this part of the chapter is to identify the factors that affect the core of human dignity despite the fact that India is in the globalization and the digital era. In the complexity of the 21st century India, broadly the following four factors that disturb the very essence of human being are highlighted: i) increase of poverty amidst plenty; ii) disparity despite unity; iii) discrimination despite gender-equity; and iv) fundamentalism amidst religious pluralism.

Increasing Poverty amidst Plenty

The biggest problem the 21st century India has raised to human conscience is the increase of poverty in the midst of plenty. Despite India being one of the fastest growing economies, globalization and free market economy, the poor are not only further marginalized but also made aware of the fact that they are dispensable. Though India has a history of significant cultural heritage, it has been always challenged by the reality of grinding poverty. Poverty disrupts the very fabric of human relationship. The globalized market has created wealth for a rich minority and reinforced the fate of a poor majority. Indian markets are flooded with poor quality foreign products, affecting not only the Indian industries but also loss of livelihood of many poor workers. Poverty is a global phenomenon – India has almost one third of the poor of the world. In 2010, the World Bank stated, "32.7% of the total Indian population falls below the international poverty line of US$ 1.25 per day, while 68.7% live on less than US$ 2 per day."[36] Poverty is also dehumanizing because it involves the denial of human rights (*SRS* 15).[37] Therefore, it is evil and scandalous. There exists a big gap between economic growth and poverty, between the rich and the poor.

The operating value system seems to be: you are what you have and the basic view of society is the tendency to accumulate material wealth and consider it equal to growth and prosperity. "The poor do not have the means of leading a truly human life. They are often politically powerless, socially discriminated against and culturally deprived."[38] Evidently, the poor in India are not just economically deprived but are socially ostracised as well. In a way, the causes of poverty in India revolves round two main factors, one being the cultural factor and the other the structural factor. The cultural factor is dominated by the social structures and relations. The apathy induced by a fatalistic understanding of the doctrine of *karma* and the caste system generates an 'artificial' poverty between people belonging to different castes. The structural factor refers to "structural factors inherent to either the economy and/or to several interrelated institutional environments that serve to favour certain groups over others, generally based on gender, class, or race."[39] Despite the advancement in science, technology and industry, 21st century India still struggles with its poverty.

Unemployment

Increasing unemployment is closely connected with poverty in the context of India.[40] Still, there are millions of people in our country who sort through piles of garbage in search of the bare necessities of life. Hundreds of thousands die every year for want of sufficient food and nutrition. Therefore, unemployment is more than an economic problem, since it brings with it "series of negative consequences for individuals and for society prompts one to question seriously the type of development which has been followed over time (*SRS* 18). Justice seems to be silenced; the rich are getting richer at the expense of the poor, who are more and more reduced to a kind of "fuel" for the production processes of economic and social elites.[41] Poverty amid globalization forces the workers to migrate from their homelands in poorer areas to more developed towns and cities in search of employment. Migration also results in longer working hours, poor living and working conditions, social isolation and poor access to basic amenities. They have very little bargaining power, and therefore, are very vulnerable. Their problems are enormous: poverty, agony, pain, loneliness, exploitation, humiliation, insecurity, dependency, poor sanitation, unhealthy hygiene situation, exposed to disease and so forth. The migrant workers in many cases leave their families and live temporarily in another country, thus disrupting the family and social fabric of their home communities.

Therefore, in the Indian scenario, poverty and unemployment are crucial social problems that are mutually interwoven in the lives of the common people. These problems in turn bring in other calamities like sickness, broken families, and so on.[42] Ultimately people on the edges of life exhibit the vast discrepancy between the rich and the poor as the external reasons for social injustice, cultural nationalism, ethnic consciousness and above all finiteness of human life. Unemployment is an important factor that causes poverty in India. Poverty and unemployment are the two most formidable problems of the Indian economy. Developing employment opportunities has been an important objective of development planning in India. Though employment has increased over the years, growth in the population, defective planning, joint family system, caste system, preference for white-collar jobs and the labor force have aggravated the unemployment problem year after year.[43] The growth in labour force in India is much higher than the growth of jobs. Actual growth in employment figures in India has mostly fallen short of estimated figures.[44]

In the socio-cultural context poverty is more primordial and of far reaching consequences than the attendant economic poverty. A dire existential need is presumed to become more human, since the human being is not human enough, though they have the potency to become human. The situation of a majority of the Indian women, especially of those belonging to *Dalit* and Adivasi communities is most dehumanizing. Economic deprivation is a result of socio-cultural and political discrimination and marginalization. On the economic front, one can still speak of feminization of poverty and labour, because more and more women are being added to the number of poor and the unemployed.

Marginalization

To be on the margin is a way of systematic devaluing. Being there signifies being less, being over-looked, not having any importance. The marginalized live under the yoke of age-old caste system and oppression. They are the victims of economic self-centeredness, cultural alienation and political and religion's domination. Discrimination is seen not only at the caste level, but also at the emerging class level. Marginalization is a state of deprivation of basic human rights. It is a state of structured or unstructured exclusion of vulnerable people from their rights and privileges.[45] It is also described as a social process where people are relegated to the fringes or 'margins' of society. It is defined as processes, in which individuals or communities are socially excluded, systematically blocked from, or are denied access to participation in social and political processes which are basic to integrate with society.[46] "The victims on the margins do not have any space, any role in the planning for their future; they are left behind and even deliberately muscled out."[47]

The people at the margins in India are the Tribals, the *Dalits*,[48] poor farmers, the child labourers, the prostitutes, the trafficked women and their children, the refugees, the orphans, the drug addicts, the leprosy patients, the street children, those who suffer from HIV and AIDS and so on. The 'poor' in India are not just economically deprived but are socially ostracised as well, and what determines their worth is not so much their economic status as their social status. That is, the poor are themselves not as poor but are 'marginalized'. In short, *Dalits* are a typical marginalised group of India, characterized by convergence of multiple marginalities and cumulative inequalities. This context of multiple dimensions of oppression and subjugation, deprivation and marginalization has given rise to and shaped many peoples' movements in India. India has witnessed the rise of many subaltern[49] groups that find in Jesus a new inspiration and empowerment to carry on the struggle for their own liberation.[50] On the top of the list of the marginalized are the women,[51] whose humanity is not recognized as equal to that of men even in the 21st century India. These are the ones who are denied of rights, especially the right to human dignity and common livelihood.

Disparity Despite Unity

The unjust disparities include socio-cultural and religious conditions of India. Economic inequality is also linked to the social inequalities.

The way people behave socially, through racist or sexist practices and other forms of discrimination, lends itself to affect the opportunities, and wealthy individuals can generate them for themselves.[52] The massive poverty of India's people is not the only element in India's chain of bondage. The assignment of basic rights among various castes is both unequal and hierarchical. The system is maintained through the rigid enforcement of social ostracism (a system of social and economic penalties) in case of any deviations. Inequality is at the core of the caste system.[53]

Even though the government of India wishes others to believe that India is a secular country and is above caste and religion, the fact remains that the elite of Indian society, both in the government and outside, continue to think, judge and evaluate everything from an ancient caste point of view, which necessarily keeps the Indian people unique in the way they rate members of their stratified caste communities. Therefore, poverty is not the only element in India's chain of bondage, but other links reinforce its fearsome hold. The hierarchical ranking of various castes and sub-castes constitutes another essential element and the very structure of this institution. "Instead of dispersed inequalities, we find in caste a system of accumulative inequalities, where social, economic and political power is concentrated into the hands of the same group."[54] There is poverty in other parts of the world, but poverty combined with caste is found only in India.[55] One of the characteristics special to India is its caste system.

Caste System

The caste system is a social disparity[56] in India that stratifies various social groups, with a set of upper castes, "backward" castes, and the most oppressed group, the *Dalits*. Brahmins are the uppermost caste, enjoying the benefits of the privileged social group for centuries. George M. Soares-Prabhu says that "Caste defines the typically Hindu (indeed Indian) world view, determines the type of relationships that exist in Indian society, and gives concrete expression to both India's religiosity and its poverty. India's religiosity is a caste religiosity; India's poverty is caste poverty. Therefore, caste determines the shape of India's poverty."[57] Caste system and the law of *karma* add a *swadeshi* touch to the oppression of India's poor. Caste as summarized by Rayan still holds true in the Indian context:

> Caste is a powerful, divisive, and oppressive institution, deeply entrenched in the very flesh of the people and infecting all the limbs and movements of the nation. Indian caste has its peculiar features; it also has elements in common with racist and classist structures elsewhere. Used for long as a tool and technique for dividing and conquering, caste still acts as the main obstacle to the unity and organization of all the exploited for an effective struggle against oppression.[58]

Rayan compares caste to a powerful, divisive and oppressive institution, which is deeply embedded like a thorn in the flesh of the Indian people and affecting not only the very core of Indian life but like a virus is infecting almost every Indian. Soares-Prabhu compares the caste system to a huge cloud of smog that hangs over an industrial city, which pollutes its every nook and corner. It pervades every social class and infects all Indian religions. He says that even Christianity is not spared from being a victim of caste-system in some parts of India.[59]

Though the negative effect of caste system is reduced to some extent in urban areas, still it is prevailing in rural areas. The caste system entwined with poverty and ruled by patriarchy has created a stratified society based on inequality and hierarchy.[60] As discussed earlier, the caste system owes its origin to the four groups that were formed out of the body of Brahmā/Hari, the creator God, which is documented in the Rig-Veda.[61] On the basis of their graded caste status, they were made to bear extreme kinds of disabilities in the form of oppression for centuries, which made them almost lose their humanness.[62] What makes it a very rigid social system is its concept of purity and pollution.[63] Furthermore, 'casteist' mentality is very much operative in Christianity in India, especially in areas like the choice of marriage partners, distribution of property and so forth. Caste influence prevails in ecclesial circles too. It's an undeniable fact that the caste system has an adverse influence on the *Dalits*;[64] especially Christian and Muslim *Dalits* are the victims of illegal discriminatory practices. They are denied access in the Scheduled Caste list, deprived of government benefits such as job opportunities, educational benefits, or reservation of seats in the political sphere. Despite its constitutional abolition in 1950, the practice of "untouchability" or rather the imposition of social disabilities on persons by reason of birth into a particular caste remains very much part of rural India.

Discrimination on the basis of caste has been all-pervasive; it is seen not only at the caste level, but also at the emerging class level. It is to be noted that the doctrine of *Karma* is of great antiquity in India. Invariably, every person believes that whatever action is done by an individual has an impact on the future; the doctrine holds that that if the *karma* of an individual is good enough, the next birth will be rewarding, and if not, the person may be degenerated into a lower life form and reactions may come in the form of disease, poverty and so on.[65] The nature of the caste system is such that social, economic, political, and cultural-religious exploitation are so intimately intermingled. Rayan contends:

> What is specific and intolerable is their supposed untouchability. This is an ideology fabricated by the powerful to legitimize the enslavement of the ethnically and /or socially 'other'. On that basis the 'other' has been deprived of all human rights. Hence, rejecting various traditional names, these 'others' call themselves "*Dalits*", meaning the crushed, the broken, the oppressed.[66]

The formation of political parties and the introduction of so-called democratic politics hardly changed this caste-culture. Strangely enough the party leaders, to manipulate the *Dalit* votes, give speeches about banning untouchability, but practically each one of them operates in the same culture of 'touch me not'.[67]

Exploitation of *Dalits*

Being a *Dalit* is a social experience of "brokenness, oppression and dehumanization,"[68] as they occupy the outer strata in the caste system. Thus the *Dalits* are both economically and socially marginalized. "They have been excluded from the caste system, hence out-castes; declared ritually unclean, hence untouchables; and pushed out from fear of pollution to live on the outskirts of villages, hence, segregated."[69] They number around 167 million. In today's context as it was before, they are the most marginalized and manipulated ones. The official statistics of crimes against SCs rose to 47,064 in 2014 from 39,408 in 2013. In 2012 there were 33,655 crimes against *Dalits*, about the same as in 2011.[70] *Dalits* have been known in India by different names. Subsequently, the name 'Dalits' was made current in the late century by the *Dalits* themselves, to demonstrate the rejection of derogatory names given by outsiders and further, to refer to their pain, suffering and hope for liberation.[71]

The *Dalits* endure the most inhumane forms of oppression and exploitation within a lifelong imprisonment of the caste hierarchical society. It was Arvind Nirmal, a *Dalit* theologian, who coined the term Dalit theology at the beginning of the 1980s. He enumerates six meanings of the term *Dalit*: "firstly, the broken, the torn, the burst, the split, secondly, the opened, the expanded, thirdly, the bisected, fourthly, the driven asunder, fifthly, the downtrodden, the crushed, the destroyed, and sixthly, the manifested, and the displayed".[72]

In other words, *Dalits* are outcast and poor, because they, according to the architects of the system, are not fit to be included in the fourfold graded caste structure of the traditional Hindu society. *Dalits* are systematically brainwashed in order to maintain the status quo. Attempts at breaking the caste barriers by conscientious thinkers and social reformers and Christian missionaries have always met with résistance.[73]

However, efforts were made by the Church in India to relate Christian revelation to the *Dalit* situation prior to 1970s. A large number of *Dalits* took the initiative to receive baptism from 1850-1930, because of their search "for a greater sense of personal dignity and self-respect, improved socio-economic status, education for their children, healing from sickness, solidarity in times of suffering and death, protection from oppression and an end to exploitation."[74] The then missionaries took it as a challenge to articulate the liberative aspects of the gospel long before the emergence of modern *Dalit* Christian theology.[75] Prior to 1986, Rayan spelt out a theology about the *Dalits* and for the Indian Church. He challenged the Indian Church to make a preferential option to identify with and join the *Dalit* struggle for a new human history of dignity, equality, justice and liberation. He further contended that the God of the Bible had established this history through the incarnation, ministry, death and resurrection of Jesus Christ who chose to become a *Dalit*.[76] Looking ahead towards the future of India, Felix Wilfred in his book *Dalit Empowerment* considers its two-fold radical aspects - transformation and healing that makes *Dalits* the hope of India:

> Firstly, given their epistemological advantage of being on the margins and having knowledge of the present situation which others do not have, they will create a new India – an India that faces boldly radical transformation in its culture, society and religious practices. The struggles of *Dalits* and their empowerment, then, go far beyond their situation, touching upon the future shape of the country and strengthening the dreams of a different India. Secondly, a society that suffers from the phobia of the pollution of other human beings warrants a radical healing. It is difficult to comprehend a society where some can thrive, derive pleasure and be privileged at the cost of the other who is considered as impure. Obviously, a society with this sort of syndrome calls for a healing touch.[77]

Eventually, stagnation and social immobility which result from the rigid and oppressive system of caste no doubt play an important part in the increase of poverty. The effects of caste system in India (practised but not acknowledged officially), for example, permeates so easily into one's way of perception, thinking and decision making that seeks to place one person on a state of advantage over another.

In addition, the oppression experienced by *Dalit* women is different from that of non-*Dalit* women. For a *Dalit* woman, her primary identity is that of a '*Dalit*' rather than that of a woman. It is her Dalitness that is the major cause of her devaluation and dehumanization. Since our society is not only a male dominated society, but an upper caste male dominated society, a *Dalit* woman's problems are unique, as she is *Dalit* among *Dalits*. A *Dalit* woman's life is the most unprotected and insecure in our society. Millions of *Dalit* women live in an atmosphere of constant violence in their homes and in the society at large. Their struggle for survival is as complex as their existence. Too often we hear that *Dalit* women are molested, raped, abused and subjected to all kinds of sexual crimes and even murdered. *Dalit* women are marginalized economically and socially.[78] The social immobility engendered by caste, contributes to India's poverty, since these are seemingly the crucial, vulnerable realities which are affected by and in turn affect other areas.

The Constitution of India says, "The State shall promote with special care the educational and economic interests of the weaker section of the people, and in particular, of the Scheduled Castes and the Scheduled Tribes, and shall protect them from social injustice and all forms of exploitation."[79] Social inequalities pave the way for social discriminations such as gender inequalities, racial discrimination, economic deprivation and so on. The realization of such liberation presupposes introspection into one's own religious ethos and practices. Gender discrimination does not seem to decline, on the contrary newer forms of discrimination are added to the persisting old ones.

Discrimination Despite Gender Equity

Discrimination of women is an age-old social problem.[80] Gender inequality being a fact of history, gender status should not be an obstacle to harmonious living. "Gender inequality permeates all aspects of life. Socialization of women and men in gender role stereotyping is a major characteristic of patriarchal conditioning."[81] First and foremost, gender equality is a matter of human rights. It is also a driver of development and progress.[82] As we glance today the revolutionary changes that have taken place in the situation of women, it is perceivable that women have come a long way to be where they are today. A woman is held in esteem when she is seen as a mother, because she brings to light each person in agony and ecstasy at birth, the prototype of all forms of birthing. As girls, they are beautiful and fabulous little angels in hundreds of fanciful costumes which the boys can only envy. But the irony of the situation is that only a few dare to be different.[83]

Women in contemporary Indian society are constantly confronted with the double standards of an androgynous social system. She has value attached with a man as daughter, wife, mother and sister. The burning issues of women in India are: violence to women, impact of economic globalization, lack of health care poverty and illiteracy. Gender discrimination in India constitutes one of the major concerns in the current development paradigm. Discrimination in the workplace is a general phenomenon in India/Asia. Occupational segregation and cultural norms also often shut women out of jobs without sufficient reason. A recurring theme in the lives of many women is that of sexual harassment by their employers, bosses or co-workers, which often goes unreported for fear of losing employment.

Though the situation of women in India/Asia is still in great need of alleviation, there is a heightened awareness among groups and individuals, governments, NGOs and the Church, which have created structures and programs to improve the situation. Religious congregations of women and associations of major superiors have been in the forefront of raising consciousness and advancing the cause of women.[84] Several legislations have been passed in India to bring about changes in the status of women and to prevent offences such as dowry, *sati*, rape, molestation and immoral trafficking,[85] but the crimes are on the increase. Moreover, the household chores and bringing up of children are unpaid for, and unrecognized as labour, their economic contribution remains underestimated. The strong patriarchal bias of Indian culture continues to dehumanize the Indian women.[86]

The rise in religious fundamentalism which reinforces gender discrimination, legitimizing it in the name of religion that has further negative repercussions for women and egalitarian enterprise.[87] In addition, the dominating social structures owned by men, control and manage financial, intellectual and ideological resources as well as the labour, fertility and sexuality of women, and thus propagate gender discrimination. The culture of domination and marginalization which embody ideas, beliefs, values, traditions, rules, norms, perspectives (ideologies) that prefer males/sons have been styled in the culture of patriarchy.[88]

The World Bank in its 2012 report on "Gender Equality and Development" estimated that over the last two decades around 2.5 lakh girls were killed in India each year because of their sex.[89] As per McKinsey Global Institute Report in 2013, The Power of Parity, India ranks 141st out of 142 nations and 2062 districts in the world that are categorized as gender critical when it comes to health and survival of women as compared to men.[90] The status of women in India is linked to their access to resources and education, employment opportunities and leadership in religious and political spheres. The Indian Constitution provides specifically for gender equality, affirmative action, freedom and security of the person and socio-economic rights. It not only grants equality to women but also empowers the State to adopt measures of positive discrimination in favour of women.

But in reality, women are underrepresented in governance and decision making positions. In 2010, only 9% of Parliament seats, less than 6% in Cabinet positions, less than 4% of seats in High Courts and the Supreme Court and less than 3% of administrative and managerial positions are with women. Women do get elected to positions of power at the grassroots governance institutions largely due to reservations, but are mostly proxy candidates and the husbands, sons or other elite men actually continue to perform as leaders.[91] It is also a matter of human rights and a driver of development progress.

Today, women enjoy constitutional rights such as equality before law, freedom from discrimination on the grounds of sex, equal opportunities in matters related to employment under state, equal pay for equal work, right to work, education and public assistance and provision for just conditions of work and maternity reliefs.[92] Despite these efforts, overt and covert manifestations of gender inequality persist. Many women are not able to access the constitutional rights because of the discrimination and oppressive social and religious beliefs and practices.

Female Foeticide and Infanticide

Female infanticide, sex selection, wife battering, dowry harassment, rape and many other dehumanizing acts are regularly experienced by women. Culture is the dominant factor which dictates what women are to be and to do. The place of honour given to women in Indian culture does not match with practices imposed on them. For example, the neglect of the girl child, the female foeticide and infanticide all testify to the fact that women are considered less in comparison to the importance given to the male. Can we say that Indian culture is unfriendly to a girl-child?

With the advancement of science and technology, human life is threatened in its most safest haven, the mother's womb. Humans choose to annihilate its own offspring, where it is voiceless, make the tiny baby powerless. In a society infected by 'macho-patriarchal insanity' discrimination of a girl child begins on the lap of the mother.[93] The family which is often seen as a place of nurture and care is often a site of violence. Today female foeticide is an established phenomenon.[94] This disparity between individuals is constructed socially and biologically, based on gender.

According to the National Crime Records Bureau of India, reported incidents of child abuse in 2015 were as follows: 10,854 rapes, 8,930 assaults on women, and 3,350 cases of sexual harassment. According to the Union Ministry of Health and Family Welfare, there were 726,993 abortions done in India between April 2016 and April 2017.[95] According to the United Nations, sex ratio is defined as the number of males per 100 females. Sex Ratio of India is 108.176, i.e., 108.176 males per 100 females in 2020. It means that India has 924 females per 1000 males. India has 48.04% female population compared to 51.96% male population. India has 54,197,555 more males population than females population.[96] Through dominating social structures men own, control and manage financial, intellectual and ideological resources as well as the labour, fertility and sexuality of women, and thus perpetuate gender discrimination. Gender inequality has led to various other types of discriminations and as a result, sexual abuse, rape and women trafficking are tolerated without any guilt.

Human Trafficking

Trafficking of human beings is not a new phenomenon. Historically, it has been linked to slavery which involved the sale and purchase of human beings as cattle, treating them as commodities that could be bought and sold. The owner maintained absolute right over the slaves, who were considered his private property. "Human Trafficking' is modern day slavery. It is best defined as 'the trade in humans, most commonly for the purpose of sexual slavery, forced labour, or commercial sexual exploitation for the trafficker or others."[97] According to 2016 estimates of the United Nations Office for Drugs and Crime (UNODC): 51% of identified victims of trafficking are women, 28% children and 21% men; 72% people exploited in the sex industry are women; 63% of identified traffickers were men and 37% women; and 43% of victims are trafficked domestically within national borders.[98] Human trafficking is "an open wound on the body of contemporary society, a scourge upon the body of Christ, and it is a crime against humanity that requires continued global and local cooperation between the Catholic Church and law enforcement."[99]

The advances of transportation technology have extended human trafficking to an unprecedented scale.[100] Cedric Prakash, a well-known human rights activist, writes:

> India is regarded as the South Asian hub for human trafficking. Thousands from rural India are lured daily by human traffickers to the big towns and cities with the promise of good job, more money, so on. Most of the victims are women and children who are helplessly trapped in bonded labour, prostitution rings and other various activities.[101]

The National Crime Records Bureau reveals that in March 2017 India's Ministry of Women and Child Development told the Parliament that there were almost 20,000 women and children who were victims of human trafficking in the country in 2016.[102]

The deplorable practice of trafficking of women, girls and boys in several regions of our country is a terrible blot on the social structures. A large number of victims from poor and deprived families and tribal areas are lured or forcibly transported to cities and towns for exploitation called 'sex work' and 'cheap labour'.[103] The pressing need to migrate in search of work creates a fertile ground for traffickers and unscrupulous agents to exploit this need and profit from it.[104] While it may seem that migration and trafficking are distinct and separate, they are at the same time integrally connected.

The oppression of women often seems to go hand in hand with the destruction of nature and environment. Women are considered the primary users of natural resources (land, forest, and water), because they are the ones responsible for gathering food, fuel, and fodder. Hence they are directly affected by environmental degradation caused by deforestation, wanton destruction of natural resources for industrialization, construction of hydro-electric plants, depletion of water, mining and excessive use of toxic chemicals and pesticides in agriculture.[105] The cry of the earth is the cry of the poor.[106]

Another most striking feature in the modern society is reducing humankind to a mere mass. The growth of cosmetic industry goes with the parallel and associated rise of beauty competitions, where model winners are chosen more and more from the developing countries to advertise these products. The development of technology threatens us with a doom that the instrument that was to bring ever greater freedom to human beings has now become the means to their enslavement. So the human element disappears, the spirit crumbles under so much lavish externality, and reverence for life declines.[107]

Human trafficking is a particular type of such movement in that it commodifies human life. There may be innumerable causes: The pressing need to migrate in search of work creates a fertile ground for traffickers to exploit this need and profit from it; The rising consumerist culture that makes inroads into the villages through television and cinema. It has become a strong incentive for parents and families to sell their children especially daughters or send them out in search of a livelihood.[108] Thus, discrimination is seen not only at the caste level, but also at the emerging class level. Issues of culture, religion, ethnic and other forms of identity have become highly politicized due to rising religious fundamentalism that reinforces control over women, keeps them confined to roles that perpetuate their subordination and prevents them from full enjoyment of their human rights.[109] The appropriate question at this moment would be: what are the factors responsible for societal disparities?

The factors responsible for graded/societal inequalities are cultural stereo-types. They are the following: First, in the patriarchal[110] culture with its structure and existence, women are dominated over by the socially powerful sphere of the upper levels of hierarchical caste system, as well as they are discriminated within the social sphere of the poor.[111] The system of patriarchy finds its validity and sanction in our religious beliefs, whether it be Hindu, Muslim, Christian or any other religion. Second, an obsessive preference for sons which is deeply rooted in India's patriarchal society. It is perceived in the attitude and atmosphere in the family and society – how it differs when it comes to welcoming the new born child. Patrilineal families promote at least one son in order to continue the familial line; many sons constitute additional status to families.[112] Third, the influence the *Manusmṛiti* (or 'Laws of Manu') has contributed to the prevailing patriarchal cultural bias against women in India. It emphasizes the total submission of wives to, and dependence on wives on their husbands. The Laws of Manu warns women not to perform any sacrifice, vow or fast without the permission of their husbands.[113] Fourth, the prevalence of dowry system since the *Vedic* period (1500-600 BCE) which is practiced by all castes and is generally practiced among all both in urban and rural areas in India. "The practice of dowry demeans women by signifying that the value of women is so low that she becomes acceptable to another only when her family is able to satisfy his greed for the latest gadgets of materialistic fancy,"[114] and the list will go on and on.

Women in general are stepping out of the restricted space of domestic walls to wider horizons in life in affirming their personhood and equality with men. But in reality, in most socio-cultural communities in India, their rights are limited by religious, cultural and traditional practices that are based on patriarchal norms.[115] On the one hand, they experience a sense of achievement at the new vistas and opportunities open to them in the socio-economic, political and other spheres. On the other, there is a feeling of frustration at the growing gender discrimination. Violence in the form of female foeticides, infanticides, dowry deaths, bride burnings and other forms of physical and sexual abuse defies analysis. The need of the hour would be to gather transforming presence to affirm women and girl children as valued human beings capable of contributing towards the advance of society, nation and the world at large.

Fundamentalism Despite Religious Pluralism

Plurality of religions is not treated as a problem in the Constitution but as an asset. The Indian Constitution gives the right to establish and strengthen religious pluralism in India by guaranteeing freedom of religious in its Part III. Articles 25 to 30 of the Constitution guarantee freedom of religion for all religions.[116] The essence of secularism in India is to recognize and preserve the different types of people, with diverse languages and beliefs and place them together so as to form a whole and united nation. In that sense, secularism implies equality of all religions and religious tolerance. It does not mean being irreligious or anti-religious. Secularism stands as one of the basic pillars of Indian Democracy. Moreover, it is not on grounds of religiosity or respect for religion but in the interest of diversity and pluralism.[117]

Michael Amaladoss, an eminent Indian theologian, highlights the different forms fundamentalism takes in different places: One, threatened by modern scientific discoveries or by liberal cultural and political ideologies, some believers hang on to what they consider the fundamentals of their religion. They may organize themselves to defend their belief. They may be perceived as conservative or revivalist; Two, a particular group of people, gathered together in the name of religion, ethnicity, caste, and language may think that they share the same economic and political interests which they seek to pursue and defend, together. This is more commonly called communalism. This may happen when there are wide economic and social disparities in society and a group feels unjustly exploited and/or discriminated against; Three, a communal group may imagine itself as a nation, discovering its historical roots. A very powerful force that can weld such a group together is religion. Such a group may fight for autonomy or independence or seek domination over other groups. Finally, a group with a strong identity looks on other groups, not only as different, but as inimical to their interests. In a religious setting the others can be demonized, when one group thinks that God is on its side. This can lead to defensive or aggressive violence, particularly when it experiences itself as the victim of deprivation, injustice and oppression. Indiscriminate violence against the innocents is called terrorism.[118]

Religious fundamentalism is a response to the threat of the diversity of identities that exist at any given time, in any given place. The situation deteriorated for a number of reasons, but chiefly because of the corruption of morality brought about by the increasing presence and takeover of political power by the 'enemies'.[119] Today fundamentalism and the political use of religion have resulted in inter-religious conflicts, more or less violent, which are aggravated by the acute atrocities and barbarous torture in various parts of India. This is clear from the Hindu Right Wing's propaganda through pamphlets, books, audio and video tapes, speeches, and so on which reveals a concerted effort to invoke a golden age where Hinduism reigned supreme and Hindu principles were firmly in place, governing the society.

Religious fundamentalism is often a national project, in that it often aspires to create a different kind of 'national identity' that will serve as an answer to the crisis that has gripped many modern nation-states. While purporting to address social, cultural or economic inequalities among communities, religious fundamentalism, in actual fact seeks to impose a new hegemonic order. In order to assist this project, religious fundamentalism invokes mythical memories of a perfect age where religious principles were followed to the book and all was well with the world.[120]

While claiming to address social, cultural or economic inequalities among communities, religious fundamentalism in reality seeks to impose a new hegemonic order. It sees contemporary science and theology as a threat to its perpetuity. It is assumed that religious fundamentalism gives rise to violence. Religious fundamentalism is closely associated with communalism that makes one believe that one's own religion alone is true.[121]

Communalism

The term Communalism is widely used across South Asia to describe the systematic misuse of religion for political purposes.[122] Communalism is one of the most complex problems that India is facing. This is generated when individuals belonging to one religion develop excessive affinity to their religion and hatred towards other religions. This kind of feeling promotes religious fundamentalism and fanaticism and proves to be dangerous for the unity and integrity of the country.[123] It is more so for a country like India where people of all major religions of the world live. In India, however, the word communal has come to acquire a reversed and largely negative sense, that of socially divisive and politically regressive activities. According to Pritam Singh, the reason for the linguistic anomaly is a legacy of India's anti-colonial struggle for national independence. Singh in *Economic & Political Weekly* magazine writes as follows:

> During India's movement for independence, many of the legislative, judicial, and administrative policies and instruments that the British rulers adopted in response to demands, generally from non-Hindu religious communities for protecting their interests came to be called "communal." The meaning of the word communal in that context was understood by the British, the minorities in question, and democratic-minded people in India as something that implied defending the democratic rights of the vulnerable or potentially vulnerable minorities with religious identities.[124]

The terms *communalism* and *fundamentalism* are almost synonymous in their meaning and application.[125] There is a very narrow division between the two alternatives that differentiate fundamentalism from communalism.

> The ideology of communalism tries to mobilize the people of similar religions by making them believe that their secular interests are similar. On the other hand the secular interests of the followers of other religion are different. Fundamentalism derives political principles from a sacred ancient text. It tries to evoke an utopian past mentioned in the sacred religious text at the cost of modern structures, institutions and rights. One of the defining characteristics of fundamentalism has been that adherents often see themselves as the guardians of the truth, usually to the exclusion of others.[126]

Rising fundamentalism and communalism threaten to tear the social fabric and the secular character of India. Prof. Khwaja Abdul Muntaqim, in his lecture "Challenges to Constitutional Mandate for Religious Harmony" said:

> In our country, communal violence had assumed the form of a multi-factorial disorder, though we Indians were considered as one of the most tolerant nations in the world. These factors were divisive, mostly hidden and sometimes open. Communal propaganda, communal instigation by individuals and so-called political leaders, indifferent attitude of law enforcement agencies, delayed justice and poor rate of conviction and misuse of religion had greatly contributed to the prevailing situation. He held that divisive forces and religious fanatics were raising their ugly heads. Such elements were bent upon polluting the atmosphere. They were demolishing religious places, desecrating deities and resorting to loot and arson, besides killing innocent people by applying most inhuman methods.[127]

The important link is between communal and political loyalties. "Communalism has been described as a sectarian exploitation of social traditions as a medium of political mobilization. This is done to punish the interests of the entrenched groups. Thus communalism is an ideology used to fulfil socio-eco-politico hopes of a community or social groups."[128] It relies on the constant creation of a set of enemies who were/are responsible for all that goes wrong in this world. Obviously, communalism is seeking to destroy the fundamental character of Indian society - its historical legacy, cultural complexity and political institutions. It presents "the whole history in the communal colour, one community making a selective use of religious doctrines to 'build an enemy image' of the other community." This image building of the other community creates permanently a hostile atmosphere in the society,[129] thus crafting out of it a shocking socio-political movement under the concept of 'Hindutva', which in turn becomes antithetical to the fundamentals of secularism envisaged in the Indian Constitution. Therefore the only way to rectify this situation is to eliminate the enemies one by one and at the same time to adhere to the religious principles it describes as the only correct ones.

The CBCI discussed in 2010 about the negative impacts of Fundamentalism and Communalism, namely in the guise of making a 'Hindu Rashtra' and of upholding what they regard as Indian culture. Violent and heinous activities are on the increase. Today India's secular nationalism is facing an onslaught from not only those who oppose secularism as a political doctrine and policy but also from those who consider it as a convenient umbrella for protecting their communal interests.[130]

Terrorism

Terrorism is "the use or threat of violence to create fear and alarm."[131] It is generally accepted that terrorism occurs when an ardent believer in a system - either religious or political – uses force or violence at any cost to threaten others who do not share their view. Terrorism has one main goal: to throw society into chaos.[132] The contemporary era is getting so accustomed to hearing about terrorist attacks such as car bombings and suicide bombings that we have become more or less insensitive to the immense damage and destruction done to human lives and property in almost every such attack.[133] In different parts of the country, religious minorities are attacked causing physical harm and damage caused to church property. The violent atrocities against the minorities, the desecration of churches, and the fear of reconversion (*ghar vapsi*) and the cow vigilantes (*gau rakshak)* violence are perhaps some of the glaring examples of this. What about the silence and insensitivity of the political leadership to a string of attacks on five churches and a Christian school in Delhi? The ongoing issues of violence against minorities and women, and the culture of rape in India raise legitimate questions about human rights. Take for example, the case of an eight year old girl, who was brutally gang raped and murdered in Rasana village near Kathua in Jammu Kashmir on January 17, 2018. Did these heinous acts of desecrating the sentiments of minorities leave one spellbound and speechless?

Human life is under a serious threat because of the growing violence in several parts of the country.[134] The burning and destruction of various Churches and burning of Christians, in Odisha's Kandhamal District in 2008;[135] the vandalization of Christian Churches and the murder of Christian priests and missionaries are some of the manifestations of "hate campaign" organized by the Hindutva. The focus of Hindutva campaign is "*Brahminic* ideology," which upholds the supremacy of the upper castes.[136] In addition to what is said above, the ideology of patriarchy creates myths of female inferiority and a culture of silence of women. Practices of child marriage, *sati*, dowry deaths, ban on widow remarriage, female foeticide and infanticide are violations of fundamental human dignity and they are expressions of a violent society.[137] Terrorism is a steadily growing intimidation to the world today and thwarts peace in this beautiful world.[138]

The above analysis reveals that the dehumanizing systems are on the increase. The 21st century has thrown up a whole host of challenges: i) the advent of globalization due to which, the technology that we have and the power that we manifest are superb; ii) people and communities are coming closer to one another, and differences are slowly giving way to collaboration, convergence and communion; iii) the human person, living in an era of fast paced development in all spheres of life, often finds that life's demands for progress and cares of the world require more energy and attention, rather than to give oneself to God, self and the other. and iv) we live at a time when authority is in question, patriarchy remains, and women have the gifts we need. Despite the rapid socio-economic, political, and religio-cultural changes brought about by globalization, the distribution of such changes remains uneven. As a result there still exists widening inequalities between men and women and within the different subgroups, within the categories called caste, creed, and gender.

Discrimination against women is an issue for our consideration. Increasing number of women are demanding that they be recognized as equals and that their dignity and rights as human persons be upheld by society. Poverty together with social injustice and unjust distribution of wealth is deeply dehumanizing as it stands in the way of their progress towards growth and wholeness. The truth of the matter is that we are living at a time when every single life-support system on this planet is on a decline.

We have discussed that staggering poverty, caste based discrimination, gender inequalities and violence against minorities are the four major issues of the 21st century India. The above analysis shows that these four issues are interrelated, and have to be addressed together. These are but some of the present day problems that become the locus for theologizing and creating a new society. Similar are the features that can be found in the 21st century Church in India. Indian Christian women of today are influenced by the contemporary society in which they live. But the contemporary society, in turn, is influenced by its past history and tradition. The situation of the Church and identifying its fundamental challenges in relation to Christian women in India in today's milieu will be explored in the second half of this chapter.

3. The Church in the Contemporary India

The Church in India is as old as Christianity itself. Tradition ascribes the introduction of Christianity to India to the Apostle Thomas, one of the 12, giving India the Syro-Malabar Church and the Syro–Malankara

Church.[139] Our Christian faith was nourished and strengthened by many great saints like St. Francis Xavier who is Patron Saint of Missions.

The total population of India today is estimated to be 1.21 billion with a decadal growth of 17.70%, representing a full 17% of the earth's population.[140] Accordingly, Hindus comprise 79.80%, Muslims 14.23%, Christian 2.30% (29,138,323 million), Sikh 1.72%, Buddhist 0.70%, Jains 0.37% and others 0.66%, and unspecified 0.24%.[141] Christianity is India's third largest religion with approximately 27.8 million, comprising 2.3 percent of India's population. The number of Christians in India is 2.78 crores. There are around 17.6 million Catholics[142] in India. The five southern states: Tamil Nadu, Kerala, Karnataka, Andhra Pradesh and Telangana account for 12.80 million, that is, 46 percent of India's 27.80 million Christians. Among them Kerala alone is home to 22.07 percent of the total number of Christians in the country, followed by Tamil Nadu with 15.88 percent. The seven North-Eastern States account for 28.1 percent of the Christian population. Goa accounts for 1.3 percent of Christian population in India. The rest of the country is home to less than 25% of the total number of Christians in the country.[143]

Unity in Diversity for a Mission

The Catholic Church in India consists of 174 dioceses across India of which 132 are Latin Church, 31 are Syro-Malabar, and 11 are Syro-Malankara. Together they form the Catholic Bishops' Conference of India (CBCI),[144] and a communion of three Individual *sui juris* Churches.[145] The three Individual *sui juris* (Ritual) Churches have their respective Episcopal Bodies: Conference of the Catholic Bishops of India (CCBI) for the Latin Church, Syro-Malabar Bishops' Synod (SMBS) for the Syro-Malabar Church and Holy Episcopal Synod for the Syro-Malankara Church. Latin, Syro-Malabar and Syro-Malankara, all these Churches, while remaining juridically distinct, are under the headship of the Bishop of Rome, the Pope.[146] Most Christians in India are Catholics of the Latin rite. The Eastern rite of the Church includes the Syro-Malabar and the Syrian Malankara Church, which are prominent in Kerala.

Other Christian Churches include the Mar Thoma Syrian Church, Church of South India (CSI), the Church of North India (CNI), Indian Pentecostal Church and other evangelical groups.

Apart from the Churches of the three rites, there are the upper and the lower social classes in each Church; there are the two orders of the Church laity and clergy and to narrow down the whole paradox, there are women and men in the Church. The Catholic Church operates on a hierarchy with the Pope at the top and laity at the bottom.

The Church on the one hand, is by her very nature missionary and universal since, according to "God's design" has her origin in the mission of Jesus Christ and the Holy Spirit (*GS* 2) which is all-inclusive. The Church as the sign of Jesus' abiding presence among us "continues and unfolds in the course of history the mission of Christ himself" (*AG*, 5). On the other hand, the Church "forms part of the civil society," because Church is "first and foremost members of the civil society in India and then only members of the Catholic Church." Therefore, it is the task of the Church to be involved and to "strengthen the civil society imprinting Jesus' prophetic vision"[147] of partnership with her values, attitudes and norms of conduct subverting the dominant culture.

New Horizons as Dynamic of the Milieu

Change, renewal, adaptation, creativity fidelity, and men and women as equals are some of the characteristics of the Second Vatican Council,[148] a significant milestone in the history of modern day Church. This wave has given a deeper understanding of the person and message of Jesus, reclaiming the prophetic role in faithfulness to the evangelizing mission of the Church.[149] Reading the signs of the times, we can say that the 21st century is the century of women. The election of Pope Francis has inaugurated a new era for the entire Church. The examples of Pope Francis calling upon women to play a greater role and giving more importance and participation for women, including the women in washing of the feet is an epochal change.

The 28th Plenary Assembly of the CBCI, held in Jamshedpur in February 2008, on the theme "Empowerment of Women in the Church and Society." Added to this, on 8th December 2009, the Catholic Bishops' Conference of India issued a document titled "Gender Policy of the Catholic Church of India."[150] Women still feel controlled under a "patriarchal and androcentric, with men in the dominant role and women in a position of subversive."[151] Pope Francis desires and calls for an inclusion of women in the life of the Church: More widespread and inclusive female presence, many women involved in pastoral responsibilities, in the accompaniment of persons, families and groups as a well as in the theological reflection.[152] Pope Francis during his meeting with heads of religious orders of women which was held in the Vatican in May 2016 opened the door for discussion about female deacon. But it was only a step on a long road to let women serve in a role reserved for men.[153] Moreover, today women themselves are collectively awakened globally and locally, still their voices not heard, experiences and abilities are not fully documented in the life of the Church.

Rayan in his article "Sociological Factors and the Local Church as Eucharistic Community" says that the Catholic Church is guilty of classism, casteism, and sexism. Freedom and equality are not valued and the central place which should be given to the human person is taken by laws and systems.[154] Rites, casteism and inequality in the Church are the important issues of the time that play a vital role affecting the life of the Church in India. Casteism within the Church is a scandal to the followers of Jesus and his message.[155] Factors like liberation theology, feminist theologies, and ecotheology have encouraged religious women in the Church to reconstruct their understanding, reassessing mission priorities.[156] The Church in India is indeed at the cross-roads and in many areas, at its defining moment.

Women in the Church

Developments in the contemporary era have given rise to a band of women and men in the Catholic Church who hold the view that Christian faith and practice are to be in line with the emancipation of women with an the assurance of equal rights for them. The biblical account Gen 1:27 reveals not only the fundamental equality of man and woman but also their personal character. Their partnership "constitutes the first form of communion between persons" (GS 12). Woman represents a particular value by the fact that she is a human person, and at the same time, by virtue of her femininity. In spite of man and woman being created equal by God, unfortunately, both in history and in today's world there is gross discrimination against women. Generally, we can say that the Christian tradition has preserved a certain amount of ambivalence with regard to women. In principle, there must be equality of sexes. But in practice, women's subordination to men is maintained.[157] Though women religious study theology, the number of those who take up theological studies is still insignificant compared to the large number of women religious in India.[158]

The Catholic Church in India has promoted the empowerment of women over the years and has made a noteworthy contribution to it, particularly in the field of education and health care. Worthy of mention is the pioneering work of the missionaries who were the first to promote girls' education in India. The first ever girls' school opened in India by the Missionaries was at Kottayam, Kerala in 1819. As per the CBCI Commission for Education and Culture report there are a total of 54,937 Catholic Educational Institutes in India.[159]

In India, while great women foundresses of Catholic religious orders showed both character and charism to instil in Catholic women religious a sense of worth and dignity by bringing theological studies at their reach. "Institute *Mater Dei* was launched in 1964, toward the end of the Vatican Second Council. It was an answer from among women religious to bring about the much-needed renewal in religious life as the council envisage. *Mater Dei* Institute aims to renew Religious life in the light of Vatican II. Ever since 1964, *Mater Dei* Institute has given theological formation and training to more than 6,000 women religious from India and the neighbouring"[160] Today women excel in every field not only in the secular world but also in Sacred Sciences, including Theology.[161] Women religious are playing a vital role in the life and formation of the Church.[162] Women religious render yeoman service to people by staffing their hospitals in towns, and their dispensaries and health clinics in the villages.

While being appreciated for women's compliant service and passive presence in the congregation, "they are barred from ministerial roles and decision-making processes."[163] Those women fully conscious of their full value of personhood and the depth of their historical victimhood are awakened to new forms of ministry.[164] Women were challenged to affirm their ontological and theological goodness, their rights to be respected in the ministry and the need to break free from those age-old limitations. With a dictum "the liberation of women has to be achieved by women themselves", the women were challenged to recognize that the only way to freedom and equality is an integral part of Christian freedom.[165] Another development, Indian feminist theology has its origin in the feminist theology that developed in the West, especially in the United States of America.[166] The 21st century women are still claiming their rightful space and place in the Church as well. Do women really experience affirming atmosphere in the Church? Does the Church really foster a sense of dignity among women that eventually leads to a participatory Church? If so, is the Church providing enough space for women-participation?

The 21st century Church in India echoes a parallel to the above reflection by taking note of the growing multiculturality around and the continuing dehumanized situation. Hence the modern context becomes a challenge for an ongoing witness to the person and message of Jesus in today's Church. A critical appraisal of the Indian ecclesial scenario with a view of the task ahead, becomes a theological imperative in our times. Therefore, understanding the dynamics of the milieu in which we live and adhering to a foundational vision of the Church which is based on the basic principles of human solidarity, equality, dignity are of immense importance. It would enable us to work towards shaping a holistic and inclusive vision of humanity that would guide in the process of transformation as well.

4. Identifying the Concerns of Women in the Church

Vatican II categorically stated that all forms of discrimination are contrary to God's plan.[167] Changes are taking place in the Church. Women's role and functions are determined partly by their gender and partly by the limits imposed by the culture, which they accept for reasons untold.[168] A detailed study of women in contemporary Indian Church would be a herculean task. Moreover, this section of the chapter has a very limited purpose. Hence the task here is to consider the Christian women in the 21st century in India followed by the concerns of women in the Church with a view to proposing a vision and praxis for a collaborative and all inclusive Church in the 21st century India.[169] The most important issues at stake are grouped under three significant concerns: i) patriarchal ideology ii) domination iii) sub-ordination. Against this background, the thesis raises the question: How effective and relevant is the person and message of Jesus Christ in the Church in India in moving out of dichotomy to partnership and collaboration? Church in India/Asia as a whole acknowledges that the contribution of women is often undervalued or ignored and this has resulted in a spiritual impoverishment of humanity. The Church in India, in this multifaceted context, is challenged to the growing awareness of the basic equality of women and men, together with the realization of their complementary roles and functions both in society and in the Church.

Patriarchal Ideology

Patriarchy is defined as a system of male dominance legitimized within family, Church and society through superior rights, privileges, authority and power vested in the male.[170] In the words of Elizabeth Johnson, patriarchy is a form of social organization in which power is always in the hands of the dominant man or men, with others ranked below in a graded series of subordinations reaching down to the least powerful who form a large base.[171] Deriving from the Greek word *patriá*, which means family or clan (from *pater*, father), and - *arkhēs*, ruler, the term 'patriarchy' designates the structure of male dominance over women, both in the family and in society at large. It can be deployed to signify male dominance at the institutional level and can have extended substantial legal, political and economic privileges to men as a group and maintain women in a marginalized position.[172] In other words, in patriarchy, men are considered to be "subjects" and "normative" human beings, with the result that women are infantilized and treated as less than fully human objects who exist for the sake of benefiting men.[173]

With the impact of Vatican II, the Church has tried to break with its feudal past and move to freedom and democracy at least in spirit, but in practice it still needs to cut itself from the clutches of patriarchy. Continuing the flow of thought, Joan Chittister very aptly enunciates the four interlocking principles on which patriarchy rests: dualism – some things are good and some things are bad; hierarchy – things have value in ascending order; domination – some people have the right to control other people, and essential inequality – some things are simply lesser forms of life than others.[174] Sandra Schneiders compliments:

> Patriarchy is the basic principle underlying not only the subordination of women to men, but of one race to another of colonies to master colonies, of children to adults, of nations to divine right monarchs, of believers to clergy. In other words, patriarchy is the nerve of racism, classism, colonialism, and clericalism as well as sexism. Fundamentally, patriarchy is a masculine power in which all relationships are understood in terms of superiority and inferiority, and social cohesion is assured by the exercise of dominative power.[175]

This patriarchal ideology is a major cause of the violation of the women's right to equality and therefore women are often pushed to the most marginalized groups and are denied access to resources, justice, and leadership.

Gender sensitivity comprehends the ability to recognize and highlight existing gender differences with a view to deconstructing biased gender stereotypes that are social, cultural and religious constructs.

Deconstructing gender stereotypes includes a radical attitudinal change towards women, re-defining roles of women and a respectful sensitivity to womanhood.[176] Rayan in his article "Hierarchy-Religious Relationship in the Context" reflects deeper on the indispensability of being related and on the need for openness. He identifies that "the Church was brought forth into history by the Holy Spirit falling on the whole assembly in the upper room and enriching everyone with new dreams and visions. There is among us a kind of organic unity within which we share the same life-source with Christ Jesus."[177] Complementing on what is said above, Schüssler Fiorenza claims - only when the most marginalized and - those who are relegated to the bottom of this *kyriarchal* structure - are positively affirmed can the biblical promise of freedom, justice and well-being for all be made concretely present.[178] In this context Monteiro states:

> Church today is impoverished and incomplete because it follows one mode of being Church, the patriarchal mode which is the unquestionable and accepted norm. Women are consulted but neither their voice is considered nor accepted in decision-making and decision taking. Women are invited to catechize but are not permitted to proclaim the Word and share their unique God-experience. Women are included in pastoral services but excluded from active ministerial responsibilities.[179]

Women are dehumanized both in religion and society.[180] Just as patriarchy pervades all areas of women's life in society, so too Church structures and doctrines control and domesticate Christian women.[181] Church's structures and various related problems such as androcentrism and misogynism challenge the equality of women with men.[182] The important aspects presented here will highlight the existence of patriarchal ideology in the Church.[183]

Fiorenza, in her first book, *In Memory of Her*, contends that Christianity was not originally patriarchal because "the Jesus movement in Palestine was an alternative prophetic renewal movement within Israel", that had "announced the in breaking of God's *basileia* as good news to the impoverished and outcast among its own people." [184] Moreover, "in the fellowship of Jesus, women apparently did not play a marginal role, even though only a few references to women disciples survived the androcentric tradition and redaction process of the gospels.[185] According to Fiorenza, it was the post-Pauline and pseudo-Pauline tradition that eliminated women from the leadership of worship and community.[186] She further says that the patriarchal-societal ethos, in the long run, replaced the genuine Christian vision of equality.[187] As Monteiro says, "the pyramidal structure of the Church can be traced back to the Judaic world where Christianity found its inception and from where it appropriated much of the first century Hebrew cultural and religious traditions."[188] As a result, patriarchy developed into a system of human relationships built on hierarchy and subordination.

Domination

The issue of women in the Catholic Church continues to be a vital one. That, due to a system of social structures and practices in which men dominate, oppress and exploit woman's experiences and calibre are by and large ignored by patriarchal cultures.[189] A cursory glance at the organizational structure of the Church would reveal that societies in general and various organizations within the society whether religious, social, political and economic or cultural are structured hierarchically that give the impression that it is a fact that should be accepted uncritically. No wonder then, the Church, though a mystery and yet an organization[190] has its leadership at almost every level clergy-centred; laity in general and women in particular still remain powerless at the bottom of the Church structure.

According to the national survey initiated by 'Streevani' in 2013, on the role of women in the Church in the light of the CBCI Gender Policy document, indicates that less than half (45%) the respondents think that women and girl children are discriminated against in the Church.[191] Still according to the national survey only 165 of the respondents are familiar with "the Gender Policy of the Catholic Church of India". Only about 35% of them believe that the parish has taken the initiative to address issues of women's representation in parliament, equal pay for men and women and just wages for Religious women employed in Church organizations. There is greater need of the importance to ensure the protection of rights of women. For achieving an appropriate equilibrium between the ideas, the principles and the reality about gender justice related issues, the perceived deficiencies confronting fundamental gender and justice related issues; two fundamental issues like women representation and equality of wages are not satisfactorily addressed by the Church. Discrimination against women in the Church is an experienced reality.[192]

Rayan views the Church as "a critical or class ecclesiology with unequal division of religious work, and with the control of means of religious production in the hands of one group."[193] Rayan elaborates on the hierarchic character of the Church:

> The Church is hierarchic means that it has a sacred beginning (hieraarche) in God's will, in Jesus' ministry and the presence of the Spirit; it is sacred in its origins and foundations, and in the evolutionary dynamism the Spirit imparts to it. It also means that the Church is well-ordered fellowship endowed with diverse gifts and tasks co-ordinated in love for service and growth of the whole. Jesus thought of his Church as a circle of friends: You are my friends. I chose you (Jn 15:12-16).[194]

The Indian Christian Women's Movement was launched on January 11, 2014 the final day of the four-day conference on "Paradigm Shift in Vatican II and Its Impact on Women." The statement from the participants of the conference, 113 women and seven men, said: "We were challenged to change our patriarchal mind-set, to develop a feminist way of thinking, to create gender sensitivity, promote the use of inclusive language, break boundaries and move into a new way of being and doing,"[195] The *CBCI Gender Policy* articulates an inclusive vision that speaks up for an equal dignity and call to discipleship of equals. And yet in reality this vision needs to be actualized.

Subordination

The women in the Indian Church are no better off than they are in the society at large. Women do not take part in basic policy decisions; their decision-making power is limited to the practical implementation of plans. The many problems that affect the lives of women in society are also existent in the Church. This is because the social customs and traditions prevalent in society have seeped into the Church structures and into the minds of the members of the Church as well. Another area that needs a special attention is the theological formation of women. On the one hand there is no provision of employment opportunities to earn their livelihood and on the other women lack confidence and initiative to venture into newer ways of getting involved in life.

A system or an ideology in which the Church identifies men with Christ, the head, and women as the body that is subordinate and dependent ultimately leads men only to exercise leadership at all levels. Patriarchy which has widened its scope over the centuries, has led to an over-arching system of graded subjugation and oppressions. This exclusion has been often justified by quoting Scripture out of context. Hence, the Scripture is used as an important source and legitimizer of excluding and alienating women from the leadership roles in the Church.[196] This makes it imperative for both women and men, to identify attitudes that are discriminatory and dehumanizing to women, especially when these attitudes are seemed to have legitimized by Scripture. Patriarchal ideology claims divine legitimacy for women's victimization in the social and religious spheres.[197] Rekha Chennattu offers a neat synthesis saying, "Patriarchal cultures regard women as psychologically sentimental, intellectually inferior, socially marginal, religiously impure and culturally insignificant, and thus incapable of leadership."[198]

Monteiro in her article notes that the twenty-first century is witnessing "an authority-freedom conflict in various areas of life-relationships: the family, the school, work, society and the Church. The silent exodus of Christ's followers from the Catholic Church is an exasperated expression of 'enough is enough' against the cold fortress structures of patriarchal dominion and clerical domestication of ecclesial life."[199] Monteiro further says:

> Although Vatican II describes the Church as the People of God and emphasizes the equal dignity of all its members (LG 9-17; 32), the same document reaffirms the authority of the patriarchal hierarchy (18-19) and fails to recognize the importance and the place and status of women in the Church. As long as authority is understood and practised as 'power over' the community and remains only in the hands of one section of the community, the essence of Church as communion is undervalued.[200]

Following the same line of thought John Paul II in his Apostolic Letter *Mulieris Dignitatem* highlights the essential equality of man and woman since both are created in the image and likeness of God. Reading the signs of the times, John Paul II addressed the "Letter to Women" on the occasion of the 4th World Conference of Women in Beijing, 1995.[201]

The two analyses made so fare, that is, a brief overview of the Indian reality and the Church in the 21st century India show clearly the life of those who are on the periphery, the lot of the *anawim* and their dignity do not count in reality. The above discussion on the essential issues of the 21st century Church in India has identified the changing role of women in the Church as one of the most significant trends of the current era. The main concern of women is the increasing clericalization and centralization of power in the Church. Still the struggle continues between implementing the complementarity of women and the acceptance of equal partnership of women in the Church. Perhaps one of the reasons for the exclusion of women in the decision making bodies of the Church is the ban on ordination to women.

Conclusion

The analysis made above of the present situation gives us a brief overview of the 21st century India, the context in which this study is situated. The first section of this chapter focused on the analysis of the socio-economic and cultural context of the present day India. On the one hand, India has a long tradition of deep cultural and religious plurality that seeks integration and ultimate liberation. On the other, there is the challenging life situation of massive poverty and oppression, due to caste system and gender inequality which stands in need of immediate liberation. India is characterized by innovations, inventions and new discoveries; India seems to have all the basis of its economy right, the information technologies have brought about a revolution in modern life and so on. It also examined how these factors contribute to the dehumanizing of human beings.

In the second section of this chapter our focus was on the women in the 21st century Church in India. There is a growing awareness among the women today that they are not given their rightful place in life and in the Church. This divide poses a great challenge to the Church as it seeks to affirm the equal dignity of all persons. The observation is that the dehumanizing systems are on the increase. Can we still say that we are living in a globalized world, where degeneration or distortion in different spheres of life is the norm?

Next the focus would be a theological investigation of the Christological writings of Rayan and Fiorenza. While responding to the socio-religio-economic contexts of their specific milieux, Rayan and Fiorenza have offered an alternative and comprehensive approach towards human dignity and solidarity enshrined with dynamism of emancipation.

Endnotes

[1] Gender is a word often used today. For the purpose of this chapter it is important to define what "gender" is. It is a set of "stereotyping" – a social construct. Gender is the way in which a culture interprets the behavioral, cultural or psychological traits typically associated with one's sex and so encodes it within that culture that it is eventually seen as "God-given," or received as a gift from God. In this thesis, the terms like gender and feminist have been used with a personal interest in the equality between women and men and an unceasing effort to break open the boundaries that are of human constructs.

[2] The ones on the periphery of today's India still suffer due to all forms of oppression – religious, social, cultural, economic, political, and the challenge of the integral liberation of the victims should be the concern of all citizens of India irrespective of caste, creed and gender, so that our common search for human wholeness in freedom and dignity is accomplished.

³ Dietmar Rothermund, *India: The Rise of an Asian Giant* (New Haven and London: Yale University Press, 2008). Through the lens of India's past, Dietmar Rothermund offers a new perspective of India today and a fascinating look into the nation's future.

⁴ World Population Review, "India Population 2019," http://worldpoplulationreview. com/ countries/india/ (accessed September 13, 2019).

⁵ Alex Gray, "The world's 10 biggest economies in 2017," *World Economic Forum,* 9 March 2017, https://www. weforum.org/agenda/ (accessed June 18, 2017).

⁶ Resources, "President's address on the eve of Republic Day 2017," *The Hindu,* 25 January 2017, http://www.thehindu.com /news/resources (accessed April 14, 2017).

⁷ Global village is a phrase credited to be coined by the Canadian, Marshall McLuhan, in 1962. Predicting the effects of technological advances in electronics growth long before the explosion of the Internet McLuhan coined the phrase. Marshall McLuhan, *The Gutenberg Galaxy: The Making of Typographic Man* (London: Routledge and Kegan Paul, 1962), 31.

⁸ Michael Amaladoss, "Globalization from the Perspective of the Victims of History." *Integral Liberation* 1/3 (1997): 131.

⁹ According to Stanislaus, "A materialistic outlook on life, consumerism, individualism, and competition pinning only profits and business developments are some of the characteristics of this culture. In this process, not only monopoly has grip, but also money plays a pivotal role in society. Thus ethical and moral values are not respected; the poor countries are victimized in this process." Lazar Stanislaus, "Challenges to Mission and Characteristics of a Missionary," *WW* 34/1&2 (January 2001):1-2.

¹⁰ Poverty is often defined by one-dimensional measure, such as income. But no one indicator alone can capture the multiple aspects that constitute poverty. 'Multidimensional poverty' is made up of many interlocked dimensions. First, although poverty is rarely about the lack of one thing, the bottom line is lack of food. Second, poverty has important psychological dimensions such as powerlessness, voicelessness, dependency, shame and humiliation. Third, poor people lack access to basic infrastructure–roads, transportation, and clean water. Fourth, poor health and illness are dreaded almost everywhere as a source of destitution. Finally, the poor people rarely speak of income, but focus instead on managing assets – physical, human, social and environmental – as a way to cope with their vulnerability. Cf. Narayan, D., R. Patel, K. Schafft, A. Rademacher, and S. Koch-Schulte, *Voices of the Poor: Can Anyone Hear Us?* (New York: Oxford University Press and the World Bank, 2000), 4-5.

¹¹ India has been ranked 37th out of 103 nations in the 2017 global Multi-dimensional Poverty Index (MPI), according to a new report by the Oxford Poverty & Human Development Initiative. Accordingly, MPI for 2017 includes 103 countries, covering 76 per cent of the world's population. According to the estimate, 31 per cent of the 689 million poor children live in India, followed by Nigeria (8%), Ethiopia (7%) and Pakistan (6%), noted the survey, 2017. A multidimensionally poor child is one who lacks at least one-third of ten indicators, grouped into three dimensions of

poverty: health, education and standard of living. Cf. Staff Reporter, "India has 31% of world's poor kids" *The Hindu, 19 Kolkata*, 03 June 2017, http://www.thehindu. com /todays-paper/tp-national/india-has-31-of-worlds-poorkids/article18710738.ece (accessed December 21, 2017).

[12] Commenting on the plight of the neglected and discarded poor in today's globalized world, Jon Sobrino and Felix Wilfred said: During feudal times poor tenants were wanted, though they were subjugated; in the industrial capitalism, workers were wanted, even though they were often denied just wages. But today, with globalization, we have reached a situation where the poor ones are not wanted. Jon Sobrino and Felix Wilfred, "Introduction: The Reasons for Returning to This Theme," *Concilium* 5 (2001):14-15.

[13] Ramachandra Guha, "Ten Years of Change: Politics and Play," *The Telegraph* 36/30 (5 August 2017). https://www.telegraphindia.com/opinion/ten-years-of-change/cid/1461144 (accessed October 23, 2017).

[14] Willi Lambert., *Directions for Communication: Discoveries with Ignatius Loyola* (Bangalore: Claretian Publications, 2001), 44.

[15] Gali Bali, "Leadership in the Church in India Today," in *The Church in India in the Emerging Third Millenium* ed. Thomas D'Sa (Bangalore: N.B.C.L.C., 2005), 315-329.

[16] Jacob Parappally, "Social and Ecclesial Movement," in *Retelling the Story of Jesus: Through the Stories of People*, eds. Antony Kalliath and Thomas D'Sa (Bangalore: Sugranth Subodhana Publications & NBCLC, 2011), 413-414. India is also blessed with various ecclesial movements like Catholic Charismatic Movement, Basic Christian Communities, Focolare Movement, Neo-Catechumenate, Jesus' Youth, All India Catholic University Federation, Mission League, and Catholic Youth Movements.

[17] Prasad Lankapalli, *Hindutva Challenge: Christian Response as a Call to Community* (Delhi: ISPCK, 2014), 75-76.

[18] Arun Kumar, "Economic Consequences of Demonetisation–Money Supply and Economic Structure," *EPW* 52/1 (January, 2017):31-36.

[19] World Bank. "World Development Indicators Database, 2017," 28 April 2017, http://data. worldbank.org/ data-catalog/GDP-PPP-based-table(accessed June 26, 2017).

[20] The First Advance Estimates of GDP have been released in accordance with the release calendar of National Accounts. Accordingly, real GDP or GDP at Constant Prices (2011-12) in the year 2019-20 is likely to attain a level of [1] 147.79 lakh crore, as against the Provisional Estimate of GDP for the year 2018-19 of [1] 140.78 lakh crore, released on 31st May 2019. The growth in real GDP during 2019-20 is estimated at 5.0 per cent as compared to the growth rate of 6.8 per cent in 2018-19. Press Information Bureau Government of India, "First Advance Estimates of National Income," 2019-20, 7 January, 2020, https://pib.gov.in/pressreleaseshareaspx?PRID=1598643 (accessed April 20, 2020).

[21] According to IMF World Economic Outlook (April-2019), GDP (nominal) per capita of India in 2019 at current prices is projected at $2,199. India is the projected to become fifth-largest economy of the world. But, due to its huge population of more than 1.37 billion, India is at 145th position in term of GDP (nominal) per capita.

On the basis of PPP, GDP per capita of India is projected at 8,484 International Dollar in 2019. World rank is 126 and Asian rank is 31. Ministry of Statistics and Programme Implementation, "IMF World Economic Outlook" (April-2019) http://statisticstimes.com/ economy/gdp-capita-of-india.php (accessed March 23, 2020).

[22] India is the fastest-growing trillion-dollar economy in the world and the fifth-largest overall, with a nominal GDP of $2.94 trillion. India has become the fifth-largest economy in 2019, overtaking the United Kingdom and France. The country ranks third when GDP is compared in terms of purchasing power parity at $11.33 trillion. Caleb Silver, "The Top 20 Economies in the World," https://www.investopedia.com/insights/ worlds-top-economies/ (accessed March 25, 2020).

[23] This report is based on a master set of data that has been compiled by an Inter-Agency and Expert Group on Millennium Development Goals Indicators led by the Department of Economic and Social Affairs of the United Nations Secretariat, in response to the wishes of the General Assembly for periodic assessment of progress towards the MDGs. Cf. United Nations, "Goal 7–Ensure environmental sustainability," in *We Can End Poverty: The Millennium Development Goals Report 2014* (New York: United Nations, 2014), 9, http://www.un.org/millenniumgoals/2014%20MDG%20 report/ MDG%20 2014 % 20English%20web.pdf (accessed March 27, 2017).

[24] Neo-liberalism refers to "a theory of political economic practices that proposes that human well-being can best be advanced by liberating individual entrepreneurial freedoms and skills within an institutional framework characterized by strong property rights, free markets, and free trade." David Harvey, *A Brief History of Neoliberalism* (New York: Oxford University, 2005), 2-3.

[25] C.T. Kurien, "Economic Growth and Poverty in India," *Religion and Society* 55/4 (December 2017): 45.

[26] The Constitution of India uses the word secular in two different meanings. One, in the Preamble it is used to refer a neutral way of life (*Panth nirapeksha*); two, in Article 25 it is used to mean non-religious or worldly (*Laukik*). M.P.Raju, "Indian Secularism and Christians as a Minority," *Smart Companion India* 81/8 (August 2017): 10.

[27] Peter C. Phan, and Jonathan Y. Tan, "Interreligious Majority-Minority Dynamics," in David Cheethan, Douglas Pratt, and David Thomas, eds. *Understanding Interreligious Relations* (Oxford: Oxford University Press, 2013), 222.

[28] Louis Dumont, *Homo Hierarchicus: The Caste System and Its Implications* (Chicago and London: The University of Chicago Press, 1980), 21.

[29] The word "caste" has its roots in the Latin word '*castus*,' which means pure or chaste. It was first used by the Spanish as '*casta*,' meaning tribes, species or races, and was used in reference to the mixed breed between Europeans, Indians and Africans. The Portuguese used this word around the seventeenth century in the Indian context "to denote the Indian institution, as they thought such a system was intended to keep purity of blood" Shridhar V. Ketkar, *The History of Caste in India*, vol. 1 (New York: Taylor & Carpenter, 1909), 12.

[30] V. Balakrishnan Nair, *Social Development and Demographic Changes in South India: Focus on Kerala* (New Delhi: M.D. Publications, 1994), 97-99.

[31] The 2011 Census was the fifteenth nationwide Census carried out in India. The first was held in 1881, although it was not able to cover all of British-held Indian Territory. The first comprehensive nationwide Census was carried out under the auspices of Lord Ripon, the British Viceroy of India at the time, and counted a population of 288 million in 1881. Since then, Census has been held every ten years in India. cf. India Population, "World Population Review," 26 October 2016, http://worldpopulation review.com/countries/india-population/ (accessed June 26, 2017).

[32] In 1976 the term "secularism" was formally introduced in the Indian Constitution and India was declared a secular republic. "Indian secularism is intractably linked to a profound religious diversity and it is committed to respecting many values such as freedom and equality understood broadly to allow autonomy of religious communities and their equal status in society. It recognizes not only individuals' right to express their religious beliefs but also the right to religious communities to establish and maintain the educational institutions essential for the survival and preservation of their specific religious traditions, as well as their access to public funds. Moreover, secularism is designed to combat both the phenomena of discrimination within religions…" Nishant A Irudayadason, "The Role of Religion in Indian Secularism," *Smart Companion India*, 8/2 (February, 2017):12-13.

[33] Fundamentalism is a term drawn from Protestant Christianity. It is an American coinage that refers to a group of early twentieth-century Protestant activists who organized against Darwinian evolution and who championed the literal reading of the Bible. Dinesh D'Souza, *What's So Great about Christianity?* (Mumbai: Jaico Publishing House, 2008), 2.

[34] The Preamble of the Constitution of India says, 'We, the people of India, having solemnly resolved to constitute India into a sovereign socialist secular democratic republic and to secure to all its citizens: justice, social, economic and political; liberty of thought, expression, belief, faith and worship; equality of status and of opportunity; and to promote among them all fraternity assuring the dignity of the individual and the unity and integrity of the nation; in our constituent assembly this twenty-sixth day of November, 1949, do hereby adopt, enact and give to ourselves this constitution.' "Preamble" Constitution of India, 1950. Article 15 of the Constitution provides for prohibition of discrimination on grounds of sex apart from other grounds such as religion, race, caste or place of birth. Article 15(3) authorizes the State to make any special provision for women and children.

[35] Jyoti Pinto, "Does Religious Life have a Future?" (225-240), in *Women as Equal Disciples: Unfinished Task of the Church*, eds. Virginia Saldanha, Varghese Theckanath and Julie George (Delhi: Media House, 2016), 228.

[36] Venkata Subrahmanyam, C.V. and K. Ravichandran, "The Role of Universities in Rural Development," *Journal of Business and Management*, 8/5 (Mar-Apr. 2013): 23-27, http://www.iosrjournals. org/iosr-jbm/papers/Vol8-issue5/D0852327.pdf?id=5180 (accessed December 20, 2015).

[37] John Paul II, "*Sollicitudo Rei Socialis:* on Social Concern," in *Essential Catholic Social Thought*, ed. Bernard V. Brady (Maryknoll, New York: Orbis Books, 2008), 215.

[38] Kurien Kunnumpuram, *Towards a New Humanity: Reflections on the Church's Mission in India Today* (Bombay: St Pauls, 2005), 31.

[39] Gregory Jordan," The Causes of Poverty Cultural vs. Structural: Can There Be a Synthesis?" (Spring 2004): 22. https://pdfs.semanticscholar.org/8fb8/95114065cfd4464821cac28a56aec3868ae7.pdf (accessed September 2, 2019).

[40] Kunnumpuram, *Towards a New Humanity*, 201.

[41] For in Leonard Boff's reflection: "The millions of starving persons in our world question the quality of our bread: it is bitter because it contains too many children's tears; it is hard because its substance embraces the torture of so many empty stomachs." His reflections call one to a collective conversion that leads to transformation of the society. Leonard Boff, *The Lord's Prayer: The Prayer of Integral Liberation*, trans. Theodore Morrow (Maryknoll: Orbis Books; Indore: Satprakashan Sanchar Kendra, 1983), 109.

[42] Jose Pulickal, *Dynamics of Jesus Community: Towards the Discipleship in Lucan Theology* (Bangalore: Asian Trading Corporation, 2007), 260.

[43] Meenu Agrawal, "Synopsis" *Economic Reforms, Unemployment and Poverty: The Indian Experience* (New Century Publications, 2008)

[44] In India, a person working 8 hours a day for 273 days in a year is regarded as employed on a standard person year basis. Thus, a person to be called an employed person must get meaningful work for a minimum of 2184 hours in a year. The person, who does not get work even for this duration, is known as unemployed person. A person having worked for an hour or more on any one or more days during the reference period gets the employed status. Prabhat Chaudhary, 'Impact of Economic Liberalization on Employment Generation in India' Chaudhary Charan Singh University, Meerut, 10 March 2010, http://hdl.handle.net/10603/ 24233 (accessed August 19, 2017).

[45] Jose Kalapura, "Christianity and Marginalized Communities" in India: A Subaltern Historical Overview," in *Indian Church History Review* 43/1 (2009):7-36

[46] Azra Abidi, "Educational Marginalization of Muslim Girls: A Study on the Role of State and Religion," JOSR 5/ 4 (Jul-Aug. 2015): 62.

[47] Felix Wilfred, "The Margins: The Site of God's Visitation - A Meditation," *TMILL* 11/4 (1999): 117.

[48] *Dalit* is a term that literally means crushed or broken, denoting the oppressed existence of communities in India who were until recently known as the untouchables. *Dalit* (Sanskrit *dalita*, 'split, broken, and crushed') is a general term for the most disadvantaged hereditary groups (caste, jāti) in Indian society. In simple terms, the caste system can be understood as the division of society into four occupationally determined, hierarchically structured and hereditary in nature social groups: the Brahmins (the priests), the *Kshatriyas* (the warriors), the *Vaisyas* (the merchants) and the *Shudras* (the laborers and craftsmen). *Dalit* are subjected to a variety of oppressive caste practices such as being denied access to basic amenities like water or worship

in village temples. Their touch is polluting. Although this pollution is attributed by some to their occupations, such as working on leather and other work involving dead cattle, the consumption of meat and toddy, the principle of purity and pollution places it in their birth. Cf. Dermot Killingley, "*Dalits*," in *Encyclopedia of Hinduism*, eds. Denise Cush, Catherine Robinson, Michael York (London: Routledge, 2008) 158.

[49] The term 'subaltern' is from Ranajit Guha who first used it in the late nineteen-seventies. In the context of south Asia, subaltern refers to the subordination of South Asian society under British colonial rule. It also means the power of the indigenous elite over other sections of the population. Subaltern groups are those assigned inferior rank by the dominant group. Ranajit Guha, "Preface," in *Subaltern Studies* I: Writings on South Asian History and Society (Delhi: Oxford University, 1982), vii, 1-8, as cited in *Quest for Identity: India's Churches of Indigenous Origin: the "Little Tradition" in Indian Christianity Quest*, Roger E. Hedlund (Delhi: ISPCK, 2000). In terms of Christian institutions in India, perspectives arising "from below", through local initiative, may be classed as subaltern. Because they are not imposed but they are the expression of local people who are not so privileged, marginalized or oppressed. Hedlund, *Quest for Identity*, 9-10.

[50] ITA, "The Significance of Jesus Christ in the Context of Religious Pluralism in India," *TMILL* 1/4 (October-December, 1998): 88-96, quoted in Felix M. Podimattam, *Global Spirituality: Ecumenical, Inter-religious, and Continental Spirituality* (Delhi: Media House, 2005), 35-36.

[51] Shalini Mulackal, "Church's Dialogue with the Marginalized," *AJTR* 58/1 (January 2013): 8-19.

[52] CTI Reviews, *Social Inequality, Patterns and Processes*, 5th edition (Cram101 Textbook Reviews, 2016), 66.

[53] G. Cosmon Arokiaraj, "Addressing Caste Discrimination within Indian Church," *FORUM of Religious for Justice and Peace* 30 (Jan-April, 2017): 15.

[54] Ashwini Deshpande, *The Grammar of Caste: Economic Discrimination in Contemporary India* (New Delhi: Oxford University Press, 2011), 37.

[55] Jose Thayil, "The Experience and Expression of the Divine: A Dalit Perspective," in *Cross-Cultural Encounter, Experience and Expression of the Divine*, Conference Series, eds. Mohan Doss and Andreas Vonach (Innsbruck: Innsbruck University Press, 2009), 81.

[56] Social disparity refers to relational processes in society that have the effect of limiting or harming a group's social status, class, and circle such as access to voting rights, freedom of speech and assembly, access to education, health care, quality housing so on and so forth and reasons for social inequality are different in India, which are often broad and far reaching. Reviews, *Social Inequality, Patterns and Processes*, 6.

[57] George M. Sores-Prabhu, "The Indian Church Challenged by Poverty and Caste," in *Biblical Themes for a Contextual Theology Today*, vol. 1, ed. Isaac Padinjarekuttu (Pune: Jnana-Deepa Vidyapeeth, 1999), 143.

[58] Samuel Rayan, "Theological Priorities in India Today," in *Irruption of the Third World: Challenge to Theology: Papers from the Fifth International Conference of*

Ecumenical Association of Third World Theologians, 1981, eds., Virginia Fabella and Sergio Torres (New York: Orbis Books, 1983), 33.

[59] George M. Soares-Prabhu, "From Alienation to Inculturation: Some Reflections on Doing Theology in India," in *Biblical Themes for a Contextual Theology Today: The Collected Work of George M. Soares Prabhu* (Pune: JDV Theological Series, 1999), 86

[60] Pinto, *Encountering Christ in the Suffering Humanity,* 10.

[61] Rig-Veda 10.90.12 is the only one passage in the Rig-Veda which mentions the four castes. Ralph T.H. Griffith Trans., *The Hymns of the Rigveda,* vol. II (Benares: E.J. Lazarus & Co., 1926), 519.

[62] K. P. Kuruvilla, "*Dalit* Theology: An Indian Christian Attempt to Give Voice to the Voiceless," as cited in *New Challenges for Dalit Theology: The Changing Face of the Indian Society and the New Challenges for Dalit Theology,* ed. Jesudas M. Athyal, *Presented at the International Consultation on, 'Dalit* Theology and A Theology of the Oppressed'* (Chennai: Gurukul Lutheran Theological College, 2004).

[63] They were not allowed to own any land and denied education too. "The Vedas, symbolizing learning, was out of bounds for the *Dalits,* the hearing of which was to be punished with pouring lead into the ear and the reciting of which was to be punished by cutting off the tongues." F. Devashayam, "Pollution, Poverty and Powerless: A *Dalit* Perspective," in *A Reader in Dalit Theology,* eds., Arvind. P. Nirmal and V. Devashayam (Madras: Christian Literature Society, 1990), 10.

[64] Pauline Chhakkalakal, *Discipleship: A Space for Women's Leadership? A Feminist Theological Critique* (Mumbai: Pauline Publication, 2004), 28-29.

[65] Karma is the sum total of one's action in previous birth, determining one's unalterable future destiny. Mahendra Kulasrestha, ed. *Culture India: A Compendium of Indian Philosophy, Religions, Arts, Literature and Society* (Delhi: Lotus Press, 2006), 55.

[66] Samuel Rayan, "Jesus and the Struggles of the Masses in India," *TMILL* 11/1 (1990): 22. See also, George Oommen, "The Emerging *Dalit* Theology: A Historical Appraisal," *Indian Church History Review,* 34/1 (June 2000): 19-37.

[67] Kancha Ilaiah, *The State and Repressive Culture: The Andhra Experience* (Hyderabad: Swecha Prachurenalu, 1989), 45.

[68] Samuel Rayan, "The Challenge of *Dalit* Issue: Some Theological Perspectives," in *Dalits and Women: Quest for Humanity,* 117-137, ed. V. Devashayam (Madras: Lutheran Theological College and Institute, 1992).

[69] Kalarikkal Poulose Aleaz, "Some Features of *Dalit* Theology," *AJT* 18 (2004): 164.

[70] Besides, National Crime Records Bureau (NCRB), statistics show that 2,233 *Dalit* women were raped in 2014, up from 2,073 in 2013, 1,576 in 2012, 1,557 in 2011, 1,349 in 2010 and 1,346 in 2009. Kidnappings and abductions also went up in these years, barring in 2012 when there was a marginal decline. Against 755 kidnappings/abductions in 2014, there were 628 in 2013, 490 in 2012, 616 in 2011, 511 in 2010 and 512 in 2009. Cf. Bharti Jain, "Crimes against Dalits rose 19% in 2014, murders rose to 744," *Times of India* (Oct 22, 2015) http://timesofindia.indiatimes. com (accessed April 21, 2017).

[71] Historically, *Dalit* protest and resistance movements went through several phases. Bhakti movements within Hinduism between the 14th and 16th centuries symbolized the low castes' aspiration for an egalitarian society and religion. Eventually these movements were either suppressed or co-opted into the mainstream by the dominant castes or by British colonialism. Oommen, "The Emerging *Dalit* Theology," 19. The first significant attempt at conscientising and mobilizing the subaltern sections in the colonial period was the Satyashodak Samaj led by Jotirao Phule (1827-1890), the social reform leader of Maharashtra.

[72] Nirmal states that Jesus identified himself with the "*Dalits*" of his day, and in his "Nazareth Manifesto" (Lk 4:18–19), he promised liberation for the prisoners. On the cross "he was the broken, the crushed, the split, the torn, and the driven asunder man –the *Dalit* in the fullest possible meaning of that term." Therefore, it is "precisely in and through the weaker, the oppressed and the marginalized that God's saving glory is manifested or displayed. This is because brokenness belongs to the very being of God." As cited in Volker Küster, *The Many Faces of Jesus Christ: Intercultural Christology* (Maryknoll, New York: Orbis, 2001), 164, 172.

[73] For example, the religious movement like Buddhism, Jainism, *Bhakti*, the social movements of *Brahmo Samaj by* Ram Mohan Roy, Sri Narayan Guru, were attempts to break the caste system.

[74] John C. B. Webster, *The Dalit Christians: A History* (Delhi: ISPCK, 1994), 40-41, 45.

[75] Webster, *The Dalit Christians*, 202-206.

[76] Samuel Rayan, "The Churches and Justice to Christians of Scheduled Caste Origin," *WWW* 11/6 (July, 1978): 227-239.

[77] Felix Wilfred, *Dalit Empowerment* (Delhi: ISPCK, 2007), 6-7.

[78] Bama Faustina, "Caste Discrimination from a Woman's Perspective," *FORUM of Religious for Justice and Peace* 30 (Jan-April, 2017): 10.

[79] Article 46 in the Constitution of India 1949.National Commission for Scheduled Tribes: Government of India, "Constitutional Safeguards for STs," https://ncst.nic.in/content/constitutional-safeguards-sts (accessed April 15, 2020).

[80] The ritual status of women in early and middle Vedic times was virtually equal to that of men. Women enjoyed enormous freedom and power during this age. Consequently, during the late Vedic period (900-500 BCE) the scene was totally changed. Names of Sita, Savitri, Damayanti and Draupadi are constantly cited as exemplary characters to be emulated. Somen Das, *Christian Ethics and Indian Ethos*, (Indian Society, 1989), 156; See, Lynn E. Gatwood, *Devi and the Spouse Goddess: Women, Sexuality and Marriage in India* (New Delhi: Manohar Publications, 1991), 29. Both the *Sruti* and the *Smriti* literature of Hinduism failed to advocate the rights and equality of women. On the contrary, they considered them as slaves to be exploited and oppressed. Das, *Christian Ethics*, 158; furthermore, Muslim women of India to a certain extent enjoyed freedom during the periods of Sultanate of Delhi and the Mughal period. But ever in history they were suffering under the clutches of religion and its practices. Even in the present day the practices like *pardah* system, shariat, child marriage, polygamy etc., affected the status of women and they are still

victims of rape, dowry death and so on. Asghar Ali Engineer, ed. *Problems of Muslim Women in India* (Hyderabad: Orient Longman Limited, 1995). Thus, the oppressive patriarchal values are the reasons for the low status and dignity of women in India.

[81] Kochurani Abraham, "The Role of Women in the Catholic Church," in Kurien Kunnumpuram & Evelyn Monteiro, *Towards the Full Flowering of the Human: Interdisciplinary Studies on the Empowerment of Women* (Bandra, Mumbai: St Pauls, 2011), 54.

[82] For more than 30 years, UNFPA has advocated for women and girls, promoting legal and policy reforms, gender-sensitive data collection, and supporting initiatives that improve women's health and expand their choices in life. Helen Clark UNDP Administrator, "Foreword" *UNDP Gender Equality Strategy 2014-2017*, http://www. am. undp.org/content/dam/armenia/docs/ (accessed July 6, 2017).

[83] The improved societal control and societal legislations have played a vital role in bringing a change. They have fought, conquered and travelled many roads unknown to be in the position that they are today. Woman's struggle begins from the time when she gets attached to her mother's womb and lasts till her last breath. But for a few women like Medha Patkar, Arundathi Roy, Sr Rani Maria and Sr Valsa, the journey was difficult. By no means is this list exhaustive.

[84] Amelia Vasquez, "Sixth Plenary Assembly: Workshop Discussion Guide Women and the Church's Service to Life in Asia," *FABC Papers*, no. 72 (January 1995):2-6.

[85] P.C. Tripathy, *Contemporary Social problems and the Law* (New Delhi: A.P.H. Publishing Corporation, 2000), 1.

[86] Shalini Mulackal, "Who is Jesus for Indian Women? A Feminist Critical Enquiry" *VJTR* 80/6 (2016): 435.

[87] At a more subtle level, we see the growth of the cosmetic industry with the parallel and associated rise of beauty competitions, where model/winners are more and more chosen from the developing countries to propagandize these products. At a more direct level, we are witnesses to continuous trafficking young girls and growing violence against women.

[88] CBCI Commission for Women, *Gender Policy of the Catholic Church of India* (*Delhi*: CBCI Centre, 2010), 3-4. The Gender Policy of the Catholic Church of India is a first in the universal Church. it has taken into account the situation of women in India.

[89] Satyabrata Paul, "Statistics of Gender Bias," *The Hindu* (June 2, 2016): 4.

[90] As a whole the country ranks 127th on gender inequality index and 114th on gender gap in the world. The report claims that only 30.3% of women are in the workforce in India, as per the World Bank WDI report among the eight South East Asian countries and ranks 134th in the world when it comes to economic participation of women. Nepal has the highest with 83.1% women formally employed. Aparajita Ray, "India Ranks 127th on Gender Inequality Index out of 142 Countries," *The Times of India*, 12 November 2015, http://timesofindia.indiatimes.com/ (accessed April 7, 2017).

[91] CBCI Commission for Women, *Gender Policy of the Catholic Church of India*, 3-4.

⁹² Faustina, "Caste Discrimination from a Woman's Perspective," 12.

⁹³ Samuel Rayan, "Editorial," *JD* 17 (1987): 99.

⁹⁴ Tripathy, *Contemporary Social problems and the Law*, 2-3.

⁹⁵ Namita Kohli, "10 and Mum," *The Week* 35/33 (August 13, 2017): 22-27; Namita Kohli, "Failure to Deliver," *The Week* 35/33 (August 13, 2017): 28-29.

⁹⁶ According to the United Nations, data on Sex ratio India is at 189th position out of 201 countries in terms of female to male ratio. Among Asian countries, India is at 43th position out of 51. Ministry of Statistics and Programme Implementation, "Sex ratio of India" *United Nations (World Population Prospects 2019)* 18 March 2020 http://statisticstimes.com/demographics/sex-ratio-of-india.php.(accessed April 25, 2020).

⁹⁷ Cedric Prakash, "Stop Human Trafficking Now!" *Indian Currents* 29/31 (July 31, 2017): 18.

⁹⁸ UNODC, "Global Report on Trafficking in Persons 2016, *UNODC Research* https://www.unodc.org/documents/data-and-analysis/glotip/2016_Global_Report_on_Traffickingin _persons.pdf (accessed April 20, 2020).quoted in Prakash, "Stop Human Trafficking Now!", 18.

⁹⁹ Carol Glatz, "Pope Francis: Human trafficking is an open wound on society," *Catholic Herald*, 10 April 2014, http://www. catholicherald.co.uk/news/ (accessed April 8, 2017). This is what the Pope said at the Pontifical Academy of Sciences to participants in an international conference on combating human trafficking, which was organized by the Bishops' Conference of England and Wales and Cardinal Vincent Nichols of Westminster in April 10, 2014.

¹⁰⁰ As the International Labour Office rightly points out, in the process of searching for economic opportunities, some migrants are coerced into work they did not choose willingly. They have been deceived about the nature of their work or conditions of their employment contract; they work under threat subjected to violence, and are confined to their workplace or do not receive the wage that was promised to them. Cf. Bryn William-Jones, "Concept of Personhood and the Commodification of Body," *Health Law Review* 7/3 (1999): 11-13.

¹⁰¹ Cedric Prakash, "Crime against Humanity," *The New Leader* 130/14 (July 16-31, 2017): 10-13. AMRAT is a network of over fifty religious Congregations of South Asia, with a 'collaborative commitment' to address the issue and to put an end to this modern-day form of slavery and exploitation. Prakash, "Stop Human Trafficking Now!" 19.

¹⁰² Prakash, "Crime against Humanity," 10-11. More than 21 million people across the world are victims of human trafficking. They are de facto 21st century slaves. More than 10,000 children go missing every year. Almost half of them are never traced. Forced labor constitutes India's largest trafficking problem; men, women, and children in debt bondage are forced to work in brick kilns, rice mills, agriculture, and embroidery factories. Most of the untraced children become victims of human trafficking, slavery, begging and prostitution. Kailash Satyarthi, "Free Children from Chains: India and the World need Multi-dimensional Strategy to Stop Human

Trafficking," *The Telegraph*, 3 August 2017. The writer is 2014 Nobel peace laureate and founder of Kailash Satyarthi Children's Foundation.

[103] CBCI Commission for Women, "Gender Policy," 31.

[104] Enakshi Ganguly Thukral, ed. "The Trafficked Child" in *Children in Globalising India: Challenging Our Conscience* (New Delhi: HAQ, Centre for Child Rights, 2002), 258.

[105] CBCI Commission for Women, "Gender Policy,"24-25.

[106] Kunnumpuram, *Towards a New Humanity,* 12.

[107] Hans Lilje, "The Crisis of Modern Man," *Christian Century* 64/47 (1947): 1395.

[108] Enakshi Ganguly Thukral, ed. "The Trafficked Child," in *Children in Globalising India: Challenging Our Conscience* (New Delhi: HAQ centre for Child Rights, 2002), 258.

[109] Sahaya Mary, "The Emerging Challenges to Christian Mission and Women's Response," in *The Emerging Challenges to Christian Mission Today*: Revisioning Mission from Religious, Cultural, Historical & Women Perspectives, eds. S.M. Michael & Jose Joseph (Pune: Ishvani Kendra, 2016), 67-70.

[110] Patriarchy refers to the male domination both in public and private spheres. In this way, feminists use the term 'patriarchy' to describe the power relationship between men and women as well as to find out the root cause of women's subordination. Patriarchy, in its wider definition, means the manifestation and institutionalization of male dominance over women and children in the family and the extension of male dominance over women in society in general. Abeda Sultana, "Patriarchy and Women's Subordination: A Theoretical Analysis," *The Arts Faculty Journal*, (July 2010-June 2011): 2-3. https://www.banglajol.info/index. php/AFJ/article/view/12929/9293 (accessed April, 2018). For a detailed explanation see section 1.4.1. Patriarchal Ideology.

[111] V. Geetha, *Patriarchy, Theorizing Feminism* (Calcutta: STREE, 2007), 4.

[112] Sudhir Kakar, "Feminine Identity in India," in *Women in Indian Society: A Reader*, ed. Rehana Ghadially (New Delhi: Sage Publications India Pvt. Ltd., 1998), 47.

[113] The Laws of Manu states "though of bad conduct or debauched or even devoid of good qualities, a husband must always be worshipped like a god by a good wife" (*Manusm[iti* V: 154). Arthor Coke Burnell, *The Ordinances of Manu: Translated from the Sanskrit with an Introduction*, ed. Edward W. Hopkins (London: Kegan Paul, Trench, Trübner, & Co. Lt. 1891), 131, 150-156.

[114] Ananatnand Rambachan, "A Hindu Perspective," in *What Men Owe to Women: Men's Voices from World Religions*, eds. John C. Raines and Daniel C. Maguire (Albany: State University of New York Press, 2000), 17-40.

[115] Caritas India, the developmental wing of the Catholic Church in India, has always searched for avenues to make her presence felt in the hearts of the economically, socially and culturally marginalized through her partners in different regions and dioceses. Caritas India's commitment to Gender equality is rooted in the biblical vision of the wholesome human being, created in the image and likeness of God. It provides a framework for removing this inequality and attempts to eradicate gender

discriminatory attitudes. Caritas India, "Gender Policy," www.caritasindia.org/support/ gender policy.pdf (accessed December 18, 2014).

[116] Article 25 of the Constitution of India states, "Subject to public order, morality and health and to other provisions of this part, all persons are equally entitled to freedom of conscience and the right freely to profess, practice and propagate religion; Nothing in this article shall affect the operation of any existing law or prevent the State from making any law-(i) regulating or restricting any economic, financial, political or other secular activity which may be associated with religious practice; (ii) providing for social welfare and reform or the throwing open of Hindu religious institutions of a public character to all classes and sections of Hindus." Dr Pawan Kumar, "Religious Pluralism in Globalized India: A Constitutional Perspective" *Journal of Humanities and Social Science* 3/3 (Sep-Oct. 2012): 5.

[117] Raju, "Indian Secularism and Christians as a Minority," 13.

[118] Michael Amaladoss, "Responding to Fundamentalism," *Jivan* (January, 2009): 25-26.

[119] Bina Srinivasan, *Negotiating Complexities: A Collection of Feminist Essays* (New Delhi: Promilla & CO Publishers in association with Bibliophile South Asia, 2007), 182.

[120] Srinivasan, *Negotiating Complexities,* 181.

[121] Franz Xavier Scheuerer, *Interculturality: A Challenge for Mission of the Church* (Bangalore: Asian Trading Corporation, 2001), 29.

[122] In the rest of the world, especially beyond South Asia, this word tends to relate to social unity and cohesion, and to socially progressive and collective modes of thinking and activities: communal agriculture, communal ownership of land, communal irrigation, communal kitchen, communal leisure, communal singing and communal dancing, etc. In all these examples, the word communal suggests public sharing in contrast with private and individualistic pursuits, a positive connotation that implies cooperation and mutual tolerance. Pritam Singh, "Institutional Communalism in India," *EWP* 1/48 (July 11, 2015): 48.

[123] Social Science, "National Integration and Secularism" in *Contemporary India: Issues and Goals* Module 4: 202-219. http://www.nios.ac.in/media/documents/ secsocscicour/english/lesson-24(acessed August 21, 2016).

[124] Singh, "Institutional Communalism in India," 49. Thus, communalism in India has, as noted earlier, a colonial legacy wherein the rulers (Britishers) used religious contrasts, existing among the different communities to their advantage by giving them prominence.

[125] Bernard D'Samy, "Communalism and Religious Fundamentalism in Asia," in *Religion and Politics in Asia Today* (Bangalore: Dharmaram, 2001), 220.

[126] Ankur Aggarwal, "Secularism, Communalism and Fundamentalism," 2 May 2015, http://lordkrishn aias.blogspot.in/2015/05/secularism-communalism-and.html (accessed August 18, 2017).

[127] Khwaja Abdul Muntaqim, "Challenges to Constitutional Mandate for Religious Harmony" *IOS organize lecture*, 17October 2015, https://www.iosworld.org/ Challengesto_Constitutional Mandate_ for_ Religious_Harmony.php (accessed June

23, 2017). Abdul Muntaqim in his lecture on the one hand upheld the essence of secularism in India to be the recognition and preservation of different types of people with diverse languages and different beliefs, and placing them together so as to form a whole and united India. On the other, he pleaded for immediate enactment of the "Prevention of Communal and Targeted Violence (Access to Justice and Reparations) Bill, 2011" against the backdrop of incidents of communal violence against Muslims in different parts of the country.

[128] Unit 3, "Fundamentalism, Communalism and Secularism," https://reliableandvalid. files. Word press.com/2016/06/unit-32- (accessed August 18, 2017).

[129] Muricken, "Foreword" in *Secular Challenge to Communal Politics*, xiv.

[130] D R Goya, "Communal Challenge to India's Secular Nationalism," in *Religious Fundamentalism in Asia* ed. V. D. Chopra (New Delhi: Gyan Publishing House, 1994), 20.

[131] Teacher Guide, "Fundamentalism and Terrorism," http://www.distributionaccess. com/ new/pdf (accessed August 21, 2014).

[132] Guide, "Fundamentalism and Terrorism".

[133] Vimal Tirimanna, "Can the War against Terrorism be won?" *VJTR* 6/7 (July 2004): 521-539.

[134] None of us can forget the violence unleashed against Christians in Odisha and in other parts of the country some of which are documented. Christians are targeted in a systematic manner since the 1990s in Gujarat.

[135] Francis Gonsalves, "Carrying in our body the Marks of His Passion," *VJTR*, 72/11 (November, 2008): 801-807. "Attacks on Churches Decried." See *The Hindu: Special Correspondent, Hindu-Christian meet takes stand against 'compulsory conversions'* September 30, 2008.

[136] Joseph Lobo, *Encountering Jesus Christ in India: An Alternative Way of Doing Christology in a Cry-for-life Situation Based on the Writings of George M. Soares-Prabhu* (Bangalore: Asian Trading Corporation, 2004), 57, 58

[137] On August 3, 2017, the National Council of Churches in India (NCCI) – a forum representing 14 million Protestant and Orthodox Christians in India – has sought a law against violence targeting minorities. The forum states: "What makes us feel so exasperated is that the state and central governments are not taking severe action against the different expressions of vigilantism." "Christians Seek Law against Violence Targeting Minorities," *UCAN India*, 7 August 2017, http://www. ucanindia. in/news/ (accessed August 10, 2017).

[138] Willi Lambert, *Directions for Communication: Discoveries with Ignatius Loyola* (Bangalore: Claretian Publications, 2001), 44.

[139] Francis Thonippara, "St. Thomas Christians: The First Indigenous Church of India," in *Christianity is Indian: The Emergence of an Indigenous Community*, ed. Roger E Hedlund (Delhi: ISPCK, 2000), 60-61.

[140] Census Data 2011-Government of India, *The Census Data* 2011, http://censusindia. govt.in/ (accessed January 14, 2016). The current population of India is 1,377,529,845

as of Sunday, April 26, 2020, based on Worldometer elaboration of the latest United Nations data. World Meter, "Elaboration of data by United Nations, Department of Economic and Social Affairs, Population Division. World Population Prospects: The 2019," Revision. .https://www.worldometers.info/world-population/india-population/ (accessed April 25, 2020).

[141] Religion Data-Census 2011, "Population Census 2011," https://www.census2011co. in /religion.php accessed September 26, 2018).

[142] Etymologically the term "Catholic" means "according to the whole" (*kath' holou*), hence, universal, entire, and complete. The Church is broadly inclusive because it is spread across the face of the globe and open to people of every race, gender, nationality, language, and social condition. Catholicity in this sense is opposed to every kind of sectarianism or religious individualism. According to the Second Vatican Council, the Church is not bound in an exclusive way to any one culture, but can enter into communion with various cultures on their own terms (*GS 58*). Avery Dulles, "Catholicity and Catholicism," *Concordia Theological Quarterly* 50/2 (April 1986): 81-83.

[143] S.M. Michael, "Intercultural Living for Effective Mission in the Postmodern World," *VJTR* 81/2 (February, 2017): 88-89.

[144] CBCI, *Gender Policy of the Catholic Church of India* (New Delhi: CBCI Center, 2010), 8.

[145] *sui juris* Churches means Churches "of one's own right/law," or "of a particular nature." This means that they have their own particular liturgy, theology, spirituality, and code of law that set them apart. Another term applied to all of these Churches is "autonomous", meaning that they have their own laws, different from the Code of Canon Law governing the Western Church. The Western Church of Rome, the largest *sui juris* Church, and the other 19 *sui juris* Eastern Churches comprise the Roman Catholic communion Churches. Kath Engebretson, Marian de Souza, Gloria Durka, Liam Gearon, *International Handbook of Inter-religious Education*, (Dordrecht: Springer, 2010), 132.

[146] John M. Huels, "Title I: Ecclesiastical Laws," in *New Commentary on the Code of Canon Law*, eds. John P Bea, James A Coriden, and Thomas J. Green (New York: Paulist Press, 2000), 57.

[147] X.D. Selvaraj, in his article describes civil society as a public space not only between the state and the market in which people debate and tackle action, but it is also a society which provides ample space for open and public dialogues, discussions, counter-cultural movements and protests. X. D. Selvaraj, "How Prophetic is the Church in India Today," in *The Church in India in the Emerging Third Millennium*, ed, Thomas D'Sa (Bangalore: N.B.C.L.C., 2005), 501.

[148] Henceforth Second Vatican Council will be referred to as Vatican II

[149] Melpa Lopez, "Emerging Challenges to Christian Mission: Women's Perspective," in *The Emerging Challenges to Christian Mission Today: Revisioning Mission from Religious, Cultural, Historical & Women Perspectives*, eds. S.M. Michael & Jose Joseph (Pune: Ishvani Kendra, 2016), 63.

[150] CBCI Commission For Women, *Gender Policy of the Catholic Church of India*.

[151] Inigo Joachim, "Empowering Women," Presented at Catholic Bishops Conference of India (CBCI) Meeting at Jamshedpur, Scriptural Spiritual and Theological Foundations, http://inigoJoachim.com/ empowering-women, (accessed October 23, 2007).

[152] Pope Francis, "Pope Francis: women must truly participate in Church and Society," https://www .youtube.com/watch?v+c7mt_WnQnqM, (accessed February 25, 2015).

[153] Ordination of Women, "Pope Francis to consider ordaining women as deacons," https://www.the guardian.com/world/2016/may/12 (accessed May 15, 2016). Deacons are one of the three "orders" of ordained ministry in the Church, after bishops and priests and can fulfill some but not all of the duties of priests including preaching, conducting baptisms and serving Holy Communion.

[154] Samuel Rayan, "Sociological Factors and the Local Church as Eucharistic Community," *VJTR* 40 (August, 1976): 307-312.

[155] S.M. Michael, "Christian Vision of Human Life and *Dalit* and Tribal Responses to Christianity in India," in *Church in India Tomorrow: A Roadmap for her Mission and Ministry in the Third Millennium* eds. Bishop Gregory Karotemporel, Jacob Marangattu and Paul Vithayathil (Rajkot: Deepti Publications, 2011), 244 -245.

[156] Susan Elizabeth Smith, *Women in Mission: From the New Testament to Today* (New York: Orbis Books, 2015), 167.

[157] Leonardo Boff, *The Maternal Face of God: The Feminine and Its Religious Expressions* (San Francisco: Harper & Row, 1987), 70.

[158] In this context we may note with satisfaction the contribution of *Mater Dei* Institute of Goa in educating women religious in the field of theology.

[159] CBCI Commission for Education and Culture, "The Contribution of the Indian Catholic Church in the Field of Education" http://www.cbcieducation.com/ contribution.aspx (accessed July25, 2018). More information can be found at www. cbcieducation.com/contribution.aspx.

[160] Matters India, Institute that strengthens Indian women religious, *Matters India* January 2, 2015 http://mattersindia.com/2015/01/institute-that-strengthens-indian-women-religious/ (accessed August 30, 2019).

[161] Inigo, "Scriptural and Theological Foundations," *VJTR* 72 (2008): 465-475.

[162] Some notable feminist theologians in India are: Sr Pauline Chakkalakal, Sr Evelyn Monteiro, SCC Rekha M. Chennattu, RA, Sr Pushpa Joseph Sr Shalini Mulackal, Sr Kochurani Abraham, and Sr Philomena D'Souza.

[163] Evelyn Monteiro and Kochurani Abraham, "Statement of the Indian Theological Association," in *Concerns of Women: An Indian Theological Response* (Bangalore: Dharmaram Publications, 2005), 216.

[164] It was in 1982 that a few like-minded Christian women got together and started Women's Institute for New Awakening, India. The 'Women's Institute for New Awakening' (WINA) women took their cues from some well-known western women theologians. The purpose was to bring about an awareness of women's place in the

Church as well as in society in India. Being led by the Spirit, WINA organized four workshops on theology: i) Human liberation of women, Bombay, in 1988; ii) Women doing contextual theology, Bangalore, in 1989; iii) Woman and her God Experience, Khandala, in 1990; and iv) Liberating ourselves-Indian women breaking free of patriarchy, Bombay, 1993. B. S. Chandrababu, L. Thilagavathi, *Woman: Her History and Her Struggle for Emancipation* (Chennai: Bharathi Puthakalayam, 2009), 524-525.

[165] The coming together of feminist theologians in the 1980s was "a new axe laid to the root" of the current one-down position of women in the Church. Pearl Drego, "The Feminist View-Point," *VJTR* 48/3 (March, 1984): 114.

[166] In the mid-1960s the second wave of American feminism burst upon the scene with the publication of Betty Friedan's Feminist Mystique in 1964. In 1975, the first Women's Ordination Conference organized by Catholic nuns and lay women, drew 1300 people to Detroit and set the ordination issue in the broad context of a new concept of ministry. In the early 1970s there was a great influx of women into seminaries - the number of women seminarians doubled between 1972 and 1975. In September 1983, the Women's Theological Center opened in Boston with a year-long program, integrating theory and praxis, spirituality and ministry, in a feminist perspective. Janet Kalven, "Feminist Theology in the United States," *VJTR* 48/3 (1984): 126-27.

[167] Therefore, "the Church reproves, as foreign to the mind of Christ, any discrimination against people or any harassment of them on the basis of their race, color, and condition in life or religion. Accordingly, following the footsteps of the holy apostles Peter and Paul, the sacred Council earnestly begs the Christian faithful to "conduct themselves well among the Gentiles" (1 Pet 2:12} and if possible, as far as depends on them, to be at peace with all people (see Rom 12:18) and in that way to be true daughters and sons of the Father who is in heaven (see Mt 5:45)" (NA 15), also see GS 29.

[168] The cultural and social roles that the women have to play in their daily life affect their nature while cultural pressures reinforce role stereotypes. Thus certain qualities are developed in the female to prepare them for motherhood and bring about their complete economic and physical dependence on the male.

[169] The basic questions that require to be answered in this section of the chapter are: what is the relevance of Jesus and his message to women in the Church in today's milieu? Will the all-inclusive vision of Jesus Christ reflected in the writings of Samuel Rayan and Schüssler Fiorenza bring back the Church to her original image?

[170] Virginia Saldanha, "Christian Discipleship: Women's Perspective," (454-473) in *The Church in India in the Emerging Third Millennium*, 457.

[171] Elizabeth A. Johnson, *She Who Is: The Mystery of God in Feminist Theological Discourse* (New York: The Crossroad Publishing Company, 2001), 23. The adjective is patriarchal, the system is patriarchy.

[172] Maja Mikula, *Key Concepts in Cultural Studies* (Basingstoke: Palgrave Macmillan, 2008), 149.

[173] Orlando O. Espín, James B. Nickoloff, *An Introductory Dictionary of Theology and Religious Studies* (Collegeville: Liturgical Press, 2007), 1011. Women in India are still classified as less valuable, less strong, economically less attractive and not suitable for public leadership roles.

[174] Joan Chittister, "Women and Moral Leadership," (published in October 25, 2016) https://youtube/ Mg8OU_43s2cExcerpt_Joan_Chittister_Women_Moral_Leadership/ (accessed August 8, 2017); see also J. Chittister, *Heart of Flesh: A Feminist Spirituality for Women and Men* (Ottawa: Novalis, 1998), 25.

[175] Sandra Marie Schneiders, *Women and the Word: The Gender of God in the New Testament and the Spirituality of Women* (New York: Paulist Press, 1986), 13.

[176] Evelyn Monteiro, "Who Will Break Down the Wall?" in *Dreams and Visions: New Horizons for an Indian Church*, eds, R. Rocha, Kuruvilla P. (Pune: Jnana-Deepa Vidyapeeth, 2002), 248; see also Varkey Cardinal Vithayathil, "Foreword," to *Gender Policy of the Catholic Church of India* 2010, ix-xi.

[177] Samuel Rayan, "Hierarchy-Religious Relationship in the Context," in *It Shall Not Be So Among You* (Hyderabad: A Forum Publication, 1999), 89.

[178] Elisabeth Schüssler Fiorenza, *Sharing Her Word: Feminist Biblical Interpretation in Context,* (Boston: Beacon Press, 1999), 28-36.

[179] Evelyn Monteiro, "Towards Partnership in a Participatory Church: A Feminist Dream and Vision," in *Concerns of Women: An Indian Theological Response*, eds. Evelyn Monteiro & Kochurani Abraham (Bangalore: Dharmaram Publications, 2005), 107.

[180] One of the reasons why women feel dehumanized is that women as a whole were discriminated at the conceptual as well as at the empirical level-at the theological as well as at the practical level. Eventually, they were deprived of power and privileges for centuries. A plethora of prohibitions and consequent inhibitions afflict women all over the world. Women have internalized the imposition from outside and this has resulted in an inferiority complex. Cf. Somen Das, *Christian Ethics and Indian Ethos* (Delhi: ISPCK, 2001), 151.

[181] Pauline Chakkalakal is of the view that with a clearly fabricated theology and the incorporation of the oppressive socio-cultural norms, the Church continues to deny women access to positions of authority and leadership and thus in decision making. Chakkalakal, *Discipleship a Space for Women's Leadership*, 36.

[182] The hierarchical attitudes of different religious people bring exclusive and violent tendencies among the people and it causes fragmentation and dehumanization in the society of human beings. Religion seems to become now a source of exploitation and distress for many and a threat to equality and social order. T Johnson Chakkuvaracka, "Glimpses of the "Feminine" in Indian Religion and Society: A Christian Perspective," *JJT* 44/1&2 (2002): 79-93.

[183] Women's theological voices are emerging in every continent of the world. New theological visions are being born out of the womb of women's experiences of suffering, pain and struggles. Women all over the world recognize that traditional expectations of long-suffering and sacrifice, which have been imposed on women, can no longer be accepted. Cf. Ofelia Ortega, *Women s Vision: Theological Reflection, Celebration,*

Action (Geneva: WCC Publication, 1995), viii. The women's movement in India has moved to a new phase of maturity, in attempting to formulate a feminist political methodology to understand the roots of oppression of women and other oppressed groups in Indian society, particularly tribals and *Dalits*. A feminist hermeneutics of suspicion in India is (therefore) based on a new understanding of biblical and extra-biblical history in order to discover the liberating possibilities of the gospel for today so as to challenge a society which has so devalued women's labour, their sexuality and their dignity as human persons. Aruna Gnanadason, "Feminist Methodology: Indian Women's Experience," in *Confronting Life: Theology Out of the Context*, ed. M. P. Joseph (Delhi: ISPCK, 1995), 184.

[184] Elisabeth Schüssler Fiorenza, *In Memory of Her: A Feminist Theological Reconstruction of Christian Origins* (London: SCM Press, 1983), 99-100.

[185] Elisabeth Schüssler Fiorenza, "Interpreting Patriarchal Traditions," in *The Liberating Word*, ed. Letty M. Russell (Philadelphia: Westminster, 1976), 52.

[186] For instance, in the first and most precise form of the domestic code given in Col 3:18-4:1, she finds that the writer of the Colossians not only spiritualizes and moralizes the baptismal community's understanding of the tradition of discipleship in Galatians 3:28, but also makes this Greco-Roman patriarchal household ethic a part of the Christian social ethic. She insists, however, that such a reinterpretation of the Christian baptismal vision did not happen before the first century, and, therefore, had no impact on the earlier Jesus' tradition. Fiorenza, *In Memory of Her*, 252.

[187] This phenomenon is observed in the Letter to the Ephesians as well as in the Pastoral Epistles, Ephesians 5:21-33 takes the household-code pattern and reasserts the submission of the wife to the husband as a religious Christian duty. In the Pastoral Epistles, we find further patriarchalization not just of the Christian household but also of the church as "the household of God." Fiorenza, *In Memory of Her*, 290.

[188] Monteiro, "Towards Partnership in a Participatory Church," 108.

[189] Shalini Mulackal, "Creation of a Just and Compassionate Society," *Journal of Dharma* 41/4 (October-December, 2016): 362-363.

[190] Jacob Parappally, "Hierarchical Structures in the Church: Implications for Gender Relations," (136- 148), in *Gender Relations in the Church: A Call to Wholeness and Equal Discipleship*, eds., Astrid Lobo Gajiwala, Varghese Theckanath and Raynah Braganza Passanha (Delhi: Media House, 2012), 136.

[191] Adopting a convenient sampling, ninety nine dioceses across the country were covered. The survey found that "only 16% or 142 of the 1000 participants had read the Policy. 40% or 370 had heard about the policy and 44% or 488 had not heard about the document. Given that 63% of the respondents were women, the ignorance about a document" that pertains to them, especially given the extent of context of the discrimination and submissive status of women, is of concern. Julie George, "Women Living the Legacy of Vatican II: Gender Policy of the Catholic Church," in *Women As Equal Disciples, Unfinished Task of the Church*, eds. Saldanha, et al. (Delhi: Media House, 2016), 22-23. The study was undertaken with dual intent of ascertaining the

familiarity of the Church members with the Gender Policy, as well as of gathering their perceptions and beliefs about gender justice related issues

[192] Julie SSpS, "Women Living the Legacy of Vatican II," 30, 39.

[193] Samuel Rayan, "The Ecclesiology at Work in the Indian Church," in *Searching For an Indian Ecclesiology: The Statement, Papers and the proceedings of the Seventh Annual Meeting of the Indian Theological Association*, ed. Gerwin Van Leeuwen (Bangalore: ATC, 1984),197-198. Further Rayan says that "the authoritative witnessing-teaching begins beautifully with our mothers. Office-bearers in the Church, bishops and popes, can only build on the foundations parents lay." Rayan, "Hierarchy-Religious Relationship in the Context," 90.

[194] Rayan, "Hierarchy-Religious Relationship in the Context," 90-91.

[195] Anto Akkara, "Indian Church conference leads to national Christian women's movement," 15 January 2014, http://www.catholicherald.co.uk/news (accessed August 24, 2016).

[196] S. M. Schneiders, *The Revelatory Text*: Interpreting the New Testament as Sacred Scripture (New York: Harper Collins, 1991), 180-182.

[197] Pauline Chakkalakal, "Discipleship of Equals: A Biblical-Theological Perspective," in *Women as Equal Disciples: Unfinished Task of the Church*, eds. Saldanha, et al. (Delhi: Media House, 2016), 244.

[198] Rekha Chennattu, "Women in the Mission of the Church: An Interpretation of John 4," Paper presented at the Conference on "Mission in Asia in the Third Millennium: Models for Integral Human Liberation", Sanata Dharma University (Yogyakarta, Indonesia: April, 14-17 1999), 1-12.

[199] Evelyn Monteiro, "The Silenced Speak: A Feminist Perspective on Authority," in *Towards the Full Flowering of the Human: Interdisciplinary Studies on the Empowerment of Women*, eds. Kurien Kunnumpuram SJ & Evelyn Monteiro SCC (Mumbai: St Paul Society), 2011, 199-200.

[200] Monteiro, "The Silenced Speak," 202-203.

[201] John Paul II, *Letter of Pope John Paul* II (Bombay: Pauline Publications, 1995)

Chapter 2

Samuel Rayan's Interpretation of Jesus

Introduction

This chapter focuses on the Christological reflections of Samuel Rayan. It is worthwhile to reflect on the theological vision of Rayan who is greatly affected by the reality of fragmentation within Indian society. Rayan will certainly go down in the history of the Church in India as a liberation theologian, who toiled passionately and creatively to bring home the liberative message of Jesus to the struggling masses. He sought to justify Christian involvement in developmental schemes as the work of the Spirit of God uniting the human and the divine, grace and nature, the sacred and the secular.[1]

This chapter has set its border to study Rayan's Christological understanding which is firmly rooted in Scripture and tradition. Accordingly this chapter commences with a brief profile of Rayan and then goes into the development of his understanding of the dignity of the suffering masses. There after certain aspects of his theological method and factors that have influenced his theological horizon, contributing to the development of his Christological reflections which will be discussed. This chapter also reflects on some of the key theological expressions and the need for a new and appropriate language, which is specific to Rayan. Subsequently the sources of his theological framework will be considered and then his interpretation of Jesus Christ will be explored. Finally an attempt is made to understand the relevance of this radical following of Jesus for us who live in the 21st century India with its own unique problems and issues.

The sources used in this study are the following: *Breath of Fire: The Holy Spirit: Heart of the Christian Gospel*,[2] *Bread and Breath*,[3] *The Search for an Asian Spirituality*,[4] and his articles published in various books and journals, including *Selected Writings of Samuel Rayan*,[5] *Collected Writings of Samuel Rayan SJ*,[6] and *The Vision of a New Church and a New Society*,[7] and other recent works on him. In short, an attempt is made to study and reflect on the Christological writings of Rayan in relation to the person and message of Jesus for the Church in India today.

1. Biographical Sketch of Samuel Rayan

When the liberation theology began spreading over the rest of the continents from Latin America, it was the voice of Rayan,[8] along with other Indian Jesuit theologians, which gave an Indian face to liberation theology in India.[9] Rayan has achieved considerable distinction as a liberation theologian, and is acclaimed as such in his *festschrift*[10] by well-known international theologians such as Gustavo Gutierrez, Jon Sobrino, James Cone and Kosuke Koyama. Rayan is one of the first Indian theologians to welcome the Latin American liberation theology and the Christian option for the poor and oppressed. Rayan's concern for the poor and his awareness of Marxist analysis gave him a natural affinity to Latin American liberation theology.[11]

Rayan was born in Kumbalam, near Kollam, Kerala, India, on July 23, 1920. He entered the Society of Jesus in 1939, was ordained a priest in 1955. He did his doctoral studies in theology at the Gregorian University, Rome from 1958-60.[12] What stands out most in his life is his closeness to people. From 1960 to 1972, he was advisor to the Kerala Branch of Catholic Student Movement, the AICUF.[13] He has served as Principal and Professor of Theology at Vidyajyoti, Delhi from 1971 onwards. Rayan has substantially contributed to Indian Christian Theology and has been one of the first Catholic members of the World Council of Churches' Faith and Order Commission from 1968-1982. He served as the first Principal of the Indian School of Ecumenical Theology in Bangalore from 1988-1990.

Rayan is one of the founding members of the Ecumenical Association of Third World Theologians (EATWOT). He is also well respected as one of the great Christian interpreters of Christian faith in the Indian context. He became the spokesperson for Indian theologians as well as for third-world theologians.[14] He was a member since 1976 of the Indian Theological Association (ITA) and sectional editor, 1971-'96, of *Jeevadhara*, a Journal of Theology.[15] He is regarded as one of the first theologians to adopt a new and different approach to theologizing. He sought to understand and interpret the Christian faith in the light of the religious and secular realties of India.[16] Rayan pioneered a reinterpretation of the Eucharist, the central act of the Church's life, as a redistribution of the world's wealth inspired by the Spirit's mission of liberation.[17] In 2009 Rayan returned to Kalady in Kerala [18] and called to his eternal reward on 2 January, 2019.

Although Rayan has published only a couple of books *Breath of Fire: The Holy Spirit: Heart of the Christian Gospel* and *The Anger of God*, he has received enormous appreciation for all the articles he has published in India and abroad in English and Malayalam. Besides, he has often been a spokesman for Indian[19] and Third World theologians.[20] His articles in Christian theology were always characterized by his respect for the rights and dignity of the human person.[21] The underlying theme of his theological writings in English and Malayalam is a postcolonial thrust that seeks to decolonize and liberate Asian theology in general and Indian theology in particular.[22]

Subsequently, Rayan made a name internationally in 1971 with his paper presented in the *International Review of Mission* to the Commission for Social and Economic Development Activities, Second Meeting, Rome.[23] In this paper, he considered the meaning and purpose of mission. He argued that it springs from the divine mission of the Son and the

Spirit continues it, making it present in history (AG 2, 6) with the new awareness of God's action in all the historical and social situations. In the same year he wrote a seminal paper,[24] which gave theological justification for mission involvement in development far ahead of the Synod on Evangelisation (1974) and the landmark document, *Evangelii Nuntiandi* (On Evangelization in the Modern World).[25] This paper made such an impact that it resulted in Rayan's first visit to the USA and a further paper on "Evangelization and Development." [26]

Rayan, being a mystic, poet and visionary, and with his rare qualities of heart and mind, his remarkable power of expression, and blazing zeal for mission, promotion of justice, peace and human dignity, puts it in a poem: "Rice is for sharing, bread must be broken and given. Every bowl, every belly shall have its fill, to leave a single bowl unfilled is to rob history of its meaning; to grab many a bowl for myself is to empty history of God."[27] One of the major discussions during the *National Seminar* on "Samuel Rayan and His Contribution to Indian Christian Theology"[28] held from Dec 28-31, 2014 at Christ Hall, Calicut, paved the way to think of Rayan as a prime path-finder of *Dalit* who in India are to get a lion's share of the experience of God's unconditional love and care. For Rayan, the rootedness in reality is the external manifestation of faith in the God of Justice.[29] Kurien Kunnumpuram, who is well acquainted with him for many years, writes about Rayan:

> He has had close relationships with many priests and lay people. He has conducted theology courses and renewal programmes for thousands of men and women religious. Over the years he has maintained frequent contacts with social activists - visiting them in the place of their involvement, inspiring and guiding them in their work, as well as listening to and learning from them. He has a special concern for certain groups of people – the poor, the youth and women. It is because Rayan was able to approach the Christian faith from the point of view of the people especially the oppressed and the marginalized people that his theology is so living and relevant.[30]

In addition, "Rayan's writings are poetry in prose and paintings in words. They are experiences expressed in ordinary and yet in captivating images, symbols and metaphors." Moreover, they "spring from a heart that knows deeply the presence, pain and power of the Holy Spirit who has been journeying along human history and is actively involved in contemporary life situations."[31]

Apart from his creativity and novelty, Rayan is known for his exceedingly remarkable closeness to people on the peripheries. He acquires an appreciation of beauty and a contemplative life. He has also a strong sense of truth and justice and a concern for the suffering of others, which led him to liberative action.

2. Theological Framework of Samuel Rayan

A spontaneous question one might ask at this juncture is, 'How does Samuel Rayan approach theology? What is his understanding of theology?' Rayan describes what he means by 'Doing theology in India':

> Theology is to be understood as reflection on our faith-experience in the light or shade of life lived in its actual context, with its problems, struggles, tears, and hopes; it is a reflection on life in the light of faith. We bring the two – life and faith – to face each other and to dialogue, questioning and critiquing each other, exploring each other's depths and enriching each other, challenging each other. Theology is the spark that leaps up at the point of their encounter. The fact is that theology anywhere, anytime, is born of two interlacing experiences: of the faith and of the reality of life.[32]

Theology emerges from the encounter of life and faith.. The task of such a theology is to champion a whole new social order of justice and not merely nominal freedom and equality, and people's power and social structures are important concerns. As a result, theology is challenged for an insertion into the concrete and daily life of the people, especially of the most marginalized and oppressed in society.[33] Furthermore, Rayan writes with clarity and precision:

> We want a theology to be at the service of life and to human wholeness. We want a theology that will be at the service of life with its many needs and spiralling possibilities as well as its transcendence and its endlessly expanding quest and onward thrust. In other words, our theology will be at the service of those who work, suffer, and hope, those who struggle for justice and human dignity for all women and men.[34]

At the heart of Rayan's theology is the understanding that God works through the marginalized. Hence, Rayan says: "the concern of the Church is not Christians but the poor; its struggle is not for itself but for the liberation of all men and women who are held captive. The task of the Church is to champion a whole new social order of true and not merely nominal freedom and equality and people's power"[35]

From this we gather that the concrete human person struggling for dignity and wholeness is at the centre of Rayan's theological enterprise. Indeed, he reads the Bible and interprets it through the Indian eyes. Kurien Kunnumpuram writes about this:

> Samuel Rayan's theologizing is deeply rooted in his life, his land and his commitment to Jesus. Born and brought up in a village in Kerala, he devoted many years to the study of Malayalam literature. He mastered Sanskrit and is well read in Indian religions and philosophy. Rayan is not the first thinker to do theology in an Indian way. Others before him sought to relate the Christian faith and the gospel way of life to the religious and cultural context of India. What Rayan seeks to do is to interpret the Christian faith in the light of both the religious and secular realities of the land. And this effort has given shape to a theology which is truly Indian and genuinely Christian. [36]

Rayan's two main concerns have been the interpretation of Christian faith in the multi-religious context of India, and the development of a theology for the creation of a just and more humane society in our land. As a result his theological thinking which resonates with the hopes and aspirations of the masses makes him understand and interpret the Christian faith in the light of the religious and secular realities of our country. Therefore, the following section deals with Rayan's theological method, including his understanding and use of social realities, as well as the factors that have influenced his theological vision. Therefore, the need for a new set of terms that Rayan has incorporated into his theology,[37] and his passion for a Spirit-led theological horizon are taken up.

2.1 Theological Method

For Rayan method is the way theology is done.[38] Method implies a direction, and liberation is the direction. For him, theology is latent in people's struggles. Its primary expression is the transformation seen in the life of men and women committed to justice and liberation.[39] For Rayan, to understand the theological method is to situate oneself in the wider world of realities and concerns where theology belongs. He took seriously people's experiences and struggles and studied carefully in the light of faith. From the encounter and mutual challenge of realities of life and faith, a theology emerges like a flame; a new understanding emerges both in life and faith. One is able to discern the presence and action of God's Spirit in justice, freedom and fellowship. Eventually the Paschal mystery is enlivened.[40] As a result, "theology has its roots in a Divine-human encounter, a face-to-face meeting of God" and humans.[41]

The starting point of his theological reflection is from below, from life's realities, from the "profound and enriching questions" which are posed by these realties, and it proceeds to an equally "profound and enriching" re-reading of scriptures and doctrines, in view of action to humanize the situation further.[42] Hence, theology is born of Theo-praxis, right action - all struggles for liberation, justice, dignity and community are right actions. The most significant contribution to Indian theology by Rayan is his method of theologizing in India.[43] Rayan was engaged in forging what he called an inductive-liberationist method in theology, beginning from below.[44] Rayan's method of theologizing can be summarized in the following words:

> The context for Rayan is primarily the Indian context which is to be understood in two senses: one is concerned about the vital issues in the Indian societal context; the other, it draws from the Indian Context as its theological resource. While remaining thus rooted, his reflections have a pan-Asian and cross-cultural quality about them; he is aware that the Indian context cannot be grasped adequately unless it is placed within the wider Asian context, and still more, in the global Third World context. [45]

Therefore the starting point of theology is the struggle of the people. Hence, a critical understanding of the historical context is one of the essential conditions. By articulating a theological basis for collaboration among followers of all faiths and ideologies, a common effort is to be made for the liberation of the downtrodden and the building of a free and equal social order for all people. Hence, every bit of his theological writings emphasizes the local and the contextual and takes every concrete historical situation seriously. His theological method gave priority to praxis and experience over theory and external authority.

A Critical Understanding of the Historical Context

Rayan's experience-based theology does not start from an "a *priori*, doctrinal abstract," approach, but it "starts from the concrete reality" of experience, which is "subversive of abstract principles". Hence at the very outset Rayan highlights two phases within the experience-based approach: "The first phase raises questions, seeks to criticize and unravel, to speak and to formulate. It then deepens into the second phase, which is one of contemplation, adoration and silence."[46] Therefore, his theology is so living and relevant. For Rayan, it is in the depths of suffering, struggling, wrestling with God that the Spirit meets people and that a theology is born.[47] If theology is, as it should be, an experience-based reflection oriented to change and transformation, then it needs to be pursued in the immediate context of life.[48] Taking the 'context' seriously leads Rayan to categorically assert that if a theology has to be relevant it has to respond to both the living experiences of the people and of the faith traditions.

Scientific Reading of the Word of God

According to Rayan, the resources relevant and common to Christians the world over to reconceive theologies in India/Asia are the faith, the Judeo-Christian Scriptures, and the historical experiences of the churches. But the Indian/Asian resources include: our people, the sacred writings of other religions, the spiritual history of the people and the liberative potential of their traditions.[49] The poor exist within every religion, and as the people through whom God's action is most decisively effective, they are to be validated as theologically significant in themselves. Being rooted and grounded in God-experience, and of his passionate attachment to the fascinating personality of Jesus, Rayan not only sought deep insights into Scripture, but turned inside in meditative reading of the Bible that has enabled him to gain such insights into it that are rarely found elsewhere.[50] In his own words:

> Relevant love-action in today's world is action for justice and liberation, action for the destruction of systems that legalise and perpetuate the robbing and spoliation of entire classes and races of people who are then left behind broken and maimed by the wayside; and action finally for the construction of new patterns of working and relating which would answer to human need and to the dignity and destiny of men and women.[51]

Rayan's theological thinking which resonates with hopes and aspirations of the masses, made him understand and interpret Christian faith in the light of the religious and secular realities of our country. Indeed, Rayan reads the Bible and interprets it through the Asian eyes. Hence, Rayan is of the view that a theology which does not take these hard realities of life seriously could be considered at best irrelevant.[52] In fact, theology for Rayan is embedded in social justice and it is more life-transformative than an intellectual assent. He affirms:

> When we stand for justice and freedom and for people's right to life with dignity, we stand for those realities and values in terms of which all faiths portray the mystery of the divine. In all faith traditions the divine or god is conceived as the absolute 'yes' or affirmation of goodness, justice, freedom, love and life, and as the absolute 'no' or negation of evil, oppression, deprivation and domination. That is why for Jeremiah to "know" God is to "do" justice. When we stand with the oppressed we stand with the ones who always take their side and acts for their liberation.[53]

Therefore, for Rayan, the poor and the oppressed have the sense and the sensitivity, the affinity to God's presence and action in history. They are the ultimate theologians of the New Testament. People's movements which represent the struggles of the poor are theologically significant for Rayan, for they are "the primary *locus theologicus*–the point from which God acts and speaks in history here and now. Hence, Rayan insists on the need for the analysis of social reality prior to the scientific reading of the biblical texts. All the rest like exegesis, analysis, archaeology are meant to enable one to commune with historical reality and with the divine that constitutes the depth of reality, and to take our stand at God's and people's side."[54] The poor and the marginalized are also the spaces of "action for a new social order" of God's *Reign*.[55]

Accordingly, Rayan pays special attention to the liberation praxis of the downtrodden. Praxis [56] becomes central to his theological method.[57] Praxis is not only mediation which changes reality in a small way, but praxis is thought emerging in deed and deed evoking thought. Moreover, a theology that discerns God's presence and sheds light on reality, arouses consciousness and denounces all that is dehumanizing and unjust and thereby announces prophetically the freedom, the dignity, the human right that the realm of God enshrines.[58] Rayan's ability to combine these two, which is based on his re-reading of the Bible and the sacred writings of other religions so as to emulate Jesus, is his greatest strength.[59] Therefore, at the heart of Rayan's theology is the understanding that God works through the poor people.

Fundamental to the whole of Rayan's theology is his belief in the mystery of the human person as God's gift and grace, and therefore he champions the cause of the life, dignity, rights and freedom of human persons wherever they are in fetters. It is the poor and the marginalized who are the chief source of theology, the chief record of God's self-revelation and intervention in world history. For, he believes in the indomitable power of determination in the people and their movements for liberation gushing forth in India and in other parts of the world; he sees in them the sign of hope for a new and humane social order.

A Deep Commitment through a Life of Involvement

For Rayan, theological method is not only the way of doing theology as a disciplined knowledge, but it is also the process and the manner of theologizing. The Statement of the National Seminar on People's Theology[60] held on June 8-11, 1991, at Theology Center, Kottayam, on the one hand, affirms life-experience, commitment, involvement, and struggles of people as the condition, basis and starting point of people's theology, and on the other rejects the traditional theological method and its matrix. The traditional theological approach begins with Scripture and Tradition and is speculative, abstract, and its doctrinal formulations have as its main preoccupation other-worldly concern and safeguarding of orthodoxy. Thus an adequate tool for people-centred theologizing is lacking.[61] The starting point of Rayan's theology is the life of the people, especially of the marginalized groups with their struggle and quest for justice and dignity. A necessary condition for developing a valid theology of the people is a deep commitment to the people through a life of involvement.

Accordingly, the act of theologizing will consist in listening to each other, facilitating reflection and articulation and thus becoming capable of working towards integral liberation. In this process people will learn to re-read their religious scriptures, their inherited traditions, myths and symbol systems. A critique of existing ideologies and theological methodologies which are based on discrimination against women, caste hierarchies, ethnic domination and dogmatic absolutism becomes the essential requirements for the birthing of People's Theology.[62] Being convinced of this evolving and networking approach, Rayan says:

> Theology will connect hope and freedom in history; connect eschatology and struggle for justice now; connect the *Reign of God* and social change. It will also clarify the relationship between God and freedom, and freedom and life. God is indeed the basis of the rights and freedom of the oppressed. God's freedom is for People. To be Christian is to be free; and to be free for the Kingdom is to Christian. To be Christian is to be human because the locus of freedom is the Kingdom of God.[63]

Rayan is deeply convinced that a theology capable of serving the wholeness of life will be ever springing forth at the meeting point of faith and the reality of our country. The encounter of these two will illumine each other's depths, question and challenge each other, enable each other to a new self-understanding, to fresh interpretations of human hope, to committed action and profounder silence.[64] Hence, commitment for Rayan is the first act of theology. In an article he wrote in 1983, he explains his theological method:

> We are convinced that our theology will remain an unfinished endeavour, open-ended and hopeful of correction, improvement, and growth. Because, historical reality keeps evolving and changing, and because we are all conditioned by our situation and class position, we recognize the need for ongoing criticism and revitalization of our approaches to theology.[65]

This commitment is implied in and demanded by our faith-commitment to God in Jesus Christ. It calls for a continuous solidarity with the oppressed to promote freedom and a participative society. The assumptions with which Rayan begins reveal that the method he uses has a symbiotic relationship with people's struggles and people's movement. Consequently, the struggles of the people are the starting point of theology. Hence, the primary *locus theologicus*: the point where God acts and speaks in history here and now, that is, the poor and the marginalized are the "chief source of theology, the chief record of God's revelation and intervention in world-history".[66] In other words, his method is one that would make a meaningful contribution to the march of the people toward full humanity in freedom and dignity.[67]

Accordingly, we can identify three procedures in Rayan's method: First, the point of departure is the people, the human experience of poverty, oppression and suffering. He begins his theology from the world of realities and concerns of the poor in India. In that world of uncertainties and decisive concern lies salvation. Second, the basis of his method is the theology of salvation. Rayan holds that "salvation is God's gift offered within the uncertainties of life". Third, the way of life is compassion, justice and fellowship of God. In other words, the situation is analysed and judged unacceptable both from the human point of view and from the perspective of faith in God. Rayan's developed notion is that the situation is seen and faced as one that we can and will change and as one which "God is already transforming through justice, freedom and fellowship", and that God is in favour of poor people. Fourth, to "recognize and celebrate the critical awareness, the struggle for change and the seeds of liberation" hidden therein.[68]

From the above discussion it is quite obvious that Rayan is convinced of two guidelines for his theological method: First, Christ must be interpreted not in relation to "the India of the past, of the Rishis and the Upanishads" but to "the India today, of the factories, five year plans and atomic reactors".[69] Second, "the method has to be existential, responding to actual, live situations." Accordingly Rayan envisions a task which is to be shared by all, irrespective of religion, and confronts the situation of tension, and dialogues in order to learn to understand, and to re-interpret the Christ reality as called for by concrete experiences and encounters. What is to be noted carefully is that though Rayan is primarily interested in the socio-economic and political dimensions of contemporary India, he still promotes a theology which reflects not only the poverty but also the religions of India/Asia because he sees these as tools for liberation.[70] Therefore, Rayan's approach revolves around the basic conviction that God became human in Jesus to reveal to humanity how God is involved in the struggles and sufferings of people to let them experience God's liberating love.

2.2 Reasons and Influences for the Choice of Method

Having gained some insights into the theological method of Rayan, the liberation theologian. Let us consider the influences which gave him the socio-economic political perspective inherent to his stand. This section, we focuses on the five challenges of his time that have fashioned his ideals and vision.

Boyhood Experiences During Anti-colonial Struggle in India

Rayan's life is the matrix of his theology. Born and brought up in a village in Kerala, he was deeply rooted in Indian culture. He devoted many years to the study of Malayalam literature. He mastered Sanskrit and knew well Indian religions and philosophies. He thus acquired a great familiarity with the religious and cultural tradition of this land. In addition to his childhood experiences, two important events deeply influenced his early years: on the one hand, India's struggle for national liberation from British colonial domination and on the other, the successful though painful victory of the depressed Ezhava community[71] of the State of Kerala which led to their social and economic liberation from age-old discrimination and humiliation that was based on caste prejudice. "The Ezhava community was enslaved and oppressed, treated as untouchables and denied elementary amenities of life."[72]

Certainly, the experiences during the anti-colonial struggle in India and elsewhere enabled him to grow ever more conscious of the dehumanized situation of the marginalized. Rayan from his early years knew more at first-hand about the cruelties of oppression and unjust treatment of the poor and the marginalized who kept fighting for survival and human dignity. In the midst of all this pain he also came to know the power of an intense spirituality exhibited in the lives of such men as Sri Narayana Guru and Mohandas Gandhi, individuals who were able to retain their serenity in the midst of suffering.[73] Therefore, choosing the margins as the site of theologizing activity enabled him to witness closely the day-to-day life situation of wo/men living there, not only as victims but also as agents who take charge of their lives and were capable of interpreting their lives. The attitudes and perceptions about life that Rayan experienced during these years lie at the basis of his own theological views which were only to emerge later.

Peasant Culture in a Catholic Atmosphere

Having been brought up in a distinctively Catholic atmosphere within a culture that was pervaded by Hinduism, Rayan developed an absorbing interest in all the facets of religion, including liturgy, prayer, the Bible, the saints, and even Hindu myths and stories. This sensibility, together with his awareness of the poverty and oppression that surrounded him in the caste-ridden Hindu society, instilled in him the dream of a society based on human equality and dignity, a dream that has remained with him throughout his life.

Rayan sensed an increased awakening and reaching out for freedom on the part of marginalized people, a movement that will continue to grow. It is the task of the liberation theologians to support the people in their aspirations and to articulate the theological content of their dreams. During Rayan's 12 years as chaplain to the more than fifteen thousand Catholic university students in Kerala, his political and social interests became pronounced and consciously linked with his theological views. Rayan realised that faith, to be meaningful, had to have social-political repercussions. "Living and searching with fiercely honest youth helped make theology earthly-historical and render the Bible open-ended, unfinished."[74] Besides, it was his growing interest in literature, especially poetry and myth that developed in him a feel for religious symbolism as well as a sense of mystery pervading all things. This factor which he himself traces back to his rural peasant culture helped him to rise above any narrow view of religious orthodoxy and enabled him to discern the spiritual potential in Asian religious traditions. Therefore, Rayan believes that all religions carry a latent theology of liberation.[75] It was later with the benefit of hind-sight that he realized how these attitudes and dreams tallied with his understanding of the Christian faith and how a theology of liberation lay latent in the ongoing struggles of the oppressed.

The Influence of the First Generation Liberation Theologians

In the early 1970s, Rayan was introduced to the International Conference of the EATWOT. It was in the Dar Conference in 1976 that the EATWOT came into being. Rayan says that from the start the movement was ecumenical in every sense of the word. He was concerned to reject foreign theological imports and imitations, and to develop a new form of theology that, in the context of contemporary India, placed the hopes, the disappointments, the struggle, and the suffering of men and women in the center. He considers those theologies that originated in Europe and were brought to India/Asia by colonial era missionaries inadequate to our Asian context. It is because their eyes failed to notice the suffering people, including the victims of colonialism, the Crucified of Calvary. Rayan says that they failed to be prophetic, failed to develop a prophetic vision and voice. This was the time when Rayan interacted with the first generation of the liberation theologians, Gustavo Gutierrez in particular, at meetings of EATWOT, which was set up specifically to bring Latin American theologians together with those from Africa and

Asia.[76] He claims that his interactions with them have helped him to evolve "a theology of human well-being on earth".[77] Under the influence of Gutierrez and other liberation theologians, and of his study of the Bible, Rayan could realize that the *Reign of God* is a gift received in history and that it implies the establishment of justice in the world.[78] The exposure to the liberation theologians of Latin America made a deep impact on the mind of Rayan.

Rayan is fascinated by Jesus' dream of a new human community; it becomes foundational as reflected in his commitment to and work for the liberation of the oppressed and the downtrodden. Rayan's theology considers that true spirituality is found not in the devaluation of the historical life and material existence but it is found where the peoples' life in its wholeness is taken into account. For Rayan theology is an articulate discourse of the ultimate, unconditional dimension of reality,[79] and the most important thing about the gospel was that it should be good news to the poor.[80] Rayan is rightly called a liberation theologian;[81] because he looked at Jesus as fostering values like justice, solidarity and intervention on behalf of life and human dignity. He emphasized the indispensable privilege of the poor and their cultures, religions and struggles as theologically significant. The poor are to be perceived as a 'privileged locus' of God's incarnation in history. In this process the person and event of Jesus Christ is our norm. God's history is our history; God-with-us (Emmanuel).

Radical Commitment to the Person of Jesus

Rayan's theology is very much influenced by the historical Jesus' radical concern for the poor. His understanding and interpretation of Jesus based on the New Testament witness about the person and mission of Jesus and in Christian faith-tradition, is in constant dialogue with the context of his life. In the context of his time, that is, the foreign rule, oppression and social hierarchical differences, Jesus wanted to abolish all categories of domination, oppression and marginalization. For Rayan, Jesus is a man of freedom who was able to identify himself freely and authentically with the poor, their longing and struggles. Jesus initiated a movement of radical love and radical action.[82] Therefore, the commitment to Jesus demands a commitment to struggle with and for the exploited, and all victims of social, cultural, religious and political discrimination and oppression.

Furthermore, Jesus' place in the life of Rayan is derived from the Gospel portrayal of the man Jesus whose intervention on behalf of life and human rights was radical. He was deeply influenced by Jesus who lived in solidarity with the outcast, the oppressed and the victims of his time. Mt 25:31-46 describes Jesus' struggles and his participation in people's struggles and movements for food, clothing, housing, health, freedom and fellowship. Rayan wrote:

> By associating with the "least of these" he [Jesus] set them free; he recognized their humanity, acknowledged their dignity, and affirmed their worth. He awakened their selfhood, rebuilt their pride, and assured them of their status as daughters, sons, and citizens before God. He challenged them to live accordingly to open freedom and to refuse every enslavement.[83]

The core of Jesus' concern reveals his 'compassion' which Rayan paraphrases as "a special self-communication of God, of divine love and compassion, of solidarity with human beings, with the poor in particular, in their humiliation and suffering and struggle for justice."[84] His fascination for Jesus can be summarized thus: For Jesus, human person is great and unique with capacity, worth and dignity (*imago Dei*). Jesus' heart beats for all women and men the world over down to the dawn of time. Therefore, Rayan is emphasizing the truth that "the locus of our encounter with God is present history and the persons making it."[85] He finds meaning and depth in Jesus' own way of doing theology which is illustrated in his reply to the followers of John the Baptist (Mt 11:1-4). Here, there is "the engaging invitation to see and hear and touch what is present, and to understand and interpret it."[86] Similarly "theology is the interpretation of seen events - the blind recovering their sight, the lame waking, the dead rising to life, and the poor hearing good news that is hope-giving."[87] The Christ event provides a way of seeing, and we call it faith.

Therefore, Rayan begins by dissecting the reality of brokenness from various socio-political and religious angles, and relates it with caste-like formations worldwide. He then leads us to the social order in Palestine in the time of Jesus to take note of similar traits by exploring the gospels. He ascertains the mind of Jesus who by his birth, his miracles aimed at breaking the culture of silence, and who submitted himself as an outcaste to be sacrificed outside the gate. For Rayan, conversion of heart implies also Christians' action for transforming the social order and to uphold the language of the Cross in solidarity with the victims of caste ideology. Furthermore, he says that it is the Cross of the out-caste that bears the promise of the new earth and the new India with a human heart, a heart of flesh, full of *karuna* sensitive to the all-encompassing Brahman, and realizing advaita and brotherhood and sisterliness at all levels of life and relationships.[88]

Accordingly, Rayan gives importance to such stories which reflect the compassion and mercy of Jesus like the feeding of the Five Thousand, parable of the good Samaritan, Last Judgment, and Jesus' discourse on the priority of the human being over Sabbath.[89] The climax of Jesus' solidarity with the poor is visible in its final and ultimate expression on the Cross. Hence, Rayan is of the opinion that the salvation is a present experience of "human wholeness, and meaningful human existence".[90] It is the historical Jesus who motivates Rayan in the task of liberating the poor and establishing their rights and their human dignity. His theological reflections are founded on his Christological reflections. That is how Rayan looks at Jesus' mission of the ushering in of the *Reign of God*, which is the core of Christian life.

The Reflections on the Holy Spirit

In the biblical sense the Holy Spirit is active together with the Father and the Son from the beginning to the completion of the divine plan of salvation, and the Holy Spirit continues to be active in the on-going history.[91] The New Testament presents Jesus as one who is anointed, shaped and led by the Spirit (Lk 1:35; 3:21-22; 4:1;14:18-19; Jn 3:34). The Spirit-experience with God the Father as His sole authority becomes the foundation of Jesus' ministry from the moment of his conception in the womb of Mary to his death and resurrection. Rayan says that the Spirit's presence and gifts were experienced as transformative of persons and "constitutive of the Church as mission with dissent and conflict. The Spirit is not apart from the uplifting of Jesus on the Cross and his struggle unto death in defense of people's dignity, freedom and future of the dispossessed in particular."[92] For the first Christians the Holy Spirit was a source of new life, of power and courage, of liberation and of freedom from fear of elemental forces and of exodus from known life to a leap into faith.[93]

Rayan proposed a Spirit-Christology with a twofold purpose: primarily to reveal Christ in his humanity "in relief the significance of Jesus for society and social change."[94] In other words, it is to enhance the liberation, for the socio-political and economic liberation of the oppressed; secondarily, to replace 'the Christology from above' (Logos Christology) with 'the Christology from below'.[95] He portrays the Spirit as a 'breath of fire', who empowers us in committed historical action. For Rayan, the Spirit is the One who gives people the dream of a new society and empowers them to bring about their own liberation.[96] He considers the annunciation as a second act of creation by the Spirit, because the Spirit is at work in Jesus from annunciation, not just from baptism. From the moment of baptism the Spirit took charge of the ministry of Jesus, of his life and his mission.[97] The Spirit-experience is, for Rayan, the starting point of Pneumatology.[98] Therefore, for Rayan mission is the extension in space and time of the Incarnation of God's Word, and those who engage in it are co-workers of the Spirit, provided they live in the Spirit.[99] Thus the Spirit is the initiator of fresh beginnings and the source of being and life, the mother of the living earth, who unites God's people, connects human race and gives a ministry of life-giving.[100]

2.3 Need for a New and Appropriate Language

In the preceding sections, the discussion was centred on the context of Rayan's theological journey followed by the factors that influenced his vision. It was also pointed out that according to him, theology is an unfinished endeavour and open–ended growth as the historical reality keeps evolving and changing. This leads him often to make use of unfamiliar terms and integrate new concepts into his theology. His goal is the birth of a new humanity that would go hand in hand with the emergence of a new language.[101] It is the language evolved from the lifestyle of the people, the language of the heart, of the hands, of the womb; a body language, a language embodied in stories, parables, myths and metaphors.[102] Rayan reads the Bible and interprets it through the Asian eyes. He bases his dream of a new humanity upon Jesus' dream, a dream that would concern people, assimilate genuine search for freedom and fellowship. It is a language that would integrate the music of different dialects into a rich symphonic composition. Ultimately, that which would lead people to sing a song as ancient as their own quest for communion with the cosmos and its inhabitants. Hence we consider some of the terms or the concepts he frequently employs in his theology.

Bread and Breath

The phrase "Bread and Breath" is an expression fashioned in Samuel Rayan's own poetic imagination and an inversion of a line from a poem by Gerard Manley Hopkins, "God! Giver of breath and bread." This expression "suggests the two main poles around which Samuel's own theological reflections turn: the question of Bread for all, with justice this demands at all levels of our national and international society, and the role of the Spirit, the inspiration which faith and God's action provide for a commitment to those who go hungry."[103] Rayan sees the metaphor of bread and breath as symbols of life to motivate and to seek human well-being and encounter the Spirit in one's neighbours. It is in this sense, for Rayan, sharing bread, living for the other are authentic signs of the presence of the Spirit.[104] Therefore, breaking bread with or for one another is a characteristically human and humanizing act which Christ has made the hallmark of discipleship. Bread itself is a community reality, and a social product. In and behind every slice of bread is the presence of many hands, many tears, the toil and sweat of many men and women. Therefore every piece of bread is the fruit of widespread collaboration, which is the point of reference for human and cosmic energy.[105]

Rayan interprets the Spirit as a "breath of fire", which enables in "the recreation process and is present in committed historical action."[106] or Rayan, commitment is taking sides with the oppressed classes, the marginalized and despised cultures. Thus, the phrase 'bread and breath' calls for an effort which brings about a redistribution of our resources to the total and complete liberation from all that alienates human beings so that the world may be transformed in the direction of God. 'Bread and Breath' indeed stands for the Eucharist which is the sacrament of total involvement and global presence of Jesus Christ.

Sharing of Rice

The expression 'sharing of rice' springs from the great demand of the Kingdom, which implies an insertion into the concrete and daily life of the people, especially the most marginalized and oppressed members of society. The expression reflects the basic concern of the masses of everywhere: the concern both for food and fellowship, care and concern.[107] Hence, to use one's autonomy, to deny others access to the countries' resources is to make oneself a god. If we fail in the concerns of God for his creation, God can ask, "Where are you?" (Gen 3:9). The earth is our mother, not for conquest, not for sale, not to be grabbed, nor to be squabbled over. What is essential for life has to remain common, universally accessible and free like sunlight, air, water and the earth. For Rayan, justice is part of the contemplative life:

> People are sacred. Women and men are made in the image [and likeness] of God. Men and women not simply as individuals, but as community, are the only image and symbol capable of pointing to the Mystery of the Divine with any relevance and meaningfulness. It is in respecting, loving, serving, liberating and waiting upon the mystery of this image that we come to discover and experience the divine with an ever-deepening, creative sense of the real. Communities of men and women are the only place of life-giving encounter and communion with God.[108]

Therefore, God is to be discovered in the process of committed action to build history, the struggle of a people for justice and freedom.[109] It is the sign of God's gift, a sign of mutual gift within a community. In this context, sharing of bread[110] is not an empty ritual, but a symbol of freedom and liberation among the children of God who live by sharing and participation. Rayan visualizes the mystery of salvation in the sharing of Jesus, wherein Jesus identifies himself with the bread: "I am the bread of life" (Jn 6:35) and same is true in Jesus' words, "this is my body for you" (Lk 22: 19). "The experience of his mystery on earth is bound up with shared bread and food for the people."[111] Meal is a means of sharing life, of giving to one another, of experiencing belongingness.

Perceiving theology as a reminder of the great demands of the Kingdom, Rayan advocates insertion into the concrete and daily life of the people, especially of the most marginalized and oppressed members of the social body, as central to the Christian faith.[112] Rayan puts it poetically: "Rice is for sharing; bread must be broken and given. Every bowl, every belly shall have its fill, to leave a single bowl unfilled is to rob history of its meaning; to grab many a bowl for myself is to empty history of God."[113]

Response-ability

Response-ability is a theological term used during the opening address given by Samuel Rayan on the occasion of the Third Asian Theological Conference in 1989.[114] He understands spirituality in terms of two related ideas or realities or activities, namely openness and response-ability. He writes response-ability with a hyphen in order not to restrict its meaning to accountability. Rayan defines spirituality as "response-ability, which consists in our willingness and readiness to respond to significant realities and situations of import for life." This spiritual concept is what makes for fuller life, for finer humanity, and for a new earth.[115] Spirituality is thus "openness to reality" and a "humanizing response to the same."[116] It means to be open to changes, open to the complexity of life, to the surprises of life, and to a God full of surprises. In this way spirituality[117] will be continually renewed by the discovery of new perspectives and new dimensions of life.

Rayan understands spirituality as the ability to respond to the many different dimensions of reality, to different things, events, and people. This includes the ability to respond to the realities of other faiths, their spiritual horizons and insights. Such spirituality, Rayan believes, is not just the spirit of many a biblical story like the exodus, the Lord's Prayer, and the Good Samaritan but it is also characteristically Asian.[118] 'Response-ability' will thus address not only to reality's present but its past and future as well; it will speak to the personal no less than to the structural. Rayan, therefore, interprets "spirituality" as "response-ability", i.e., the ability to respond to the call of God.[119] The whole of human life with its struggle coupled with the trust placed on God is spirituality.

Rayan suggests that spirituality be understood and described in terms of those two related ideas. "Openness" is being truthful in humility, acknowledging God's greatness and the sacredness of all human life. It calls for study, analysis, and evaluation of reality. The more adequate and authentic the response, the deeper is the spirituality. Rayan, therefore, interprets "spirituality" as "response-ability", i.e., the ability to respond to the realities that challenge us,[120] it's an ability to respond to the call of God.

Decolonization of Theology

Historically, colonialism has been a "policy of acquiring or maintaining colonies" with a view to their exploitation, especially economic, their dignity, corrosion of the freedom, life and culture of their original inhabitants. Under colonial domination, the exploited and the marginalized people's creativity is crippled, and resourcefulness deteriorates, gradually paving the way to greater dependence at all levels of life and in all areas of existence.[121] Lack of equitable development and progress across the country has led to some youth taking up arms to demand justice and rights in many parts. At the same time, the innumerable insurgent groups have turned the less developed and segregated geographical parts of the Indian continent into a battle field. As a result, development is hampered. To reach out to the other in need, people on the margins one needs to decolonize one's mind from all that is "me and mine." It is to renounce, to let go of the selfish and limited self so as to enter into an opening new realm in which "all life takes on a completely new meaning; the real sense of our own existence, which is normally veiled and distorted by the routine distractions of an alienated life…sees everything transfigured in God coming from God and working for God's creative redemptive love."[122]

The process of decolonising theology is not new, nor confined to India.[123] The immediate question would be "what do colonial theologies mean?" For Rayan, colonial theologies are those theologies that originated in Europe and were brought to Asia by colonial-era missionaries and that the colonial administrations found it convenient for keeping the locals subservient to colonial rule.[124] According to Rayan, in Indian/ Asian situation "either the theological soil of our Christian existence has been used to grow foreign crops which we do not need or use; or it has been left fallow while theologies raised abroad were imported, and were borne by us as a burden, and not assimilated as nourishment nor welcomed as a force for social change." Consequently, Rayan says:

> Colonial mission and theology committed the *a priori* error of taking for granted that God had never been here, that Christ had not preceded them, that they have never been savingly active in its history, that the Spirit has never been in liberating and life-giving dialogue and communion with the hearts and dreams of the men and women of this land. They did not look for God's presence and action here to acknowledge it and give thanks. Their eyes failed to discern in the suffering people, including the victims of colonialism, the Crucified of Calvary.[125]

Besides, colonial mission and theology "did not know what to do with people's struggles for freedom from colonial domination and oppression." In addition, Rayan says that "they failed to be prophetic, failed to develop a prophetic vision and voice."[126] Hence, there is the imperative to decolonize theology.

Mission in the Spirit

Rayan uses the concept of "mission in the Spirit" as the integrative centre of his thought. Rayan's distinctive contribution has been to create a Pneumatology of mission in which the Spirit impels the struggle for liberation. This thought becomes clear even from the title of his masterpiece, *Breath of Fire: The Holy Spirit: Heart of the Christian Gospel* based on a retreat he gave at Maryknoll, New York, in June 1975.[127] The title further shows that Rayan founded his liberation theology on the mission of the Spirit. For Rayan, the Spirit is the breath of God by which we breathe. It is the yeast of new life that invigorates the bread, which is the earth, and brings about a redistribution of its resources to the benefit of all.[128] Besides, Rayan's distinctive contribution has been the liberation pneumatology which revolves around the symbols of Bread and Breath. It poetically combines the two natures of Christ, the immanence and transcendence of God, and the liberative and evangelistic dimensions of mission.[129] It is the breath of fire that energizes the presence and activity of God, and avoids dualism, individualism, secularism and elitism. It is the wind of God that transfers the unjust structures that oppress the poor and frees them to experience the good news of the *Reign of God*.[130] Rayan's awareness of the Spirit's activity in the world as Liberator, and presence as Creator brings together action for human welfare with aesthetic and mystical concerns. "The experience of the Spirit is the starting point and this experience offers a new vision to orient oneself and urges the believers to work towards building a new society based on the values of the *Reign of God*."[131]

The mission is God's. God sends the Son and the Spirit, and through the Son in the Spirit God sends forth creation. According to Rayan, "the overall mission of the created universe is to be a translation of the eternal Word of God. Its mission is to be a revelation, a manifestation and a proclamation of God's face and mind, of God's beauty and wisdom, of God's power and wonder and of God's inmost reality as love."[132] Rayan discerns the Spirit at work in movements for the liberation of the poor and oppressed.

For Rayan, mission is a mystery that is rooted in the Trinitarian sending within the Divine.[133] For him this triune communion is a source of inspiration for social transformation. He writes: "each particular reality has a share. Each is on a mission to the rest. Every creature has something special, some gift, some experience, some promise or challenge or good news for its fellow creatures. God's varied gifts are so distributed that creatures need not only God but each other with an intricate web of cosmic interdependence, of give and receive, of mission and ministry."[134]

Rayan takes the cue from José Comblin, and continues to examine the effects of the presence of the Spirit in the world and the Church: "The experience of the Spirit launches men and women out into the world to bring about a new creation; the Spirit's action in the Church is subordinate to this goal of new creation." [135] The Spirit does it as though imbibed with super human energy to tackle super human tasks. The Spirit actually generates a new human being. The Holy Spirit is the presence in our own time of the *Reign of God*. The Holy Spirit is seen as the one who permeates all aspects of life and all spheres of reality: one who brings about wholeness and harmony though dialectically through conflict and pain, through the dynamics of the Cross. Therefore, mission is "the extension in space and time of the Incarnation of God's Word. It is like the Incarnation, the work of the Spirit. Those who engage in it are co-workers of the Spirit. This they can be only to the extent they live in the Spirit…"[136] This life in the Spirit empowers the individuals and the societies to transform the poor of the societies as a sign of furthering the *Reign of God* through Jesus.

Basing on the Nazareth Manifesto (Lk 4:16-30) Rayan reflects on 'mission in the Spirit' in a threefold way: i) the goal of the mission is specifically to the poor, the oppressed, the enslaved, the hopeless, and the powerless. It is to bring to such people the glad tidings that they have rights and equal dignity; that God holds out to them the possibility and the hope of a fuller, more human life from now on; that God is with them in their struggle to win back their freedom and make their own history. Understanding human situations is also part of bringing the glad tidings; ii) the content of the mission is freedom: liberation from oppression; freedom to be human; freedom to see things for ourselves; to walk before God in dignity; to take responsibility for one's life and one's destiny, and to shape both in partnership with God. For, God is still working with people to liberate and make them whole through Jesus. It is the mission of the Church and of all the disciples of the Lord; and iii) the relation between the goal of the mission and its content. The glad tidings that the Church brings to people are tidings about the heart of God, what God thinks about them; their history, their goings and comings, what God's plans are for humankind. In that sense the Good News is a revelation of the depth of God, of the profound and interior designs for God's people.

The question is: who can delve into the heart of God? It is the Spirit alone who can delve into the heart of God. Therefore, "without being endowed with the Spirit, without an experience of the Spirit, and without knowing what the Spirit knows of the heart of God, there can be no mission."[137] Rayan relates the Annunciation to Mary and the Jordan experience of Jesus as proofs of being taken up to the sphere of divine in and through the Spirit. First, the story of annunciation which begins with the salutation to Mary in a unique way: "The Holy Spirit will come upon you, and the power of the Most High will overshadow you" (Lk 1:35). Rayan says that the word whom God sends into the world can become a saving mission in the world only through the creative overshadowing of the Spirit. The chief message is that mission and Spirit go hand in hand. Second, the Jordan experience of Jesus is one of anointing by the Spirit, and this coming of the Spirit marks the beginning of Jesus' mission. It was indeed "the moment of His Commissioning, or the moment of the manifestation of his mission." It begins in the womb of God, and what is born of God becomes a historical reality within human space and time only in and through the Spirit.[138]

According to Rayan, mission in the Spirit is to be understood as reflection on our faith-experience in the light or shade of life lived in its actual context, with its problems, struggles, tears, and hopes; it is a reflection on life in the light of the Spirit. It is the Spirit who marks the new movement, and makes the Christian movement specifically Christian. The Spirit always builds community and sends forth those who have had this experience to build further community. Rayan concludes that listening is an essential part of mission, listening to the Spirit in self, in others, in cultures, and in events. Therefore mission always starts with the Spirit. It grows in the Spirit through the witnessing in human hearts and it culminates in the Spirit in a life of freedom and sacrificial living in community, the kind of life that Jesus lived.[139] The concern for humanity is based on Jesus' dream of a new human community, built on freedom, love and meaning and on a personal experience of God finding therein a deep respect for the human person and humanity, which is the core of his Christology. The chapter, further, explores Rayan's interpretation of God and Jesus Christ.

3. Rayan's Interpretation of God and Jesus Christ

To understand the Christology of a theologian, we need to know his/her theological vision and the corresponding experiences. Theological vision refers to the God concept i.e., the dominant image of God which serves as an inspiration and the particular aspect of the mystery of the life and mission of Jesus. The basic questions one might ask at this juncture are: What was the theological vision of Samuel Rayan and what were the corresponding experiences? Who is the God of Samuel Rayan? Where are we likely to meet our God? Or where are we to look for our God? Prior to exploring the Christological images of Rayan, it is essential that we know his understanding of God. Hence, what follows is his understanding of God and Jesus Christ that would be relevant for human well-being on earth, particularly to the present context in India, which is the thrust of the thesis as indicated in the general introduction.

3.1 The God of Samuel Rayan

Rayan was captivated by the mystery of God with us and God for us. He was drawn more often to a God who is constantly in search of humans. The process of liberation brought about by God contains several theologically significant aspects: God is interested in the affairs of the world of humans; God takes the initiative and expects a human response in faith; God intervenes in the history of humankind in concrete historical contexts; God responds to human helplessness with compassion and love as well as brings about justice in unjust situations; God enters into dialogue with humans in executing his plans; God reveals through his elusive name his abiding presence among his people; God's plan of salvation for all humankind also includes social justice and liberation from the dehumanizing slavery of all kinds. The God he encountered through Jesus Christ in the Gospels was primarily a God who made a difference in the life of Rayan.

Rayan qualifies his God experience by saying:

> God is Spirit, God is mystery, and we know very little about him, only what he reveals about himself. In our present condition God manifests himself to us in signs and symbols, and the finest symbol and sacrament of God upon earth is the human person. It is within human experience and within the human phenomenon that the Spirit of God is partially seen and experienced by us. Hence, the central emphasis in the biblical tradition and in other traditions as well, is centred on the neighbour, on loving one another. It is in the neighbour that God is met and distantly and obscurely, but significantly, experienced by people. We therefore, see the importance of looking at people, attending to their life and personal experiences. The more people love and are open to one another and to reality, the more transparent they are, the more the mystery of God shines through them. Among all the human beings the finest self-manifestation of God is Jesus of Nazareth.[140]

Thus, Rayan understands that "we come to the presence of God as we grow in the ability to experience ourselves in community," and "God lives in friendships, in kindness, in relationships of forgiveness, of openness and of sacrificial living for others. That is where God makes his dwelling, is met and is properly worshipped."[141] For, God is interested in the human reality as a whole and in the quality of its existence. Thus, God is present and active through human beings of all faiths in the fight against oppression and injustice, because it disrupts God's purposes in this world.[142] Consequently, it is the liberating action of God in history which becomes enfleshed in Jesus Christ.

3.2 The Jesus of Samuel Rayan

Rayan's contemplative experiences convinced him more and more that Jesus not only dwelt among us but preferred to be poor; preferred to live with the poor and the marginalised. Accordingly, this section explores Rayan's Christological insights by employing a contextual-liberationist approach advocated by him. It will be developed in five stages: Jesus is the flesh translation of Divine Compassion, Jesus is the Truth that sets us free, Jesus is the friend of the outcast, Jesus is the daily Bread, and Jesus is a Spirit-filled person.

Jesus: The Flesh-Translation of Divine Compassion

Rayan offers an all-pervading meditation on *Jesus the Flesh-Translation of Divine Compassion*.[143] He explains that the Christian community sees in Jesus God's compassion translated for us in the idiom of our own flesh and blood, and our fragility and brokenness, our freedom, our lovability and our responsibility in regard to God, our fellow humans and the rest of creation. Rayan's deep insight into the biblical texts, especially the Gospels, shows that the God he encountered through Jesus Christ in the Gospels was primarily a God of compassion.[144] His sustained search to contemplate the face of a compassionate God confirmed him more and more that Jesus dwelt among us as "a Flesh Translation of Divine Compassion." For Rayan, Jesus is compassion enfleshed who became human to reveal to us a God who is involved in the inhuman sufferings of the masses to become authentically human.[145]

Rayan maintains that in Jesus God's compassion became visible and tangible to us in what he calls the three movements. The first is the mystery of the Incarnation as compassion, namely, God's compassion translated into flesh; it empowers us and teaches us the virtues that generate life and compassionate love.[146] In Jesus, God becomes an 'insider', God-with-us (Immanuel) in our lives, and commits Himself to be with us always.[147] According to Rayan, the Incarnation of the

Word is compassion because it brings God to our side, to pitch his tent among us, to become Immanuel. Moreover, it is an image of the self-emptying of the Divine to take on the image of the enslaved human with a view to restoring the divine image in us (Rom 8:29; Phil 2:6-11; 2 Cor 3:18; Col 3:10). In other words, Incarnation is identification with the dispossessed and the discarded, the victims of death-systems (Mt 25:31-46); and that is compassion.[148] Thus, if the very fundamental option of God to incarnate as a human being is inspired by compassion, all the other minor options within that, in order to fulfil this fundamental option also are manifestations of God's compassion.[149]

The second is found in the Gospel of Mark, that Jesus himself comes to the Jordan and joins the company of all those coming from the region of Judea and the city of Jerusalem to hear John, to confess their sins and to be baptized by John. Here is a 'movement' on the part of Jesus "into the experience of the other to be present and in solidarity and communion of experience,"[150] and this movement for Rayan is compassion.[151] Jesus' solidarity with the people, demonstrated at his baptism through which he identifies himself with the conversion movement of the people (Mk 1:4-9), reveals the Divine compassion. From then on, in Jesus, all those who came to him with their suffering - the hungry, the blind, the widows, the public sinners, and those afflicted by leprosy - were given a revelation of the divine compassion that led God to enter our humanity. Furthermore, Rayan says that Jesus' table fellowship with the outcasts (Mk 2:15-17), all his invitations to "come and dine with him" (Jn 21:1-14) as well as the last supper are the moments that reveal the extension of Jesus' humanity. It is important to underscore here that in the cure of the sick, or the feeding the five thousand, the deep compassion of moved Jesus effected these miracles.[152]

Rayan sees the Cross as God's compassion,[153] because the Cross of Jesus reveals the suffering of God for humanity who makes his own the pain of his earthly family.[154] Calvary is divine self-identification with every kind of historical suffering and humiliation. Therefore,

God's presence is to be found in the midst of the suffering community, grieving and partaking in their suffering, just as it happened on the Cross of Jesus. The compassion exercised by Jesus led him to conflicts (Jn 1:5). Jesus' solidarity with the oppressed led him to confrontations with the theological establishment (the scribes). Jesus wished to free people from the burdensome interpretation of the rituals and the moral law (Mk 2:1-3, 6), the religious leaders, their misuse of the Temple (Mk 11:15-18) and the political establishment of his time (Lk 13:31-33). It was the natural outcome of a life of solidarity (identification) and conflict (confrontation) with the rich and the powerful that leads inevitably to the fatal confrontation, which could only end in a foreseen and freely accepted death on the Cross. The Cross then, truly reveals the compassionate face of the Father.

The third, the Mystery of the resurrection of Jesus is compassion because the revelation of God-with us is realized; he becomes the key to enter with Him into the sufferings and hope of His people.[155] According to Rayan, the resurrection shows that Jesus redeems the situation of hopelessness by being there, because where he is, is after all not quite hopeless. In radical compassion "Jesus enters into our situation of fear and frustration," accompanies us to the bitter end and effects a breakthrough. "This multi-faceted compassion of Jesus offers the key to the Resurrection. Because, for Rayan it is above all the revelation and realization of God-with-us, and the token of it is that the presence of Jesus has become interior to our consciousness, interior to our freedom, not doing things for us as we remain passive but empowering us."[156] Hence, in the total self-gift of his compassion Jesus acts most divinely and becomes most imitable even when he is risen from the dead.

Rayan understands the Resurrection "as the completion of this incarnational involvement. By his resurrection, Jesus is released from the confines of local particularity in order to become really present to the whole of history. He still walks with us as we in our sadness leave Jerusalem and continue our quest. He is where we gather together, he is one with naked and hungry people, he is in the bed-ridden and those detained in prisons."[157]

We may summarize the Jesus of Rayan thus: in Jesus God becomes God-with-us, the Incarnation of the Word is compassion by which God takes the side of humanity, pitches his tent among us to become Immanuel. Jesus is the embodiment of divine compassion in the world. Jesus is the flesh translation of God's compassion. In Jesus, God's compassion became visible and tangible for humanity. By entering into our world and becoming one of us, God let us know for sure that in Jesus, God is neither a stranger, nor an outsider but the embodiment of divine compassion in the world.

Jesus: The Truth that Sets Us Free

The exact exegetical implications and context of 'truth' may be debated. However, Jesus' purpose of communicating a liberating sense of being loved by God was plainly clear to his believers. Moreover, Jesus came to share the love of his *Abba* (Jn 3:16). As the Gospels describe, the foundation of his freedom was the experience of being loved as the Son. Further, his *Abba*-experience empowered Jesus and enabled him to widen his horizons and see beyond the boundaries set by humans. Freedom provides that avenue to go forth with a sense of determination. The mission of Jesus was and is to disclose the truth about God and human beings. What is this truth about God and human beings? Rayan, in his article, "The Truth that sets us Free," seeks to understand Jesus' claim to be the truth. Jesus is the one chosen to become the truth of God's saving relationship to humanity.[158] "The Jesus-truth is seen to be concrete, historical, action-based and oriented towards the transformation of the world and the liberation of the people."[159] According to Rayan the reference is to God's attitude to the world, to the forgiving love in which God invites and gathers humanity in Jesus. It is this that Jesus reveals, bears witness to and embodies in his life and in his personal relationships (Jn 18:37). Truth, accordingly, is what gives authenticity and substance to one's well-being.

Jesus of Rayan is the friend of the outcastes, associating himself with the ostracised, welcoming the publicans and the prostitutes, restoring the human dignity and honour of women, widows, the children and the poor as the striking images of bringing in dignity and freedom to the victims.[160] Rayan interprets Jesus as the friend of the outcast in the context of caste system, a system of taboos based on purity, pollution and untouchability. He says that Jesus chose to be a friend of the outcasts in order to break open their prejudiced minds and make room for a new world which is free and equal. In this endeavour, Jesus lived with the masses, taught them through their metaphors and parables, challenged and led them to liberation. [161] The Word becomes incarnate and inculturated by identifying with the poor and the lowly, emptying himself and becoming a slave. Jesus made the culture of the masses his own.[162] Jesus touched the lepers (Lk 5:13) and let prostitutes (Lk 36:50) and women with haemorrhage tou2ch him (Lk 8:43-48).[163]

For Rayan, Jesus is bold to suggest to people that they are, and therefore should become, the salt of the earth and the light of the world. His trust in people is so great that he cannot but expect and demand from them everything that is sublime, refined, admirable and beautiful.[164] The question therefore, that arises is, what would be some of the basic features that disclosed the truth that set people of his time free? Rayan sets it forthrightly as Jesus' table fellowship with prostitutes, tax collectors, and sinners that had a tremendous meaning.[165] Moreover, table fellowship in the Jewish religious world-view also symbolized the eschatological community which is a fellowship with God (Cf Isa 25:6; Mt 8:1; Lk 22:30). [166] By sharing a meal with 'sinners', God's solidarity is vividly painted as far more superior to any other action.[167] When Jesus defied the powers that be of state and of temple, and forgave and loved and released into the lives of the poor a new hope and joy and creative strength, Jesus set aside sacred laws, religious traditions, holy practices and all authorities and claims which enslaved and diminished people. Such was the freedom that Jesus offered and which served as the personal foundation of being ready for a transformative mission.

Reflecting further Rayan says that it is in the passion and death of Jesus, truth-disclosure reached the epitome of truth:

> The crucified Jesus is the truth of God's forgiving love; of God's solidarity with our sinful and suffering existence; of God's resistance to every power of state or church which oppresses and humiliates people; and of God's affirmation of freedom and of people's right to love and worship in joy without being manipulated by Mammon, Temple, Sword or Experts on God. In the resurrection, finally, the Jesus-Truth becomes the Spirit of freedom and joy and of joyful struggle for dignity, released into the lives of the poor and the powerless.[168]

Truth meant for Jesus to suffer in solidarity with the victims and positively to do something constructive to empower them.

Rayan makes note of the constitutive elements of Jesus' way of truth, as the gospel of John says Jesus is the Truth (Jn 14:6). For instance, firstly, the truth of Jesus is perceived against the background of the poor and the marginalized of his time. It is in solidarity with the victims that the truth of Jesus is built. In the first place the Jesus-way of truth passes, by deliberate option, through the land of the broken. Therefore, Jesus' major concern was the people on the periphery.[169] The marginalized, oppressed and honourless sectors of society, together with God's will to liberate and lift them up are constitutive of the truth of Jesus. Jesus hears their cry, answers; their questions in their midst he moves, and their dignity and freedom he struggles for. In other words, the truth of Jesus cannot be comprehended apart from the poor, the lower classes and the wretched of his time. For, Jesus was not only reaching down even to the lowest level of human society, but he was disclosing the truth of God and of the people, and was manifesting that truth in his own life and person.

Secondly, Jesus breaks all the rules of Jewish society in his preferred association with social outcasts and prostitutes, his fellowship with the disreputable and the social outcasts. He is completely out of place according to Jewish cultural perception. Jesus' own emphasis lay on the primacy of mercy over every sort of temple sacrifice. He broke with relatives and family ties and called not his blood relatives but his disciples his true family. Doing God's will was the mark of the true relative of Jesus. Accordingly, he went on to define relationships in terms of openness and obedience to God's word and will (Mk 3:21, 31-35; Jn 7:3-8; 20:17; Lk 11:27-28).

Thirdly, Rayan presents the image of 'Jesus the Truth that sets us free,' in the context of two kinds of kingship.[170] The truth of Jesus' kingship is "expressed in poverty and in the washing of one another's feet, in resistance to injustice, in witnessing to freedom, in love unto death in a struggle for people's liberation. The truth of Jesus' kingship consists in the breaking of the son-of-David idol and identification of himself with the Suffering Servant (Mk 8:31, 33; 9:33-37; 10:35-45; 14:10-11)."[171] Fourthly, truth in Jesus had to die and rise. Christ emptied himself and shared human being's destiny in suffering and death to pay the price of humans' sin. Even at the point of terrible suffering and humiliation Christ's sacrifice on the Cross was his ultimate love to respond to the love of the Father on behalf of fallen humankind; it becomes Jesus' act of solidarity with humankind by embracing human suffering in order to transform this condition of human embodiment into the Trinitarian life of love. The proof of this event is the resurrection that happens in the heart of the Cross and the struggle where the New Humanity of freedom and love is revealed. It is in following Jesus in a life of solidarity and conflicts that we understand Jesus and his way of truth.

Lastly, Rayan considers the medium Jesus used to communicate. Direct exchange and oral communication was his method. Jesus toured the length and the breadth of Galilee, visited every village and town, contacting people, experiencing reality directly and at first hand, rendering services and pressing everyone to personal reflection and decision which might enable them to shake themselves free of oppressive powers, to exercise their freedom in loving one another, and so begin to be authentically human. Everywhere Jesus talked to people, told stories, proposed parables. The parables of Jesus through the use of various imageries not only speak of the essential role of nature in making the earth habitable, but also in revealing the presence of God in the natural world. Moreover, Jesus' extensive travels in the countryside and involvement with the deprived people of society who earned a living from the bounties of nature, made it possible for him to observe from close quarters the role of nature in agricultural activities. They thus came naturally to him to be used as metaphors in his parables proclaiming the *Kingdom of God*,[172] to an audience predominantly consisting of peasants and others who belonged to the deprived and alienated social groups.[173]

Being the revelation as well as the praxis of the truth which sets people free, Jesus relates directly to the oppressed who need liberation and transformation. Jesus calls for a two-fold reversal: one that affects the poor and the marginalized in which they will become the inheritors of the divine blessings with a transformation in their entitlement. The other, affects the rich and the powerful ruling class whose lives have to be transformed from a desire for acquisitiveness to a willingness to share. The call is for a reversal and return of every human being irrespective of their class, longing to overcome their own values and to attain the divine values. The truth is that Jesus has been sent to bring good news to the poor, to open prisons, liberate captives and set the downtrodden free (Lk 4:18).

Jesus: The Immanuel – God-with-Us

According to Rayan, Jesus is the Immanuel or God-with-us from his birth and to the end as per his promise to his disciples that his presence continues to be with them "to the end of time" (Mt 28:18-20). The incarnation of God's Word is not becoming "just a human being, but flesh, a weak human being, a member of the powerless, suffering, oppressed and fragile class."[174] The incarnate Word was truly a "flesh of the poor," sharing the sufferings and plight of the poor and the oppressed. "Jesus becomes a slave, an oppressed person, an outcaste." Jesus is flesh, "carrying in his corporate personality all flesh, all who are weak and vulnerable, the powerless multitude of the wretched of the earth."[175] His *sarx* is a "divine sharing in the powerlessness" of the poor.[176]

The incarnation is that event where the second person of the Trinity, the Word, became flesh and dwelt among us. As the Gospel of John states: "In the beginning was the Word, the Word was with God, and the Word was God" (1:1). "And the Word became flesh and lived among us..." (1:14). Jesus' Immanuel presence among us of God in Jesus is a dynamic one. One that identified with the poor and the lowly, emptied himself and become a slave. He sat in the homes of tax collectors and sinners who were considered outcasts on account of their profession; he ate with them and made them welcome in his own home. He asks for and accepts water from "a woman of Samaria" (Jn 4:7, 9). He went all over Galilee, visited all its towns and villages, and walked among the common people, walked with the harassed and the oppressed and the wretched of the earth (Lk 8:1; Mt 4:23; 9:35-37). He walked with them in recognition of their dignity, to bring them honour, to awaken in them a new sense of their own worth.

In the light of above reflections it can be stated that Jesus' presence was with those who needed him the most, especially the poor, the marginalized, the oppressed and the disciples on their way to Emmaus. His walks and ways were a challenge to the leaders of his times. His mission of solidarity was marked by the movement from the center to the periphery, reached its climax in his death on the Cross where he identified himself absolutely and totally with the poor and the oppressed. Therefore Rayan says,

> Even without the Resurrection the death of Jesus would be more than the death of the thousands who have been crucified; it would still be the most shattering affirmation of the downtrodden and the most explosive protest of the poor. The Resurrection revealed that Jesus' options had God's approval and that Jesus' death was God's own decisive and critical intervention in the human situation and in human tragedy.[177]

Jesus took a stand against oppression and wretchedness. He stood for the people, their dignity and their freedom. He expressed solidarity with them in radical ways throughout his life, beginning with his '*Dalit*' birth in a stable and ending with his shameful death on the Cross.

Jesus: The Daily Bread

Rayan speaks of Bread[178] as the symbol of all human food, the food that we cannot do without. To eat bread means to have a meal. Jesus calls "himself the bread of life, the True Bread," "Bread of God that has come down from heaven" (Jn 6:32-35). It is in the deep awareness of his own identity that Jesus understands his mission as well. Jesus is moved at the sight of people harassed and dejected, left like sheep without a shepherd, destroyed by thieves and bandits and abandoned by hirelings (Mt 9:36; Jn 10:2-10). Therefore, after healing Jairus's daughter Jesus tells her parents to "give her something to eat" (Mk 5:43); when he saw the great crowd that had nothing to eat, he said: "I feel sorry for these people, they have nothing to eat. If I send them off home hungry they will collapse on the way."(Mk 8:2).[179]

By sharing a meal with the sinners, Jesus vividly portrayed God's love and solidarity as condescending. It reaches down even to the lowest level of human society. Therefore, "Jesus is the Word become flesh, now become Bread. Of the Word, the Flesh is the sacrament, and of both the sacrament is Bread." Moreover, Jesus loved to dine. Food was for Jesus "a sacrament of equality and friendship, and a shared meal a place of recognition and honour."[180] This Word-Flesh-Bread has been sent by the Father to feed the world and foster life. Jesus is the bread and support of all forms and levels of life that comes from God.

Therefore, Rayan reflects deeply on the discourse on Bread of Life, wherein Jesus called himself the Bread of Life. "Take, eat, this is my Body, my Self, he said (Mt 26: 26). He said: 1 am the living Bread; my flesh is real food, my blood is real drink; whoever eats me will draw life from me (Jn 6:51-57). The claim is that Jesus himself is the bread, the rice, the food and the basis of life." It is in terms of life and its nature Jesus understands and identifies himself as well as his mission: "I came that they may have life, and have it abundantly" (Jn 10:10). Hence, Rayan comes out with the image of Jesus the Daily Bread. By "giving himself as Bread, Jesus is inextricably linking his person and mystery with the foundations of our life, with its material and economic roots.

If Jesus is the Bread of life, and that affirmation is understood in all its depth and width, then bread has, the economy has, Christological dimensions; and the Christ reality has economic implications."[181] The Incarnation is very real and present, and reaches to and touches every fibre of our being.

Jesus: The Spirit-filled Person

In his book *Breath of Fire,* Rayan observes that "the Holy Spirit, the Spirit of God and of Jesus Christ" as the "heart of the Christian hope".[182]The Scripture reveals to us that from the moment of his conception in his mother's womb Jesus was overshadowed by the Spirit. His baptism affirms it further: "during that time Jesus came from Nazareth into Galilee and was baptised in the Jordan by John. Immediately on coming up out of the water he saw the sky rent in two and the Spirit descending upon him like a dove. Then a voice came from heaven: You are my beloved Son…" (Mk 1:9-11). Being convinced of the biblical indication of the specific vocation of Jesus, Rayan portrays Jesus as "He who is baptised with the Holy Spirit," the one who presents us with the basis and core of Christian identity and Christian distinctiveness.[183] In other words, for Rayan, the Spirit-experience of his Abba was the foundation of Jesus' intimate relationship with the Father, of his teaching authority, his healing power, his compassion and gentleness, of his life from birth to death to resurrection. Jesus was encountered and experienced by the people of his time as a Spirit-filled person. The Spirit is present at the public commission of Jesus on the Jordan, and takes charge of his life, in the desert and back in Galilee (Lk 4:1, 14). Therefore, Rayan affirms that the Spirit is the agent of Mission (*EN* 75).

The Spirit permeates all aspects of Jesus' life and the Spirit's activity overflows the bounds of the Christian Community; the Spirit fills the whole earth and all history. In Rayan's own words, the Christian gospel is "that our life and our word stand bathed in the Holy Spirit, the Spirit of God and of Jesus Christ. This is the central point of God's redemptive activity. It is the basic experience of salvation. It is the heart of the Gospel and of Christian hope".[184] This, in his view, is uniting the human and the divine, grace and nature, sacred and secular.[185] Rayan succinctly describes: "the Spirit is the nonconformist manner in which Jesus moved with bad characters, and ate with social outcasts; and the way he broke all Sabbath laws and traditions in the service of life and the affirmation of the dignity of women and men. In his defiance of Herods, Pilates and Priests, Jesus is the symbol of the Spirit."[186] Jesus' ultimate expression on the Cross, Rayan describes, as "the supreme symbol of the Spirit: the Crucified One with his word of forgiveness for his killers, his caring for others, his independence and freedom and the surrender of his life in faith to God. If Jesus' life was the dance of the Spirit on our earth, Calvary was its culminating, crowning movement."[187]

Rayan considers Jesus on the Cross as the Lord of the dance as well as cosmic dance blossoming into the resurrection: "A cosmic dance, the rhythm of which reverberates in every fibre of the universe and keeps throbbing in the centre of every spirit and in the heart of every particle of matter. A dance of blood and travail, that gave birth to the New Age of freedom and abounding in life and the outpouring of the Holy Spirit."[188] The resurrection was Jesus' fullest and most decisive experience of the Spirit, an experience which wholly transformed him to provide humanity with a decisive future, which indeed is the work of the Holy Spirit. Rayan wants to emphasise that "Jesus is pre-eminently the man of the Holy Spirit, the giver of the Spirit, the dispenser of the gift of the Spirit, and it is he who makes it possible for us to share in the Spirit of God".[189] And the resurrection scenes are nothing but the dances performed to a different tune. Perhaps we can justifiably say that the Holy Spirit was the way Jesus walked and lived his mission-existence.[190]

What does Rayan mean by Cross as the cosmic dance? By this, he means that the Cross of Jesus blossoming into the resurrection is the supreme affirmation of life, freedom and joy.[191] For Rayan, Pentecost reveals "the whole meaning of Jesus for human history and destiny" as the disciples are then empowered to participate in his mission.[192] It is affirming the reality that the central message of the New Testament is the Christ event, the Incarnation and Redemption through Christ.

As a result, the Spirit occupies a significant place in Rayan's theological horizon too. Rayan looks upon the Holy Spirit as the initiator of fresh beginnings.

In the light of what has been said so far, there is no doubt that Rayan describes Jesus as related to five key events in the Gospels, the annunciation, the baptism, the Cross, the resurrection and the Pentecost. He considers the annunciation a second act of creation by the Spirit because the Spirit is at work in Jesus from annunciation, his baptism in the Jordan confirmed his Spirit-filled nature.[193] The baptism of Jesus was not the first but a fresh, more personal experience of the Spirit which guaranteed the coming of the Spirit upon us and on Earth. According to Rayan, Jesus' intervention on behalf of life and human rights was radical. He sided with the poor, loved the unloved, and those deemed unlovable. Jesus was in solidarity with the outcast, the oppressed, and the victims of history's slavery and untouchability systems.

4. Implications of Rayan's Christology

An analysis of the Christological insights of Rayan reveals that he considers the dignity of the human person as a gift of God. Thus he cries for the dignity of human life, human rights, and human freedom wherever they are denied. It is the historical Jesus who motivates him to be involved in the task of liberating the poor and establishing their rights and their human dignity. No doubt his theological reflections are founded on his Christological reflections. For him Jesus is a man of freedom who was able to identify himself freely and authentically with the poor, and with their longing and struggles.

Rayan interprets Jesus as the initiator of a new social order. It is similarly noteworthy that for Rayan, Jesus was not simply "God's eternal Word in a particular cultural clothing," but a "deeply historical, densely human reality, a sharer in our bodily existence and earthly conditions, flesh of our flesh, man among men, like us in all things though never sinning, never closing himself to God. His body was of this earth, fruit along with us of its evolutionary process."[194] He lived with the masses, taught through their metaphors and parables, acted on their behalf, challenged them and led them to liberation.[195] The Word becomes incarnate and inculturated by identifying himself with the poor and the lowly, emptying himself and becoming a slave. Jesus made the culture of the masses his own.[196]

For Rayan, the struggles of the poor are theologically significant as they are not only "the chief record of God's self-revelation in world history," but because they are also the spaces of "action for a new social order" of God's Reign.[197] Thus the incarnation, for Rayan, is an "incarnation into the poor." Rayan's theology is deeply grounded in the very mystery of incarnation. The human person struggling for dignity and wholeness is at the centre of Rayan's theological enterprise. It offers an avenue to examine how those who are downtrodden and marginalized today can continue living out the socio-political reality of the vision of the new social order. The incarnation of the church in a local context cannot happen in alienation of the poor and their realities.[198] The new social order was a society of love and service, a world in which everyone is loved and respected.[199] Jesus' interaction with the poor, the children, the women, and his table fellowship show that the ones Jesus wished to bring into his society are those who count for nothing in the world's eye.

Thus, the implication of Jesus' praxis and words is that he has a radically new image of God. In other words, Jesus' praxis and his concept of the reign of God would not have been possible without a totally new image of God. According to Rayan, the early Christian community "encountered Jesus as the Word of God, as something God was [is] saying to them, a Word about God's own self and about us humans and our world and history and destiny. They knew him as God's Word of love and forgiveness, compassion and peace, spoken into their hearts and lives; a life-giving Word at the foundational level of creation and the crowning Word at the level of redemption (Jn 1:1-3)." Indeed, Rayan thinks that Jesus probably understood himself as "the Father is in me and I am in the Father" (Jn 10:38). In the midst of a broken world of hunger, misery and tears Jesus is compassion. Compassion is his name.

One could echo Jesus and add: "Whoever experiences my compassion, experiences the compassion of the Father who sent me and is in me."[200] Jesus, in his humanity, manifested his Christic identity and made God visible and experiential to humankind. Thus, Jesus is the incarnate presence of God for our times. Jesus becomes the model in taking a stand with the millions of the marginalized and the oppressed to support the cause of God's work of mercy and compassion.

Significantly, Rayan takes delight and inspiration from Jesus who made it a point to decolonize the religion and the theology of the people, which had been occupied by royal, priestly and wealthy settlers from the time of Solomon. Power centers molded religion for the socio-religious periphery. Worship was centralized to suit monarchical politics. Religion became priest-ridden and expensive, legalistic and burdensome. It had its outcasts and untouchables. Jesus marginalized the temple and all priestly pretensions. Relationships have priority over offerings to God. "Rules of purity and pollution were not decisive at the level of the heart. With such teaching and corresponding practice, Jesus' work of decolonizing and revising traditional religion and theology was so far-reaching that, while the liberated people rejoiced, the powers that be decided to rid society of the radical prophet."[201]

Therefore, the central concerns of the theological pursuit of Rayan is to construct autonomous indigenous theologies which address the challenging issues that are encountered by the marginalized, and criticize the status quo. His prime concern is to propose alternatives. Rayan's personal commitment to Jesus and his faith-experience of God in Jesus is the basis and foundation of his theological pursuit. In this process the person and event of Jesus Christ is our norm. God's history is our history; God is with us (*Emmanuel*). In this context it is good to look at a provocative question, which Samuel Rayan asks: "if Jesus were born in India, would he be in caste or an outcast? What would be his choice?"[202] Hence, theologizing in India, the interpretation of the mystery of Jesus Christ and the self-understanding of his community take place in a multi-religious context and in a situation of massive poverty and oppression. It is in such contexts "that the true God can emerge and be met. The living God in Jesus is one who fosters life and takes sides with those who struggle for food, freedom, and dignity against all systems of death and subjugation."[203]

Conclusion

This chapter began by introducing the focus of Rayan, as it is necessary to briefly sketch some biographical notes and some basic factors that have shaped his Christological framework. The chapter described that while Rayan's approach to a Christological framework has distinctive features that lend themselves to developing a Mission of the Church in the emerging 21st century India, they include: 1) the basis of Rayan's theological thinking: it lies in the dignity of the human person as a gift and grace of God; 2) Rayan has a passion for the person of Jesus, and his faith-experience is the basis and foundation of his theological vision; 3) Rayan cries for the wholeness of humanity; and 4) Rayan allows himself to be led by the Spirit. That is why he could convincingly say that Christology is to be read not with the scientific eye, nor with the techniques of swift diagonal reading, but with the heart which alone sees reality truly and tastes it.[204] The examination of the few concepts frequently used by Rayan, and the other terms in use to which he gives special importance in his theological search reveal that Rayan has a unique way of describing what he means by doing theology in India.

Rayan portrays Jesus as the one who provides the pressing challenge for today and summons to the effect that primacy is given to the quest for the justice of God which is God's fidelity to every creature God has loved into existence. To give heed to Jesus' invitation to love one another as He loved implies providing health, bread, rice, liberty, honour and acceptance to the neglected masses of the people who needed them to become fully themselves and know themselves and one another as God's children.[205]

To the extent people wake up to the truth of their situation or reality, to that extent Jesus Christ becomes relevant. In other words, the immediate need of the hour is to develop a critical consciousness, pay serious attention to existential issues; recognize therein their dignity and their vocation to live as God's friends and co-operators in the fashioning of the new age. What follows next is an exploration of the writings of Fiorenza and the relevance of her insights to our context.

Endnotes

[1] Samuel Rayan, "The Basic Dilemma," extract from longer paper on "Development and Evangelization," in *The Church and Development Dilemma*, ed. Tony Byrne (Eldoret, Kenya: Gaba Publications, 1971), 42, 45.

[2] Samuel Rayan, *Breath of Fire: The Holy Spirit: Heart of the Christian Gospel* (London: Geoffrey Chapman, 1979).

[3] John, ed. *Bread and Breath*

[4] Samuel Rayan, "The Search for an Asian spirituality of liberation" in *Asian Christian Spirituality: Reclaiming Traditions* eds. Virginia Fabella, Peter K. H. Lee, David Kwang-sun Suh (Maryknoll, New York: Orbis Books, 1992).

[5] Samuel Rayan, *Selected Writings of Samuel Rayan*, vol. I-III ed. Kurien Kunnumpuram (Mumbai: St. Pauls, 2013).

[6] Samuel Rayan, *Jesus: The Relevance of His Person and Message for our Times*: *Collected Writings of Samuel Rayan*: vol. I-III ed. Kurien Kunnumpuram (Delhi: ISPCK: 2013).

[7] Kunnumpuram, ed. *The Vision of a New Church and a New Society.*

[8] For this part of the biographical details I depend largely on the following sources: *SEDOS* bulletin Vol. 29/6&7 (June & July, 1997); John, *Bread and Breath*; and Kurien Kunnumpuram, "Introduction" in *Jesus: The Relevance of His Person and Message for our Times*, 7-12.

[9] Other important scholars and thinkers associated with Indian liberation theology are Sebastian Kappen, George M. Soares-Prabhu, Michael Amaladoss, and Felix Wilfred. Indian because it is an Indian heart that listens to the cry of the poor and oppressed, reads the signs of the times in India, and provides a context to understand the situation from the down-side of history.

[10] John, *Bread and Breath.*

[11] Rayan, "Theological Priorities in India," in *Irruption of the Third World*, eds. Fabella and Torres, 39-40.

[12] Georg Evers, "Samuel Rayan: Theologian from India," (March 1, 2006) http://www.forum-weltkirche.de/de/personen/13889.samuel-rayan-sj.html (accessed July 26, 2015); Kunnumpuram, "Introduction," in *Jesus*, 1.

[13] SEDOS Resource Persons "Samuel Rayan SJ," *SEDOS Bulletin*, 29/6&7 (June & July, 1997): 164. Rayan's thesis was entitled *Vincent Taylor's Interpretation of Christ's Death as Sacrifice*. Vincent Taylor, Methodist, a specialist in Mark's Gospel. This piece of information is gathered from the thesis: Nicholas Tharsiuse, *Christian Faith*:

A Liberative Praxis: Theology of Samuel Rayan (ISPCK, 2015), 3. All India Catholic University Federation (AICUF) is a movement of university students with a vision for a new and just society. Progressing in a history of constant rediscovery and re-creation, the AICUF ever tries to link itself to the emerging needs and realities of the university, the Church and wider society.

[14] Kunnumpuram, "Samuel Rayan: A Great Indian Theologian," in *Bread and Breath,* 19-20.

[15] SEDOS "Samuel Rayan," 3.

[16] Kunnumpuram, "Samuel Rayan," in *Bread and Breath,* 19.

[17] Samuel Rayan, "Baptism and Conversion: the Lima text in the Indian Context," in *A Call to Discipleship* ed. Godwin Singh (Delhi: ISPCK, 1985), 186.

[18] Kunnumpuram, "Introduction" in *Jesus,* 9-10.

[19] Rayan, "Theological Priorities in India Today," in *Irruption of the Third World,* 30-41.

[20] Samuel Rayan, "Reconceiving Theology in the Asian Context," in *Doing Theology in a Divided World,* eds. Virginia Fabella and Sergio Torres (Maryknoll, New York: Orbis Books, 1985), 124-142.

[21] P.R. John, "Images of Jesus Christ in India: in the Writings of Samuel Rayan" *VJTR* 68/7 (2004): 499-500.

[22] Miguel A. De La Torre, *Introducing Liberative Theologies* (Maryknoll, New York: Orbis Books, 2015). The term 'Colonial' theologies will be taken up later in section 2.1.

[23] Samuel Rayan, "Mission after Vatican II: Problems and Positions," *IRM* 59 (October 1970): 414-426.

[24] A paper presented to the Commission for Social and Economic Development Activities, Second Meeting, Rome, 24th - 28th April, 1971; Samuel Rayan, "Development and Evangelization: A Theological Sketch" (Lumen Institute, Cochin, Kerala, India, 1971); Barbara Hendricks, M.M. "Life, Work and Word: The Contribution of Samuel Rayan SJ to the Renewal of US Missionaries," in *Bread and Breath:* ed. John, 6-17.

[25] *Evangelii Nuntiandi* is an Apostolic Exhortation issued on 8 December 1975 by Pope Paul VI on the theme of evangelization. It affirms the vocation, identity and role of the Church as bringing the Good News into all strata of humanity, and through its influence transforming humanity from within and making it anew.

[26] Speaking of Rayan, Sr Hendricks says, "In the 1970s Rayan's paper was probably one of the most widely spread and eagerly read documents among missionaries in the U. S. A. as well as among church personnel in social ministry and in other countries where U.S. missionaries had an outreach." Cf. Sr Barbara Hendricks, "Life, Work and Word: The Contribution of Samuel Rayan, to the Renewal of U.S. Missionaries," in *Bread and Breath: Essays in Honour of Samuel Rayan, on the Occasion of his Seventieth Birth Anniversary,* ed. T. K. John (Anand: Gujarat Sahitya Prakash, 1991). x.

[27] Samuel Rayan, "Meditation: Worship Him with Bread and Rice," *VJTR,* 50/6 (July, 1986): 312-316.

[28] The thrust of the National Seminar held on "Samuel Rayan's Theological Writings" from Dec 28 to 31, 2014 at Christ Hall, Calicut, Kerala, was to honour the well-known Jesuit theologian of Kerala province by assessing his contribution to Indian Christian Theology. The papers, twenty two in number, were meant to study Rayan's theological writings and to assess his contribution in Indian Christian theology. The papers have been suitably presented in four parts, namely: Theological Themes, The Church and its Mission, Approach to the Bible, and Theologizing in India. Kunnumpuram, ed. *The Vision of a New Church and a New Society*, i.

[29] Ben Jose, "A New Light to Enlighten the Indian Church: The Significance of Samuel Rayan SJ," *AJRS* 60/2 (March 2015): 5-8.

[30] Kunnumpuram, "Samuel Rayan," 19-20.

[31] Mohan Doss, "The Spirit of Life: Rayan's Thoughts on the Holy Spirit," in *The Vision of a New Church and a New Society*, ed. Kunnumpuram, 39-65.

[32] Samuel Rayan, "Doing Theology in India," in *Theologizing in Context: Statements of the Indian Theological Association*, ed. Jacob Parappally (Bangalore: Dharmaram Publications, 2002), 11-22. This article was originally published in *Socio-Cultural Analysis in Theologizing*, ed. Kuncheria Pathil (Bangalore: Indian Theological Association, 1987), 12-32.

[33] Nicholas Tharsiuse, rightly states that in view of achieving his objective, that is, a close connection between Christian faith with a special emphasis on social justice and socio-historico-political existence in India, Rayan's writings from the early 1970s until 1981 focused predominantly on the existential approach to Christology from which flows the value and centrality of persons in the plan of God and the mission of the Church as well as Rayan's prophetic critique of the Church in India. Tharsiuse, *Christian Faith*, xxviii.

[34] Rayan, "Re-conceiving Theology in the Asian Context," 124.

[35] Samuel Rayan, "The Justice of God," in *Third World Liberation Theologies: A Reader*, ed. Deane William Ferme (Maryknoll, NY: Orbis, 1979), 354.

[36] Kunnumpuram, "Samuel Rayan A Great Indian Theologian," 18-19.

[37] Terms will be explained in the chapter under, 2.2.3 'Need for a New and Appropriate Language.'

[38] Rayan's approach to Christology stems from his theological methodology which is reflected in his many articles, especially in the following articles: Samuel Rayan, "Theological Education in the Social Context of India Today," in *Theological Education in India Today, The Statement, Papers and Proceedings of the Eighth Annual Meeting of the Indian Theological Association, Pariyaram, Kerala, Dec 28-31, 1984*, ed. Felix Wilfred (Bangalore: ATC, 1985), 12-32; Samuel Rayan, "Re-conceiving Theology in the Asian Context," "The Irruption of the Third World – A Challenge to Theology," *VJTR* 46 (1982): 106-127; Samuel Rayan, "The 'How' of Third World Theologies," in *The Third World Theologies in Dialogue: Essays in Memory of D.S. Amalorpavadass* ed. J.R. Chandran (Bangalore: EATWOT, 1991); Samuel Rayan, "Commonalities, Divergences, and Cross Fertilization among Third World Theologies," in *Third World Theologies: Commonalities and Divergences* ed. Abraham K.C. (Maryknoll: Orbis

Books, 1990), 195-213; and Samuel Rayan, "Third World Theologies: Where Do We Go From Here?," *Concillium* 199 (1988): 127-140.

[39] Rayan, "Commonalities, Divergences, and Cross-fertilization among Third World Theologies," 200-201.

[40] Rayan, "The 'How' of Third World Theologies," 63, 65.

[41] Rayan, "Doing Theology in India," 11-12.

[42] Rayan, "The 'How' of Third World Theologies," 44.

[43] However, independently of what was happening in Latin America at the end of 1960's and early 1970's Rayan started theologizing precisely from praxis. Rayan has developed a theology that is supportive of peoples' movements. Leonard Fernando, "Indian Christian Theology" *Class Notes*, 11 November 2011, http://leocpps.blogspot. in/2011/11/class-note-on-indian-christian-theology.html (accessed August 28, 2017).

[44] Deane William Ferm, *Profiles in Liberation: 36 Portraits of Third World Theologians* (Eugene, Oregon: Wipf & Stock Publishers, 2004), 104-105.

[45] P.T. Mathew, "Exploring the Realm of Implicit Theologies: Reflections on Samuel Rayan's Method of Theologizing," in *The Vision of a New Church and a New Society*, 310-311.

[46] Samuel Rayan "Wrestling in the Night," in *The Future of Liberation Theology: Essays in Honour of Gustavo Gutiérrez*, eds. Mark H. Ellis & Otto Maduro (Maryknoll: Orbis, 1989), 454.

[47] Rayan, "Wrestling in the Night," 450 ff.

[48] Wilfred rightly summarizes in the following words: "Theology is intrinsically connected with integral life and the name of the Divine and its image, the human beings. If so, then the focus is more than academic centres of theological learning; it is a life-context of the people. It is that people who fight for freedom and struggle for justice that are the subjects of theology." Felix Wilfred, *Beyond Settled Foundations: The Journey of Indian Theology* (Madras: Department of Christian Studies, 1993), 85.

[49] Rayan, "Re-conceiving Theology in the Asian Context," 132.

[50] Kunnumpuram, *Jesus,* 12.

[51] Samuel Rayan, "Christian Participation in the Struggle for Social Justice: Some Theological Reflections," *CM* 38/7 (August, 1974): 282-296.

[52] Samuel Rayan, "Irruption of the Poor: Challenge to Theology," *Concillium* 197/5 (1986): 101-102, 106.

[53] Samuel Rayan, "Spirituality for Inter-Faith Social Action," in *Liberation and Dialogue*, ed. X. Irudayaraj (Bangalore: Claretian Publications, 1989), 65-66.

[54] Samuel Rayan, "Analysis of Society and Indian Theology," in *Socio-Cultural Analysis* ed. Kuncheria Pathil (Bangalore: Indian Theological Association, 1987): 144-145.

[55] Rayan, "The March Has Begun," *JD* 9 (1979): 180-181.

[56] In Rayan's theology 'praxis' refers to the real, active living out of faith in God here and now. Rayan, "Re-conceiving Theology in the Asian Context," 133; see also Nicholas Tharsiuse, "The Social and Liberative Consequences of Samuel Rayan's Theology" in *The Vision of a New Church and a New Society*, 204, 202.

[57] A brief evaluation of the liberationist approach of the Pontifical Biblical Commission includes elements of undoubted values which reflect in almost all the major works of Rayan. They are: the deep awareness of the presence of God who saves; the insistence on the communal dimension of faith; the pressing sense of need for a liberating praxis rooted in justice and love; a fresh reading of the Bible which seeks to make of the Word of God the light and nourishment of the people of God in the midst of its struggle and hopes. Ref: Joseph A. Fitzmyer, *The Pontifical Biblical Commission: "The Interpretation of the Bible in the Church": Text and Commentary* (Rome: Gregorian Biblical Bookshop, 1995), 94-95.

[58] Rayan, "Re-conceiving Theology in the Asian Context," 131.

[59] Although Rayan's theologizing is within the ambit of the EATWOT theological process, he still brings in nuances about Indian theologizing. Accordingly, the Word of God for Rayan is found not only in Scriptures but also in people's religious stories and practices.

[60] Rayan, "The National Seminar on People's Theology," *JD* 22 (1992): 169-239. This national Seminar was held to mark the twentieth year of the publication of the Journal *Jeevadhara*. The Final Statement of the Seminar, put out by the participant theologians and activists, belonging to various movements, religions and ideologies, would serve as the starting point of the discovery of the theological method of Rayan.

[61] Rayan, "The National Seminar on People's Theology," 231, 237-238

[62] Furthermore, Rayan has found in Marxist social analysis a useful tool for evaluating the weakness of capitalism and colonialism, and the power that the economic system has as a means of enslaving or liberating human beings. Ferm, *Profiles in Liberation*, 105.

[63] Rayan, "Decolonization of Theology," *JPJRS* 1/2 (July 1998): 147, 151.

[64] Rayan, "Re-conceiving Theology in the Asian Context," 124.

[65] Rayan, "Theological Priorities in India Today," 41.

[66] Rayan, "The March Has Begun," 161-188.

[67] Developing a theological method is an important item on the EATWOT held in Geneva, which is in line with the spirit of Rayan. Tissa Balasuriya affirms that "one of its key perspectives of is that deep commitment to liberation from oppression is the first act of Christian faith. The life of Jesus bears witness to this. Theology has to flow as a faith reflection from such commitment to love of neighbor." This means that experience of the life of faith in the difficult circumstances of our unjust world is an essential factor in theologizing. The inductive method is therefore indispensable for theology. Tissa Balasuriya, "A Third World Perspective," in Virginia Fabella and Sergio Torres, eds. *Doing Theology in a Divided World* (Maryknoll, New York: Orbis Books, 1985), 198.

[68] Rayan, "The 'How' of Third World Theologies," 43, 47-48.

[69] Samuel Rayan, "Interpreting Christ to India: Contributions of Roman Catholic Theological Seminaries," *IJT* 23/4 (1974): 229.

[70] Rayan, "Interpreting Christ to India," 230-231.

[71] During the anti-colonial struggle in India, the people were made to imagine the 'nation' as the only form of freedom. All other imaginations were thought to be 'non-national' and apolitical. Accordingly, the Ezhava movement appeared as a peripheral 'socio-reform movement' whose disunity or rupture within the entity ran the risk of destabilizing the very existence of India and therefore, what happened at the macro-level within communities was being enfolded into major historical narrative of Indian nationalism as 'socio-reform movements'. But, in the South Indian state of Kerala one such 'reform movement' occurred within a lower caste called the 'Ezhavas'. Cf. J. Raghu, "'Community' as de-imagining Nation: Relocating the Ezhava Movement in Kerala", in *Development, Democracy and the State: Critiquing the Kerala Model of Development* ed. K. Ravi Raman (New York: Routledge Taylor & Francis Group, 2010), 40-45. The Ezhavas were at the top among the *avarnas*. The *avarnas* means lacking *varna*. They are the class of untouchables. They suffered many disabilities along with the other non-caste Hindus. They had to keep themselves at least thirty six feet away from a Nambudiri and twelve feet away from a Nair (the major non-Brahmin caste). Women of these communities also suffered a lot under the clutches of the high caste. G. Rajendran, *Ezhava Community and Kerala Politics* (Trivandrum: The Kerala Academy of Political Science, 1974), 24.

[72] The removal of all discriminations and the attainment of total liberation was the result of a prolonged struggle by the Ezhava community inspired and led by a whole galaxy of charismatic persons like Sri Nārāyana Guru (b. 1856), Dr Palpu (b. 1863), Kumaran Āsān (b. 1873), T. K. Madhavan (b. 1885), P. Kuruppan (b. 1885), and Sahōdaran Ayyappan (b. 1889). Samuel Rayan. "People's Theology," JD 22 (1992): 185-186.

[73] Ferm, *Profiles in Liberation*, 103.

[74] Ferm, *Profiles in Liberation*, 104.

[75] Ferm, *Profiles in Liberation*, 103.

[76] Samuel Rayan, "Asian Theological Conference: A Reflex of its Dynamics," *VJTR* 43/6 (July 1979): 246-260.

[77] Samuel Rayan, "Human Well-Being on Earth and the Gospel of Jesus," *JD* 5/7 (Jan-Feb 1972): 36.

[78] Rayan, "Christian Participation in the Struggle for Social Justice," 288.

[79] Gustavo Gutiérrez, "Theology as Wisdom," in *Bread and Breath* ed. John, 4-3.

[80] Kirsteen Kim, "The Holy Spirit in Mission. Where and How is the Spirit Working in Religions, Cultures and Movements for liberation?" *Connections* 2/10 (Spring, 2001): 25.

[81] George Gispert-Sauch, "Asian Theology", in *The Modern Theologians: An Introduction to Christian Theology in the Twentieth Century* ed. David F. Ford, 2nd Edition (Oxford: Blackwell Publishers, 1997), 460.

[82] Rayan, *Breath of Fire: The Holy Spirit*, 203.

[83] Samuel Rayan, "Outside the Gate, Sharing the Insult," in *Leave the Temple: Indian Paths to Human Liberation*, ed. Felix Wilfred (Maryknoll, NY: Orbis, 1992), 135

[84] Rayan, "Decolonization of Theology," *JPJRS* 147.

[85] Rayan, "Theological Priorities in India Today," 37.

[86] Rayan, "Theological Priorities in India Today," 37.

[87] Rayan, "Theological Priorities in India Today," 37.

[88] Rayan, "Outside the Gate, Sharing the Insult," 144.

[89] Rayan, "Human Well-Being on Earth and the Gospel of Jesus," 41-45. Therefore the core of human person in Rayan's theology is endowed with value and sacredness, rights and dignity.

[90] Rayan, "Christian participation in the Struggle for Social Justice," 288-295.

[91] This part of the section on Rayan's refection on the Holy Spirit largely depends on the following sources: The paper entitled "New Efforts in Pneumatology" by Rayan at a Jesuit Congress on Ecumenism in 1999, in Kurien Kunnumpuram, *Collected Works of Samuel Rayan* Vol III, 77-112; *Breath of Fire: The Holy Spirit: Heart of the Gospel and Christian Hope*; "A Spirituality of Mission in an Asian Context," *SEDOS Bulletin* 29/6 &7 (1997): 194-206. Rayan prefers to use the feminine pronoun for the Spirit.

[92] Rayan, *Breath of Fire: The Holy Spirit*, vii. Rayan 1974a: 231

[93] Rayan, "New Efforts in Pneumatology," 90.

[94] Rayan, Samuel "Interpreting Christ to India: Contributions of Roman Catholic Theological Seminaries", Indian Journal of Theology 23/4, (1974a): 231. 223-31..

[95] Two categories of Christologies: one, Christology from above begins with Jesus as divine, then tries to understand his humanity; and two, Christology from below begins with Jesus as human, then tries to understand his divinity. both the approaches are to recognise both natures in Jesus: human and divine. A right understanding of Christ leads to the right understanding of God. Therefore, Christology becomes the starting point for theology. The first major attempt to express in precise language the New Testament's dual emphasis on Christ as both a human being and a divine figure came to be known as *Logos* Christology, for the simple reason that these early fathers adopted the Johannine concept of Logos. It has been a dominant way of interpreting Christ's incarnation, and it has taken various forms throughout history. Veli-Matti Kärkkäinen, *Christology A Global Introduction* (Grand Rapids, Michigan: Baker Academic, 2013), 65, 67.

[96] Rayan, *Breath of Fire*, vii. A number of published doctoral theses explain the Spirit-Christologies of Indian theologians. For instance, Kirsteen Kim, *Mission in Spirit: The Holy Spirit in Indian Christian Theologies* (Delhi: ISPCK, 2003) and Christina Manohar, *Spirit Christology: An Indian Christian Perspective* (Delhi: ISPCK, 2009).

[97] Rayan, *Breath of Fire*, 5-6, 8.

[98] Doss, "The Spirit of Life, in *The Vision of a New Church and a New Society*, 38.

[99] Samuel Rayan, "Local Cultures: Instruments of Incarnated Christian Spirituality" *SEDOS Bulletin* 29/6&7 (1997): 210.

[100] Rayan, "The Search for an Asian Spirituality of Liberation," 17. Spiritual life, according to Rayan, is the whole of human life inspired and led by the Spirit that people are spiritual in their struggles for daily rice, in their devotion to their children,

in their love for one another, in their simple prayers, their trust in God, and the responsibility they assume for new generations of people.

[101] Rayan, "Theological Priorities in India Today," in *Irruption of the Third World*, 40.

[102] Rayan, "Analysis of Society and Indian Theology," 147-148.

[103] John, *Bread and Breath,* xii. The bread of which the 'our Father' speaks is inseparable from the Kingdom; in other words, the bread is an integral part of the eschatological *Reign of God* inaugurated by Jesus' preaching and miracles.

[104] Rayan, *Breath of Fire,* 25-26.

[105] This understanding of the earth as a theological and liturgical reality has made Rayan a leading voice in ecotheology in ecumenical circles. Samuel Rayan, "The Earth is the Lord's" in *Ecotheology: Voices from South and North* ed. David C Hallman (Maryknoll: Orbis Books, 1994), 130-148.

[106] Rayan, *Breath of Fire,* vii.

[107] St Basil the Great is apt in saying: "The bread in your cupboard belongs to the hungry; the coat unused in your closet belongs to the one who needs it; the shoes rotting in your closet belong to the one who has no shoes; the money which you hoard up belongs to the poor." Boff, *The Lord's Prayer*, 84-85.

[108] Samuel Rayan, "The Justice of God," in *Living Theology in Asia,* ed. John C. England, (London: SCM Press, 1981), 213.

[109] Rayan, "Re-conceiving Theology in the Asian Context," 139.

[110] Bread has a very great significance in Christian tradition and history. In the Old Testament God gave the hungry Israelite people sojourning in the desert *manna* and the meat of the quails to nourish them and strengthen them. But God strictly prohibited them from hoarding for tomorrow, but they had to eat for the day.

[111] Rayan, *Breath of Fire: The Holy Spirit,* 116-117.

[112] Janina Gomes, "Theologian finds gospel in life of the people," *National Catholic Reporter*, May 12, 2000..http://www.natcath.org/NCR_Online/archives2/2000b/051200/051200o.html (accessed June 2016).

[113] Rayan, "Meditation. Worship Him with Bread and Rice," 312-316.

[114] Third Asian Theological Conference was held at the Ewha Women's University Retreat Center near Suanbo, Korea from July 3 to 8, 1989, focused on articulating spirituality grounded on praxis, so as to advance Asian People's liberation from all forms of domination. This gathering was not an isolated one, but was built on two previous meetings that formed part of the Asian program of the Ecumenical Association of Third World Theologians (EATWOT) held in Sri Lanka in 1979 and in Hong Kong in 1984 respectively. Virginia Fabella, Peter K.H. Lee, David Kwang-sun Suh, *Asian Christian Spirituality: Reclaiming Traditions* (Maryknoll, New York: Orbis Books, 1992), 2.

[115] Rayan, "The Search for an Asian Spirituality of Liberation," in *Asian Christian Spirituality*, ed. Fabella et al., 25, 3, 11-30

[116] According to Rayan, reality refers to everything – from sand and stone and the earth, through grass and trees, through worms and birds and their songs, through

human beings, their lives, their history, on to the ultimate Mystery we call God. In other words, the above mentioned perspective is shared by all mystical thought, for example, a stanza from *Auguries of Innocene*: "To see a world in a grain of sand, and a heaven in a wild flower, to hold infinity in the palm of your hand, and eternity in an hour." William Blake, "Auguries of Innocence," in Poets *of the English Language* (Viking Press, 1950). Openness is in Rayan's words "letting reality, significant for personal and social life and for the health of the earth, come and invade, enter, affect, disturb, challenge, mold and move us to joy, to tears, to anger, to action." Rayan, "The Search for an Asian Spirituality of Liberation," 22.

[117] Spiritual life is human life, the whole of human life inspired and led by the Spirit, the energizing presence and activity of God. The Spirit is the breath of God by which we breathe. It is the divine sea of life in which we live and move and have our being.

[118] Colony and 'colonial' derive from *colonia* via *colonus* 'farmer' from *colere* to 'cultivate'. Rayan, "The Search for an Asian Spirituality of Liberation," 28-30.

[119] Rayan, "The Search for an Asian Spirituality of Liberation," 25.

[120] Rayan, "The Search for an Asian Spirituality of Liberation," 25.

[121] Rayan, "Decolonization of Theology," 140.

[122] Kurien Kunnumpuram, ed. *In Spirit and Truth: Indian Christian Reflections on Spirituality and Worship: Selected Writings of Samuel Rayan, SJ.*, Vol II (Bandra, Mumbai: St Pauls, 2012), 42-43

[123] Decolonizing theology has been implicitly present and evolving within all theologies for instance, within slave revolts, ancient and recent, in Rome, in Rio, in Maryland, in Neo-Cartegena, in Carolina, in Auschwitz, in 'Gulag Archipelago'; and within peasant rebellions the world over against feudal lords and land mafias; within protests against oppression, within resistance to domination; and within movements of liberation from colonial and neo-colonial exploitation. One may recall the indigenous tribes that resisted Columbus' scheme to scoop up gold and collect slaves; and others who fought Cortes and Magellan; and the freedom fighters from Simon Bolivar to Che Guevara and Fidel Castro (Latin America); A. Cabral, P. Lumumba and M. Machel (Africa); and the anti-apartheid struggles of the Children of Soweto, of Steve Biko, of Nelson Mandela, and the tribes and organizations which made them (South Africa); and, of course, our own liberation movements led by Tilak, Gandhi and Nehru, Phule, Ayyankali, Narayana Guru and Ambedkar. Rayan, "Decolonization of Theology," 141.

[124] Torre, *Introducing Liberative Theologies*, 56-57.

[125] Rayan, "Decolonization of Theology," 141, 145.

[126] Consequently, Rayan says that "colonial theology was unable, in particular, to take note of and speak to our roots in the spiritual culture of this land. It did not know how to relate to the history of India's quest for the Ultimate Mystery: to India's experience of the Divine; to the symbols of that encounter in its sacred texts and worship forms; to the profundity and beauty of these symbols; and to the saints and seers of this land. Operating from within the West's mercantile framework, the

churches (from west Asia and Europe) saw themselves as bringing God and Christ in their ships to these godless shores. They failed to honour the biblical truth that it is always God that leads peoples, brings them together and gives them to each other". Samuel Rayan "Decolonization of Theology," in *Quotations on Terrorism*, ed. Harry Kawilarang (Victoria, British Columbia: Trafford, 2004), 425.

[127] Rayan, *Breath of Fire, viii, 2.*

[128] John, "Forward" to *Bread and Breath,* xi-xii.

[129] While Bread in Rayan's thought refers primarily to the Spirit as liberator, Breath draws attention to the role of the Spirit as Creator. The Spirit is the "breath" or yeast of new life that invigorates the "bread," which is the earth, and brings about a redistribution of its resources to the benefit of all. Cf. Kirsteen Kim, "Indian Contribution to Contemporary Mission Pneumatology," in *Ancient World: Reader, 5th edition*, eds. Robert Winter, Stephen D. Morad and Beth Snodderly (California, Institute of International Studies, 2004), 292.

[130] Rayan, "The Search for an Asian Spirituality of Liberation," 20.

[131] Doss, "The Spirit of Life,", 38-39

[132] Rom 1:19-20; Wis 13:1-9. In other words, creation's mission is to bear witness to God that God is present and God cares.

[133] Rayan, *Breath of Fire,* 104-105.

[134] Rayan, "A Spirituality of Mission in an Asian Context," 199.

[135] Joseph Comblin, *Holy Spirit and Liberation* (New York: Orbis Books, 1989), 4-8 as quoted in Rayan, *A Spirituality of Mission in an Asian Context*, 205.

[136] Samuel Rayan, "A Spirituality of Mission in an Asian Context," *SEDOS*, (1999), # 16a https://sedos mission.org/old/eng/rayan2.htm (accessed March, 2018).

[137] Rayan, *Breath of Fire,* 95-97.

[138] Rayan, Breath of Fire, 99.

[139] Rayan, *Breath of Fire,* 102, 105, 108.

[140] Rayan, *Breath of Fire,* 18.

[141] Rayan, *Breath of Fire,* 20, 24.

[142] In this view, God is understood to be leading everything and everyone to the final consummation to which all are summoned. In this perspective, different religions provide a common spiritual foundation to a common commitment to the task of liberation. The task therefore, is to work as partners in building this *Reign of God.* Geomon Kizhakkemalayil George, "The Immediacy of Presence in the Experience of God: An Indian Christian Perspective," in *World Christianity in Local Context: Essays in Memory of David A. Kerr*, vol.1, ed. Stephen R. Goodwin (London: Continuum, 2009), 174-176.

[143] Samuel Rayan, "Jesus: A Flesh-Translation of Divine Compassion," *JD* 26 (1996): 212-229.

[144] Traces of this understanding of God's compassion in Jesus are found in Henri Nouwen, et.al, in their book *Compassion.* They say that as soon as we call God, "God-with-us," we enter into a new relationship of intimacy with him. By calling him

Immanuel, we recognize that he has committed himself to live in solidarity with us, to share our joys and pains, to defend and protect us, and to suffer all of life with us. The God-with-us is a close God, a God whom we call our refuge, our stronghold, our wisdom, and even, more intimately, our helper, our shepherd, our love. We will never really know God as a compassionate God if we do not understand with our heart and mind that "he lived among us" (Jn 1:14). His compassion is anchored in the most intimate solidarity, a solidarity that allows us to say with the psalmist, "This is our God, and we are the people he pastures, the flock that he guides (Ps 95:7). Cf. Henri J. M. Nouwen, M. Donald P. McNeill, and Douglas A Morrison, *Compassion: A Reflection on the Christian Life*, (New York: Doubleday Image Books, 1982), 13-15.

[145] Ben Bose, "A New Light to Enlighten the Indian Church: The Significance of Samuel Rayan," 5-8.

[146] All religions speak of the greatness and absoluteness of God, also of His omniscience and limitless love. What is unique in Jesus' life and message is his 'Self-emptying love' or self-giving love'. (Phil 2:5-11). Joseph Prasad Pinto, OFM Cap, *Journey to Wholeness: Reflections for Life in Abundance* (Bombay: St. Pauls, 2006), 186.

[147] Rayan's reflections capture Jesus' concern for people: In his view Sabbath is for man (woman); Sabbath and sacrifice, temple and altar, priests and hierarchies, churches, institutions, laws, liturgies, traditions, definitions, creeds and cultures are all for all, and the community of women and men and the wholeness to all. Samuel Rayan, "The Underlying Philosophy of Jesus Christ," *The Rally* (Dec. 1974-Jan. 1975): 5.

[148] Rayan interprets that "the incarnation is God's reaffirmation in tenderness of the world in the power of love, and a reaffirmation in compassion of human existence God had set within the world. Work for human well-being will correspond to this divine 'Yes' to the world". Rayan, SWSR –III, 95. Therefore, what is done to the least of human beings is done to the person of Jesus, Son of Man, and Son of God.

[149] Jesus becomes the radical praxis of God's compassion: "the prophet of compassion" of Marcus Borg, "the Compassion of God" of Monika Hellwig and "the Inclusive Praxis of Wholeness" of Elisabeth Schüssler Fiorenza. Cf. Marcus J. Borg, *Meeting Jesus Again for the First Time* (San Francisco: Harper San Francisco, 1994), 46-68. Fiorenza, *In Memory of Her*, 119-130.

[150] Rayan, "Jesus: A Flesh-Translation of Divine Compassion," 213.

[151] Monica Hellwig says, that in his baptism at Jordan Jesus shows "sensitivity, vulnerability to be affected by the experience of the other. That is what compassion implies". Monika K. Hellwig, *Jesus: The Compassion of God* (Wilmington: Michael Glazier Inc., 1983), 121.

[152] Henri Nouwen says, "when Jesus was moved to compassion, the source of all life trembled, the ground of all love burst open, and the abyss of God's immense, inexhaustible, and unfathomable tenderness revealed itself". Cf. Nouwen, et.al, *Compassion: A Reflection on the Christian Life*, 16.

[153] Doss compliments Rayan saying that Jesus' identification with the poor, and his confrontation with the religiously and politically powerful of his time, led him inevitably to the conflict that culminated on the Cross. Mohan Doss, ed. *Led By the*

Spirit: Mission, Spirituality and Formation (Delhi: ISPCK, 2008), 100; Further he says, Jesus' solidarity with the poor found its final and ultimate expression on the Cross. Mohan Doss, *Christ in the Spirit: Contemporary Spirit Christologies* (Delhi: ISPCK, 2005), 167.

[154] Speaking about the significance of Dalit theology, Rayan puts it that God in Jesus suffers outside the camp like the Dalits. Rayan, "Outside the Gate, Sharing the Insult," 141-142.

[155] Rayan, "Jesus: A Flesh-Translation of Divine Compassion," 228.

[156] Hellwig, *Jesus: The Compassion of God*, 107-108.

[157] Samuel Rayan, "Flesh of India's Flesh," *JD* 33 (May-June, 1976): 260-261.

[158] Samuel Rayan, "The Truth that sets us Free," *JD* 14/81 (May, 1984): 206-230.

[159] Samuel Rayan, "Editorial," *JD* 14/81 (May, 1984).

[160] Rayan, "The Truth That Sets Us Free," 210.

[161] Rayan, "The March Has Begun," 182-186.

[162] Rayan, "Inculturation and Peoples' Struggles," *IMR* 19 (1997): 42.

[163] The woman in this story was excluded from social contact. In Jewish society menstruation made women unclean and removed them from religious worship for each month. In the case of this woman's condition, however, it made her continually unclean. Cf. Michael Keene, *St Mark's Gospel and the Christian Faith* (Cheltenham: Nelson Thornes, 2002), 74.

[164] Samuel Ryan, "Spirituality," *Voices from the Third World,* 10/3 (September, 1987): 62-63.

[165] Jesus' table - fellowship with prostitutes, tax collectors, and sinners had a tremendous meaning – he was elevating them to his status circle and expressing his solidarity with them. This resulted in a special focus on the purity of one's everyday food and of one's companions at every meal. Cf. S. Scott Bartchy, "Table Fellowship," in *Dictionary of Jesus and the Gospels*, eds. Joel B. Green and Scot McKnight (InterVarsity Press: Downers Grove, IL, 1992), 796.

[166] Jacob Neusner observes that this zeal for ritual purity extended so far that the Pharisees viewed the tables on which they ate their meals as representations of God's altar in the Jerusalem Temple. Jacob Neusner, 'Two Pictures of the Pharisees: Philosophical Circle or Eating Club?' *Anglican Theological Review* 64 (1982): 525-38.

[167] Joseph Lobo has tried to illustrate the table fellowship of Jesus that "the radicality of this practice comes to light when we realize that it is the host who blessed the bread, broke it and shared it with the guests. Hence in a table fellowship with the outcasts, Jesus ate the food blessed and shared by the socially polluted hosts." Lobo, *Encountering Jesus Christ in India*, 391.

[168] Rayan, "The Truth That Sets Us Free," 211.

[169] Albert Nolan's interpretation of Jesus goes along with Rayan's interpretation when he argues that the major theme of the gospel narrative is Jesus' concern for the poor and the oppressed, his dealings with the hungry and his love for and service to the miserable, the lepers, the cripples, the blind, the lame, the outcasts, prostitutes

and tax collectors, the persecuted, the downtrodden, the deranged, the least' and the lost, the widows, the rabble, the demoniacs, those who labour and are burdened, the harassed sheep, the sheep without shepherd, the condemned, the bereaved. Albert Nolan, *Jesus Before Christianity* (New York: Orbis Books, 1976), 21.

[170] One is the kingship of those who wield power with their basis in wealth and arms, one which imposes itself and rules by force. It contradicts the truth of the people and ultimately of God (e.g., Pilate). The other kind of kingship which tallies with truth and chimes with the footsteps of Jesus is one proper to every woman and man who loves, to everyone who has a heart human enough to feel, to suffer with others. Such is people's participation in the royalty of God (John 18 and Luke 23). Cf. Rayan, "The Truth That Sets Us Free," 214.

[171] Rayan, "The Truth That Sets Us Free," 215.

[172] As the *Kingdom of God* has a masculine and geographical overtone, henceforth, we prefer to use the phrase *Reign of God*.

[173] Rayan, "The Truth That Sets Us Free," 219.

[174] Rayan, "The March Has Begun," 188.

[175] Rayan, "Outside the Gate, Sharing the Insult," 137, 140.

[176] Rayan, "People's Theology," *JD* 22 (1992): 197. In this article Rayan enumerates some of the People's Movements in India and their significance for theology.

[177] Rayan, *Breath of Fire: The Holy Spirit*, 129.

[178] Samuel Rayan, "Jesus and Our Daily Rice," *JD* 25/147 (May 1995): 235-251.

[179] Rayan, "Jesus and Our Daily Rice," 239, 240-241.

[180] Rayan, "Jesus and Our Daily Rice," 240, 254.

[181] Rayan, "Jesus and Our Daily Rice," 239, 241.

[182] Rayan, *Breath of Fire*, 2.

[183] Rayan, *Breath of Fire*, 31.

[184] Rayan, *Breath of Fire*, viii, 2.

[185] Rayan, "The Basic Dilemma," 42, 45; P R John, rightly points out in his article that contemplating the spiritual heritage of India, Rayan could even say that a genuine inter-religious Christology will have to center on the Risen Lord who is Spirit and the life-giving *Prâna*, who is no longer known according to the flesh, who abides in the believer and is *Antaryâmin* or as the Indweller who bestows on wo/man the divine *Prâna* and commands a non-localised worship in Spirit and in Truth. Cf. Samuel Rayan, "An Indian Christology: A Discussion of Methods," *JD* 1/3 (1971): 229 as cited in P.R. John, "Catholic Christology and the Challenge of Religious Pluralism," *VJTR* 76/9 (2012): 942.

[186] Samuel Rayan, "Symbols of the Spirit," in *Collected Writings of Samuel Rayan*, vol. III ed. Kunnumpuram, 120.

[187] Jyoti Sahi, "Indian Symbols of the Holy Spirit" in *JD* 45 (May-June 1978): 245-246. From Jyoti Sahi's point of view "when the multitude looked on Jesus, they looked on him as on a dancer filled with the fire of the Holy Spirit. And this dance was infectious." Further Sahi observes that in the Indian art the central figure is the

dancing body. Hence "the figure of the dancer reveals the presence of the inspiring Force, in the same way as the dancing tree reveals the movement of the wind".

[188] Kurien Kunnumpuram, ed. *God's Hope Becoming Visible: Indian Christian Reflections on some Relevant Issues of our Times: Collected Writings of Samuel Rayan*, vol. III (Delhi: ISPCK: 2013), 138.

[189] Rayan, *Breath of Fire*, 31.

[190] Doss, "The Spirit of Life," 44

[191] Kunnumpuram, *God's Hope Becoming Visible*, 120.

[192] Rayan, *Breath of Fire*, 106.

[193] Rayan, *Breath of Fire*, 5-6;

[194] Rayan, "Flesh of India's Flesh," 260.

[195] Rayan, "The March Has Begun," 182-186.

[196] Rayan, "Inculturation and Peoples' Struggles," *IMR* 19 (1997): 42.

[197] Rayan, "The March Has Begun," 180-181.

[198] This is well summarized by Albert Nolan: "When God's kingdom comes, God will replace Satan. God will rule over the whole community of humankind and confer the kingdom or ruling powers upon those who will serve God's purposes in society. And evil will be eliminated and people will be filled with the Spirit of God." Nolan, *Jesus before Christianity*, 81.

[199] John Crossan gets it right when he states, "the Kingdom is a Kingdom of nobodies." John Dominic Crossan, *Jesus: A Revolutionary Biography* (San Francisco: Harper, 1994), 266.

[200] Rayan, "Jesus: A Flesh-Translation of Divine Compassion," *JD* 224.

[201] Rayan, "Decolonization of Theology," *JPJRS*, 150.

[202] Samuel Rayan, "Outside the Gate: Sharing the Insult," *JD* 11 (1981): 203-231.

[203] Rayan, "Irruption of the Poor: The Challenge to Theology," 106.

[204] Samuel Rayan, "Editorial," *JD* 21 (1991):184.

[205] Samuel Rayan, "Asia and Justice," *VJTR* 50/7 (1986): 352-364.

Chapter 3

Elisabeth Schüssler Fiorenza's Interpretation of Jesus

Introduction

The history of Christianity tells us that there have been significant feminist[1] movements that have profoundly influenced the Christian tradition, and women who have been involved in the struggle for equality in humanity in order that both men and women can reach full humanity.[2] Feminist theology is one such movement shaping the future of the Christian tradition. It embraces the lived reality of a rainbow of experiences of women and men which become the starting point to the reflection that empowers the combat for transformation. It goes without saying that the faces of Christ will also change according to the context. Consequently, the Christ who is emerging is more inclusive, speaks more deeply and challengingly than ever before. Elisabeth Schüssler Fiorenza is a key figure within Feminist Theology. Her principal tool is a hermeneutics of suspicion,[3] a tool which has effectively revolutionized biblical studies. Her stance is that of a critical historian seeking to discover the role of women within the history of the Church. To get an overall picture of the theological vision of Fiorenza is probably a herculean task. In order to introduce the focus of the present research it is necessary to briefly sketch some biographical notes and some basics in her theological reflections.

In this chapter, we attempt to decipher the Christology of Schüssler Fiorenza. Our main sources to analyze this theme will be her four major works, namely *In Memory of Her,*[4] *Discipleship of Equals,*[5] *Jesus: Miriam's Child, Sophia's Prophet,*[6] *Jesus* and *the Politics of Interpretation*[7] and her most recent works.[8] Hence, this chapter begins with a brief biographical profile of Fiorenza and the development of her understanding of theological framework. It is followed by certain aspects of her theological vision and method which would help us to decipher the development of her feminist Christological method that, in her opinion, more adequately addresses issues of diversity and marginalization. An attempt is made to spell out the factors that influenced her theological horizon. Further, her need for formulating new and appropriate language, which she terms as neologisms, will also be considered. This is followed by a discussion of her interpretation of God, and of Jesus Christ, singling out five components for our consideration. Finally, an attempt is made to understand the relevance of her insightful theology for us who live in the 21st century with its own unique problems and issues.

1. Biographical Sketch of Schüssler Fiorenza

The 1980s witnessed the publication of many studies in the area of feminist reconstructions of early Christianity and feminist hermeneutical theory. Both in terms of methodology and in terms of historical-critical research and exegesis Fiorenza's work has received acclaim.[9] Fiorenza can certainly be viewed as one of the key contributors to the field of feminist theology. She identifies herself as Catholic and her work is generally in the context of Christianity, although much of her work has broader applicability.

Fiorenza is a Romanian-born German, feminist theologian, currently Krister Stendahl Professor of Divinity at Harvard Divinity School. She is a German trained New Testament historical critic and a liberation theologian. She is the only woman ever to be the President of the Society of Biblical Literature.[10] Having been educated in the 20th century Catholicism, Fiorenza has witnessed the period of transition in the Church. The Second Vatican Council's emphasis on retrieving the horizontal character of the Church as the people of God has empowered her to critically study the role of women in the Church. Moreover, the major emphasis in her work has been on a reformation of ecclesiology[11] that would give proper attention to the ministry of women in the Church.[12]

By adopting a liberationist approach to feminist hermeneutics Fiorenza has aligned herself with the plight of the poor and dispossessed. Her scholarship is magisterial and her scholarly work encompasses not only the New Testament spheres, but also a rather wide range of social and religious interests.[13] For the first time, a powerful defense of new theological emancipatory models of hermeneutics, critical method, historical reconstruction and an application of these models are found in a single book.[14] Fiorenza has been the recipient of numerous awards and guest professorships and has been honored by her colleges in three *Festschriften*.[15] In 2011 she received the Jerome Award from the Catholic Library Association, in recognition of her outstanding contribution and commitment to excellence in scholarship which embody the ideals of the Catholic Library Association.[16]

Fiorenza was born into a family of ethnic Germans, but born in Cenad (Tâşnad),[17] in the Banat region of the Kingdom of Rumania on April 17, 1938. It was then colonized by the Austro-Hungarian Empire under Maria Theresa and the communities living there.[18] So she is partially an offspring of a colonizing people who were mostly farmers trying to pacify the land.[19] Fiorenza was born in the same year as the Kristallnacht.[20] The coincidence of her birth-year with Kristallnacht has increased her awareness of the violence instigated in the name of Christianity, of the need to include the voices of others in biblical scholarship, and of the responsibility of religious to contribute to a more humane world.[21]

In 1960s Fiorenza became the first woman in Würzburg, Germany, to complete the full academic program in theology at a time when because of her gender she was excluded from the articulation of theology and church leadership by church law and academic convention.[22] It is said that her academic path was marked by success in the midst of great challenges.[23] In 1970, she as a woman privileged by education and race, completed her doctorate in New Testament studies on the understanding of priesthood in the Book of Revelation.

Fiorenza achieved considerable distinction as one of the key contributors when it comes to the field of feminist theology, and it is acclaimed in her *festschrift* that Fiorenza's scholarship is a pioneering force in the twentieth-century biblical interpretation.[24] Fiorenza came of age during a time when feminist theology as a discipline did not exist; she helped create it. Many historians of the past 50 years have identified the birth of feminist religious thought with Mary Daly's act of protest when she walked out of Harvard chapel in the late 1960s. If Mary Daly's act and writing sparked the movement, it was Fiorenza who gave a strong scripturally based skeletal structure and flesh and brought it to life.[25] Fiorenza worked to recover, rename, and reimagine women's role in the history of Christianity.

Subsequently, in the 1970s, Fiorenza and Carol Christ were the first co-chairs of the Women's Caucus for Religious Studies in the American Academy of Religion and the Sisters of Biblical Literature. In 1988, she was appointed as the first Krister Stendahl Professor of Scripture and Interpretation at Harvard Divinity School. Fiorenza was not only instrumental in creating structures and programmes that empower feminist and wo/men in the academy and in ministry but she also initiated a doctor of ministry program for Feminist Liberation Theology and Ministry during her tenure at Episcopal Divinity School. She also co-founded the *Journal of Feminist Studies in Religion* and continues to be the senior editor of that Journal. She also co-initiated and co-edited the issues on feminist theology in the International Journal *Concilium*.[26]

With the publication of her masterpiece, *In Memory of Her: A Feminist Theological Reconstruction of Christian Origin,* Fiorenza marks a milestone in feminist interpretation of the Bible. In the book Fiorenza uses a form of the historical-critical method assessments of sociology and critical theology, and the principles of the women's liberation movement to consider the beginnings of Christianity. It is here that she proposes the need for a reconstruction of early Christian origins, particularly with regard to Jesus' treatment of women and the status of women in the early Church. In Fiorenza's words, her primary objective in *In Memory of Her* is "to reconstruct early Christian history as women's history in order not only to restore women's stories to early Christian history but also to reclaim this history as the history of women and men." Further on in her work, she attempts to reconstruct women's history as "the history of the discipleship of equals."[27]

Fiorenza summarizes the nature of her contribution in *In Memory of Her*.[28] Such a feminist reconstruction of Christian origins requires a disciplined historical imagination that can make women visible not only as victims but also as agents. It is not surprising to find that the list of Fiorenza's publications, both in English and German, is extensive, and her career is studded with awards, scholarships, guest professorships, and other signs of academic recognition. What emerges in her writings is the historical and theological roads leading to and from the New Testament and the effect of Christianity on gender. Moreover, they lay out insightful analysis of the status of women in the Church perceived through a valid scholarly lens of a critical feminist thinker.

2. The Theological Framework of Fiorenza

Fiorenza's theological interest was Ecclesiology that made her way into American academics in the 1970s.[29] This was the time when the second wave of feminism really began to flourish and when the first attempts at articulating feminist theology emerged. Therefore, from the very beginning of her career, ecclesiology has been of prime interest for Fiorenza.[30] The all-encompassing thesis in her ecclesiology is that the church is called to a discipleship of equals and that this identity cannot be completely realized until women are fully included in the *ekklesia*.[31] She believes that this notion of the Church as a discipleship of equals is rooted in the biblical traditions, and her work as a biblical scholar has focused on exposing and developing these historical roots.

Fiorenza's early feminist theological work stressed that feminism is characterized by a concern for the emancipation of wo/men.[32] The resources for her theology are wo/men's experience and praxis. She is critical of feminist theologies that emphasize interpersonal interpretation and connectedness to the detriment of the struggle against socio-political, kyriarchal structures of domination.[33] Fiorenza utilizes biblical criticism and theological hermeneutics as intellectual tools in emancipatory struggles against all forms of oppression. In solidarity with "the least of these" who struggle for survival and justice, the majority of whom are women and their dependent children, she seeks to examine the ministry of Jesus and the earliest Jesus movements to show the gospel to be God's vision of an alternative community and world distinguished by wholeness and inclusiveness.[34] Therefore, she argues that a different theoretical framework is required.[35]

According to her, biblical interpretation for liberation should engage in critical analysis of the "politics of otherness" inscribed in the Christian scriptures.[36] However, her theology is done as a critical response to 'otherness'; so her prime metaphor does not focus on the crisis of identity, but on the struggle for identity by those who have been marginalized by diversity. She directs her critical theological gaze towards the complex relational axis of power and domination that frame and support Western Christianity. She claims only when the most marginalized others – those who have been relegated to the bottom of this kyriarchal structure – are positively affirmed can the biblical promise of freedom, justice and well-being for all be made concretely present.[37] Speaking about the significance of her theological vision, Francis Schüssler Fiorenza rightly says in his article *From Interpretation to Rhetoric: The Feminist Challenge to Systematic Theology,* "From the beginning two elements characterized Fiorenza's vision: one is an egalitarian vision of the church that affirms the equality of all human persons and the full discipleship of women; the other is a critical method of interpretation that is evident in her feminist hermeneutics and rhetorical analysis."[38]

In the face of such an analysis of the fundamental and pervasive nature of gender-based oppression and the role of Christianity in legitimizing and thus perpetuating this oppression, Fiorenza proposed substantive changes in the way in which theology should be approached and understood. Therefore, she insists that this experience must be systematically reflected upon if it is to become the starting point of feminist theology.[39] With community as the locus of authority, Fiorenza bases her feminist method of biblical interpretation on the experience of women. According to her, feminist theology is based firmly on a vision and commitment to 'an emancipatory ecclesial and theological praxis'. From this we can gather that Fiorenza's position is that she finally rejects those biblical texts that conflict with the experience of wo/men under kyriarchal social systems, thus creating a canon within a canon. She considers some texts usable and others unusable based upon experience. Only when theology is on the side of the outcast and oppressed, as the teaching of Jesus was, can it become fully incarnational and Christian. Therefore, Christian theology has to be rooted in emancipated praxis and in solidarity so as to be authentically Christian.[40]

Fiorenza's major emphasis in her work has been on women in the Church. She consistently contends for a reformation of ecclesiology that would give proper attention to the ministry women have done and are doing in the Church. Therefore, in this section the study is centred on the theological method of Fiorenza, including the way she understands and uses the category of experience, as well as the factors that have influenced her theological vision. Some of the terms that she has incorporated into her theology are also explored.[41]

2.1 Theological Method

As we have already noted in the preceding section, with the publication of *In Memory of Her*, Fiorenza's place in the development of feminist theology[42] and feminist biblical interpretation becomes obvious. *In Memory of Her* proposes not simply an argument about wo/men's place in the Church's ministry and history, but a methodology within which her overall project sketches its central task.

Methodology is important because it enables the researcher to ask and begin to answer important questions. It can be defined as a set of linked procedures that specify how to reach a particular kind of analytical conclusion. For Fiorenza it's a work of reconstruction that is feminist and historical, whose goal is to disrupt prevailing interpretive discourses. Hence, the core of her academic project is the recovery of women's voices in the history of the Church in a distinctively feminist-theological key.[43] Fiorenza describes her particular perspective as a critical feminist theology of liberation, like that of traditional liberation theology which addresses experience primarily in socio-political terms.[44] This definition, she says, grew out of her experience as a Catholic Christian woman who is indebted to historical-critical scholarship, critical theology, and political as well as liberation theology.[45] Fiorenza says that she stands in agreement with black theologian James Cone who considers the Bible and biblical faith as sources along with other sources like the history and culture of oppressed peoples.[46] Moreover, he employs a method of correlation that seeks theological answers to the experience of suffering specific to black people, incorporating scripture and contemporary existence as corroborative and correlative authorities.[47] Although Fiorenza's approach is very much in keeping with Segundo's position,[48] she would not adopt his term "fountainhead of our faith" to describe the Bible. An additional thing to point out about Fiorenza's work is that it has elements of liberation theology – she is clearly influenced by Latin American liberation theologians such as Juan Luis Segundo.[49] In Fiorenza's work, she seeks to alleviate problems of sexism in Christianity and liberate the marginalized (in particular, marginalized women).

Fiorenza looks to the Bible to interpret it in a way that is redemptive and liberating to women, rather than demeaning and degrading. Unlike many secular feminists, she does not dismiss the Bible outright simply because it has sexist elements. Instead, Fiorenza tries to emphasize what is good about the Bible while also taking what can be seen as negative and puts it in the correct historical context. Fiorenza's methodology makes three basic moves: the first is to problematize the category "woman", the second focuses on historical-critical interpretation in biblical studies, and the third centers her work on the project of liberation. [50]

Problematization of the Concept Wo/man

The first is to problematize the category "woman", drawing attention to the ways race, ethnicity, class, and religion contribute to the marginalization of every one of the oppressed whether male or female. The category "woman" today is used interchange-ably with female/feminine and thus has become a "naturalized" generic sex-based term, although until very recently it was utilized as an appellation for lower-class females only. Until very recently, the term "Lady" had been restricted to women of higher status or educational refinement. It also functioned to symbolize "true womanhood" and femininity. Strictly speaking, slave women and alien resident women were not considered to be wo/men. They were "gendered" not with respect to slave or alien resident men but with difference in "nature" from not only elite men but also from elite women.

As a result, the relations of domination and subordination have produced not only male-female and male-male but also female-female "natural" differences. All other women are marked as "inferior" on grounds of race, class, religion or culture. They are seen as the others of the feminine other, the "lady." Hence, they are not mentioned in historical records at all. Such a rendering of the basic category of feminist analysis i.e., "woman" as problematic has introduced a crisis into the self-understanding and practices of feminist liberation theory. As a result of this issue, Fiorenza does something unique when she writes the word "woman" or "women." Instead of the word "women," she writes "wo/men," in order to include the men who are hurt by the patriarchal structure in society and the Church. [51] Fiorenza says that she seeks to mark this crisis by writing wo/men in a broken form in order to complete the category of "woman" as a social construct and also to indicate that wo/men are not a unitary social group but are fragmented by structures of race, class, ethnicity, religion, heterosexuality, colonialism and age. In so doing, Fiorenza emphasizes the double risk in which wo/men of color find themselves, and at the same time widens the scope of her analysis to include the problem of men's marginalization. She sees women's experience as normative within her theology and attempts to maintain the distinctiveness of women's dignity within that category.[52] Hence instead of referring to the power structure that must be resisted as "patriarchal," Fiorenza uses the term *"kyriarchy"*[53] to describe the system as she sees it.

Historical-Critical Biblical Interpretation

The second step focuses on historical-critical interpretation in biblical studies and the use of history in systematic theology. The particular brand of feminist critical hermeneutic of liberation seeks to create and incorporate a mode of biblical interpretation that "can do justice to women's experiences of the Bible as a source of empowerment and vision in our struggles for liberation."[54] The question therefore, that arises is, what would be the key to biblical interpretation? A key to Fiorenza's biblical interpretation is her analysis of the suffering in the world as the result of kyriarchal oppression and her assessment of the role she believes the Bible has played in sustaining such oppression.[55] Therefore, she concludes that "only the nonsexist and nonpatriarchal traditions of the Bible and the nonoppressive traditions of biblical interpretation have the theological authority of revelation if the Bible is not to continue as a tool for the oppression of women."[56] Thus, for example, Fiorenza questions biblical scholarship that claims to render the meaning of the text. She emphasizes the shaping of the resources used by all scholars of the Bible and early Christianity by centuries of interpretation and mediation by the church. Thus she seeks not to construct an accurate account of Christian beginnings but to persuade her audience to rethink Christian history. For this she proposes a new methodology for interpreting the Scriptures.

Fiorenza says that the Bible must be read in a deconstructive way as well as a reconstructive way. Hence, she proposes the need for a "critical feminist biblical interpretation for liberation," which includes a seven-fold hermeneutical strategies to help her read Scripture in a way that complements the needs of feminist theology: A hermeneutics of experience that socially locates experience, a hermeneutics of deconstruction, a hermeneutics of suspicion, a hermeneutics of assessment and evaluation, a hermeneutics of re-imagination, a hermeneutics of reconstruction, and hermeneutics of change and transformation.[57]

Fiorenza describes in several of her writings the "rhetorical"[58] use of the Bible as a root metaphor for change and the *ekklesia* of equals - as described in several other sources. Thus she places the burden of proof not on the feminist scholar, who would be required to produce evidence for wo/men's agency in early Christianity; instead, Fiorenza sets it forthrightly on the shoulders of those scholars who would deny wo/men's role in the shaping of Christian belief and practice. In this way Fiorenza believes to shape her methodology,[59] by rooting this understanding of experience in a form of community which she calls the '*ekklēsia* of women'.[60]

The Project of Liberation

Fiorenza's third methodological move centers her work on the project of liberation. She presupposes that Christian struggles and arguments for liberation originated long before Jesus' birth, and continue into the present toward the future. This belief stamps her theological method: rather than looking for clues to the liberative message of the Gospel, she begins from the perspective that Jesus' place is within the trajectory of liberation that commences with Israel and continues through the Church after Jesus' death, resurrection, and ascension.[61] Fiorenza notes a fundamental distinction between many feminist writers and liberation theologians: the use of God and the Bible in theological method. Liberation theologians are generally more optimistic than feminists, seeing the God of the Bible as a God of the oppressed and the Bible as a weapon in the struggle for liberation.[62]

Fiorenza rightly affirms that Feminist theology presupposes as well as has for its goal an emancipatory ecclesial and theological praxis. Therefore feminist theology correctly maintains that it is not enough to include some token women in the male dominated theological and ecclesial structures. What is necessary is the humanization of these structures themselves. In order to move towards a "whole theology," women and men, black and white, privileged and exploited persons, as well as people from all nations and countries, have to be actively involved in the formulation of this new theology, as well as in the institutions devoted to such a "catholic" theologizing.[63]

Fiorenza holds firmly that the biblical scholars and the early Christianity through their interpretation, and the mediation of the Church down the centuries have shaped the sources of Christianity. Her radical starting point for biblical and theological research namely, that a generation of scholars who take women's place in the history of Christianity for, granted, have shaped the very resources, has given a wakeup call to empower and uphold human dignity unto the margins. The purpose of such biblical interpretation for liberation, according to Fiorenza, is to interpret daily life in the global village with the help of the biblical God of justice and salvation. It is not only to inspire Christians to transformation with the biblical vision of a world freed from the structural sin of patriarchal domination but also to give dignity and value to the life of exploited women in those struggles, which ultimately lead to an experience of the image of God in our midst.[64] Thus, Fiorenza is convinced that the biblical interpretation is for liberation ought to become the starting point of feminist theology.[65] Consequently, she proposes a shift into a rhetorical space for an interpretation that questions reconstructive methods and models in biblical or theological scholarship.

To conclude, the assumptions with which Fiorenza begins reveal that one of the methods she uses is the reconstruction of the historical origins of early Christian communities and the historical suppression of wo/men's voices. Another key feature of her method is the use of language to express the instability of concepts otherwise taken for granted. It also becomes clearer that she doesn't require a specifically Christian framework for the development of her vision. Her goal is to establish a new paradigm for the biblical interpretation that will more adequately address the experiences and concerns of women.[66]

2.2 Reasons and Influences for the Choice of Method

Fiorenza looks towards a more egalitarian form of Christianity, similar to that of Christ's original group of followers. She calls this ideal a "discipleship of equals."[67] In this section, we shall focus on five challenges that have fashioned her ideals and vision.

Childhood Experiences During the World War II

Fiorenza's writings clearly show a two-fold challenge: on the one hand, she witnessed all the tragedies; on the other, the experiences have planted in her a deep concern for the oppressed and forgotten people whom she noticed, remembered, and whose pain, problems, and traumas she grew conscious of, which later developed into a critical feminist theology of liberation. By considering a few stories of her childhood, we can discover the genesis of this consistent and fervent concern Fiorenza has for the oppressed and forgotten members of society.[68] The effects of war shaped not only her theology, but her personality as well. Fiorenza reminisces about her childhood: "The characteristic elements of my work have their roots in this experience of war displacement, migration and xenophobia."[69] The ideals she learnt as a child from her mother and grandmother about "human dignity and claim to justice" must have seemed to Fiorenza to be in conflict with the realities of Europe during the war.[70]

Further Fiorenza says that the women in her family, her grandmother and mother, as well as the other women she travelled with, as having created for her "a ring of safety and love". War-torn Europe contributed to the development of her consciousness of the pain and suffering of others, and "inspired her not to forget the forgotten; not to overlook their suffering; and not to demean, diminish, or disregard those who live under oppressive societal structures." [71] In other words, the lessons of her childhood resonate in her writings. Fiorenza's early childhood experiences as a refugee helped shape her life as an adult and a feminist, and planted within her a concern for those in need that grew and flourished over the years.

Although Fiorenza's refugee experience occurred towards the end of World War II, certainly it was not the last military conflict to produce significant refugee populations.[72] Passion and persistence have played a big part in everything she has done. Despite the opposition, Fiorenza never compromised the lessons she learnt as a child. Her childhood memories of the horrible effects of the war, on herself, her family, and other victims of the war shaped the development of her critical feminist theology of liberation, and "planted in her a deep concern for oppressed and forgotten people."[73]

Positively, the experiences during the World War II helped her grow ever more conscious of the situation of women in kyriocentric societies, which also symbolizes the profound influence that her childhood experiences had on her construction of a critical feminist hermeneutics of liberation. Furthermore, an early instance in which she began to question the teachings of the Church was when she was a young girl. Glen Enander in his book recounts that she even became suspicious whether she was not divinely punished after she dressed up in an outrageous costume, painted her face, and laughed as loud as she could in an empty Church. This suspicion later became a "major element in her critical feminist hermeneutic of liberation,"[74] giving her the distance and freedom needed in order to recognize the androcentric dimensions of biblical texts, interpretations, and traditions.

The Existence of the Women's Liberation Movement

In addition to her childhood experiences as a refugee, the women's liberation movement also played an integral role in Fiorenza's life and in her biblical interpretations. In 1960, the world of American women was limited in every respect, from family life to the workplace.[75] In 1962, Betty Friedan's book *The Feminine Mystique* captured the frustration and even the despair of a generation of college-educated housewives who felt trapped and unfulfilled. Friedan stunned the nation by contradicting the accepted wisdom that housewives were content to serve their families and by calling on women to seek fulfillment in work outside the home. While Friedan's writing largely spoke to an audience of educated, upper-middle-class white women, Fiorenza's work had such an impact that it is credited with sparking the "second wave" of the American feminist movement. Now a new generation would take up the call for equality beyond the law and into women's lives.[76]

From the late 1960s to the 1980s there was a dynamic women's movement in the United States. Culturally persuasive and politically capable, on its liberal side this movement included national organizations and campaigns for reproductive rights, the Equal Rights Amendment (ERA), and other reforms. On its radical side it incorporated women's liberation and consciousness raising groups, as well as cultural and grassroots ventures. The women's movement likewise comprised innumerable assemblies and organizing projects in the professions, unions, government bureaucracies, and other institutions.[77]

In addition, two events turned out to be decisive for Schüssler Fiorenza personally as well as for the improvement of feminist studies in religion and feminist theology. Fiorenza would say the 1971 Atlanta[78] and the 1972 Grailville[79] meetings were vital moments for sowing seed of women's activist theological and women's cultural religious studies in the United States. Fiorenza says that it was here that the awakening of a feminist consciousness probably first occurred noticeably in the United States of America, when women, as women, started to take part actively in the religious sphere. Speaking about its significance Schüssler Fiorenza says that the experience of the wo/men's movement in religion empowered her to re-conceptualize her own self-understanding as a theologian.[80]

Eventually Fiorenza finds inspiration for her Christology from a speech given in 1852 by Sojourner Truth, *"Ain't I a Woman?"*[81] Fiorenza argues that Sojourner Truth applies a critical evaluation to those people who have articulated Christological doctrine and roots her Christological understanding in her own experience of liberation as a source of empowerment. Truth experienced Jesus as present in her greatest hour of need, thus anchoring "the articulation of Christology in the revelatory struggle of women for survival and well-being."[82] Although Truth does not call for a development of women's Christology in place of a kyriarchal Christology constructed by male clerics, she insists that the best response is a praxis of liberation.[83] Therefore, Fiorenza would advocate a critical evaluation of the doctrine itself and understands a feminist liberationist exploration of Christian scriptures beginning not with the biblical text but with a critical articulation and analysis of the experiences of wo/men.[84]

A Critical Response to 'Otherness' and the Struggle for Identity

Fiorenza personally felt the marginalization of the *Kyriocentric* bias in the German educational system, an experience that would shape her work and efforts to change the hermeneutics and teaching styles of biblical studies at the university level. Although she became aware of this bias in Germany, her move to the United States showed her that the German educational system was still more "academically inclusive." Fiorenza was "shocked" by the divisions within biblical studies in the United States, such as the division between theology and exegesis or historical criticism. Unlike in much of the scholarship in the United States, Fiorenza adopted a pluriform approach, using various methods of interpretation. Her work is often considered unique and original. She had to develop and provide her own theoretical tools in her critical feminist theology.[85]

In like manner, Fiorenza guides her critical theological gaze towards the complex social hub of power and domination that frames and supports Western Christianity. She insists that these kyriarchal connections keep up structures and states of mind that imprint contrast as mediocre with a specific goal to dominate and marginalize otherness. In other words, the truth of otherness can only authentically be found and retained through its diversity.[86] Fiorenza claims that only when the most marginalized others are positively affirmed can the biblical promise of freedom, justice and well-being for all be made concretely present.[87]

Fiorenza further describes and contextualises the situations of oppression and marginalisation of wo/men and other non-persons. She scatters her critique of the marginalising relationships of Western culture by way of a tensive symbol[88] that she names the most marginal of others in Western culture as the 'poorest most despised wo/men on earth.'[89] Fiorenza contends that if the biblical promise of freedom, justice and well-being is to be made historically present with any authenticity it must first be made present in the lives of these wo/men. Fiorenza understands it as a feminist reality, construct and vision that aims to make present a radical democracy that "brings people together as citizens" and is "realised again and again" in the struggle to 'change relations of domination, exploitation and marginalisation.'[90]

Limitations of the Preceding Model of Biblical Interpretation

Since the reconstruction envisioned by Fiorenza is intended to transform and re-conceive early Christian history, she explores the interplay of the interpretative models developed within the feminist paradigm with biblical-historical theoretical approaches. Fiorenza perceives the preceding sets of models as important but limited. Hence, she briefly reviews different models of biblical interpretation. For instance, firstly, the model of doctrinal hermeneutical interpretation, which she calls the doctrinal approach, understands the Bible in terms of divine revelation and canonical authority. Nevertheless, it conceives of biblical revelation and canonical authority in a-historical and dogmatic terms. According to Fiorenza, "the biblical text is not simply a historical expression of revelation but revelation itself."[91] Fiorenza is of the view that the doctrinal hermeneutical interpretation model is important yet limited. It is important because it takes historicity seriously by acknowledging the temporal situating of the interpreter and the illuminating potential of the interpreter's biases. Yet it is limited because it does not take history seriously, that is, the model refuses to dig into the depths of the cultural, political, and societal contexts of texts and interpreters.[92]

Secondly, the model of positivist historical exegesis was developed in confrontation with the dogmatic claims of Scripture and the doctrinal authority of the Church. Its attack on the revelatory authority of Scripture is linked with an understanding of exegesis and historiography that is positivist, factual, objective, and value-free. Modeled after the rationalist understanding of the natural sciences, positivist historical interpretation seeks to achieve a purely objective reading of the texts and a scientific presentation of "facts."[93]

Thirdly, the dialogical-hermeneutical interpretation is predominant in biblical scholars.[94] It takes seriously the historical methods developed by the former model, reflects on the interaction between the text and community, or text and interpreter.[95] For Fiorenza, this model is important, yet limited. It is vulnerable to ideological distortion unless and until it is practiced from the perspective of a marginalized community and its aspirations for justice and liberation are taken seriously. Fourthly, the model of biblical interpretation is that of liberation theology, which recognizes that all theology is by definition "always engaged for or against the oppressed" and challenges the so-called "objectivity and value neutrality of academic theology". She sets feminist theology within liberation theology.[96]

Consequently, Fiorenza provides a model for the imaginative critical reshaping of Jesus through her imaginative and critical feminist reconstruction of early Christian origins. She is for re-conceptualizing its act of critical reading as a moment in the global praxis for liberation. The model she proposes is one that locates revelation not in texts but in Christian experience and community. Fiorenza, therefore, appeals to biblical theological scholarship to develop a paradigm for biblical revelation that understands the New Testament not as an "archetype" – which establishes an unchanging timeless pattern but as a "prototype" – which is open to change and transformation.[97] Moreover, Fiorenza says that the Bible is to be understood as a formative root-model rather than to be obeyed as the normative archetype of Christian faith and community. It has to derive theological authority from women's experience of God's liberating presence in today's struggle to end patriarchal relationships of domination.

In the discipleship of equals the role of women is not peripheral or trivial, but at the center and thus of utmost importance to the praxis of "solidarity from below." For example, the Pauline letters apply missionary titles and characteristics as co-worker-Prisca (Rom 16:3-5; Acts 18:2), brother/sister-Apphia (Philem 1:2), *Diakonia*-Phoebe (Rom 16:1-2), Lydia (Acts 16; 14) Nympha of Laodicea (Col 4:15) and apostle (Junia) to women as well as men.[98] This is obvious from the story of Syrophoenician woman (Mk 7:24-30; Mt 15: 21-28), who makes an argument against limiting the messianic table community of Jesus to Israel alone. She safeguards he inclusive discipleship of equals called forth by Jesus.[99] The Markan Gospel speaks of women disciples who followed Jesus from Galilee to Jerusalem and accompanied him on the way to the Cross and witnessed his death. According to all the four gospels, women fulfill the criteria of apostleship enumerated by Paul and Luke. [100] For Fiorenza, the location of revelation is not in biblical texts but in "the life and ministry of Jesus and the movement of women and men called forth by him" and she is convinced about "the egalitarian reality of the early Christian movement"[101] that would shape her formulation of a feminist model of historical reconstruction.

The Quest for the Historical Jesus

The quest for the historical Jesus has been underway in waves. The "old quest," [102] which flourished through much of the nineteenth century, was replaced by a period known as the time of "no quest" in the history of Jesus scholarship. The quest for Jesus was launched about 1775, the same time as when the United States was being founded. Johannes Weiss (1863-1914) stands as a towering figure at the beginning of the twentieth century. Weiss reacted to the optimism of nineteenth-century theology by rediscovering Jesus as an eschatological prophet,[103] and sought to understand his mission and message within the framework of imminent eschatology, which was comprehended as the heart of Jesus' message and the conviction animating his mission. [104]

It was, however, the renowned Albert Schweitzer who interpreted and propagated some of these ideas of Weiss, and who challenged the nineteenth-century research into the historical Jesus by focusing on the imminence of the *Reign of God*.[105] Schweitzer believed that the whole life, work and teaching of Jesus was dominated by his expectation of the end of this world as we find it in Jewish apocalyptic. Subsequent researches rejected many of Schweitzer's arguments, especially Jesus' change of mind, but retained the conceptual model of eschatology or apocalyptic. Successively, Borg in his article on "North American Scholarship" on the historical Jesus suggests that two questions central to 'the renaissance of Jesus research' concern: Jesus' eschatology and his relationship to the social world. According to him, it is the weight assigned to these questions which separates the works of the five scholars he was reviewing.[106]

Accordingly, Fiorenza's work reflects the changes occurring within the discipline in three ways. She notes with approval the shift from a theological paradigm to a more historical one, from "almost sixty years of focusing predominantly on theological-kerygmatic issues" to the historical task of searching for "the social context and matrix of early Christian literature."[107] Finally through feminist, perspective, Fiorenza brings to her reading of the New Testament texts the awareness that these texts are both androcentric and patriarchal.[108] In her portrait of Jesus, Fiorenza defines social reality as the movement around Jesus.[109] Using sociological models as a way of ordering data from the earliest traditions, she sees the group around Jesus as "an inner-Jewish renewal movement." As "an alternative prophetic renewal movement within Israel"[110] and intrinsically sociopolitical, it articulated an ethos and followed an alternative social praxis. Her feminist perspective enabled her to see the movement's challenge to patriarchy and argue convincingly that women were prominent among the first followers of Jesus in the "discipleship of Jesus," and that they were the central figures[111] in the early Christian missionary movement.

In addition to the movement around Jesus, Fiorenza correlates Jesus' frequent use of the wisdom in parable, in which he speaks of the "gracious goodness of God," with texts in which Jesus speaks of the wisdom of God as "Sophia,"[112] and argues that Jesus perceived God "in a woman's *Gestalt* as divine Sophia."[113] She concludes that the earliest movement understood Jesus "as Sophia's messenger and later as Sophia herself" and that Jesus probably understood himself "as the prophet and child of Sophia."[114] His proclamation of the gracious goodness of God called into existence "a discipleship of equals" based upon "a vision of inclusive wholeness." His purpose was the creation of such a community within Israel for the sake of the renewal of Israel.[115] In this way Fiorenza believes that Jesus' *praxis* and vision of the *basileia*[116] he proclaimed and lived was a present reality with a deep socio-political dimension. Jesus was a prophet of wisdom in that he was a spokesperson for Sophia and that he was a social prophet who subverted the dominant structures of the time with a different vision of reality and human community.

2.3 Need for a New and Appropriate Language

Fiorenza, through her writings, has contributed greatly, in terms of both the formative development of the notion of 'feminist theology' and the development of biblical feminist hermeneutics with her feminist informed re-constructionist approach to early Christian history. She considers that the limits of language also are created from the limits of androcentric aspects. For that reason, an important aspect of her Western feminist theological method is the issue of language.[117] Hence, Fiorenza often coined new words and incorporates her new terms into her theology and seeks to implement her neologisms in life and mission, developing her own method of theology.[118] This is significant because she is going outside of what is considered normative. Fiorenza changes terms and expressions to avoid falling into language traps that she thinks contribute to patriarchal norms. Fiorenza makes use of the biblical text that is enhancing as well as inclusive: "We are no longer subject to a disciplinarian, for in Christ Jesus you are all children of God through faith. As many of you as were baptized into Christ have clothed yourselves with Christ. There is no longer Jew or Greek, there is no longer slave or free, there is no longer male and female; for all of you are one in Christ Jesus" (Gal 3:25-29). She does this to include people of various socio-political and ethnic groups, such as men and women in the Two-Thirds World.[119] Accordingly, the following terms are defined to clarify their use in this study and to minimize misunderstanding and ambiguity.

Kyriarchy

One of Fiorenza's fundamental insights was the identification of "*Kyriarchy*"– a neologism coined by her and derived from the Greek word for "lord" or "master" (*kyrios*) and "to rule or dominate" and *archia*, meaning "rule or government." It seeks to redefine that there are multiple, intersecting forms of oppression in the world, not just the oppression of men over women.[120] She coined the word *kyriarchy* because no other English word seemed adequate to express the concept. In contrast to patriarchy, which is generally interpreted as the power of all men over all women, *kyriarchy* denotes a socio-political structure in which elite men rule over both males and females. *Kyriarchy* implies that women and men are controlled and oppressed by the structural system, since it "connotes a socio-political system of domination and subordination that is based on the power and rule of the lord/master/ father."[121] Therefore, Fiorenza considers that the word "*kyriarchy*" means a more historically accurate reality.

Patriarchy has a biological concept of gender built into it, but *kyriarchy* refers to socially produced domination in which gender is only one factor among many others, such as social position and wealth. For her the terms wo/men and *kyriarchy* are linked; she sees feminism as something that raises the consciousness of both females and males and helps them understand the oppressive structures that entangle them.[122] Fiorenza incorporates an understanding of domination and oppression that goes beyond this; in other words, *kyriarchy* and patriarchy are two separate and significant terms, but *kyriarchy* is intended to be more comprehensive.[123] Fiorenza has developed the concept of *kyriarchy* in order to comprehend the complex and interlocking systems of oppression that are embodied in sexism, racism, classism, colonialism and nationalism.[124] In spite of this inclusive definition, Fiorenza speaks primarily in terms of women's oppression.

Wo/man-wo/men

Wo/man-wo/men[125] is a way of writing proposed by Fiorenza, to indicate that the category "wo/man-wo/men" is a social construct. It is grammatical gender issue that she addresses in the way in which she handles the word "woman". Instead, "man" is used as both the generic term for humanity and specifically the term for the male gender. As a result of this issue, Fiorenza does something unique when she writes the word "woman" or "women." Instead of the word "women," she writes "wo/men", in order to include the men who are hurt by the patriarchal structure in society and the Church.[126] Fiorenza contends that "wo/men" is therefore to be understood as an inclusive rather than as an exclusive universalized gender term.[127] She adds the slash symbol partway through the word women (and also woman) in order to highlight that there are differences within and between women. Fiorenza first began using this spelling of wo/men in *Jesus: Miriam's Child, Sophia's Prophet: Critical Issues in Feminist Christology*.[128] The broken form of the word immediately calls attention to itself thereby inviting the reader to reflect on its meaning.

Furthermore, the term "wo/men" means "people" in a broad sense, including men, women, feminists of any gender, and non-feminists and it is meant to convey diversity. Fiorenza stresses the diversity of factors by which wo/men are defined; not only by gender but fragmented by structures of race, class, and colonization.[129] She deliberately uses the term "wo/men" instead of the generic term "men", in an inclusive way to lift into consciousness, she says, "the linguistic violence of so-called generic male-centred language."[130] In Fiorenza's words:

> My way of spelling "wo/men" seeks to underscore not only the incoherent, destabilized character of the term "wo/man"–"wo/men" but also to retain the expression "women" as a political category. Since the term "wo/man"–"wo/men" is often read as referring to white wo/men only, my unorthodox writing of the term seeks to draw the attention of readers

that kyriarchal structures that determine wo/men's lives and status also have an impact on men of subordinated races, classes, countries, and religions, albeit in a different way. [131]

Hence, in breaking up the category "wo/men," her intention is to construct an inclusive term in which to make room for all women, as well as for men oppressed by patriarchal structures.

The *Ekklēsia* of Wo/men

Fiorenza is committed to the transformation of the Christian tradition through a critical engagement between the social-political-historical context of contemporary Western life and the biblical promise of freedom, justice and well-being for all.[132] A key symbol in this critical work of Fiorenza is the creation of '*ekklēsia* of wo/men' – a legitimate democratic, egalitarian space where the historical experience and religious agency of wo/men and other non-persons can be truly affirmed.[133] Fiorenza holds up the biblical vision of the *ekklēsia* as a critical reminder to keep focused on the struggles of those who strive for the emancipatory practices of radical democracy. While doing so, she roots this understanding of experience in a form of community, which she names *ekklēsia of wo/men*.[134] The Greek word *ekklēsia* is understood by her as "assembly, gathering or congress of full citizens." In Pauline understanding it is the very name for the Christian community. Hence, Fiorenza says that the best translation of *ekklēsia* is not "church"[135] Even though the English word 'church' is generally used to translate *ekklēsia*, linguistically 'church' is not derived from *ekklēsia* but it derives from the Greek word *kyriakē, that is,* belonging to the *kyrios* (Lord) who in Roman imperial times was the propertied man, slave master, father and head of household.[136] A close look at, the translation of *ekklēsia* as "church" is misleading, as the word "church" in English entails two contradictory meanings. One derives from the *kyriarchal* model of household of antiquity which was governed by the lord/master/husband/father, to whom freeborn men and women, workers and slaves (both men and women) were subordinated. The other meaning of Church (*ekklēsia*) connotes the equality of its members in terms of citizenship and friendship.[137]

Fiorenza says further that the expression *ekklēsia* of wo/men is not to be understood analogously as meaning Church of wo/men that is exclusive of men. Rather, the notion is a contradiction in terms. In Fiorenza's own words:

In order to raise into consciousness the masculine over-determination of catholicity in mainstream theological discourses and ekklesiatical representations I have coined the expression *ekklesia gynaikôn*, the *ekklēsia of wo/men*, as a linguistic and theological means of conscientization. Since the signifier 'woman' is still used to draw the exclusive boundaries of Church, it is important to mark linguistically the difference between Church as Roman kyriarchal institution and Church as *ekklesia*, the people of God. I have introduced the notion of ekklesia of wo/men as a means of conscienticization that articulates a different ekklesial catholicity. This is justified because official Roman documents still speak of the Church as 'mother', and 'she', and 'sister', making it common sense that all male hierarchy consists only of fathers, sons, and brothers.[138]

Consequently Fiorenza seeks to communicate a vision that connects struggles for a more democratic and egalitarian Church. Biblical interpretation, according to Fiorenza, is best understood as searching for Divine Wisdom; accordingly, the radical equality of the *ekklēsia* of wo/men is theologically grounded in the fact that we are all created in the image and likeness of God and have received the multi-faceted gifts of the Spirit.[139]

Therefore, for theological reasons, Fiorenza prefers to refer to the Church as '*ekklesia*' rather than as 'church', because she understands there to be a significant ideological distinction between the two terms. Furthermore, she describes the *ekklēsia* of wo/men as a rhetorical space which asserts women's theological authority to determine the interpretation of Christian Scripture, tradition, theology, and community.[140] Hence, the *ekklēsia* of wo/men is Fiorenza's site of transformation and the goal is wo/men's self-affirmation, power, and liberation from all kyriarchal alienation, marginalization and oppression.[141] *Ekklēsia*, then, is a move for Fiorenza, not only of empowering wo/men, but a corrective to the deformation of the historical consciousness that has eliminated women's and nonpersons' victimizations and struggles from the ecclesial memory.[142]

For Fiorenza, *ekklēsia* then is a term which evokes continuity and connection with the early church communities. The *ekklēsia* of women refers to the 'discipleship of equals', which is the vision she postulates as a crucial component of Christian development in the first century. This image, then, is focused on women's emancipatory struggles. Therefore, to bring this history to conscious memory is a means to empower and validate the present *ekklēsia* of wo/men.[143] Hence, the constructive aim of *ekklesia* of wo/men is not to gather over and against men, but to provide a space in which women can regain their spiritual and ecclesial authority so that true mutuality can become a reality.[144] The *ekklesia* of wo/men seeks to embody this political reality, not because it becomes an end in itself, but because the *ekklesia* of wo/men might ultimately transform the kyriarchal church into the discipleship of equals, a renewed vision for the Church.

G*d

Fiorenza stresses the way in which language constructs reality. She insists that human language is inadequate for expressing the divine reality. She states in her book *Wisdom Ways* that her way of spelling G*d seeks to mark and make conscious this inadequacy of our language about the Divine. "It seeks to indicate that G*d is ultimately unnamable and ineffable."[145] G*d is "in a religious sense unnamable" and belongs to the "realm of the ineffable." God is not G*d's "proper name." Writing the word "G*d" in this fashion visibly seeks to "destabilize our way of thinking and speaking about the Divine."[146] Therefore, Fiorenza uses this incomplete form of the word to highlight the fact that "G*d is not fully representable or describable in our limited language." This is akin to Jewish custom of not fully spelling out the name "G*d."[147] It is an indication that we can only say who G*d is not, rather than who G*d is, since our language is unable to comprehend and express the

Divine.[148] It indicates the insufficiency and inability of human language to adequately name the Divine.[149]

Wisdom-Sophia

Although Sophia is clearly not a term unique to Fiorenza, it nevertheless is important for her portrayal of Jesus. Like Elizabeth Johnson, Fiorenza employs the concept of Wisdom as a hermeneutical clue for discovering who Jesus was and can be for wo/men.[150] However, in contrast to Johnson, Fiorenza does not see Jesus as Wisdom personified, but as Wisdom's messenger. This is a very subtle but important distinction; Johnson sees the incarnation in traditional terms, but substitutes Sophia for *Logos* as the divine hypostasis being incarnated in Jesus, whereas Fiorenza sees Sophia/Wisdom as G*d, who sends Jesus as her representative and not as an incarnation of Sophia/Wisdom herself.[151] Fiorenza identifies historical theological discourses that seek to articulate the significance of Jesus with the help of the traditions of Divine Sophia. The G*d of Jesus was a Sophia-G*d characterized by an all- inclusive love, for "Sophia-G*d recognizes all Israelites as her children and she is proven "right" by all of them" (Lk 7:35).[152] Therefore, Fiorenza employs the concept of Sophia/Wisdom "as a hermeneutical clue for discovering who Jesus was and can be for wo/men."[153] Her approach helps to see how the theological possibilities offered by divine Sophia can be realized in history. Thus Sophialogy is an important resource in Schüssler Fiorenza's theological project.[154] The characteristics of Sophia/Wisdom, as they are exemplified in the literature of the Hebrew Scriptures, suggest a divine power that is nurturing yet strong and full of compassion and commitment to her people.

In this section, we have examined some of the new terms Fiorenza has coined along with the reasons for the same, and some existing terms to which she has given special significance in her work. She incorporates her new language terms into her theology. We have also considered that Fiorenza retrieves from Scriptures inclusivity in the *basileia* vision of Jesus, and participation in the early Christian community and uses them as her vision for an inclusive wholeness.[155] The chapter further explores Fiorenza's interpretation of God in Jesus.

3. Fiorenza's Interpretation of God in Jesus Christ

Since the commencement of her career, Fiorenza has sought to find connections between women's experience and the earliest Christian message. Adapting the methods of sociology, she hypothesizes two forms of early Christianity: the "Jesus movement" in Palestine and the "missionary movement" in Greco-Roman cities.[156] For Fiorenza, the Jesus movement had a vision of inclusive wholeness, with special concern for the poor, the sick and crippled, and tax collectors, sinners and prostitutes. This group manifested "the feminist impulse within Judaism." Indeed, it was a discipleship of equals that understood God "in a woman's Gestalt as divine Sophia (wisdom)."[157] The God of Jesus was a Sophia-God characterized by an "all inclusive love," and recognizes all Israelites as her children.[158] According to her, "The Sophia God of Jesus does not need atonement or sacrifices; and that Jesus' death is not willed by God but is the result of his all-inclusive praxis as Sophia's prophet."[159] In other words, Jesus stands up against the evil of non-involvement and the notion of omnipotence that threatens the Sophia-God as well as the human being. Fiorenza has described the historical Jesus in two of her books.[160]

Through her theology, Fiorenza looks towards a more egalitarian form of Christianity, similar to Christ's original group of followers. She calls this ideal the *basileia* of God, where the *Reign of God* is realized through the values of love, equality justice, freedom and well-being, where all are treated with dignity.[161] Therefore, "in God's world women and men no longer relate to each other in terms of patriarchal dominance and dependence, but as persons who live in the presence of the living God.[162] The God of Jesus was an inclusive God who welcomed and received all people.

3.1 The Jesus of Fiorenza

In her book *In Memory of Her* - undoubtedly the best-known work throughout the world to date by a feminist biblical scholar - Fiorenza uses a form of the historical-critical method to reconstruct early Christian origins, particularly with regard to Jesus' treatment of women and the status of women in the early Church. Fiorenza's primary objective is "*to reconstruct* early Christian history as women's history in order not only to *restore* women's stories to early Christian history but also to *reclaim* this history as the history of women and men."[163] Applying historical and sociological criticism to the Gospels, she contends that the Gospels Jesus movement in a feminist key transcends the boundaries set by history, gender and doctrine. Thus, female subordination is not part of the original gospel but a result of Christianity's accommodation to Greco-Roman culture.

Given that Fiorenza does not derive her theological norms in any way from Scripture, Jesus (whether the historical Jesus or the Jesus of the gospel *kerygma*) is not normative in her understanding of Christian theology.[164] Nonetheless Jesus is important for women, because the movement that began with and around him was an egalitarian movement in which God's future; the *basileia* was communicated and promised to all the people of Israel. Christologically she considers that it is more important to focus on the witness of the earliest community gathered around Jesus, who perpetuated his message, than on Jesus himself.[165] Therefore, she even evades the issue of Jesus' maleness altogether so as to consider the question, "Can a male saviour redeem women?", [166] to be the wrong question based upon a frame of reference that assumes femininity and masculinity are ontologically predetermined.[167]

Fiorenza takes Ruether to task for her assumption of the idea of "full humanity" [168] as the lasting significance of Jesus.[169] In other words, Fiorenza seeks to shift the question from gender to that of *kyriarchal* power and asks: "can wo/men represent Christ in a kyriarchally typed symbolic and institutional system?" because that is where it is located in kyriarchal orthodoxy be it Evangelical or Roman Catholic. [170] For Fiorenza, such views are caught up in the dynamics of sex/gender system that fails to understand the concept of "humanity" and re-inscribes the kyriarchal frame of reference which understands gender as a biological given.[171]

The following section explores the Christological insights of Fiorenza, by employing the method of feminist hermeneutics of critical evaluation advocated by her.[172] It will be developed in five stages: i) Jesus is the Praxis of Discipleship of Equals, ii) Jesus is the Prophet of Divine Sophia, iii) Jesus is the Wise Teacher, iv) Jesus is the *basileia* of God, and v) Jesus is the Resurrected One.

Jesus: The Praxis of Discipleship of Equals

The term 'discipleship of equals' was coined by Fiorenza in the first edition of her seminal work on feminist theology, *In Memory of Her* (1983),[173] and mentioned regularly in her subsequent writings and the public forum. In its origins, the term refers to the community of disciples Jesus gathers around him,[174] in contrast to the natural or patriarchal family.[175] What characterizes the members is made clear from the incident in Mk 3:31-35, where Jesus explicitly redefines his family as those who do the will of God (Mk 3:35).[176] It is no longer physical ties which count, but the bonds of faith uniting those who form a circle around him (3:34b).[177] Within this community, women are included (Mk 10:30; Lk 11:28); indeed, it is obviously in their discipleship and not in their traditional role of motherhood that they are blessed (Lk 11:27-28).[178] Such in simplest sketch is the Gospel portrait of that 'discipleship community which Jesus initiated and the apostolic churches continued'.[179]

Fiorenza understands the "Jesus movement" as a renewal movement within Judaism that presented an alternative to the dominant patriarchal restrictions in that culture.[180] Jesus' vision of the reign of God includes the praxis of 'discipleship community'. She states that "well-being and inclusiveness are the hallmarks of the gospel." Fiorenza finds behind the Jesus movement "a radical Jewish democratic vision. It is the vision of the *basileia* of G*d and G*d's alternative society and world that is free of domination and does not exclude anyone."[181] Therefore, Jesus' praxis and vision and his movement are best understood as an inner-Jewish renewal movement that presented an alternative option to the dominant patriarchal structures rather than an oppositional formation rejecting the values and praxis of Judaism.[182] Thus for Fiorenza Jesus was Sophia's prophet, proclaiming a vision of the *basileia* of God that engendered a discipleship of equals, the community's praxis of inclusive wholeness subverting patriarchal relations of domination in the empire and household.

The healing ministry of Jesus, his table fellowship with sinners, and all inclusive attitude are cited as proofs of this new approach to bring about liberation and emancipation to the marginal.[183] The emancipation Jesus offers freedom from bondage, freedom to express one's own authority and transform one's context, which is understood as discipleship in Mark.[184] Fiorenza says:

> As a feminist vision, the *basileia* [kingdom] vision of Jesus calls all women without exception to wholeness and selfhood, as well as to solidarity with those women who are the impoverished, the maimed, and outcasts of our society and church. It knows of the deadly violence such a vision and commitment will encounter. It enables us not to despair or to relinquish the struggle in the face of such violence. It empowers us to walk upright, freed from the double oppression of societal and religious sexism and prejudice. The *woman-identified man, Jesus, called forth a discipleship of equals* that still needs to be discovered and realized by women and men today.[185]

For Fiorenza the crux of that renewal movement is the wholeness and holiness of all the people of Israel which in turn becomes the driving force behind Jesus' pursuit of a "discipleship of equals".

Fiorenza holds that Jesus initiated a social movement that defied the hierarchical society into which he had been born, in favour of a vision of inclusive wholeness. He sought to create a new community in which women and other basically disenfranchised people could be prominent. He denounced Jewish purity codes as preserving masculine dominance and stressed instead the wisdom tradition of Israel. Fiorenza's identifies, Jesus as part of the ongoing struggle of First Century Jewish wo/men for justice and liberation.[186]

Jesus: The Prophet of Divine Sophia

Even a cursory glance at the literature of Fiorenza indicates that she envisions Jesus as a prophet, but of a different sort. Jesus was a prophet of eschatological wisdom speaking for Sophia, the name she applies to Jesus' vision of G*d. Fiorenza in her book *In Memory of Her* argues that the Palestinian Jesus movement understood the ministry and mission of Jesus as that of the prophet sent to announce that G*d is the G*d of the poor and heavy laden, of the outcasts and those who suffer injustices.[187] With the help of the traditions of Divine Sophia,[188] she discusses the early Christian theological discourses that seek to articulate the significance of Jesus. In the fifth chapter of her book *Jesus: Miriam's Child, Sophia's Prophet*, Fiorenza tries to trace the traditions of Divine Wisdom, Sophia, in the texts of the Christian New Testament in order to reconstruct their significance in the debates and struggles with the early Christian communities concerning the meaning of Jesus.[189] Although this Jewish tradition of divine wisdom seems absent in the Christian New Testament, in her book, *Jesus*, she elaborates her thesis of *In Memory of Her*, that Sophia has been important for the early Christian theological discourse.

Consequently, she distinguishes two levels of reflections in these discourses. At the first level Jesus is understood as the latest in a long line of messengers or prophets of Sophia of God.[190] Hints of this comprehension of Jesus can be found in the expression of Jesus in the Gospel accounts. At the second level, the relation between Jesus and Sophia is shifted. He is no longer represented as the messenger or prophet of Sophia, but identified as Sophia herself. He is praised – in language and with imagery which recalls the divine wisdom traditions – as the Sophia G*d who appeared on earth and is now exalted as the resurrected Lord of the whole cosmos. This interpretation of Jesus as the Sophia of G*d, which originated in the early Christian missionary movement, is expressed in hymns and prayers, of which traces can be found in the letters of Paul as well as in the Gospel of John.[191] Her approach enables us to see how the theological possibilities offered by Divine Sophia are realized in history. She cites some of the earliest traditions of the Jesus movement and understands the mission of Jesus as that of the 'prophet' of Sophia - G*d sent to proclaim that the Sophia - G*d is the G*d of the poor, the outcast, and all those suffering from injustice.

As a result, after quoting Lk 7:35, "*Wisdom* is justified by all her children," Fiorenza makes the claim that divine Sophia served as Israel's G*d and that "the Palestinian Jesus movement understood the mission of Jesus as that of the prophet and child of Sophia," who calls forth a "discipleship of equals." [192] As Sophia's messenger and prophet, Jesus made available God's justice through his table fellowship, miracles and his ministry.[193]

Fiorenza in her book *Jesus*, also highlights Schroer's argument that "the discourse on personified Wisdom seeks to connect such an 'inclusive monotheism' with the experience of women in Israel. She locates such reflective Wisdom theology in the social situation after the exile in which women appear as religious subjects."[194] According to Fiorenza, this inclusive monotheism is of great relevance for human inclusiveness, which is expressed in the imagery of divine Sophia's cosmic house without walls and her table set for all.[195]

As discussed earlier, Fiorenza sees Sophia/Wisdom as G*d who sends Jesus as her representative and not as an Incarnation of Sophia/Wisdom herself. As a child of Sophia he stands in a long line of Sophia prophets, both men and women, sent to gather the children of Israel to their gracious Sophia-G*d. Jesus' execution results from his mission and commitment as prophet and messenger of Sophia-G*d who "holds open a future for the poor and outcast and offers G*d's gracious goodness to all children of Israel without exception". Fiorenza identifies Jesus as Sophia's 'prophet' who is sent to announce that G*d is All-Inclusive Love who brings about well-being and justice for everyone.[196] She views

Jesus as Sophia's messenger and Prophet who not only proclaimed the Reign of G*d to the poor but also made it experientially available to all through his ministry and miracles.[197] Fiorenza ascertains historical theological discourses that seek to articulate the significance of Jesus with the help of the traditions of Divine Sophia.[198]

Highlighting the similarities between Divine Sophia and Jesus, Fiorenza argues that like Sophia, "Jesus speaks in the revelatory "I am" – style, and with the symbolism of bread, wine and living water s/he invites people to eat and drink. Like Sophia, Jesus proclaims his/her message aloud in public places. Like Sophia, Jesus is the light and life of the world. To those who seek and find her/him, Sophia Jesus promises that they will live and never die. Like Sophia, Jesus calls people and makes them his/her children and friends."[199] These similarities explicate Jesus' prophetic mission being realized in history in its all-inclusive character and as a universal invitation to all to experience God's unconditional love and Justice.

Jesus: The Wise Teacher

Fiorenza understands Jesus' ministry as a movement of inner renewal within the religious structures of Judaism, of which he was a faithful adherent. This vision was a prophetic critique of the corrupt hierarchical structures that existed in the society that Jesus knew and at the same time an imaginative construct that opened up the possibility of God's own transforming rule. What is obvious is that Fiorenza carefully constructs Jesus as one who came with a view toward a Jewish discipleship.[200] So with Jesus as their teacher, they were 'disciples of equals,' a community of learners, who attempted to live his *basileia* vision.

The notion that understood Jesus as a sage and prophet of Sophia provides two images of Jesus which are not separate but interactive. "One presents Jesus as a wise teacher, who in his concrete life relates to our ongoing quest for a gracious G*d. The Sophia-G*d of Jesus loves all of humanity irrespective of their ethnic and social standing and shows concern for liberation and empowerment of the underprivileged."

The other insight presents Jesus as a powerful prophet of Divine Sophia, "whose teaching is meant not only for hearing but also to be acted upon" as Jesus' proclamation of the *basileia*.[201] Thus Jesus' Sophia-G*d calls believers to put into action the teachings of Jesus.[202] As Sophia's prophet Jesus not only proclaimed the *basileia* of G*d to the poor, the hungry, and the excluded in Israel, he also made it experientially available to everyone through his miracles and healing activities.[203]

Subsequently, Fiorenza says that the earliest tradition emphasizes that the most prominent among the children of Sophia are John the Baptist and especially Jesus, whose work continues in the Jesus communities. Therefore Jesus' ministry and teaching are here seen as greater than that of the great Wisdom teacher Solomon and as exceeding that of the prophet Jonah.[204] There are four oracles in the earliest traditions in which Sophia is said to be speaking directly.[205] The first is found only in Matthew and the words are placed in the mouth of Jesus.[206] Fiorenza says that as a wise teacher, Jesus calls the nobodies who are heavy-laden and promises them rest and *shalom*.[207] The second is in the "lament over Jerusalem," once again placed in the mouth of Jesus, who mourns the murder of her messengers.[208] Third, the prophetic understanding of the death of Jesus is also expressed in a very ambiguous and difficult saying of Jesus. And finally, the saying which is attributed to Jesus which indicates that Jesus was executed as an insurrectionist by the Romans (Mk 15:27; Mt. 27:38; Lk 23:33; Jn 19:18); it further resulted in an understanding of Jesus as a prophetic messenger of Sophia who was persecuted and killed.[209]

These four oracles speak of Jesus as standing in succession to Sophia's prophets and messengers. Jesus who opens up a future for the poor and oppressed in Israel and promises salvation and well-being to all irrespective of who they are, was one of Sophia's children who vindicated Her. Further it reveals that the execution of Jesus was the outcome of his mission as messenger and prophet of Divine Sophia.[210] Jesus' death on the Cross, was in Fiorenza's view not an atoning sacrifice required by God for humanity to be reconciled with their creator; rather Jesus' death on the Cross was merely the outcome of prophetic practices that offended and threatened those in power.[211]

Jesus: The *Basileia* of God

Jesus' vision of the *basileia*, as understood by Fiorenza, was an inclusive one. Hence instead of using the word kingdom, she retains the Greek word *basileia* but when she does use the word *basileia*, it evokes the notion of a discipleship of equals. For Fiorenza, the Greek word inclines toward a more inclusive language, a better image of the reign of the Messiah, a reminder of the 'nearness of the liberator'. The vision of Jesus and the movement that gathered around him was a possible prototype or as the praxis of inclusive wholeness.[212] For Jesus *basileia tou theou* is an alternative vision to Roman forms of imperial domination. For Jesus, God's rule is the rule of God's power of creation and redemption which mediates God's future of inclusiveness, wholeness and salvation – a religio-political vision in opposition to that of the Roman Empire.

In this context, Fiorenza employs *basileia* in her eschatological writing precisely because she thinks it echoes the same political resonance for us as it did for the early Christians, being an "imaginative" symbol of God's emancipatory empire that exposes and resists the oppressive human politics of domination.[213] She points out that "the gospel of the *basileia* envisioned an alternative world free of hunger, poverty, and domination."[214] The vision that completed Jesus as one among many in the discipleship community of equals was "the vision of the *basileia tou theou*, of G*d's different world of justice and love"[215] Fiorenza argues that the Jesus movement was one of several Jewish groups which fostered and dreamed of emancipation. In other words, Fiorenza believes in these experiences and contends that the nearness of the awaited future is the present: "the *basileia* of God is in the midst of you."[216]

Fiorenza locates the center of Jesus' vision and action in the *basileia* of God and finds four characteristics that defined his movement. First, in contrast to John the Baptist, Jesus mediated a notion of God's reign that is already in our midst and already experientially available. It is arriving and experienced in the healing ministry of Jesus. The salvation of God's *basileia* is present and experientially available whenever Jesus casts out demons (Lk 11:20), heals the sick and the ritually unclean, tells stories about the lost who are found, of the uninvited who are invited, or of the last who will be first. The power of God's *basileia* is realized in Jesus' table community with the poor, the sinners, the tax collectors, and prostitutes - with all those who 'do not belong' to the 'holy people,' who are somehow deficient in the eyes of the righteous.[217] Second, the *basileia* stands for God recreating human wholeness. It refers to human integrity, fulfilment and humanization. Third, the *basileia* is all-inclusive. It excludes no one; it is especially addressed to those who need it most, the poor and the marginalized. God's reign is "inclusive of every person in Israel and engenders the wholeness of every human being." Fourth, the *basileia* of God involves reversals of our ordinary appreciation of things. As for the praxis of the *basileia*, Fiorenza sees it addressed to three constituencies in particular: the poor, the sick and the crippled who were the partners of Jesus' ministry of healing, and the group summed up with the phrase tax collectors, sinners and prostitutes,[218] who were in need of new hope in the time of Jesus.

In general, the *reign of God* was addressed centrally to those excluded and marginalized from society, and these constituted the majority of Jesus' followers. Since the so-called crust of Palestinian society was invited by Jesus to experience the *basileia*, the whole notion of Jesus as savior of sinners is revised for Fiorenza.[219] Therefore, the whole picture of Jesus dying in order to redeem one into the *Reign of God* is put into question by Fiorenza's work of proclaiming and restoring the vision of *basileia*. The festive table image does not need a Savior who dies. Once that hope for a Savior has died, as well as that picture of a God who demands his son's death, then there is room for a different type of working hope.

Jesus: The Resurrected One

In the discussion on Jesus as the wise Teacher and Jesus as the *basileia* of G*d, an attempt was made to highlight the shifting of focus from an emphasis on the Cross to "the vindication of unjust suffering and death,"[220] as well as the notion of Jesus as Saviour of sinners. Rather than sticking to the conventional Anselmian Theology of the Cross and salvation, which comprehends that suffering is essential for salvation,[221] Fiorenza gives the empty tomb following the Resurrection as an alternative symbol. According to Fiorenza, centering the image of salvation on the empty tomb rather than on the Cross has three important meanings for wo/men. First, Jesus' suffering is not the end of the story, and the empty tomb invites us to see the same in our own. Second, the Gospel records of the disciples' discovery of the empty tomb and their almost concurrent gatherings with the resurrected Jesus indicate that Jesus is still with us, though in an unexpected way. The empty tomb, rather than the Cross, strikingly demonstrates that "Jesus' struggle did not end with execution and death." As Fiorenza says "by privileging the empty tomb as the originating space for the proclamations that Jesus of Nazareth, the Crucified One, has been vindicated, the announcement of this 'resurrection reality' opens up a road ahead into the messianic future." Third, in each of the Gospel accounts, women were the first disciples to encounter the resurrected Jesus. The empty tomb "celebrates women as faithful witnesses who do not relinquish their commitment and solidarity with those who fall victim in the struggle against dehumanizing powers."[222]

Therefore Fiorenza affirms:

> The empty tomb does not signify absence but presence: it announces the Resurrected One's presence on the road ahead, in a particular space of struggle and recognition such as Galilee. The Resurrected One is present in the "little ones," in the struggles for survival of those impoverished, hungry, tortured, and killed, in the wretched of the earth.[223]

Seen from the perspective of revelation, the Resurrection is God's definitive self-disclosure which establishes Jesus in a radically new mode of being and activity. Moreover, the power of the Resurrection cannot be measured by human mind or programs. It escapes human control, as the Resurrection of Christ brought to nothing the frail human efforts to keep Christ in the grave. Yes, the women were made the first privileged witnesses and messengers of the Good News that Jesus was living. But the Scripture also tells us that they were instructed to go straight to the Apostles with the message.[224]

To sum up, Fiorenza starts with Jesus of Nazareth using an alternative standard which she terms the *ekklesia* of women with a different assumption, that the Christological importance of Jesus is his leadership in one of many messianic movements at his time, a movement for *the basileia*, a movement which included men and women. By this she tries to portray a commitment to a specific lifestyle that is described by equality amidst diversity.[225] The Jesus who emerges from her reconstruction proclaims a kingdom without domination or hierarchy, unlike that of the Roman Empire, with a vision of the kingdom that includes the praxis of inclusive wholeness.[226]

Besides, Fiorenza points out that the emerging Galilean Jesus movement probably understood itself as a prophetic movement of Sophia-Wisdom.[227] She identifies Jesus not only as Sophia's 'prophet' who is sent to announce that God is God of all-inclusive love who brings about well-being and justice for everyone[228] but also as one who opposed the structural powers of his time by presenting an alternative system that is liberative, participatory and inclusive through his prophetic life and mission. Hence, the death and burial in her narrative lead to the climax: the empty tomb, which she takes to be historical, is witnessed by the women who come in compassion to anoint the dead body of their friend; and the narrative ends with the suggestion that Jesus has gone ahead to Galilee where the women will find him.

Therefore, for Fiorenza's historical reconstruction of Christian origins for a feminist and liberationist dismantling of the kyriocentric theology which holds women, people of colour, and the poor in bondage all over the world, is based on Jesus' vision and action in the *basileia* of God, which stands for God creating human wholeness and oneness. Fiorenza presents the dimensions of Jesus in the context of Jesus Community and its self-understanding, from its beginnings among the followers of Jesus to its fulfillment as the post-Easter Jesus movement.

4. Implications of Fiorenza's Christology

In the preceding discussion on the feminist Christology from the perspective of Fiorenza, we have made an endeavour to return to her *Basileia* Vision of Discipleship of Equals. She uses the idea of *basileia* of the Jesus movement to reject oppression and to foster the process of transformation in the Church. Fiorenza as an immigrant to the United States from Germany makes her evaluation of the subject from the perspective of Western feminist issues that relate to the Roman Catholic faith, in spite of the fact that her thoughts and systems can be connected to different beliefs too.

As we have discussed already, the God of Jesus was a Sophia-God characterized by an "all inclusive love", for Sophia-God recognizes all her children.[229] Indeed, Fiorenza thinks, that Jesus probably understood himself as a prophet, child, and messenger of Sophia-God who "holds open a future for the poor and outcast and offers God's gracious goodness" to all children without exception.[230] In her book *In Memory of Her* she uses historical critical method, assessments of sociology and critical theology, and the principles of the women's liberation movement to consider the beginnings of Christianity. Here, she posits the need for a reconstruction of early Christianity from the standpoint of the history of women.

Fiorenza understands of tradition as the legacy of those women of Jesus' movement; a tradition that must recover the footprints that were erased in the course of time. One example of the importance of this recovery is the biblical story of the woman who anoints Jesus. In the passage, Jesus responds to disciples' criticism of the woman by saying, "Truly I tell you, wherever the good news is proclaimed in the whole world, what she has done will be told in remembrance of her"

(Mk 14:9). Fiorenza being a biblical scholar, the biblical text becomes her point of departure.[231] Consequently she opts for an interpretation of Jesus that sees him as bringing about a renewal movement within Judaism. The crux of that renewal movement is the wholeness and holiness of all the people of Israel with a view that the *Reign of God* is for everyone: women and men, poor and rich, outcasts and sinners as well as Pharisees.

Using her ground breaking work *In Memory of Her* as a base, Fiorenza explores feminist Christologies in her work *Jesus: Miriam's Child, Sophia's Prophet*. With an analysis of wo/men's experience as the starting point, she utilizes clear images, for example, "into the hill country," and "the open road to Galilee," to invite readers into new spaces where images of Christ in the Scriptures can be explored from a different perspective and Christological discourses can be reconceptualized toward liberating practice. Fiorenza stresses the way in which language constructs reality. She insists that human language is inadequate for expressing the divine reality. Therefore, she uses this incomplete form of the word G*d to highlight the fact that God is not fully representable or describable in our limited language.[232]

Moreover, for Fiorenza, it is more important to focus on the witness of the earliest community gathered around Jesus, who perpetuated his message, rather than on Jesus himself. Fiorenza identifies Jesus as Sophia's 'prophet' who is sent to announce that God is God of all-inclusive love who brings about well-being and justice for everyone. Jesus becomes important for women because the movement he began was an egalitarian movement. Thus, Jesus' importance is indirect only, since feminist solidarity is not particularly with the man Jesus Christ, but with the women who gathered around him.

Conclusion

This chapter began with a brief sketch of Fiorenza's life and some basic factors that have shaped her theological-christological framework. The substance and the basic thrust of Fiorenza's feminist Christology is slightly different from those of other feminist theologians. The chapter has described that Fiorenza's approach to a theological-christological framework has distinctive features that lend themselves to developing a mission of the Church in the emerging 21st century India.

Fiorenza sets out to explore i) the theoretical frameworks of various discourses about Jesus and not to write a revolutionary biography or a post-biographical Christology. ii) With analysis of women's experience as the starting point, she invites readers into new spaces where images of Christ in the Scripture can be explored from a different perspective and Christological discourses can be reconceptualized toward liberating practice. iii) She views Jesus as the Praxis of Discipleship of Equals and Prophet of Divine Sophia who not only proclaimed the *Reign of God* to the poor but also made it experientially available to all through his miracles and ministry. iv) Examining from the perspective of feminist Christology, Jesus reinforces the courage to combat with the structural powers of his time by providing an alternative system that is liberative, participatory and inclusive through his prophetic life and mission.

This chapter focused also on Jesus' way of encountering the women of his time who provided significant space for him to address the powers of oppression which were meted out against them. And therefore, Fiorenza even evades the issue of Jesus' maleness altogether. Moreover, she considers the question, "Can a male saviour redeem women?" to be a wrong question, based upon a frame of reference that assumes femininity and masculinity are ontologically predetermined.[233] On the contrary the Jesus of Fiorenza is raised from the dead and is walking among us, and we find salvation in him. It affirms that Jesus' struggle did not end with his execution and death. The tomb is empty! But it announces the Resurrected One's presence on the road ahead, in a particular space of struggle and recognition such as Galilee. The Resurrected One is present in the "little ones", in the struggles for survival of those impoverished, hungry, tortured, and killed, in the wretched of the earth.

Having reflected on the interpretation of Jesus by Rayan in the previous chapter and by Fiorenza in this chapter, the following chapter will make a comparative study of their approaches and Christological thrusts to set the way towards the final chapter.

Endnotes

[1] For Fiorenza, feminism is a concept that raises the consciousness of both females and males and helps them understand the oppressive structures that entangle them. The use of the term "feminist" implies a liberative approach that sets forth two criteria: the liberation of the margins and the restoration of their dignity.

[2] We have examples of revolutionary feminist theologians like Mary Daly, who perceives the church as unredeemably patriarchal and defines salvation for women as freeing oneself from the misogynous chains of Christianity. There are reformist theologians such as Rosemary Radford Ruether and Letty Russell and others who seek to reclaim those elements of Christianity which are truly Christian and to eliminate those which are merely patriarchal accretions.

[3] Paul Ricoeur (1913-2005) a French philosopher coined the phrase "hermeneutics of suspicion" to draw attention to three key intellectual figures of the twentieth century who, in their different ways, sought to unmask, demystify, and expose the real from the apparent; "Three masters, seemingly mutually exclusive, dominate the school of suspicion: Karl Mark, Friedrich Nietzsche, and Sigmund Freud." Paul Ricoeur, *Freud and Philosophy: An Essay on Interpretation* (New Haven: Yale University Press, 1970), 32; Scholars in a variety of disciplines like Juan Segundo and many feminist theologians have used hermeneutic of suspicion. One among them is Schüssler Fiorenza who in her seminal work *In Memory of Her*, uses hermeneutic of suspicion as the first stage of interpreting the Bible.

[4] Fiorenza, *In Memory of Her*.

[5] Elisabeth Schüssler Fiorenza, *Discipleship of Equals: A Critical Feminist Ekklesialogy of Liberation* (London: SCM Press, 1993).

[6] Elisabeth Schüssler Fiorenza, *Jesus: Miriam's Child, Sophia's Prophet: Critical Issues in Feminist Christology* (New York: Continuum, 1995) is more than just a book on Jesus. It is part of Fiorenza's seminal work on feminist biblical hermeneutics and feminist liberation theology. Applying a hermeneutic of suspicion, Fiorenza seeks to "create a 'women' - defined feminist theoretical space that makes it possible to dislodge Christological discourses from their malestream frame of reference." This is done by locating these discourses in their socio-political rhetorical contexts; outlining a feminist method of systemic analysis of domination; and finally by discussing the concept of *ekklesia* of wo/men as the hermeneutical centre of feminist Christologies. Cf. Fiorenza, *Jesus* 3, 5.

[7] Elisabeth Schüssler Fiorenza, *Jesus and the Politics of Interpretation* (New York: Continuum, 2000).

[8] Elisabeth Schüssler Fiorenza, *The Transforming Vision: Explorations in Feminist Theology* (Minneapolis, MN: Fortress Press, 2011); *Changing Horizons: Explorations in Feminist Interpretation* (Minneapolis: Fortress Press, 2013); *Feminist Biblical Studies in the Twentieth Century: Scholarship and Movement* (Atlanta: Society of Biblical

Literature, 2014). Biography-Discussion of Work: Glenn Enander, *Spiritual Leaders: Elisabeth Schüssler Fiorenza* (Philadelphia: Chelsea House, 2005). In addition, Schüssler Fiorenza's own work in the form of *Festschriften:* will be studied.

[9] Aidan O'Boyle, *Towards Contemporary Wisdom Christology: Some Catholic Christologies in German, English and French, 1965-1995* (Roma: Editrice Pontificia Universitaĩ Gregoriana, 2003), 296.

[10] Fiorenza locates her hermeneutics in the context of liberation theology engaged on behalf of the oppressed and Elizabeth Cady Stanton's conception of biblical interpretation as a political act.

[11] Fiorenza's ecclesiology is born out of her personal experiences as a woman faced with dehumanization in society and church and a burning desire for women's liberation and wholeness. Her experience of woman in the Church is that they are dehumanized institutionally by being disqualified on the basis of sex, from access to the sacred orders and to leadership. For centuries women have been silenced and had not even access to theological education, and special authority is withheld from them. The exclusion of women from sacramental ministry, according to her, violates the equal rights women have in virtue of their baptism. Writing from the experiences of women faced with oppression, Schüssler knows the importance of making connections with our own experiences, historical struggles and feminist options in order to create visions for the future. Cf. Schüssler Fiorenza, *Bread Not Stone: The Challenge of Feminist Biblical Interpretation* (Beacon Press: Boston, 1984), 11.

[12] The recognition of wo/men as full ekklesial citizens with all rights and duties is central to this vision of a kingdom of priests, a radical democratic church. It demands a new theological articulation and self-understanding of ministry and Church. It insists with Post-Vatican II theology that ministry as a gift of the Spirit is more fundamental and comprehensive than order. Cf. Schüssler Fiorenza, "We are Church - A Kingdom of Priests" *Keynote Address for Women's Ordination Worldwide* (WOW) *Second International Conference Breaking Silence, Breaking Bread: Christ Calls Women to Lead* (Ottawa, Canada, July 22-24, 2005).

[13] All her manuscripts reveal Fiorenza's exploration of the theoretical frameworks of various discourses about Jesus and not to write revolutionary biography or a post-patriarchal Christology. Lisa Isherwood, *Introducing Feminist Christologies* (Cleveland, Ohio: Pilgrim Press, 2002), 105.

[14] Cornel West, *The Cornel West Reader* (New York: Basic Civitas Books, 1999), 380.

[15] They include, Fernando F. Segovia, ed., *Toward a New Heaven and a New Earth. Essays in Honor of Schüssler Fiorenza* (Maryknoll: Orbis Books, 2003); Briggs Kittredge, et al., ed. *Walk in the Ways of Wisdom: Essays in Honor of Schüssler Fiorenza,* and Jane Schaberg, Alice Bach and Esther Fuchs, ed. *On the Cutting Edge: The Study of Women in Biblical Worlds* (New York, London: Continuum, 200), 4.

[16] Jonathan G. Beasley, "Divinity School faculty recognized for scholarship, teaching," *Harvard gazette News*, May 16, 2011, http://news.harvard.edu/gazette/story/newsplus/divinity-school-faculty-recognized-for-scholarship-teaching/ (accessed September 15, 2015). Her on-going activity has not only borne fruit in her academic work but has

shaped the work of many other scholars who continue to interact, contest, and further develop her initial insights. Annelies Moesor, "Elisabeth Schüssler Fiorenza," in *Key Theological Thinkers: From Modern to Post Modern*, eds. Staale Johannes Kristiansen and Svein Rise (Ashgate: England/ USA, 2013), 329.

[17] There had been German communities in Romania since the time of Maria Theresia. Her small hometown was three miles from the Hungarian border and thirty miles from the border of Yugoslavia. After the Romanian government joined with Russia in declaring war on Germany in 1944, Schüssler Fiorenza and her family became refugees, fleeing from danger and violence in their home country. According to Enander, at one point her family had to beg for food and shelter during their travels, and much of their time was on a horse-drawn wagon. Enander, *Spiritual Leaders*, 16.

[18] Empress Maria Theresia (1717-1780), Archduchess of Austria and Queen of Hungary and Bohemia, was the wife of Emperor Francis I and the mother of Marie Antoinette (1755-1793), Queen of France and wife of Louis XVI. Her succession as ruler of the Hapsburg Empire led to the War of the Austrian Succession (1740-1748) and the Seven Years' War (1756-1763; Segovia, "Looking Back, Looking around, Looking Ahead: An interview with Schüssler Fiorenza," in *Toward a New Heaven and a New earth: Essays in Honour of Elisabeth Schüssler Fiorenza*, 1-32; As the Russian army advanced through Romania in late 1944, her parents fled with her from village to village to Hungary, and again to Austria and again to Bulgaria. They subsequently moved to Frankfurt, where she attended local schools. Schüssler Fiorenza arrived in the U.S. in 1970, at the age of 32. This information is drawn from "The Marty Forum: Elisabeth Schüssler Fiorenza" [*HD online*] *American Academy of Religion Annual Meeting*, Chicago, Illinois. Panellists: Elisabeth Schüssler Fiorenza, Harvard University and Judith Plaskow, Manhattan College, Sunday, November 18, 2012, https:/ /www.youtube .com/watch=8 YAwm M52wjw (accessed July 12, 2015).

[19] This information is drawn from "The Marty Forum: Elisabeth Schüssler Fiorenza," [*HD online*] She was six years old when Rumania was invaded by Russians and the German army.

[20] Kristallnacht, literally, "Night of Crystal," is often referred to as the "Night of Broken Glass." The name refers to the wave of violent anti-Jewish pogroms which took place on November 9, 1938. The violence was instigated primarily by Nazi Party officials and members of the SA (Sturmabteilungen: literally Assault Detachments, but commonly known as Storm Troopers) and Hitler Youth. Significantly, Kristallnacht marks the first instance in which the Nazi regime incarcerated Jews on a massive scale simply on the basis of their ethnicity. Hundreds died in the camps as a result of the brutal treatment they endured. Cf. United States Holocaust Memorial Museum, "KRISTALLNACHT: A Nationwide Program," *Holocaust Encyclopedia*, www.ushmm. org/wlc/en/ar ticle.php? ModuleId=10005143 (accessed October 3, 2015).

[21] Elisabeth Schüssler Fiorenza, "Biblical Interpretation and Critical Commitment," *Theological Studies* 43/1 (1989): 6.

[22] Elisabeth Schüssler Fiorenza, "Changing the Paradigms," *Christian Century* (September, 1990): 796-800, http://www.religion-online.org/showarticle.asp?title=439 (accessed February, 28, 2017).

[23] Kristiansen and Rise, *Key Theological Thinkers*, 328.

[24] Matthews et al., *Walk in the Ways of Wisdom,* 1-2.

[25] It was in 1960s when feminist thought was just emerging and feminism in the context of religion was but a glimmer in the darkness of unconscious and pervasive patriarchal flood, Fiorenza was there. This information is drawn or transcribed from her lecture. Elisabeth Schüssler Fiorenza, "The Power of the Word: Scripture and the Rhetoric of Empire," *Burke Lecture Leadership on Religion and Society*, March 3, 2007, https://youtu.be/dUDlV8B1aHw (accessed July 21, 2015).

[26] Matthews et al., *Walk in the Ways of Wisdom,* 1-2.

[27] Fiorenza, *In Memory of Her*, xiv, 107.

[28] Fiorenza, *In Memory of Her*, 351.

[29] Elisabeth Schüssler Fiorenza, "Changing the Paradigms," *Christian Century*, 107/25 (September 5-12, 1990): 797-798; Segovia, "Looking Back, Looking around, Looking Ahead: An interview with Schüssler Fiorenza," 5-13.

[30] There are of course other female New Testament scholars whose work has reached similar conclusions, such as Elizabeth A. Johnson and L. Schottroff, but to date their work has not been quite as influential as Fiorenza's. Elizabeth A. Johnson, 'Jesus the Wisdom of God: A Biblical Basis for Non-Androcentric Christology' *ETL* 61 (1985): 261-294, as cited by O'Boyle, *Towards a Contemporary Wisdom Christology.*

[31] In describing this movement as a "discipleship of equals," Fiorenza seeks to describe a commitment to a particular way of life that is characterized by equality amidst diversity. Elisabeth Schüssler Fiorenza, "Discipleship of Equals: Reality and Vision," in *In Search of a Round Table: Gender, Theology and Church Leadership, ed. Musimbi R.A. Kanyoro* (Geneva: WCC Publications, 1997): 1-2.

[32] Fiorenza once stated that theology is the product of each writer's experience and it is determined by the historical and social context of every theologian. Theology is culturally conditioned and contextually shapes, reflects, and serves a particular group's or individual's interests. Like other theologians such as Daly and Ruether, she locates particular responsibility for wo/men's oppression with Christian theology and with the associated value system and structures that embody these values. *Elisabeth Schüssler Fiorenza*, "Feminist Theology as a Critical Theology of Liberation," *Theological Studies* 36/4 (*1975*): 616, 611.

[33] Fiorenza, *Jesus* 50-53. By *kyriarchy* she means the rule of the emperor/master/ lord/father/husband over his subordinates. This is not to imply that all men dominate and exploit all wo/men without difference to culture or economic status. Whereas patriarchy implies an opposition between male and female. Fiorenza, *Jesus*, 14. For more on this term see the section on "Kyriarchy" 3.2.3.1

[34] Donald K. McKim, ed. *Dictionary of Major Biblical Interpreters* (Downers Grove, Illinois: Intervarsity Press, 2007), 899. Exported from Logos Bible Software, accessed October 21, 2016.

[35] Elisabeth Schüssler Fiorenza, "Politics of Otherness: Biblical Interpretation as a Critical Praxis for Liberation," in *The Future of Liberation Theology: Essays in Honour of Gustavo Gutierrez* ed. Mark Ellis and Otto Maduro (Maryknoll: Orbis, 1989), 311.

[36] Fiorenza, "Politics of Otherness," 312.

[37] Fiorenza, *Sharing Her Word*, 28-36.

[38] Francis Schüssler Fiorenza, "From Interpretation to Rhetoric: The Feminist Challenge to Systematic Theology," in *Walk in the Ways of Wisdom* 18-19.

[39] Experience is the ultimate authority for what is considered to be the word of God, that is, the experience of wo/men under oppression as well as experiences of God among wo/men struggling for liberation, considered systematically from within the context of women-church, determine which biblical texts are to be used in theology. Fiorenza, *Jesus*, 12.

[40] Fiorenza, "Feminist Theology as a Critical Theology of Liberation," 612, 616.

[41] Terms will be explained in the section on "Need for a New and Appropriate Language" 3.2.3.

[42] Feminist theology's task is twofold: to uncover the theologies and institutional practices which perpetuate the injustices on women and deny their full human subjectivity; and constructively, to create a liberated and liberating theology. Cf. Christopher Rowland, *The Cambridge Companion to Liberation Theology* (Cambridge: Cambridge University Press, 1999), 92.

[43] When one approaches the work of Schüssler Fiorenza, one finds a very different perspective, inasmuch as her teaching is in biblical studies and early Christian origins. Nevertheless she maintains that an artificial separation has been enforced between biblical studies and theology, and she seeks to bridge this gap by joining theological interpretation to the task of biblical exegesis. Fiorenza, *Bread and Not Stone* 130-131.

[44] Fiorenza, *Jesus*, 36-37.

[45] Fiorenza, *Bread Not Stone*, xii.

[46] Linda D. Peacore, *The Role of Women's Experience in Feminist Theologies of Atonement* (Eugene, Or: Pickwick Publications, 2010), 68. James Cone in his *God of the Oppressed*, was the first to develop a black theology of liberation, and like his Latin American colleagues, he sees the central message of the Bible as the proclamation of liberation. Although the sources of scripture and tradition bear witness to the higher source of revelation particularized and universalized in Jesus Christ, Cone considers sources such as the history and culture of oppressed peoples to have equal or greater weight. The Bible is the indispensable witness of God's revelation in Jesus, and is therefore a primary source for Christian thinking. However, revelation is incomprehensible without the "concrete manifestation of revelation in the black community as seen in black experience, black history, and black culture." Cf. James H. Cone, *God of the Oppressed* (New York: Seabury Press, 1975), 37, 9, 29.

[47] For Cone, the starting point is dialectically related to experience, and divine revelation gives it validity. In other words, because Cone has identified the central message of scripture to be God's liberation for oppressed people, and due to this fact he understands the core of black people experience to be suffering, the God of the Bible makes the experience of black people a valid place to start theological reflection. Consequently, based on these two aspects of his theology, black experience and God's revelation in scripture, Cone considers the Christian theologian's hermeneutical task to be defined by the struggle of the oppressed for liberation, while seeking to "adhere to the delicate balance of social existence and divine revelation." Cf. Cone, *God of the Oppressed*, 82, 98.

[48] According to liberation theologian Juan Segundo a specific approach called hermeneutical circle is required to liberation theology. He outlines two preconditions for such a circle: questions and suspicions arising out of our real, present situation; and new interpretations of the Bible, resulting from those questions and suspicions. In addition to these preconditions, he describes four "decisive" factors of the circle: 1) there is an *experience* of reality that leads to ideological suspicion, followed by 2) the *application* of this suspicion to theology out of which flows 3) a new *experience* of theological reality that leads to the suspicion that prevailing interpretations of scripture have not accounted for important data. Finally the hermeneutical circle is complete in 4) the "new *way* of interpreting the fountainhead of our faith (scripture) with the new elements at our disposal." Cf. Juan Luis Segundo, *Liberation of Theology* (Maryknoll, New York: Orbis Books, 1976), 8-9.

[49] Linda Hogan, *From Women's Experience to Feminist Theology* (Sheffield, England: Sheffield Academic Press, 1995), 87-88.

[50] Medi Ann Voipe, "Elisabeth Schüssler Fiorenza" in *The Student's Companion to the Theologians* ed. Ian S. Markham (West Sussex, UK: A John Wiley & Sons, Ltd., 2013), 515-517.

[51] Fiorenza, *Sharing Her Word*, 186.

[52] Elisabeth Johnson says that Feminist theology results when women's faith seeks understanding in the matrix of the historical struggle for life in the face of oppressive and alienating forces. Elizabeth A. Johnson, *She Who Is: The Mystery of God in Feminist Theological Discourse* (New York: Crossroad, 1993) 17.

[53] The term/neologism *Kyriarchy* was first used in Fiorenza's *But She Said: Feminist of Biblical Interpretation* (New York: Beacon Press, 1992). The term was coined by Fiorenza to describe the complex social order that keeps these intersecting oppressions in place. Oppression is not simply about discrimination. It is about being institutionally and systemically repressed. Unlike the term patriarchy, which refers only to institutionalized sexism, kyriarchy covers all forms of inequality. In other words, the *kyriarchy* is the social system that keeps all intersecting oppressions in place. The term will be further explained in the chapter on 'New Terminology Defined'.

[54] As liberation theology stresses God's liberating activity in history and singles out the Exodus narrative as a canon within a canon, so feminist liberation theologians seek to identify a liberating theme, tradition, text, or principle as a hermeneutical

key in order to reclaim the authority of scripture for their task. Cf. Fiorenza, *Bread Not Stone*, 5. She opposes Daphne Hampson and Mary Daly who emphasized more the contemporary religious experiences of women than the Christian past. Fiorenza holds that their position devalues women's authentic history within the biblical tradition and negates positive experiences contemporary women have in biblical religion. Fiorenza, *In Memory of Her*, xlix.

[55] Donald K. McKim, *Historical Handbook of Major Biblical Interpreter* (Downers Grove, Ill: InterVarsity Press, 1998), 607

[56] Fiorenza, *Bread Not Stone*, 60.

[57] Fiorenza, *Sharing her Word*, 77.

[58] By "rhetorical" Fiorenza means communicative practices that link knowledge with action and passion, which involves interests, values and visions. All persons who read the Bible do so from a particular context within history. Context is as important as the text. It is decisive for us how we see the world, construct reality or interpret biblical text. Elisabeth Schüssler Fiorenza, *Wisdom Ways: Introducing Feminist Biblical Interpretation* (Maryknoll, NY: Orbis Books, 2006), 96.

[59] Voipe, "Elisabeth Schüssler Fiorenza," 516-517.

[60] The notion of the "*ekklesia* of wo/men," that is the full democratic assembly of women, attempts to conceptualize a feminist space. Fiorenza says that this paradoxical expression seeks to articulate a critical democratic space from which feminists can speak in order to get involved in the theological discourses as well as for feminist discourse to articulate Christological images for change. The term is taken up in the section on 'Need for a New and Appropriate Language' 3.2.3. Fiorenza, *Jesus*, 30.

[61] Voipe, "Elisabeth Schüssler Fiorenza," 517.

[62] Fiorenza, *Bread Not Stone*, 52.

[63] Fiorenza, "Feminist Theology as A Critical Theology of Liberation," 605-626.

[64] Elisabeth Schüssler Fiorenza, "The Bible the Global Context and the Discipleship of Equals," in *Reconstructing Christian Theology* eds., Rebecca S. Chopp & Mark Lewis Taylor (Minneapolis: Fortress Press, 1994), 86-87.

[65] Fiorenza, *Jesus*, 12.

[66] Fiorenza bases her call for a paradigm shift upon Thomas Kuhn's work in which "a paradigm represents a coherent research tradition created and sustained by a scientific community". She believes that the feminist paradigm has created and is sustained by its own academic institutions and communities which need to be both strengthened and taken seriously by the patriarchal institutions. However, it is to the Women's movement, not the academy that Fiorenza wants to be accountable. Fiorenza, *Bread Not Stone*, xxi-xxii.

[67] Fiorenza, *Sharing Her Word*, 41. This will be further explained in the section of 'Fiorenza's Interpretation of God in Jesus Christ'.

[68] Fiorenza's insistence that her readers remember and think deeply about the plight of the oppressed people is found in her interviews, and in all her writings. Enander, "From Refugee to Pioneer," 16.

[69] Elisabeth Schüssler Fiorenza, "Wartime as Formative," *The Christian Century* (August 16-23, 1995): 778–779.

[70] Fiorenza, "Wartime as Formative," 1-2. As she grew up and became an adult, she pondered over and lived out those ideals, but she also remembered and suffered from the harsh realities of her youth. Enander, "From Refugee to Pioneer," 17.

[71] Enander, "From Refugee to Pioneer," 17, 18.

[72] One common problem that refugees face is the fact that they are often mistrusted and undervalued. For example, Albert Einstein, who went to the United States in 1933 to escape Nazi Germany, is a famous refugee who made great contributions to his new country. As a refugee from Tibet, Tenzin Gyasto, recipient of the Nobel Peace Prize, fostered an understanding of Buddhism and an awareness of non-violent resistance since he was being forced to flee his home country. In addition to this, female refugees can also face distinct problems because of their gender. Cf. Enander, *Elisabeth Schüssler Fiorenza* 17-20.

[73] Segovia, *Toward a New Heaven and a New Earth,* 26.

[74] Enander, "From Refugee to Pioneer," 18, 20.

[75] A woman was expected to follow one path: to marry in her early 20s, start a family quickly, and devote her life to homemaking. as someone's keeper or husband's or her children's. Cf. Stephanie Coontz, *A Strange Stirring: The Feminine Mystique and American Women at the Dawn of the 1960s* (New York: Basic Books, 2011), 42.

[76] Decades earlier, the "first wave" had pushed for women's suffrage, culminating in the passage of the 19th Amendment that gave women the right to vote in 1920. E-Collaborative for Civic Education, "The 1960s-70s American Feminist Movement: Breaking Down Barriers for Women," https://tavaana.org/en/content/1960s-70s-american-feminist-movement-breaking-down-barriers women (accessed on April 27, 2014).

[77] Recalling the vital role played by the women's liberation movement in her life, Fiorenza writes, "In my own experience, the existence of a wo/men's movement was critically important for articulating my theological self-identity in a new and different way." Ann Braude, *Transforming the Faiths of Our Fathers* (New York: Palgrave Macmillan, 2004), 138.

[78] In 1971 when Fiorenza went to her first yearly meeting of the American Academy of Religion and the Society of Biblical Literature in Atlanta, she knew about a meeting of wo/men researchers whom Carol Christ had assembled for establishing the Women's Caucus Religious Studies and the Wo/men's Studies in Religion segment. Fiorenza was chosen there with Carol as the first co-seat of the council. Cf. Braude, *Transforming the Faiths of Our Fathers,* 140.

[79] Another pivotal event took place in 1972, when a historic meeting was organized in Grailville, Ohio, by Clare Randall, general secretary of the National Council of Churches and members of the Grail. There were around 75 ladies – Jews and Christians, Protestants and Catholics, appointed priests, scholastic scholars had been united by the National Council of Churches and the Grail, a universal Catholic ecumenical

wo/men's gathering, for a workshop called "Women Doing Theology." This workshop turned out to be one of the originations of women's activist religious philosophy, which has significantly changed religious philosophy and places of worship. Braude, *Transforming the Faiths of Our Fathers*, 140.

[80] Braude, *Transforming the Faiths of Our Fathers*, 140.

[81] "Ain't I a Woman?" is the speech, delivered extemporaneously by Sojourner Truth, (1797–1883), born into slavery in New York State. Today she stands as a symbol of a strong black woman and of someone who overcame hardship and worked for equal rights; she has been recognized by the National Women's Hall of Fame. She lived to see slavery abolished. Her work served as an inspiration for supporters of equal rights who followed in her footsteps. Cf. Corona Brezina, *Sojourner Truth's "Ain't I a Woman?" Speech: A Primary Source Investigation* (New York: Rosen Central Primary Source, 2005), 46, 50.

[82] Fiorenza, *Jesus*, 59-60.

[83] Fiorenza, *Jesus*, 60. At the root of liberation theology's method is a *"nexus with concrete praxis"* According to Boff, "liberation theology is the theology of the liberation of the oppressed; the liberation of their whole person, body and soul; and all of the oppressed - the poor, the subjugated, those who suffer discrimination." Clodovis Boff, "Epistemology and Method of the Theology of Liberation," in *Systematic Theology: Perspectives from Liberation Theology* ed. John Sobrino and Ignacio Ellacuria (New York: Orbis, 1993), 10, 73, 77.

[84] Fiorenza, *Jesus*, 61.

[85] Braude, 23, 24. While Fiorenza was a pioneer and was/is outstanding in many respects, she was not alone at that time and together with other feminists she helped to forge new approaches to the Bible, tradition, church, systematic theology, and ethics.

[86] While J. B. Metz does his theology with an acute awareness of the crisis of modernity: a crisis of tradition, a crisis of authority, a crisis of reason and, ultimately, a crisis of religion, he considers the prime theological task is the struggle to become subjects before God in history. He plays out the tension of this crisis of identity through the privatization of religion. He lays emphasis on the crisis of forgetfulness of suffering and of the countless acts of inhumanity that mark Christian history. He escapes this forgetfulness of suffering through the specific symbol of Auschwitz. For Metz, Auschwitz becomes the prime symbol for the 'catastrophes' of Western history and the innocent suffering of victims. It is Auschwitz that moves him to ask the big human questions of justice, responsibility, freedom and guilt. He claims that 'if there is no God in Auschwitz, how can there be a God anywhere else?' This means, he says, that our responsibility to God, our proper response to our faith, and therefore the measure of our humanity, are gauged by our ability to be responsive to the catastrophic suffering. Cf. Johannes Baptist Metz, ed. "Theology in the Struggle," in *Faith and the Future: Essays on Theology, Solidarity, and Modernity* (New York: Orbis Books, 1995), 32-48, 52.

[87] Fiorenza, *Sharing Her Word*, 28-36.

[88] The tensive symbol is that which evokes a whole range of meanings, which can never be exhausted or adequately expressed by one referent. Elisabeth Schüssler Fiorenza, *The Book of Revelation: Justice and Judgment* (Philadelphia: Fortress Press, 1985), 183.

[89] Fiorenza, "Patriarchal Structures and the Discipleship of Equals," 231.

[90] Fiorenza, *Sharing Her Word*, 112.

[91] Fiorenza, *In Memory of Her*, 4.

[92] Cornel West, Review of Elisabeth Schüssler Fiorenza, "In Memory of Her," *Religious Studies Review*, 11/1 (1985): 1-5.

[93] Fiorenza, *In Memory of Her*, 5.

[94] The philosophical influence of Heidegger, Gadamer and Ricoeur makes biblical interpreter sensitive to the "otherness" of the text, the inescapable prejudices of the interpreter and the pervasive web of language, tradition, and community. West, *The Cornel West*, 381.

[95] Fiorenza, *In Memory of Her*, 5.

[96] Fiorenza, *In Memory of Her*, 6.

[97] Fiorenza, *In Memory of Her*, 33-34. Fiorenza envisioned her reconstruction of the early Christian origins centering on women as makers and participants in history. Accordingly, her location for revelation is not in biblical texts but in the life and ministry of Jesus and the women and men called by him.

[98] Fiorenza, *In Memory of Her*, 152.

[99] Fiorenza, *In Memory of Her*, 6.

[100] According to Paul, apostleship is not limited to the twelve. All who were eyewitnesses to the resurrection and who were commissioned by the Resurrected One to missionary work (1 Cor.9:4). According to Luke, however, only those Christians who accompanied Jesus in his Galilean ministry and were also eyewitnesses to his resurrection are apostles (Acts 1:21). Fiorenza, *Discipleship of Equals*, 83.

[101] Fiorenza, *In Memory of Her*, 33-34, 41.

[102] The term "Old Quest" refers to the constructs of Jesus, which are commonly reckoned to have been brought to an end by Albert Schweitzer in 1906. The proponents of the "New Quest" became the pioneers who moved beyond Rudolf Bultmann's "No Quest." Andries van Aarde, "Methods and Models in the Quest for the Historical Jesus: Historical Criticism and/or Social Scientific Criticism," Department of New Testament Studies, University of Pretoria, *Theological Studies* 58/2 (2002): 423. Paper presented at the International Context Group Meeting, University of Pretoria, June 12-15, 2001. This essay was first published in *Theology Today* 45/3 (October 1988): 280-292.

[103] Robert W. Funk, "Milestones in the Quest for the Historical Jesus," *The Fourth R*, 14: 4, July / August, 2001 [Online] https://www.westarinstitute.org/resources/ the-fourth-r/milestones-in-the-quest-for-the-historical-jesus/ (accessed July 2, 2016). Along with "Reading, Riting and Rithmetic," Religion is *the fourth "R"* of basic literacy. First

published in 1987, *The Fourth R* shares the latest thinking from religion scholars and writers – in non-technical language aimed at a general audience.

[104] Marcus J. Borg, *Jesus in Contemporary Scholarship* (Harrisburg, Pennsylvania, Trinity Press International, 1994), 18-19.

[105] Willem S. Vorster, J. Eugene Botha, *Speaking of Jesus: Essays on Biblical Language, Gospel Narrative, and the Historical Jesus* (Leiden, Netherlands: Brill Publishers, 1999), 307.

[106] The scholarly work of this third quest was surveyed by E.P. Sanders, B. Mack, Schüssler Fiorenza, M.J. Borg and R.A. Horsley. Cf. Borg, '*Portraits of Jesus* in *Contemporary North American Scholarship*,' 18-28.

[107] Fiorenza, *In Memory of Her*, 70-71. Her analysis of Jesus is part of a larger work treating the origins of Christianity, most relevant to her sketch of Jesus and the earliest Jesus movement.

[108] Androcentrism refers to a perspective of patriarchy to a social system. It characterizes a mind-set, patriarchy represents a social-cultural system in which a few men have power over other men, women, children, slaves and colonialized people." Fiorenza, *In Memory of Her*, 29.

[109] Fiorenza stresses that we know Jesus only through the community around him and repudiates any attempt "to distill the historical Jesus from the remembering interpretations of his first followers." Thus she does not pursue a historical Jesus separate from his followers, but Jesus whose "life and ministry is available to historical-critical reading of the earliest interpretations of the first Christians." Fiorenza, *In Memory of Her*, 103.

[110] Fiorenza, *In Memory of Her*, 102, 100.

[111] Though her claim here lacks convincing evidences or arguments, for her, the location of revelation is not in biblical texts but in the life and ministry of Jesus. Therefore, she is convinced about the egalitarian reality of the early Christian movement that would call for a radical transformation of the then hierarchical male structures of the Church. (For more explanation, see section on "Reasons and Influences for the Choice of Method" 3:2.2.).

[112] Fiorenza, *In Memory of Her*, 149-151. "Sophia" is a Greek word for wisdom; in Hebrew and Greek, "wisdom" is feminine.

[113] How would one account for Jesus' use of *Abba*? See in Robert Hamerton-Kelly, *God the Father: Theology and Patriarchy in the Teaching of Jesus* (Philadelphia: Fortress, 1979), 102. Jesus neutralizes and humanizes the patriarchy by choosing the father symbol for God. In that sense, Jesus' the use of *Abba* (Mk: 14:36) undermines the patriarchal system by downgrading the titles and reinforces the importance and essence of intimacy and personal relationship.

[114] Borg, *Jesus in Contemporary Scholarship*, 25.

[115] Fiorenza, *In Memory of Her*, 134-135.

[116] Borg, *Jesus in Contemporary Scholarship*, 25.

[117] Instead of using the word kingdom, Fiorenza holds on to the Greek word *basileia*

as it evokes in "ever new images, a realization of the gracious goodness of Israel's God and the equality and solidarity of the people of God." Fiorenza, *In Memory of Her*, 132. This will be dealt in the section on "Jesus the Basileia of God" 3.3.1.4.

[118]. Fiorenza, *Wisdom Ways,* 115.

[119] In the 1970s, women's studies distinguished social gender roles from biological sex, and by the mid-1980s gender studies emerged as a distinct field of inquiry that questions seemingly universal beliefs about woman and man and attempts to unmask the cultural, societal, and political roots of gender. Since then, gender not only has become a key analytic category alongside race, class, age, and colonialism, an analysis that has led to an "adding up of oppressions" approach, but has added to the diverse structures of domination. Fiorenza, "Between Movement and Academy: Feminist Biblical Studies in the Twentieth Century" in *Feminist Biblical Studies in the Twentieth Century Scholarship and Movement,* 6.

[120] Fiorenza, *Sharing Her Word,* 190.

[121] Fiorenza, *Wisdom Ways,* 211.

[122] Fiorenza, *Sharing Her Word,* 190. Historically, like churches and governments in the Western world the elitist notions have found the means to maintain power. These elites have defined white women along with subordinated classes, races and peoples as the "others" so as to colonize and exploit them. The result is the creation of multiplicative structures of oppression that form a complex social pyramid of graduated dominations and subordinations (sexism, racism, class exploitation, heterosexism and colonialism). As a result, Fiorenza replaces the word *patriarchy* as the usual descriptive term for this pyramid with her new word *kyriarchy* so as to communicate oppression's complexity: not all men dominate and exploit all women without difference; rather, elite Euro-American men have benefited from exploiting women and other non-persons. Cf. Donald K. McKim, *The Dictionary of Major Biblical Interpreter* (Nottingham: Intervarsity Press, 2007), 895-896.

[123] Enander, *Schüssler Fiorenza,* 7-8.

[124] Fiorenza, *Jesus,* 14. Patriarchy, according to Rosemary Radford Ruether, is the 'rule of the father,' which refers to systems of legal, social, economic, and political relations that validate and enforce the sovereignty of male heads of families over dependent persons in the household. In classical patriarchal systems, dependent persons included wives, unmarried daughters, dependent sons, and slaves, male and female. Rosemary Radford Ruether, *Women Healing Earth* (London: SCM, 1996). 205-206.

[125] Fiorenza coined the term kyriarchy many years ago in order to move beyond the gender dualism of the term patriarchy, and has been implementing an analysis of kyriarchal texts, practices and institutions ever since.

[126] 'Wo/men' is a gender-inclusive term, which also signifies more than the sum of gendered humanity: it denotes women and men, oppressed and marginalized, within kyriarchy.

[127] Fiorenza, *Sharing Her Word,* 186.

[128] Elisabeth Schüssler Fiorenza, "Reaffirming Feminist/Womanist Biblical Scholarship," *Encounter* 67, no. 4 (2006): 362.

[129] Initial definitions on "women," are found in Schüssler, *Rhetoric and Ethic*, ix; and *Wisdom Ways*, 57-59,107-109, and 216.

[130] Fiorenza, *Rhetoric and Ethic*, ix.

[131] Elisabeth Schüssler Fiorenza, *Democratizing Biblical Studies: Toward an Emancipatory Educational Space* (Louisville: Westminster John Knox Press, 2009); The *Power of the Word: Scripture and the Rhetoric of Empire* (Minneapolis: Fortress Press, 2007).

[132] Fiorenza, *Jesus*, 191, n.1.

[133] Elisabeth Schüssler Fiorenza, 'Introduction' in *The Power of Naming*, ed. Elisabeth Schüssler Fiorenza (Maryknoll, New York: Orbis Books, 1996), xxx.

[134] Fiorenza, *Sharing Her Word*, 73.

[135] In using the Greek word *ekklēsia*, Fiorenza aims to situate feminist theology in the public ground of the assembly or the congress in which all female and male citizens participate on equal footing. Fiorenza, *Jesus*, 191, n.1.

[136] Fiorenza says, that this "church" is characterized by hierarchical structures, represented by men and divided into a sacred two-class system of the ordained and the laity. Fiorenza, *Changing Horizons: Explorations in Feminist Interpretation*, chapter 15. *Changing Horizons* is the second of two volumes highlighting the ways in which Fiorenza's work constructs a critical feminist theory and praxis of liberation, in relation to the biblical text and its legacy, and in relation to the theological and ecclesial setting of today. https://books.google.co.in/ books?id=TOz75rV0GOkC&printsec (accessed October 22, 2015).

[137] Elisabeth Schüssler Fiorenza, "Women, Mission and the Catholicity of Theology," in *The Church in Mission: Universal Mandate and Local Concerns* eds. Thomas Malipurathu and Lazar. Stanislaus (Anand: Gujarat Sahitya Prakash, 2002), 155.

[138] Fiorenza, "Women, Mission and the Catholicity of Theology," 155.

[139] Fiorenza, "Women, Mission and the Catholicity of Theology," 163.

[140] Fiorenza, *Changing Horizons*, Chapter 15.

[141] Fiorenza, *But She Said*, 152.

[142] Elisabeth Schüssler Fiorenza, "The Will to Choose or to Reject: Continuing our Critical Work," in *Feminist Interpretation of the Bible*, ed. Letty M. Russell (Oxford: Basil Blackwell, 1985), 126.

[143] Fiorenza, *Discipleship of Equals: A Critical Feminist Ekklesia-logy of Liberation*, 329. Hence, Jobling J'annine states that the contemporary *ekklēsia* can reclaim the *ekklēsia* of wo/men of the first century as its own biblical forebear; the Jesus movement can be contextualized within the ecclesia's feminist vision. Cf. Jobling J'annine, *Feminist Biblical Interpretation in Theological Context* (Burlington: Ashgate, 2002), 33. Lisa Stephenson, complements in saying that the *ekklēsia* of wo/men seeks to embody this political reality, not so that it becomes an end in itself, but so that the *ekklēsia* of women might ultimately transform the kyriarchal church into the discipleship of

equals. Just as ivy envelops weeds and replaces them leaf by leaf, so too the *ekklesia* of wo/men will envelop the praxis of the kyriarchal church and replace it with a different praxis. Lisa Stephenson, *Dismantling the Dualisms for American Pentecostal Women in Ministry*, 150-151.

[144] Fiorenza understands her feminist theological reconstruction of the discipleship of equals during the first centuries of the Church to be her significant contribution toward this reconstructive process. Fiorenza, *Discipleship of Equals*, 329.

[145] Stephenson, *Dismantling the Dualisms for American Pentecostal Women in Ministry*, 159-160.

[146] Fiorenza, *Wisdom Ways*, 210.

[147] Barbara E. Reid, OP "Editors Introduction to Wisdom Commentary: "She is the Breath of the Power of God (Wis 7:25)"," in *Wisdom Commentary: Ephesians* eds. Elisabeth Schüssler Fiorenza & Barbara E. Reid, OP (Liturgical Press, 2017), xl, https://books.google.co.in/books?isbn=0814681999 (accessed August 21, 2017).

[148] Kristiansen and Rise, *Key Theological Thinkers*, 332.

[149] Fiorenza, *Sharing Her Word*, 187, n.10. Edwina Gateley suggests the spelling of God, as 'Godde' which she found in a prayer and hymn book used by a community of Sisters of the Mission in New Zealand. Gateley explains that the terms 'God' and Goddess' are not satisfactory. She was delighted to come across a word which embraces both male and female and is rooted in English far older than our current usage. Edwina Gateley, *A Warm, Moist Salty God: Woman Journeying Towards Wisdom* (Trabuco Canyon, CA: Source Books, 1993), iii n. †. Both usages remind us of what Elizabeth A. Johnson identifies as fundamental aspects of language about the divine: one, Incomprehensibility - the divine is fundamentally unknowable: *Si comprehendis, non est Deus*. Cf. *Elizabeth A. Johnson, She who Is: The Mystery of God in a Feminist Theological Discourse (New York: Crossroad, 1992)*, 104-112; two, Analogy - all speech about the divine is analogical and metaphorical. Cf. E.A. Johnson, *She Who Is*, 113-117; three, Many Names - no one image or concept suffices to comprehend the divine mystery. Johnson, *She Who Is*, 117-120.

[150] However, we use "God" as the Father and Mother, Lord of the universe, instead of G*d, in our study.

[151] In ancient Israel, Divine Sophia is "the one and only acceptable feminine image of God." She is an inalienable part of Jewish and Christian traditions because she appears in Hebrew Bible. Cf. Silvia Schroer, "Wise and Counselling Women in Ancient Israel: Literary and Historical Ideals of the Personified $o5mâh," in *A Feminist Companion to Wisdom Literature*, ed. Athalya Brenner (England: Sheffield Academic Press, 1995), 68. "Personified Wisdom appears for the first time in biblical writings from the period after the Babylonian exile." Cf. Silvia Schroer, "The Book of Sophia," in *Searching the Scriptures: A Feminist Commentary*, vol. II, eds. Elisabeth Schüssler Fiorenza, Shelly Matthews, Ann Graham Brock (New York: Cross Road, 1994), 17.

[152] Fiorenza, *Jesus,* 157. Schroer says that what the figure of Sophia-Wisdom does is to integrate masculine and feminine elements into the image of God and to connect such an 'inclusive monotheism' with the experience of women in Israel. Schroer,

"The Book of Sophia," as cited in *Mary Grey, Introducing Feminist Images of God: Introductions in Feminist Theology* (Cleveland, Ohio: The Pilgrim Press, 2001), 103.

[153] Fiorenza, *In Memory of Her*, 130-131.

[154] Fiorenza, *Jesus*, 90.

[155] Fiorenza, *Jesus, 131-132.*

[156] For Fiorenza, *ekklēsia* as the *basileia* of God is born out of her personal experiences as a woman faced with dehumanization in society and Church and a burning desire for wo/men's liberation and wholeness.

[157] Though Jesus was the inspiration for both groups, each saw Him in different ways. The Jesus group she describes as an inner-Jewish renewal movement whose integrative symbol was the *basileia* of God. Phyllis Trible, "The Creation of a Feminist Theology," *The New York Times*, 1 May 1983, http://www.nytimes .com /1983/05/01/books/the-creation-of-a-feminist-theology.html (accessed November 23, 2015).

[158] Fiorenza, *In Memory of Her*, 132, 134. But who is Sophia here? Fiorenza continues, saying that Jesus understood himself "as Sophia's messenger and later as Sophia herself."

[159] Fiorenza, *In Memory of Her*, 130-131.

[160] Fiorenza, *In Memory of Her*, 135.

[161] The first, *In Memory of Her*, appeared at the beginning of what we have called the third quest; the second, *Jesus: Miriam's Child, Sophia's Prophet*, was published in 1994. Fiorenza's intent in writing these books is to create a historical reconstruction of Christian origins which focuses on the role of women; her reason for writing is to provide grounds for a feminist and liberationist dismantling of the kyriocentric theology. However, for her, this means she begins with women's experience in order to end sexist ideals in Christianity.

[162] Fiorenza, *Sharing Her Word*, 41.

[163] Fiorenza, *In Memory of Her*, 145.

[164] Fiorenza, *In Memory of Her*, xiv.

[165] John Berchmans Barla counters the idea saying that in the mystery of Incarnation God's Word become flesh, a human person: Jesus Immanuel, God with us (Mt 1:23). In his event, God's mystery is unveiled and penetrated. Jesus is the meeting point between God's revelation and human's faith, between God's Word and human's word. He is God's definitive revelation. He is the saving mystery of God that encompasses the past, present and the future (Col 1:15-20). God continues to be present through Jesus Christ in the midst of human life and history. He is indeed the definitive, ultimate, total and supreme revelation of God. Cf. John Berchmans Barla, *Christian Theological Understanding of Other Religions According to D.S. Amalorpavadass* (Rome: Gregorian Biblical BookShop, 1999), 214. 205.

[166] Fiorenza, *In Memory of Her*, 121-122.

[167] Rosemary Radford Ruether's startling question illustrates well the dilemma feminists encounter in their consideration of the redemptive role of Jesus Christ: "Can

a male Savior save women?" Appropriating the Marxist-Liberationist hermeneutics of suspicion, Ruether begins Christology as a critical reflection on Jesus of the New Testament as traditionally interpreted and theologized by the Church. Cf. Rosemary Radford Ruether, *Sexism and God-Talk: Toward a Feminist Theology*, (Boston: Beacon, 1983), 116. As an answer to her christological question, Ruether states that Jesus' main work is to renounce hierarchy and domination, to serve and empower the oppressed. Christ's effectiveness as liberator is independent of his maleness, so Ruether concludes saying that his maleness, theologically speaking, has no ultimate significance, and concludes that "Christ is not necessarily male, nor is the redeemed community only women, but a new humanity female and male." Ruether, *Sexism and God-Talk*, 137, 138.

[168] On a personal note, we contend that our approach is consistent with the more traditional view of Christ the Saviour that on the Cross Jesus symbolizes the opposite of male dominating power. Rather power is poured out in self-sacrificing love. On the Cross one can see the *kenosis* of presence-solidarity, self-empting Jesus. In the words of Elizabeth Johnson: on the Cross *kenosis* of patriarchy is reflected. Elizabeth A Johnson, *Consider Jesus: Waves of Renewal in Christology* (UK: Geoffrey, Chapman, 1990), 111 as quoted in Mulackal, "Who Is Jesus for Indian Women? 444.

[169] For Ruether, the critical principle of feminist theology is the promotion of the full humanity of women. Whatever diminishes women's full humanity is by this criterion judged "not redemptive." Ruether *Sexism and God-Talk*, 19.

[170] Fiorenza counters the idea of ruether saying that feminist theology must be rooted in women's lives, and focused not simply on the "experience of women" but "on the experience of women struggling for liberation from patriarchal oppression for the transformation of *kyriarchy*." Fiorenza, *Changing Horizons*, 92. Fiorenza rejects Ruether's appeal to the 'full humanity of women', because Fiorenza sees it as still far too patriarchal, since humanity for her is male-defined.

[171] Countering Ruether, Fiorenza says that a feminist liberationist exploration of Christian scriptures does not begin its work "with the biblical text but with a critical articulation and analysis of the experience of wo/men." Fiorenza, *Jesus*, 61.

[172] Fiorenza, *Jesus*, 47.

[173] According to Fiorenza a hermeneutic of critical evaluation seeks to arbitrate the oppressive tendencies as well as liberating possibilities inscribed in Biblical texts, to examine their function in contemporary struggles for enhancing human dignity and their significance with wo/men of today.

[174] The phrase first appears Fiorenza, *In Memory of Her* [the first edition], xxiv.

[175] Fiorenza, *In Memory of Her*, 34.

[176] Fiorenza, *In Memory of Her*, 35. Fiorenza defines 'patriarchy' as, in the first place, 'the domination of men over women' (*Discipleship of Equals*, 359). To broaden this meaning, she has since then replaced the term 'patriarchy' with '*kyriarchy*', meaning domination in any of its forms, a term coined in *But She Said: Feminist Practices of Biblical Interpretation*, 8 and further explained in *In Memory of Her*, xviii–xxii.

[177] Fiorenza, *In Memory of Her*, 146-147.

[178] Fiorenza, *Jesus*, 74.

[179] Fiorenza, *In Memory of Her*, 146.

[180] Fiorenza, *Discipleship of Equals*, 240.

[181] Fiorenza, *In Memory of Her*, 107.

[182] Fiorenza, *Sharing Her Word*, 114, 115.

[183] Fiorenza, *In Memory of Her*, 107.

[184] Fiorenza, *In Memory of Her*, 141-143.

[185] Fiorenza, *In Memory of Her*, 318.

[186] Fiorenza, *In Memory of Her*, 153-154.

[187] Robert Lawson, Schüssler Fiorenza, "Jesus: Miriam's Child, Sophia's Prophet," *Book Review*, 25 February 2013, http://robertlawson.weebly.com/uploads/1/5/4/9/15493052/jesus-_miriams_child_sophias_prop het.pdf (accessed November 2, 2015).

[188] Fiorenza, *In Memory of Her*, 135.

[189] Divine Sophia is named Sophia in Greek, *Hohkma* (*Chokmah*) in Hebrew, *Sapientia* in Latin, and is known as Lady Wisdom in the Wisdom Literature. Cf. Grace Ji-Sim Kim, *The Grace of Sophia; A Korean North American Women's Christology* (Cleveland: The Pilgrim Press, 2002), 81-82. Divine Sophia first emerged at a time when the Israelite monarchy was lost. The Israelite prophets thus invited the Jewish people to understand the mercy of God in a more universal way, expressed "in the imagery of Sophia setting a table, summoning people to the feast from the highways and byways (Prov 9:1-6; Isa 55) followed by the New Testament imagery of the messianic banquet." Cf. Grey, *Introducing Feminist Images of God*, 103.

[190] These traditions are almost entirely lost and submerged in the Christian New Testament, whereas the figure of Divine Wisdom appears openly in Jewish discourse, albeit in a 'body of literature articulated either in the forms of instructions of a father to his son or as a fictive address to a young king.' She further quotes feminist theologians who argue that this Jewish tradition emerged in the post-exilic period and spread throughout the Jewish communities of the Hellenistic world. In the course of time, as this tradition became in many places less open to women as religious subjects, its literature came to reflect the interests of a male elite. In this tradition, Divine Wisdom is presented as G*d's presence in Israel, who 'offers life, knowledge, rest and salvation to all who will accept her.' Fiorenza, *Jesus*, 131-162.

[191] Traces of this understanding of Jesus can be found in the sayings of Jesus in the different gospels. These sayings might reflect a Saying Tradition or source which can be reconstructed as rooted in some of the earliest traditions of the Jesus movement, which consisted of Jesus' followers.

[192] Fiorenza, *In Memory of Her*, 130-140, 188-192.

[193] Fiorenza, *In Memory of Her*, 135. Fiorenza develops this in book-length form in *Jesus: Miriam's Child, Sophia's Prophet*.

[194] These early Jesus traditions interpreted the Galilean mission of Jesus as that of Sophia-G*d. Cf. Fiorenza, *Jesus, 139-140.* Further, Grace Ji-Sun Kim, a Korean-

American theologian, states how Sophia is personified in Jesus through a discussion on Jesus' identity as Sophia's 'prophet' from the perspectives of the Gospels of Matthew and John, and from the writings of Paul. She says, in the New Testament, Jesus-Sophia offers grace and unconditional love to humanity through his prophetic mission. She points out that Sophia in Jesus invites everyone into full human existence. Jesus offers the fullness of human existence through his inclusive mission, like that of Divine Sophia. Grace Ji-Sum Kim, *The Grace of Sophia: A Korean North American Women's Christology* (Cleveland: The Pilgrim Press, 2002), 114-124. John 10:10b: "I came that they may have life, and have it abundantly."

[195] Fiorenza, *Jesus, 134.*

[196] Fiorenza, *Wisdom Ways,* 27.

[197] Fiorenza, *In Memory of Her,* 135, 130.

[198] Fiorenza, *Jesus, 140.*

[199] Fiorenza summarizes the theology of the Wisdom literature: Wisdom theology with its inclusive language about the Divine seems intent on using female G*d-language for its own theological purposes. The theological discourses on Sophia speak positively about Israel's G*d in the language of their own Egyptian Hellenistic culture. Fiorenza, *Jesus, 137.*

[200] Fiorenza, *Jesus, 152.*

[201] Fiorenza, *In Memory of Her,* 105, 106.

[202] Fiorenza, *Jesus, 157.*

[203] Fiorenza, *Jesus, 157.*

[204] Fiorenza, *Sharing Her Word,* 166.

[205] Fiorenza, *Sharing Her Word,* 167. "The queen of the South will rise at the judgment with the people of this generation and condemn them, because she came from the ends of the earth to listen to the wisdom of Solomon, and see, something greater than Solomon is here!" Lk 11: 31 (NRSV).

[206] Fiorenza, *Sharing Her Word,* 168ff.

[207] "Come to me, all you that are weary and are carrying heavy burdens and I will give you rest. Take my yoke upon you, and learn from me; for I am gentle and humble in heart, and you will find rest for your souls. For, my yoke is easy, and my burden is light" Mt 11:28-30.

[208] Fiorenza, *Sharing Her Word,* 168.

[209] "Jerusalem, Jerusalem, the city that kills the prophets and stones those who are sent to it! How often have I desired to gather your children together as a hen gathers her brood under her wings, and you were not willing!" Lk 13:34.

[210] "From the days of John the Baptist until now the kingdom of heaven has suffered violence, and the violent take it by force" Mt 11:12. This saying of Jesus is bringing the Sophia and *basileia* traditions together which speaks of the violence encountered by those who struggle for the *basileia* of the Sophia-God of Jesus. Fiorenza, *Sharing Her Word,* 169.

[211] Fiorenza, *Sharing Her Word,* 170; *In Memory of Her* 135.

[212] The traditional theology of the Cross affirms that the Cross exemplifies and vindicates with absolute assurance the essence and praxis of Jesus, who in his freedom and love chooses to identify with the weak and oppose the wise and the strong. Jesus died for justice, for doing good, for taking sides with the poor, the sick, the women and the children. "By his glorious Cross Christ has won salvation for all. He redeemed them from the sin that held them in bondage. For freedom Christ has set us free." *Catechism of the Catholic Church* (*CCC*) No. 1741. From the point of view of the Swiss theologian Regula Strobel, Schüssler Fiorenza evaluates theology of the Cross and underscores the point that traditional theologies of redemption and the Cross strengthen the kyriarchal societal values and sentiments. Especially, the notion that human sin can be atoned for only through the bloody sacrifice of G*d's own son serves to support the powerful in a society whose interests in domination and profit demand a multitude of human sacrifices. In other words, such a theological belief either contributes to subjugate women under male power and women accept sufferings in their abusive relationships as G*d's will or it supports hierarchical relationships of domination. Cf. Fiorenza, *Jesus*, 101, 104. Consequently, the theology of the Cross as it is predominantly understood does not function as a salvific symbol for Schüssler in particular and some women in general.

[213] Fiorenza, *In Memory of Her*, 113-130. Some of the important signs of the nearness of the *basileia* include the healing of the blind, deaf, and the lame, the raising of the dead, the cleansing of the lepers, and the preaching of the good news to the poor (Lk 7:22), which are but images of wholeness - a restoration of humanity to individuals.

[214] Elisabeth Schüssler Fiorenza, "To Follow the Vision: The Jesus Movement as *Basileia* Movement," in *Liberating Eschatology: Essays in Honor of Letty M. Russell*, eds. Letty M Russell, Margaret A Farley, Serene Jones (Louisville, Kentucky: Westminster John Knox Press, 1999), 134-135.

[215] Fiorenza, *Sharing Her Word*, 116.

[216] Fiorenza, *Transforming Vision*, 197.

[217] Fiorenza, *In Memory of Her*, 119.

[218] Fiorenza, *In Memory of Her*, 120-121.

[219] Fiorenza, *In Memory of Her*, 120, 122.

[220] Fiorenza recommends staying in the Greco-Roman Palestinian culture for an interpretation of Jesus' death because the atonement for sin doctrine developed much later. Fiorenza, *In Memory of Her*, 130.

[221] Fiorenza, *Jesus: Miriam's Child, Sophia's Prophet*, 123-124.

[222] Jesus is both human and divine, he is able to pay humanity's debt to God, but because he is sinless Jesus also does not deserve to be punished. In this way, Jesus' death "sets right the order of justice and accomplishes redemption for human beings." Flora A. Keshgegian, "The Scandal of the Cross: Revisiting Anselm and His Feminist Critics, "*Anglican Theological Review* 82/3 (2000): 475, as cited in "Suffering Our Way to Salvation: Ivone Gebara, Elisabeth Schüssler Fiorenza, and the Adequacy of the Cross as a Symbol for Women," ed. Amy Chapman, *Lumen et Vita*, vol 1/1 (June

2011), https://ejournals.bc.edu/ojs/index.php/ lumenetvita/article/view/1698/1555 (accessed August 26, 2016).

[223] Fiorenza, *Jesus,* 123-126.

[224] Fiorenza, *Jesus,* 126.

[225] Feminist liberation therefore is something "mysterious" and so one's efforts alone are futile. Women and men are to join hands with each other for the cause of the enhancement of the oppressed even to the extent of becoming a victim after the example of Jesus for a noble cause.

[226] Fiorenza, "Discipleship of Equals: Reality and Vision," 1-2.

[227] Fiorenza, *In Memory of Her,* 119, 122.

[228] Fiorenza, *Jesus,* 94.

[229] Fiorenza, *In Memory of Her,* 130.

[230] Fiorenza, *In Memory of Her,* 130-131.

[231] Fiorenza, *Jesus, 140.*

[232] Rebecca Chabot and Sarah Neeley, "Feminist Liberative Theologies," in *Introducing Liberative Theologies,* ed. Miguel A. De La Torre (Maryknoll, New York: Orbis Books, 2015), 183.

[233] Kristiansen and Rise, *Key Theological Thinkers,* 332.

[234] Fiorenza, *Jesus,* 45.

Chapter 4

Horizons
for an Emerging Christology:
Convergences, Divergences and Synthesis

Introduction

The analysis of the situation and challenges that emerge from the twenty-first century India and the Christological pursuit of Rayan and Fiorenza in response to their respective contextsgive us a better focus on the landmark works of two prominent theologians. As the title suggests, this chapter aims at a synthesis of the two contemporary theologians: Rayan and Fiorenza. This chapter consists of two primary sections: The first section brings out the similarities as well as the differences between the theologizing processes of Rayan and Fiorenza; the second section proposes a Christology for India today that emerges primarily out of their theological pursuits. The chapter concludes with an attempt to put together some key ideas in support of our contention that the theological investigation of Rayan and Fiorenza helps us in developing a Christology for India in the twenty-first century.

1. Basic Theological Elements of Convergence and Divergence

Here we make a comparative study that focuses on what these two scholars hold in common as well as where they differ. The aim here is to be enriched, and to enhance and adhere to the vision of Jesus with reference to Rayan and Fiorenza.

Common Theological Perspectives

The essential common elements in the theological perspectives of Rayan and Fiorenza are the following:

i) The **Christian faith** runs as a backbone through their theological vision. The person of Jesus Christ encountered in the Gospel provides inspiration, insights and examples to transform society as well as the Church. They emphasize gospel-oriented radical changes and the transformation of individuals and society as a whole.

ii) **Inadequacy of the existing hermeneutics of the Bible** and Christian traditions. These scholars propose a radical way of interpreting the Scripture and a new way of theologising, by placing more emphasis on the life struggles of the people and the need to usher in God's Reign as a reality here and now.

iii) Personally they suffered injustices and discriminations due to **the prevalent socio-political oppressive patriarchal system** that is protected and perpetuated in society and even in the Church. They start their theological and Christological reflections on their own life situations, hardships, struggles, social and political oppressions around, the deep inequalities in their midst, and of the plight of the poor and of women in particular.

iv) Liberation, emancipation of the poor and wo/men are the main objectives of their Christological reflections with special reference to the social movements of their times. A common end of their theologizing is **integral all-inclusive salvation** and a bottom up approach, rather than a top-down approach, without ignoring the eschatological perspective.

v) Both are convinced that the values of the Gospel have **transformative power** to bring about a new social order.

Differing Theological Perspectives

Elements in which Fiorenza and Rayan differ significantly from each other are the following:

i) They have **different approaches to interpret the Bible**. For Rayan, the Bible and the context are the main basis for theological reflections, whereas for Schüssler, history of Israelites and early Christian community are the reference points of her liberationist theological method.

ii) Rayan emphasizes the role of the Holy Spirit in the life of the Church and the world. 'Mission in the Spirit' is Rayan's way of looking at the salvific works in the world, whereas Schüssler underscores the role of the Spirit to affirm the equality of all the baptized despite the differences in the gifts each one is endowed with.[1]

iii) Rayan **includes the plight and place of women** in his liberationist approach, whereas for Fiorenza it is **the point of departure as well as arrival in** her feminist theologizing: wo/men and their lives are the core experiences or data for theologizing.

For Rayan, the ministry and the life story of Jesus is of paramount importance in defining his Christology. But for Fiorenza, women's experience of Jesus is the starting point of her Christology. Further, it is the quest for the historical Jesus and its origin which defines her Christology.

2. Converging Themes in Relation to the Theological Vision

Although there are several points that bring them together, we shall limit ourselves to some of the theological elements that will help to perceive Christological unity between the Indian Theologian and the Western feminist theologian. Our objective is to bring out the areas where their perspectives converge in varying dimensions of their theological vision. We will consider the following five areas: i) socio-political oppressive patriarchal system; ii) religio-theological influence; iii) praxis of solidarity and identification; iv) inadequacy of the hermeneutics of the Bible; and v) all-inclusive integral approach.

2.1 Socio-Political Oppressive Patriarchal System

Fiorenza has personally suffered social and political oppressions. Both of them – Rayan and Fiorenza – have known the deep-rooted inequalities in their midst, the plight of the poor and of women in particular. Their experiences enabled them to base their theological and Christological reflections on their own life situations and experiences. From his early years Rayan had first-hand experiences of the cruelties of oppression and unjust treatment of the poor and the marginalized. Innocent people were unjustly silenced and abused. Two important events deeply influenced his early years: one, India's struggle for national liberation from the British colonial domination; two, the painful victory of the Ezhava community in his homeland, Kerala, that struggled for social and economic liberation from the age-old unjust practices of discrimination based on caste system. Rayan was aware of this socio-political context and atmosphere and was drawn to what his fellow beings were going through. He experienced his people's powerlessness that instilled in him zeal to fight for human dignity.

Rayan's childhood experiences were the matrix of his theology. He sees experience as a vital source of theology, one that is understood as reflection on life in the light of faith. Therefore, the starting point of his theological reflection is from below, from the realities of life, from the "profound and enriching questions" which are posed by these realties. Theology is the spark that leaps up at the point of encounter between the reality of life and faith.[2] Rayan's writings spring from a heart that knows deeply the presence and power of the Holy Spirit who has been journeying along human history and is actively involved in contemporary life situations. He believes it is from the experience of the poor that an authentic theology emerges. God is to be discovered in the process of committed action to build society and of involvement in the struggle of a people for justice and freedom.

During the early days of Rayan, India under colonial domination, the exploited and the marginalized people's creativity was crippled and resourcefulness deteriorated, which gradually paved the way to a mentality of dependence at all levels of life and in all areas of existence. For India, colonialism also meant that the profound experiences of the Indian mystics, the world of symbols, the rich religious texts and forms of worship were despised and rejected to make way for European theology, liturgy and spirituality. Influenced by his context, Rayan could get in touch with what his fellow brothers and sisters were going through. Consequently that became a central concern in his theological vision.

Fiorenza, as cited earlier, is an immigrant to the United States from Germany. She is a feminist liberationist theologian in the European context. She was brought up in her childhood as a refugee during the World War II. War-torn Europe contributed to the development of Fiorenza's consciousness of pain and suffering and oppressive societal structures. Her early childhood as well as later adult experiences of racism and discrimination planted within her a deep concern for the oppressed and forgotten people. She grew conscious of women's struggle for identity and freedom. Eventually that shaped her life as an adult and a feminist and later helped her develop a feminist theology of liberation. Fiorenza came of age during a time when feminist theology was yet to take shape – the discipline did not exist; she helped create it.[3] For Fiorenza, the term "feminist" implies a liberative approach that sets forth two of its criteria: the liberation of the margins and the restoration of their dignity. Feminism is a concept that raises the consciousness of both females and males and helps them understand the oppressive structures that entangle them. She undertakes a work of reconstruction that is feminist and historical, whose goal is to disrupt prevailing interpretive discourses.

The purpose of Fiorenza's project of reconstructing Christian origins is not to re-enact the pure and true church, whatever shape it might take, but to construct a political and hermeneutical agenda which has its prime locus in the reclamation and transformation of present ecclesial structures. The significance of reconstructing Christian origins is that of reclaiming women's experience of struggle against patriarchal oppression and of liberation in the past as a source of empowerment for women today.[4]

As discussed in the previous chapter, the core of Fiorenza's academic project is the recovery of women's voices in the history of the Church in a distinctively feminist-theological key. The goal of feminist theology is not 'full humanity', since humanity according to her is male-defined. 'The central spiritual and religious feminist quest', Fiorenza maintains, is 'the quest for women's self-affirmation, survival, power, and self-determination.'[5] Therefore, feminist spirituality for Fiorenza is communal, and revelation takes place not in texts or in tradition but in gatherings of women, both past and present. The remembrance of women's sufferings in religious patriarchy is explored structurally in order to set free the emancipatory power of the Christian community. For Fiorenza, this Community is theologically rooted in an egalitarian vision and in altruistic social relationships.[6]

2.2 Religio-Theological Influence

In addition to their socio-economic, religio-cultural contexts, Rayan and Fiorenza were influenced by the religious and theological contexts of their respective times. In analysing the theology of Rayan and Fiorenza the influence of Vatican II and other theological trends that became decisive at the Council were of paramount importance. Vatican II has brought a new wind of change to the Church. Most decisively, Vatican II changed the way the Church understood herself, as her identity went from being a hierarchical authority to a Church conceived as the people of God. Likewise, the pastoral constitution *GS* revealed a new perception of the world and of the mission of the Church. Needless to mention that new impetuses set in motion by Vatican II had its influence on the theologians under study.

Vatican II sought to renew the Church's life and activity in the light of the needs of the contemporary world. Vatican II emphasized the Church's missionary nature, basing it in a dynamic way on the Trinitarian mission itself. The missionary thrust therefore belongs to the very nature of the Christian life, and is also the inspiration behind ecumenism: "that they may all be one, so that the world may believe that you have sent me (Jn 17:21)" (*RM* 1).[7] Starting in the 1960s, a great wind of renewal blew through the churches. Vatican II then gave the best possible theoretical justification to activities developed under the signs of a theology of progress, of authentic secularization and human advancement.

In the years immediately following the Vatican II, Rayan made important contributions to a new understanding of "evangelization" in the Indian and Asian context by elaborating the inner link between evangelization and development. His understanding of development went to the extent of focusing on the qualitative aspects of dignity and holistic growth of the human person in harmony with society and the environment. Furthermore, Rayan as an Indian theologian saw his task of correcting the colonial structures that had first brought the Syrian liturgy and church structure to the Indian Christians, which later was replaced by the Portuguese missionaries by Latin as the language of the Church. The ecumenical openness that characterizes Rayan has gained wide recognition.

In the early 1970s, Rayan was introduced to the International Conference of the EATWOT, and the first generation of Latin American liberation theologians had an impact on Rayan's writings. Rayan, inspired by Jesus, influenced by Gutierrez, the liberation theologian, and formed by Ignatian spirituality and the context of his time, sought to understand that the *Reign of God* is a gift received in history. The implications of it are his call for the establishment of justice and fellowship within economic and political realities and concrete human relationships. Rayan writes:

> The question of justice is intrinsic to human wholeness and salvation, intrinsic to the Gospel Jesus announced and the kingdom he brought, intrinsic to his incarnate person and his risen life, to God's plans and concerns, to the love that lies at the heart of the Christian reality and to the rights, dignity and destiny of every human person and the human community.[8]

Rayan integrated liberation theology with his faith-experience. The purpose of theological thinking is to throw light on the meaning of God's presence in Jesus within economic, cultural and social realities.

Fiorenza found inspiration for her Christology from a speech given in 1852 by Sojourner Truth, "Ain't I a Woman?"[9] Influenced by Truth, Fiorenza applied a critical evaluation and roots her Christological understanding in her own experience of liberation as a source of empowerment. Moreover, Fiorenza's work has elements of liberation theology as she is clearly influenced by Latin American liberation theologians.[10]

> Since feminist theology deals with theological, ecclesial, and cultural criticism and concerns itself with theological analysis of the myths, mechanisms, systems, and institutions that keep women down, it shares in the concerns of and expands critical theology. Insofar as it positively brings to word the new freedom of women and men, insofar as it promotes new symbols, myths, and lifestyles, insofar as it raises new questions and opens different horizons, feminist theology shares in the concerns and goals of liberation theology.[11]

Fiorenza witnessed the shifts from Pre-Vatican II conservatism to the hopeful development associated with the awakening of Vatican II followed by a later conservative regression. She found an imperative in *LG* 32, establishing the equality and dignity of all human beings, based on Gal 3:28. She was influenced by the theology of Vatican II which was in process at the time of her writing, and was beginning to make its impact on the wider Church. Fiorenza's argument can be as an example of the hope for renewal expected from the developments of Vatican II. For instance, she was influenced by the Second Vatican Council's affirmation of universal priesthood of all through the sacrament of baptism. All the faithful share in the common priesthood, each in a varying form of participation in the one priesthood of Christ (LG 12, Heb 13:15).

In Fiorenza's ecclesiology, the following two elements are employed in a very particular way. On the one hand, the critical aspect focuses on the kyriarchal ideology and structures that have permeated the

Church in the course of her history. On the other hand, the liberating or energizing aspect concentrates on establishing the biblical roots of an egalitarian vision of the Church and ministry, as well as articulating how this reality can be re-visioned in the Church today.

2.3 Praxis of Solidarity and Identification

Rayan and Fiorenza rely on their Christian faith for their theologies. However, we observe a fundamental distinction between their theologies in the use of the Bible in their theological method. Scripture has a more central place in Rayan than in Fiorenza.

For Rayan, a theology relevant to the cause of the marginalized and the oppressed emerges also from the thinkers and activists in India/Asia or anywhere in the world, who in loyalty to Jesus have involved themselves in the life of the people and as partners in their struggle for justice. Jesus is present in all people's movements against all forms of domination, oppression, fundamentalism, exploitation, poverty, exclusion and discrimination based on caste, creed and gender. He is present in all women and men who struggle in life to regain their humanity and their rights to live their vocation as human persons with dignity. Rayan discerns the invisible presence of Jesus in all the struggles of people to live in dignity as humans created in the image and likeness of God. He envisages a liberative role for the theologians in general and the Church in particular in relation to the oppressed and the margins. Only through solidarity with the poor and the oppressed can the Church in India work towards emancipation of the downtrodden. In the words of Rayan: Solidarity with the downtrodden is an essential constituent of the Christian Church. It is in choosing to be identified with them that the coming reign of God is discerned, met and served. For Rayan, the struggles of the poor are theologically significant as they are not only "the chief record of God's self-revelation in world history," but because they are also the spaces of "action for a new social order," of God's Reign.[12] They are the victims of unjust social order and structures.

Appropriating the invitation to follow Jesus in accordance with letter to the Hebrews Rayan refers to the plight of the Dalits:

> Hebrews 13 urges us and the Church to go outside the camp and share the degradation of Jesus and his friends, the Jobs and the suffering servants of our times. Not in order to romanticize Dalitness, but to subvert it by loving the oppressed, rebuilding their pride, and enabling them to struggle to equality and freedom.[13]

For Rayan, the text from Heb 13:11-13 spoke about the praxis of Jesus, his suffering outside the camp. It is the episode of God in Jesus, immersing in "the Dalitness of the oppressed in order to rescue its victims and plant them in the realm of freedom, dignity and creative living."[14] The invitation is to join Jesus outside the camp and share degradation and death in the outcast place. According to Rayan, the praxis of Jesus makes it clear that discipleship and the identity of the Church consist not in sharing his throne of glory, but in sharing the cup of suffering and passion in an act of befriending, so as to join in participating in their situation and giving one's life for others.

For Rayan, commitment to the cause of the socially marginalized is an essential element of faith. The Christianness of the Church is made visible in the reliving of Christ's option for the exploited and Christ's actions for liberation are remembered and relived. To have an option for the poor, to share in Jesus' degradation outside the gate would imply a socio-cultural revolution, however fragmentary, that would liberate the oppressed and make them heirs to a world of new relationships where everyone's dignity and rights are upheld and honoured. It calls also for openness, like that of Jesus who transcended the racial and gender prejudices in his interaction with the Samaritan woman and set the servant model of leadership as the defining feature of his community of disciples.[15]

Rayan's theology is very much influenced by the historical Jesus' radical concern for the poor. His personal commitment to Jesus and his faith–experience of God in Jesus is the basis and foundation of his theological pursuit. Jesus Christ is his norm. Hence, theologizing in India, the interpretation of the mystery of Jesus Christ and the self-understanding of his community take place in a multi-religious context and in a situation of massive poverty and oppression. The context of the untold suffering of the peripheries of society with their entire existential crisis becomes the *locus theologicus*. For Rayan, Jesus brings about salvation, realises it historically, and becomes its perfect exemplar. Jesus is unique as a normative manifestation of God for Christians.

The feminist theology of Fiorenza seeks the transformation of the Western Christian tradition through a postmodern hermeneutical response that engages the metaphor of 'otherness'. Fiorenza is also concerned with the history of human suffering. However, her theology is done as a critical response to 'otherness'; so her prime metaphor does not focus on the crisis of identity, but on the struggle for identity by those who have been marginalised by diversity. Accordingly, Fiorenza directs her critical theological gaze towards the complex relational axis of power and domination that frame and support the Western Christianity. She holds that these *kyriarchal* relationships maintain structures and attitudes that mark difference as inferior in order to dominate and marginalise otherness. Fiorenza claims that only when the most marginalised others – those who have been relegated to the bottom of this kyriarchal structure – are positively affirmed can the biblical promise of freedom, justice and well-being for all be made concretely present.[16]

To find and move directly toward the reconstruction of gender equality, Fiorenza turns to Gal 3:27-28. In Christ, Christians became new creations, entered into a new family of believers, and were filled with and lived by the Spirit. Describing this reality, Fiorenza says:

In baptism Christians enter the force field of the Spirit, share in ecstatic experiences, and are 'sent' to proclaim the gospel in the power of the Spirit, attested to by miraculous signs and persuasive eloquence. They have become 'a new creation,' the Spirit-filled people. They all are equal, because they all share in the Spirit, God's Power; they are all called elect and holy because they are adopted by God, all without exception. The

> household of God concretized in the house Church constitutes the new
> family of God, where all without exception are 'sisters and brothers'[17]

Fiorenza seems to imply that all have equal access to the gifts of the Spirit because God's Spirit has been poured out on everyone.

Paraphrasing the First Epistle of Peter 2:9-10 on the occasion of *Women's Ordination Worldwide (WOW)* Fiorenza affirms that women and men are "a chosen race, a royal priesthood, a holy nation, God's own people, in order that we may proclaim the mighty acts of Wisdom-Sophia who has called us out of darkness into G*d's marvellous light."[18] Fiorenza further justifies this, saying, "these words not only have been the *Magna Carta* of the Protestant Reformation but also the guiding star of Vatican II. They affirm the radical equality and priestly dignity of the people of God, of all those called, anointed and gifted in baptism to proclaim the wonderful deeds of Divine Wisdom-Sophia around the world."[19]

It is now clear from the above discussion that, from the very beginning, Christianity was committed to a vision and practice of a radical equality that was inclusive of all. But over the course of time this democratic vision of the Church that embodied the discipleship of equals eventually got compromised. Fiorenza maintains that one can catch a glimpse of this way of life in certain biblical texts, but that these texts represent only the tip of the iceberg that breaks the surface. Her efforts to reconstruct the Christian origins are thus an attempt to uncover the remainder of the iceberg that is submerged.[20] This stance is very important for comprehending and appreciating her contribution to feminist discourse. Fiorenza further particularises and contextualises the situations of oppression and marginalisation of wo/men and other nonpersons. She claims that the lowest position of Western Christianity's kyriarchal structures will always be occupied by the poorest most despised woman. If the biblical promise of freedom, justice and well-being is to be made historically present with any authenticity it must first be made present in the lives of these wo/men. The *ekklēsia* of wo/men is Schüssler's site of transformation.

2.4 Inadequacy of the Hermeneutics of the Bible

The Bible is the indispensable witness of God's revelation in Jesus, and is therefore a primary source for Christian reflection. Both Rayan and Fiorenza emphasize the need for a continuous listening to the Scripture. They both find the existing hermeneutics of the Bible and Christian traditions inadequate and limited and propose a more radical way of interpreting the Scripture and a new way of theologising, by placing more emphasis on the life struggles of the people and the need to usher in God's reign in the concreteness of their lives and not make it an afterlife reality. A glance through all his articles[21] speak of Rayan's dependence on the Bible in delineating his methodology for theological reflection.

Although Fiorenza is a biblical scholar working primarily in the area of feminist hermeneutics, her perspective is influential for feminist theology in general. She explicates that her critical feminist theology of liberation is "indebted to historical-critical, critical-political and liberation theological analyses."[22] For Fiorenza, the critical issue for interpretation is that of securing justice and freedom for all. She argues that biblical interpretation is above all a tool for becoming aware of structures of domination. Hence, biblical hermeneutics is to be used as the base for her feminist theology. Fiorenza starts her hermeneutical consideration with the idea that "all interpretations of texts depend upon the presuppositions, intellectual concepts, politics or prejudices of the interpreter and historian."[23] As a committed Roman Catholic, her approach provides an existential challenge to her own tradition. Further, instead of writing on tablets of stone biblical hermeneutics provides bread for sustenance on the way. Thereby it creates new frameworks that allow for fluidity of margins and the forging of ever-increasing bonds.

As a result, Fiorenza appeals to an understanding of an original or authentic Christian message of equality. She contends that "women were not marginal in the earliest beginnings of Christianity; rather, biblical texts and historical sources produce the marginality of women."[24] Furthermore, Fiorenza contends that "a history of women's biblical interpretation must not be taken as identical with the history of feminist biblical interpretation. Rather, it must be subjected to a critical analysis of its implicit and explicit feminist achievements and possibilities."[25] In the context of women's struggle for self-identity, survival, and liberation in a patriarchal society and Church, she says, that for Christian women, "the Bible has been used as a weapon against us, but at the same time it has a resource for courage, hope and commitment in the struggle. A feminist hermeneutics cannot trust or accept Bible and tradition simply as divine revelation." Therefore, Fiorenza claims: "the litmus test for invoking Scripture as the Word of God must be whether or not biblical texts and traditions seek to end relations of domination and exploitation."[26]

However, one needs to take into account the influence of the Word of God on Fiorenza's vision. She confirms that the Bible has inspired and continues to inspire countless women to speak out and to struggle against injustice, exploitation, and stereotyping. The biblical vision of freedom and wholeness still energizes women in all walks of life to struggle against poverty, unfreedom and degradation. "A feminist reading of the Bible requires both a transformation of patriarchal understanding of God, Scripture, and the Church, and a transformation in the self-understanding of historical-critical scholarship and theological disciplines." Fiorenza being an industrious and creative feminist theologian, her commitment to women's liberation has "a different way and alternative perspective."[27] A question obviously arises as to how and why Fiorenza's commitment to women's liberation is different from that of other feminists. Fiorenza offers an alternative perspective to women's liberation with a feminist model of biblical interpretation. This is to unearth the biblical vision of liberation and salvation, which she developed to empower and to experience the Bible as a resource for women's struggle for liberation in her time, and it has relevance even today. As a result, she develops four structural elements which seem to emerge as constitutive for a feminist biblical interpretation.

Fiorenza utilizes a multidimensional model of a critical feminist hermeneutics, which is first of all, a **hermeneutics of suspicion** with regard to the biblical text. Then a **hermeneutic of proclamation** is to be developed, because she is aware that the Bible still functions as Holy Scripture in Christian communities and so the Word of God has to be brought to the people. As a third step she proposes a **hermeneutics of remembrance** that which moves from the biblical texts about women to the reconstruction of women's history. Finally she calls for a **hermeneutics of creative actualization** where that which has been reconstructed is articulated in an imaginative way for the ongoing history of women. Fiorenza stresses the importance of using these procedures or steps in order to look towards a tomorrow in which women are not marginalized. More specifically, she wants the actualization of the egalitarian community among Jesus' female and male followers, or as she calls it, a "discipleship of equals."[28]

Fiorenza holds the view that a critical feminist hermeneutics of liberation seeks to develop a critical dialectical mode of biblical interpretation. The Bible has to empower women to live with dignity and to continue the struggle to break open those closed patriarchal systems of Church and society. Fiorenza developed an analysis that would lift into consciousness the realization of a critical feminist theology of liberation committed to transformation. Therefore, even if one would have difficulty in accepting her approach, one would nevertheless be awakened to opt for the cause of gender justice and equality and securing freedom for all in the Church and society.

2.5 All-inclusive Integral Approach

Rayan and Fiorenza call for a holistic and inclusive approach in the field of theologizing and a bottom up approach, rather than a top to bottom approach, 'this earthly' rather than the 'other worldly'. Both of them keep liberation, emancipation of the poor and wo/men as the main objective of their theologizing and Christological reflections. They place more emphasis on the life struggles of the people and the need to usher in God's Reign in the concreteness of their lives and don't make it an afterlife reality.

Rayan is fascinated by Jesus' dream of a new human community. He looks at Jesus as one who fosters values like justice, solidarity and intervention on behalf of life and human dignity. He emphasizes the indispensable privilege of the poor and perceived them as the privileged locus of God's incarnation in history. The person and event of Jesus Christ are the norm in this process. God's history is human's history; God is with us (*Immanuel*). Hence he emphasized on an all-inclusive approach: "We want theology to be a service to life and to human wholeness. Our theology will be at the service of those who work, suffer and hope, those who struggle for justice and human dignity for all women and men."[29] Rayan is of the opinion that the starting point for theology must be from where the people are. In other words, if a theology has to be relevant it has to be at the service of life with its all-round needs and possibilities of the people. One needs to take seriously the experiences of human existence and the living experiences of faith.[30]

The basis for Fiorenza's all-inclusive approach is the *Basileia* vision of the Jesus movement and the early Christian community where she finds inclusiveness, participation, wholeness and well-being. For her the *basileia* was the prophetic-liberative central message of Jesus. She looks forward to an all-inclusive transforming vision of the oppressed subjects and stands in solidarity with all those subjects of struggles. Fiorenza argues that neither traditional biblical scholarship nor liberation theology can produce such a vision. Because for her traditional biblical scholarship is insensible to the voices of women and the marginalized, and liberation theology does not adequately emphasize the problem of gender inequality and the oppression of women. For Fiorenza, the all-inclusive transforming vision involves envisioning justice and the well-being of all irrespective of colour, creed and gender.

Fiorenza cites Lk 7:22 as the best example of 'God in the midst of us' in Jesus transforming struggling people into a new humanity.

"Go and tell John what you have seen and heard: the blind receive their sight, the lame walk, the lepers are cleansed, the deaf hear, the dead are raised, the poor have good news brought to them." Fiorenza holds up the *biblical* vision of a festive meal and table sharing to which all are invited in order to celebrate the arrival of '*basileia tou theou*', or 'the *Reign of God*'.

The God of gracious goodness was perceived by Fiorenza as the Sophia-God who according to her is characterised by an "all-inclusive love" for all. She lets the sun shine and the rain fall equally on the righteous as well as the sinner.[31] Jesus' deliberate egalitarian attitude and relations with all and especially with women point to gender equality as intrinsic to God's *basileia*. Women, too, are invited to the table.[32] The symbol of *basileia* expressed hopes for national liberation as well as the transformation of the whole creation by God's intervention. In contrast to Roman imperial domination, Fiorenza writes, the *basileia* of God:

> [It] envisioned an alternative world free of hunger, poverty and domination. This "envisioned' world was already present in the inclusive table community, in healing and liberating practices, and in the domination-free kinship community of the Jesus movement, which found many followers among the poor, the despised, the ill and possessed, the outcasts, the prostitutes, and the "sinners"–women and men.[33]

The *basileia* includes all creation and restores well-being to the subordinated and dispossessed. It stands for partnership, interdependence, equality, and mutual respect between men and women. The *basileia* vision of Jesus and the early Christian movement according to her is a realization of the "discipleship of equals." Fiorenza rightly affirms that Vatican II has rediscovered in her self-understanding as "the People of God" (LG. Ch. 2), the inclusive community-participatory model of the Church that was actualized in the early Christian movements and other reform-movements throughout Christian history. This model of the Church has no place for patriarchal hierarchy. It calls all Christians to ministry, because its constitutive sacrament is baptism.

Fiorenza bases her ecclesiology on the *basileia* proclaimed by Jesus, on the early Christian movement, and on the Council that paves the way for the transformation of the patriarchal-hierarchical church into a discipleship of equals. "The Church as the pilgrim people of God stands in continuity with Israel and in solidarity with all the peoples of the world."[34] The *ekklesia* is etymologically related to the Church understood as a political group of equal citizens.[35] *Ekklesia* is, therefore, the people of God who express their Christian faith in concrete praxis of agape, by eating together, sharing, talking with each other, experiencing God's presence through each other; in doing so, Christians proclaim the Gospel as God's alternative vision for everyone, especially the poor, the outcast, the battered, the majority of whom are women and children dependent on women. Fiorenza proposes a space to live out her all-inclusive vision, "not on the fringes of the church but as the central embodiment and incarnation of a "renewed Church" in solidarity with the oppressed."[36] This vision is a challenge to patriarchal oppression and dehumanization in the Church and society. It is a challenge to personal conversion and structural transformation, because this vision cannot be realized in the present patriarchal structures.

A radical revisioning and re-integrating of ministry in the Church is required to stop the exploitation of women, and to include them in power-sharing with men, thus paving the way to a discipleship community of equals. Jesus' vision of the *basileia*, as understood by Fiorenza, is a discipleship of equals, where the disciples experienced self-worth, human dignity, healing, justice, and well-being.

3. Diverging Themes in Relation to the Theological Vision

This section deals with divergences between Rayan and Fiorenza. We will consider the following three points of divergence:

The Conversation Partner

Fiorenza advocates women to create a space for themselves in order to address their concerns. She, in particular, addresses the Roman Catholic community, whereas Rayan's theological locus is the realm of the poor and the marginalized; he addresses those who are doing theology in these areas. Rayan sees experience as a vital source of theology, one that is understood as reflection on our faith-experience in the actual context of life experiences. He describes his understanding of theology as a critical reflection on the implementation of faith in social action. Rayan's experience-based theology does not start from an "a priori, doctrinal abstract," approach, but it "starts from the concrete reality" of experience, which is "subversive of abstract principles". For Rayan, the actual people and especially the poor and alienated are an indispensable source and place of theology. Closeness and solidarity as well as participating in their struggles is therefore, necessary for theological pursuit. Hence at the very outset Rayan highlights two phases within the experience-based approach: "The first phase raises questions, seeks to criticize and unravel, to speak and to formulate. It then deepens into the second phase, which is one of contemplation, adoration and silence."[37]

While Fiorenza embraces women's experience as normative within her theology, she attempts to maintain the distinctiveness of women's identity within that category. In other words, her work replaces the anthropological construction of woman with a political one. It is clear from her use of the spelling wo/men "to indicate that women are not a unitary social group, but rather are fragmented and fractured by structures of race, class, religion, colonialism, age and health." Women's struggle for liberation, or women-church, is normative with her theology. The significance of reconstructing Christian origins is that of reclaiming women's experience of struggle against patriarchal oppression, and of liberation as a source of empowerment for women today.[38] Fiorenza begins with women's experience and through her theology looks towards a more egalitarian form of Christianity, similar to that of Christ's original group of followers which she calls a "discipleship of equals."[39]

One of the primary things Fiorenza has attempted to do is to offer a feminist theological reconstruction of Christian origins.[40] Accordingly, Fiorenza bases her entire theological journey on a proper footing:

one, on Scripture from where she retrieves the idea of *basileia* and the early Christian movement that lived as an inclusive community; and two, in the light of Vatican II from where she takes the cue for a participatory and all-inclusive vision. The following are the measures taken by her: i), Fiorenza, in her work, seeks to alleviate problems of sexism[41] in Christianity and liberate the marginalized (in particular, marginalized women). She looks to the Bible to interpret it in a way that is redemptive and liberating to women, rather than demeaning and degrading. Fiorenza does not dismiss the Bible outright simply because it has sexist elements. Instead, Fiorenza tries to emphasize what is good about the Bible while at the same time creating an alert to what can be seen as negative. She tries to put it in the correct historical context. ii) Fiorenza creates words and phrases of her own. In order to express her thoughts or experiences in an adequate way free from the clutches of an exclusive language and patriarchal mind-set. She is further motivated in this endeavour through Jesus' vision of the kingdom which includes the praxis of inclusive wholeness.[42]

Fiorenza's vision of the Church arises from her passion to see women's experience as normative within her theology, and her desire to maintain the distinctiveness of women's dignity within that category.[43] Moreover, Fiorenza, along with the liberation theologians emphasises the importance of the context in approaching theology. Therefore, she asserts that "all theology knowingly or not by definition always engaged for or against the oppressed."[44] Her biblically founded vision of the Church is best expressed in the baptismal confession of the early Christians (Gal 3:27-29), that rejected all distinctions of gender, religion, race, class and caste. The Church that she envisages renounces all forms of oppressive practices and calls for the full ecclesial equality through the transformation of its structures.

Jesus' Death on the Cross

The Cross was an instrument of torture and execution at the time of Jesus. But it has become one of the dominant symbols of Christianity since Jesus' crucifixion nearly two thousand years ago. From the beginning, theologians have attempted to understand the meaning of Jesus' death on the Cross, and the triumph of salvation has been assumed since the beginning of Christianity. It is against this background that Fiorenza contends that the Cross proves to be an inadequate symbol for salvation.[45] Fiorenza says that part of the work of the feminist theologians has been to examine the ways in which Christianity has been used to maintain patriarchal and hierarchal systems, and to attempt to refocus the attention of the faith back on Christ who arguably sought to shatter those very systems. Within this context, Fiorenza writes:

> The notion that human sin can be atoned for only through the bloody sacrifice of God's own son serves to support the powerful in a society whose interests in domination and profit demand a multitude of human sacrifices. Most pernicious for women and subordinated men is the notion of redemption as freely chosen obedience and self-giving love. Such a theological belief also supports hierarchical relationships of domination.[46]

This interpretation of Jesus' death on the Cross creates a hypothesis that people choose obedience that requires obedience to authority rather than liberation from oppression. Fiorenza questions the assumption that the choice is both free and desired by God. That is to say that obedience to power can be seen as God's will and it is through obedience that one has the opportunity to receive salvation. Fiorenza underscores the traditional impact of the theological and Christological symbolic system that stresses that God sacrificed his own Son for our sins. Fiorenza says that this, eulogy of obedience allows for the systems of suffering and oppression present in society:

> If one extols the silent and freely chosen suffering of Christ, who was "obedient to death," (Phil. 2:8), as an example to be imitated by all those victimized by patriarchal oppression, particularly by those suffering from domestic and sexual abuse, one not only legitimizes but also enables acts of violence against women and children.[47]

Jesus' death on the Cross was in Schüssler's view, not an atoning sacrifice required by God for humanity to be reconciled with their creator; rather Jesus' death on the Cross was merely the outcome of prophetic practices that offended and threatened those in power.[48] For Fiorenza, the Cross neither invites the oppressed to question their reality and fight for emancipation nor does it function to liberate people from oppressive relationships and social structures. It only helps to maintain those very structures and live in submission to foster the circle of violence engendered by kyriarchal social and ecclesial structures.

Rayan believes that the uniqueness of Jesus lies in his suffering on the Cross in order to identify with those on the edges of life. Obviously Jesus' inclusive love holds not only the Christians but the whole of humanity together by his incarnation. He contends that the Cross, the suffering and death of Jesus are indispensable for God to have any solidarity with the poor and marginalized. Rayan says, "Without the Resurrection the death of Jesus would be more than the death of thousands who have been crucified; it would still be the most shattering affirmation of the downtrodden and the most explosive protest of the poor."[49] He explains Jesus as the one who issues summons to the effect that:

> primacy be given to the quest for the justice of God's Kingdom against the injustice, inequality, oppression and misery of the rule of Caesars and Herods and all powers which prove themselves Satanic by the deprivation, domination and wretchedness they administer; Jesus does this as He invites us to love one another as He loved by providing the health, the bread, the rice, the liberty, the honor and the acceptance of the neglected people's need to become fully themselves and know themselves and one another as God's children.[50]

Within this context, Jesus' death is seen by Rayan as the greatest crisis in the biblical story. He claims, that "was the moment of the greatest tragedy, for the people of Israel who had been living in the hope of the coming of the Messiah put that Messiah to death. This was the tragedy of a people who had been called, nurtured, and sustained by God defeating the purpose of their own call."[51] Contrary to the traditional theological view, Jesus' death on the Cross implied the end of his life (Mk12: 1-12). The death of Jesus was qualified as the death of the one sent as the Messiah of God and therefore implied also the God suffers in solidarity with the suffering humanity.[52] What actually happened was the intervention of the Holy Spirit that ignited the power of the Cross on which Jesus died. For Rayan, Spirit is life-force, energy, animation, courage, character, resolve, enterprise, grit, mettle. He affirms that salvation in Christ is an event in history, and that salvation is a cosmic event. Incarnation of God in Christ is the supreme evidence to show that there is no spirituality of an exclusively vertical dimension.[53] The Cross of Christ rooted in the world is symbolic of the redemption of the entire cosmos.

What is implied in the death of Jesus is that the poor and the marginalized of the present history are a theological, Christological reality. Their responses to situations of sufferings and hunger are theological events. Moreover, the people's struggle for justice and freedom are the best historical embodiments of God's word of human liberation and God's will to human completion. Rayan recognizes the power of the people to change their destiny, and he affirms, "the chief sources of theology; the chief 'record' of God's self-revelation and intervention in history is people."[54] To see the nature of struggle and its connectivity to the ultimate reality is what sustains the hope of God's Reign on the earth. For Rayan, unlike for Schüssler, the message of the Cross lies beyond the Cross: in the empty tomb,[55] in the power of resurrection.

The Resurrection

Although Rayan and Fiorenza have founded their respective theologies on the resurrection, Schüssler's conception of "resurrection" diverges significantly from that of Rayan. Hence, an understanding of the theological character of Schüssler's use of this symbol is vital to a proper apprehension of her work. According to her, Resurrection means that "Jesus, the Living One, goes ahead of us."[56] In contrast to the Cross, the empty tomb reveals to her that "Jesus' struggle did not end with execution and death."

For Fiorenza, an empty tomb has three important meanings for women: First, instead of placing a high value on suffering following from an emphasis on the Cross, shifting the focus results in "the vindication of unjust suffering and death." It is to say that Jesus' suffering is not the end of the story, and the empty tomb gives hope. Second, "the proclamation of the empty tomb locates the Resurrected One on earth, in Galilee," meaning to say that he goes ahead of us and that he opens up a future for us. Third, in the light of Jesus' appearance to women, the empty tomb "celebrates women as faithful witnesses who do not relinquish their commitment and solidarity with those who fall victim in the struggle against dehumanizing powers." Thereby, the empty tomb signifies not the absence but the presence of the Living one on the road ahead in all the struggles for freedom and liberation.[57] In this way she links the Cross to salvation to reclaim this space of resurrection for women's meaning-making in the face of dehumanization and oppression. Moreover, for Fiorenza, 'Resurrection reality' opens up a road ahead into the messianic future.

Rayan maintains that "the Resurrection reveals that Jesus' options had God's approval and that Jesus' death was God's own decisive and critical intervention in the human situation and in human tragedy."[58] In this endeavour the Spirit of God mediates.

> Through the Holy Spirit God raises Jesus from the dead and in the resurrection is resolved not only the crisis of Israel but of all humankind, the crisis caused by the murder of humankind's ultimate meaning. And this resolution comes about by the Spirit's opening of the prison in which humankind had shut itself, the prison of selfishness and death. In the resurrection of Jesus humankind is provided with the possibility of a future. That is why the resurrection must be seen as the work of the Holy Spirit. It is the proof that God will deal adequately with every tragedy of human existence.[59]

In the Christian tradition, the key symbol for this is the life, death and resurrection of Jesus. For, Rayan is convinced of God's liberating action in history. Rayan links the Holy Spirit with freedom and new life. He prefers to use the feminine pronoun for the Spirit. "**The Spirit lives and acts not only in the sacraments of the Church**, in sacred places, persons, sacred Scripture or confines herself to Christian churches religions and believing people. She is **present and active in all ages, all cultures and religions, for She is the atmosphere that envelops the earth, moves in the heart of every reality, and becomes the heart's**

gift to hearts across distinctions of caste, class, sex, race or religion. Rayan's reflections highlight the active presence of the Spirit. **She is resurrecting the earth and fashioning the New Age; She is coming, ever coming with justice and freedom, challenging us to the more, the greater, the finer, and the more human.**[60]

Rayan, reflecting along with Hellwig, considers the Resurrection as the symbol of compassion. And in radical compassion "Jesus enters into our situation of fear and frustration,"[61] accompanies us to the bitter end and effects a breakthrough. "This many facetted compassion of Jesus offers the key to the Resurrection. It is above all else the revelation and realization of God-with-us, and the token of it is that the presence of Jesus has become interior to our consciousness, interior to our freedom, not doing things for us as we remain passive but empowering us."[62] Therefore resurrection means that in Christ Jesus humanity and the cosmos are forgiven and accepted.[63] Hence Rayan claims that at the heart of Jesus' option lies the ruling principle of his life,[64] namely, the primacy and centrality of humans which is affirmed in the parable of judgement: "when was it that we saw you hungry or thirsty?" and in the answer "just as you did it to one of the least of these" (Mt 25:31-46).

In dealing with the theme of convergences and divergences, the focus in this section was twofold: first, to present what these two theologians have in common in terms of their theologizing approaches even though they come from different contexts, backgrounds and ecclesial settings; second, to identify the divergences likely to have arisen out of their specific cultural and religious experiences. Ultimately these reflections are undertaken in order to explore the relevance of their contributions on the life of present day Indian society and the Church.

4. A Critical Appraisal of Rayan and Fiorenza's Theological Avenues
Having dealt with the convergences and divergences in the writings of Rayan and Fiorenza that are likely to have arisen out of their specific cultural and religious contexts and perspectives, our effort in this section is to explore how they harmoniously complement each other.

This critical assessment is done with a view of evolving a Christology for today's milieu. Coming to the point of critical evaluation, we can rightly say that both the scholars are creative and industrious in their thinking. They are very much focused in their respective vision and endeavour. They are to be understood from the view point of their theological terms and the language they use.

Our aim is not to discuss which one or who is better (which is a divisive question), but focus on the commonalities shared within the social and theological construct of the corresponding milieus of Rayan and Fiorenza. Nonetheless, they don't diverge but their emphases are different.[65] Nevertheless, both are valuable in so far as they illumine the thrust of the book. Hence, the thrust of this section is to gather the fruit of chapters two and three, and to map or develop a Christology that emerges from these proponents of theology. An assessment, however, of their theological contribution has much to offer to the Indian context. In this brief section the focus will mainly be on their complementary theological horizons with a view to obtain an understanding of the person and message of Jesus Christ. Keeping this general frame in mind, we consider some points for our ongoing reflection.

Complementary Horizons

Our reading of Rayan and Fiorenza found that the Christian faith is the backbone that runs through their theological vision. We see it, for example, in their ***pro-life approach*** to the Gospel and the person of Jesus for inspiration and insights. They lay emphasis on the gospel-oriented radical changes and transformation in the individuals and in society as a whole. Their goal is the social relevance of the person and message of Jesus. Remaining faithful to their fundamental vision, they propose a more radical way of interpreting the Scripture and a new way of theologising.

The emphasis of Rayan and Fiorenza is on the experience of ***salvation here and now,*** in the concreteness of one's life, and not making it entirely an afterlife reality. This awareness leads them to a common end, that is, an integral, all-inclusive salvation in the field of theologizing. Indeed a bottom up approach, rather than a top to bottom approach lead them to underscore the powerful and transformative power of the person and message of Jesus. The Christological insights of both are very positive, down to earth, rooted in the struggles of the people. They are fully incarnational in their approach, and emphasise kenosis in mission.

In Rayan's and Fiorenza's theology, the past and present are critically reconceived in the service of a hopeful and transformative vision for a new social order. They, in their struggle for *liberation and creation of a new social order*, emphasize the role of the Risen Christ and Holy Spirit in the life of the Church and the world. The social movements are seen as actions of the Holy Spirit. The struggles are emphasized as necessary to restore the human person and to restore the rights that have been denied to people. Since the situation is unjust, it calls for subversion/alteration/ transformation. The revolt is led by God; God joins the struggle to restore humanity to their integral self.

Rayan and Fiorenza use different approaches to interpret the Bible. Both seem to agree that the essence of being relevant consists in two things: acting significantly and speaking effectively. It is sub-human to separate expressing from doing. For Rayan, the Bible and the context are the main basis for theological/Christological reflections. He was in constant dialogue with the context of his time as well as his experience of the divine. For Rayan, society and the social order means the whole humanity without discrimination of caste, creed, colour and gender.

Therefore Rayan says:

There is much Gospel work for the Church to do; many people to look after; several problems to study and solve…great suffering to share in tender compassion; much oppression to criticise and subvert and many movements for human rights, freedom and solidarity with which to collaborate. Jesus needs all of us, women and men alike to accompany him and cooperate in his project of liberating people and making the world human and whole.[66]

Moving a step further, Fiorenza emphasizes the Christian traditions, history of the Israelites and the early Christian communities as reference points of her liberationist theological approach.

Differing Perspectives

Fiorenza's interest lies in **institutional transformation** and, as a consequence, her analysis emphasizes structural and external forms of oppression. She qualifies the understanding of the concept poor from two angles: one, the poor are mostly women, and two, women are not only the 'other' but also the "other of the others." Fiorenza views the poor from the perspective of *basileia - as* "God in the midst of us" and the *ekklesia -* as a "political group of equal citizens."[67]

Fiorenza, possessing a liberationist perspective, has difficulty in accepting liberation theology's view of Scripture. Therefore, Fiorenza speaks of a feminist hermeneutics on the one hand, which shares in the critical methods of historical scholarship and theological goals of liberation theologies on the other. It can be argued that the liberation theologians focus on God's liberating activity in history, the kernel of which is found in the book of Exodus.[68] Whereas feminist liberation theologians look for a liberating theme, tradition or a text as a hermeneutical key in order to reclaim the authority of Scripture for liberation.[69] Experience of women and the experience in a form of community are considered by Fiorenza as the hermeneutical center for feminist biblical interpretation and the community as the *ekklesia of wo/men*, or "women-church."[70] This realization makes one affirm one's own dignity and respect, the worth of everyone. To arrive at her vision, Fiorenza proposes a multifaceted hermeneutic of a seven step method.[71] Therefore, the central feminist quest is the quest for women's self-affirmation, survival, liberation from the patriarchal alienation, marginalization and oppression.[72] Feminist spirituality is communal, and revelation takes place not in texts and tradition but in the gathering of women, *ekklesia* of women, past as well as present.

Rayan's theology differs from that of Fiorenza in that he starts with an analysis of the context, as he wants to respond to the cries of the people arising from it. His theology is contextual, for we can distinguish it by social groups such as the poor, women, blacks, *Dalit*s and indigenous peoples. The realities of class, caste, patriarchy and ethnicity and of local, regional and global economy are intertwined. Therefore, society for Rayan is the whole humanity without discrimination of class, creed, colour or nationality. Rayan affirms that every person is a gift of God, a reflection of the image of God. Everyone is sacred. Human persons experience their dignity and respect by living in a community that treasures every person as God's image. Such "communities of men and women are the only place of life-giving encounter and communion with God." [73]

Human society is to be free from discriminations to embody the *Reign of God*. In order to keep alive the equilibrium Rayan proposes certain directives for a new social order where equality, freedom, love, justice and peace would prevail. Rayan believes that God makes His salvation possible and available in His own time and way to all men and women everywhere throughout history.[74] Rayan sees justice as a theme not alien to God who loves us unconditionally. In His love God provides for the sustenance of every woman and man.[75] Therefore, Rayan, advocates the *Reign of God* as the epitome, as the symbol or a project of non-oppressive, just and new social order.

What Rayan wants to communicate is that the earthly society is not the end in itself for humanity but God is the foundation of human society. Therefore, the *Reign of God* as the foundation and end persuades the Church to take the task as a gift in creating a new social order based on principles of the *Reign of God* – love, freedom, justice and peace. Rayan is also aware of the struggle it entails – struggle for preservation of life giving structures of freedom, creativity, and communication at all levels, economic, political, cultural and human.[76]

Fiorenza realizes that women outnumber the rest among the poor. Therefore, for her it is the wo/men and their lives that are the core experiences or data. Their experience becomes the starting and ending of her feminist theologizing. However much she may insist on wo/men, still Fiorenza is one sided in her approach. Rayan includes the plight and place of women in his liberationist approach, whereas Fiorenza brings them rightly to prominence for a new humanity. What is lacking in Rayan is complemented by Fiorenza.

Christological Unity

Fiorenza understands the Jesus movement as an egalitarian Jewish movement of wo/men. She perceives the Jesus movement as a prophetic movement of Divine-Sophia-Wisdom. This tradition further manifests the self-understanding of the Jewish Galilean *basileia* of God movement as an ongoing and inclusive movement of prophets and messengers sent to Israel by Divine-Wisdom. The *basileia* movement is thus best understood as a Wisdom/Sophia movement in which Jesus is *primus inter pares*, that is, first among equals. The emancipatory struggle of biblical wo/men is seen within the wider context of cultural-political-religious struggle. Writing from a feminist perspective, Fiorenza sees the *basileia* of God as experienced in the healing activity of Jesus. Jesus' *basileia* makes people whole, healthy, cleansed and strong. It restores people's humanity and life.[77] It is being realized where people are liberated from oppressive power structures and dehumanizing power systems.

For Fiorenza, the resurrection of Jesus means that he is not just a memory, rather he is the Living One who is "going ahead" as a "path Finder" in the emancipatory struggle for a society of justice, liberation and freedom from *kyriarchal* oppression. He is "going ahead" in wo/men's struggle to mend the ways.[78] In other words, her perception of the Jesus movement as emancipatory *basileia* of God movement is the "envisioned" world that is already anticipated in the inclusive table-sharing, in the healing and liberating practices, as well as in the domination-free-kingship community which is a vision of God's alternative world of justice and salvation. She offers a Christology that seeks to discover the true historical Jesus - A Christology that is very much experiential and based on the pluralistic subjective feminine experience of Jesus by women in real life contexts. It is that which empowers women and liberates all the oppressed masses irrespective of race, class, colour or gender. In other words, it is a Christology that excludes none from the *Reign of God*.

As far as we have read and understood Rayan, he is very much influenced by the historical Jesus' radical concern for the poor. In the words of Samuel Rayan:

> Throughout history the masses have struggled for life, food and home, for land, honour and happiness. They have fought for freedom, dignity, community and peace. People have battled against forces of domination, oppression and exploitation; against poverty, exclusion and discrimination based on colour, race, gender and religion; against egoism, greed and hatred, and against adversities, suffering and loneliness. They have striven for meaning and truth as well as fuller knowledge, finer skills and a human future.[79]

Rayan has passionately opted for a Christology from below: A God who became a rejected human being in Jesus, a suffering and oppressed God who is one with the untouchables and outcasts of all times everywhere. A Christology that partakes in human suffering and continues to suffer wherever there is suffering and injustice and exploitation and violence, a Christology to be at the service to life and to human wholeness, a Christology that is at the service of those who work, suffer, and hope, those who struggle for justice and human dignity for all men and women. Such a Christology will be ever springing forth at the meeting point of faith and the reality of emerging India. The encounter of these two will illumine each other's depths, question and challenge each other, enable each other to new self-understanding, to fresh interpretations of human hope, to committed action and profounder silence.[80]

The Christology of Rayan is a Christology influenced by the sufferings of humanity. It is a Christology of the poor and the oppressed. Here is a Christology of divine compassion that motivates the followers of Jesus to commit themselves radically for the liberation of the poor and the oppressed. We find a Christ as the giver of the Spirit who liberates one from bondage, one who instills a responsibility for social action.

Ultimately his Christology reveals more of God in his humanity rather than in his divinity. Liberating the oppressed from the unjust structures is an indispensable dimension of the growth of the *Reign of God*.[81] The *Reign of God* is not merely a transcendent reality both now and in the future. It is also a visible reality in history and in the community. It is being experienced when God's love and concern is being concretised in the love and concern of human beings for each other.[82]

5. Critique of Fiorenza's Christology

Fiorenza makes a unique contribution to Christology. On the one hand, she looks at biblical Christology from a critical feminist perspective in the tradition of liberation theology. In view of liberating women from the patriarchal power structures operative in culture and religion, Fiorenza and many Christian feminists have begun to critique the way women were treated in the Church and in the society at large.[83] According to Fiorenza, the criterion and norm of feminist Christian theology cannot be "from the option of Jesus for the poor and outcast." Instead, feminist theology has to be grounded on "wo/men's struggles for the transformation of *kyriarchy*."[84] Therefore, I for one believe that the foundation of Christian feminist theology is not mere wo/men's struggles, but seen from the perspective of the victims, Jesus chose a life-style in opposition to unjust and oppressive systems of his time, which eventually led him to the Cross. Therefore, this section hopes to clarify or critique some of the Christological dimensions of Fiorenza.

Theology of the Cross

The death of Jesus on the Cross was a historical event witnessed by his disciples and others who were with them on Calvary. The New Testament especially the gospels and the Pauline letters report that Jesus accepted the possibility of death on the Cross out of obedience to his mission. The death of Jesus on the Cross is interpreted as an act of obedience to God; and the Cross as symbol of obedience. Fiorenza finds this interpretation as oppressive for women. But she fails to see that the Cross does not call for obedience to oppressive power structures.

In fact, on the contrary, the Cross was a loud protest of God against all exploitation. The Cross is a symbol of obedience that calls the victims and as well the oppressors to obey to the will of God, who is God of justice and love. Rayan succinctly affirms it saying that Jesus' Cross is "a symbol of defiance of and resistance to evil."[85]

Schillebeeckx states that "Jesus' death on the Cross is the consequence of a life in radical service of justice and love, a consequence of his option for the poor and outcast, of a choice for his people suffering under exploitation and oppression."[86] Therefore, "the Cross of Christ emptied of its power, [women and] man no longer has roots, [she] he no longer has prospects; [she] he is destroyed!"[87] This is the cry of the 21st century. The traditional theology of the Cross affirms that the Cross exemplifies and vindicates with absolute assurance the essence and praxis of Jesus, who in his freedom and love chose to identify with the weak and the foolish and opposes the wise and the strong. Jesus died for justice, for doing good, for taking sides with the poor, the sick, the women and the children. "By his glorious Cross, Christ has won salvation for all. He redeemed them from the sin that held them in bondage. The *Catechism of the Catholic Church* teaches: "For freedom Christ has set us free" (No 1741).

Fiorenza evaluates theology of the Cross and underscores the point that traditional theologies of redemption and the Cross strengthen the kyriarchal societal values and sentiments. In other words, such a theological belief either contributes to subjugate women under male power, and women accept sufferings in their abusive relationships as God's will or it supports hierarchical relationships of domination.[88] Consequently, the theology of the Cross as it is predominantly understood does not function as a salvific symbol for Fiorenza in particular and some women in general. Jesus' death on the Cross, was in Fiorenza's view not an atoning sacrifice required by God for humanity to be reconciled with their creator; rather Jesus' death on the Cross was merely the outcome of prophetic practices that offended and threatened those in power.[89]

According to Fiorenza, the theologically incorrect interpretation of Jesus' suffering and Cross has contributed *to the subjugation of women* in accepting the sufferings in an abusive relationship as God's will or a "misplaced notion of imitating Jesus reinforces",[90] a model *that creates* "the scapegoat syndrome for women."[91] Shalini Mulackal affirms the idea of Fiorenza saying that "Jesus' suffering and death are very significant for [Indian] Asian women. Given the situation of suffering and pain, the most prevailing image of Jesus among the [Indian] Asian women's theological expressions is the image of the suffering servant."[92] According to Anselm the way to restore God's creation and prevent human beings from being punished was Jesus Christ. For him, because Jesus is both human and divine, he is able to pay humanity's debt to God, but because he is sinless he also does not deserve to be punished. In this way, Jesus' death "sets right the order of justice and accomplishes redemption for human beings." In other words, Jesus died so that humans might live.

From this Anselmian understanding of the Cross and salvation emerges the central image of Christ on the Cross as the savior of the world [which] communicates the message that suffering is redemptive. Anselm's theory of atonement is seen as promoting the idea that "redemption and salvation are wrought through sacrifice, submission, surrender, freely chosen suffering, scapegoating, and violence against the innocent,"[93] In other words, suffering is necessary for salvation. It has come under recent criticism. Fiorenza is of the view that this interpretation of the Cross does not contribute towards the liberation of women from the oppressive structures in which they live.

In Jesus Christ, God is with all those who suffer, especially the poor, the women, the oppressed, the untouchables, the persecuted and the marginalized. For Rayan, "No Christian faith is possible in India today without identification with them and commitment to their Resurrection from the tombs in which they are held guarded by the musclemen of the ruling castes and classes according to the law and otherwise."[94] Therefore "Jesus' death is God's way of expressing his solidarity with the victims."[95]

On a personal note, I am all the more convinced that the image of the suffering servant is an act of solidarity with the victims. Solidarity in the Bible is reflected as a campaign against evil in which God sides with the poor and the oppressed, to challenge the unjust and oppressive systems. The notion of solidarity acquires a new meaning in the life, ministry and death of Jesus Christ. By his death on the Cross Jesus revealed the God of goodness and God's all-inclusive love. Therefore, Jesus death on the Cross does not encourage one to suffer for no reason rather he challenges everyone to resist injustice and dehumanizing structures of power towards the **liberation** of women and men.

In the words of Pope Francis: "We have an anchor: by His Cross we have been saved. We have a rudder: by His Cross we have been redeemed. We have a hope: by His Cross we have been healed and embraced so that nothing and no one can separate us from His redeeming love." [96] By Jesus' Cross the humanity has been saved in order to embrace hope and let it strengthen and sustain all measures and all possible avenues for solidarity, for helping us protect ourselves and others.

Empty Tomb

For Fiorenza, the resurrection of Jesus means that He is not just a memory, rather he is the Living One who is "going ahead" as a "path Finder" in the emancipatory struggle for a society of justice, liberation and freedom from *kyriarchal* oppression. He is "going ahead" in wo/men's struggle to mend the ways. [97] The tomb is empty! According to Fiorenza, it indicates the Resurrected One on earth in Galilee. Most significantly, it affirms that Jesus' struggle did not end with execution and death. But the Living One could be found only when one experiences that "he is ahead of us" and that he opens up a future for us. [98] Although, Fiorenza's attempt to sidestep the importance and relevance of the Cross and focus upon the empty tomb as an alternative symbol of salvation, and life in Christ is like seeing the world with one eye only. Empty tomb cannot be separated from Calvary. It is from Calvary one goes to the tomb/empty tomb and from the empty tomb one is guided back to meet the Living Christ. Therefore, the focus is on the Crucified Lord who confined himself to the Tomb in order to draw humanity out of death. The texts of the empty tomb tradition include the suffering, death and resurrection of Jesus.

Walter Kasper affirms that "the Resurrection is not historically verifiable, but only faith in it of the first witnesses and the fact, among others, of the empty tomb. The fact of the empty tomb would be very far from providing any proof of the Resurrection. The fact of the empty tomb is ambiguous. Even in Scripture one sees the hypotheses of theft or removal of the body (Mt 27:64; 28:1ff; Jn 20:13ff). The empty tomb is simply a sign on the way to faith and a sign for someone who already believes",[99] but it is an essentially indispensable factor. The crucified-died-risen-living Christ is one reality. It is this Jesus who tells the women near the empty tomb to go and tell his brothers that they will see him to Galilee.

The empty tomb in itself does not prove the resurrection, it is an ambivalent symbol. Because belief in the empty tomb is not a part of Christian faith. Christian faith is in the Risen Jesus. Christian faith is the effect of the appearance-experiences. The empty tomb itself is not historiographical evidence for the resurrection of Jesus; the empty tomb does not say anything about the nature of the resurrection of the risen body.[100] Seen from the perspective of revelation, the Resurrection is God's definitive self-disclosure which gathers up the earthly Jesus and establishes him in a radically new mode of being and activity. Moreover, the power of the Resurrection cannot be measured or planned by human mind or programs. It escapes human control, as the Resurrection of Christ brought to nothing the frail human efforts to keep Christ in the grave. Yes, the women were made the first privileged witnesses and messengers of the Good News that Jesus is living. But the Scripture also tells us that they were instructed to go straight to the Apostles with the message. Feminist emancipation therefore is something "mysterious" and so one's efforts alone are futile. Women and men are to join hands with each other for the liberation of the oppressed even to the extent of becoming a victim after the example of Jesus for a noble cause.

Wisdom's Messenger

Christologically, Fiorenza believes that it is more important to focus on the witness of the earliest community gathered around Jesus, who perpetuated his message, rather than on Jesus himself. Fiorenza unlike her other contemporaries, (for example Mary Daly who would contend that Jesus has no relevance for women or Reuther, who would ask whether Jesus in his maleness can help or save women), looks to the women around Jesus as indicators of Jesus' relevance. Fiorenza employs the concept of Wisdom as a hermeneutical clue for discovering who Jesus was and can be for women.[101] What does she mean here? According to her Jesus is not Wisdom personified but Wisdom's messenger. She sees Wisdom/Sophia as God, who sends Jesus as her Wisdom's representative and not an incarnation of Sophia/ Wisdom. But later with redaction of Q saying sources have shifted the focus from Jesus as Wisdom's messenger to Jesus as Sophia/Wisdom herself.[102] According to Fiorenza, Jesus was a prophet of God who saw himself as Sophia or Wisdom and led a renewal movement that stood in continuity with an egalitarian tradition within Judaism that was critical of the dominant tradition of Jewish patriarchalism. Fiorenza needs to be consistent in the use of her expressions and understanding.

Christian Women around Jesus

Fiorenza, being a feminist, views Jesus through the lens of ongoing gender discrimination. She is convinced of her stand that women were always present in the Church but their presence has been intentionally downplayed by the patriarchal ideology. Women were always around by Jesus. Therefore, Fiorenza in pursuing her hermeneutical theory with regard to the texts of the Early Christian Church believes that one must approach the text with a "hermeneutics of suspicion". Fiorenza is reluctant to perceive Jesus as divine because of the gender attributed to the divine, which makes her unwilling to see Christ as a vicarious Saviour who brings salvation to humanity, and without their participation. The death of Jesus is viewed not as salvific because of the implications that suffering is redemptive in and of itself, that validating women's unjust suffering. Nevertheless, Fiorenza does not totally abandon on the role played by Jesus, but instead incorporated as the one who goes ahead in the pursuit of women's empowerment and wellbeing. Jesus is the manifestation of the transformation of humanity in the struggle for wholeness and full humanity.

We understand the Scripture in the light of our context. Christians believe that God speaks through the Bible, because it is the normative revelation to Christians. For feminist theology, women's experience serves as both source and norm. And for Christians, Jesus Christ is the primary lens for understanding both human and divine partnership. In a patriarchal, androcentric society of the first century Palestine, where women were numbered among children and slaves as minors with diminished responsibility, and had a restricted role in worship and in public life, Jesus admitted them into his company as disciples. Therefore, the goal should not be to diminish males but to affirm both women and men along with all races and social groups.

The God-experience of Jesus and his identification with the poor and the marginalized of his time are thus joined together finding a powerful expression in three symbols all of which are basic to Christian life. The symbols are the Incarnation, the Cross and the Resurrection. The shedding of blood and sacrificing of his life on the Cross, as willed by God according to the *Kerygma*-based faith, for the redemption of humankind is a deep spiritual experience of millions even today. The Cross is therefore, the outcome of a life of solidarity with the poor and the outcast, and the resurrection of Jesus, is God's overwhelming answer to our cry for life.

A critical collaboration and coordination between the two minds – Rayan and Fiorenza – has much to offer to the 21st century society and the Church. Living in the second decade of the third Millennium, the need to search for alternative articulations of Christology is an urgent one. Every Christology has its origin in Jesus Christ. The following section of this chapter attempts to outline a Christological vision which emerges primarily from the theological vision of Rayan and Fiorenza coupled with my personal reflection. Hence, the focus is to explore who Jesus Christ is for today's India.[103]

6. An Emerging Christology for 21st Century India

Having explored Rayan and Fiorenza's interpretations of Jesus and his message in chapters two and three, the present section is an attempt to articulate some of the key features of a relevant Christology that emerge primarily from their Christological vision.[104] The Christological visions of Rayan and Fiorenza is uniquely coloured by the experiences of oppression and poverty, especially of those on the edges of society of their respective contexts. Premising upon the preceding analysis, the main thrust of this chapter is to develop a Christology for the liberation of society in India today. Before we proceed to consider the Jesus who emerges in the Christological visions of Rayan and Fiorenza, a brief discussion on the conceptual understanding of Christology will serve as a platform for our exploration of the theme. Hence this section is developed in the following way: i) concept of Christology; ii) key Christological questions; and, iii) Christological approach iv) A Christology of *Presence-Solidarity*.

Conceptual Consideration of Christology

Christology has been a subject of interpretation and reinterpretation down the history of the Church. Both at the popular and the academic levels, Jesus continues to fascinate over the minds and hearts of people. By Christology we mean a Christian theological interpretation of Jesus Christ in relation to God, human beings and the world. Each generation has answered the basic question in a variety of ways. Each one reflects something of the context one comes from and how its author experienced it. Yet each also reflects something of Jesus, who first asked this question: "Who do you say that I am?" Our question today would be: Who is Jesus for the 21st century Indian context? It is as pressing today as it was for the first Christians. Therefore there are diverse Christologies adding new voices to the dialogue about Jesus, his saving significance, and the meaning of life that has been on-going ever since his ministry began.[105] The person of Jesus Christ stands at the center of Christian faith and theology. "While no theology can confine itself exclusively to Christology, no Christian theology would be complete without serious reflection on Jesus Christ."[106] Put simply, Christianity is founded on Jesus Christ, the revelation and revealer of the Father in the Spirit. The Spirit is the bond of unity of the Father and the Son.[107] Without Jesus, there is no Christianity; and, without knowing Jesus, it is impossible for anyone to be an authentic follower of Jesus. We must, therefore, encounter Jesus in faith.

During the subsequent centuries up until now, theology has taken its point of departure from these early formulations and has refined them. Still, the search continues. Karl Rahner says that human beings by nature are self-transcending which is achieved through God's self-communication.[108] The meeting point is always in a historical context and, for us Christians, Jesus Christ embodies a unique and complete point of contact between God's self-communication and human's self-transcendence. That is, Christians believe that at a particular time in history God willed to reveal himself in the person of Jesus Christ for the redemption of humankind (*DV* 4). This man/human, Jesus of Nazareth, is God's Son. Consequently the memory of Jesus Christ "is amazingly rich, dazzlingly vivid and yet unbelievably baffling. This memory is not an event of the past but an ever present one; a memory that can never be evaporated of its depths of unfathomable mystery, that is 'Christ himself'" (Col 2:2).[109] One particular interpretation cannot capture the mystery of the person of Jesus completely. This is one of the reasons why we have many interpretations. In fact every Christology is a response to that – 'come and see' invitation of Jesus: "What are you looking for?" (Jn 1:38).

The context in which Jesus lived, related and interrelated was Palestine which at that time was a colony of the Roman Empire that imposed very heavy taxation, coupled with cultural imperialism on a people who were firmly convinced that they were a chosen people. Palestine was full of contradictions and conflicts: the rulers who are supposed to take care of the subjects preyed on them; the religious authorities who were to stand as a mediator between God and common people became rich and perverse and worshipped mammon; and a land which was a gift from God to Israelites was no more with them; they were forced to live under a foreign rule. Jesus came as the promised Prophet, Priest, and King, the one worthy and was able to live and speak the truth in every situation, able to be the mediator between God and humans, and able to reign in righteousness and peace.

For an Indian Christian theology, the Indian reality becomes the *locus theologicus* for its reflections and interpretation. As discussed in chapter one, the Indian reality encompasses two aspects: the socio-economic and political reality, and the religio-cultural reality. The underpinning incisive growth of poverty, casteism, atrocities, human trafficking, patriarchy and gender discrimination mark the socio-economic context of the 21st century India. Caste system, patriarchy and gender discrimination are resting on a religious base. The serious challenges posed by poverty, exploitation, gender discrimination, communalism and religious fundamentalism in India today call for a new approach. Christology always played a pivotal role in the discussion on the alleviation and eradication of poverty in Christian theology.

6.1 Key Questions

The key questions are the following: How am I, as an Indian Christian woman, to speak of Jesus Christ in the face of negative experiences of human life? How does one draw a Christological framework that is rooted in people's struggle for self-determination and envision a praxis of transformation? Could the Christological approach resist violence, affirm life, enthuse hope, make peace and generate equality? Hence we ask:

i)   What is our conception of this emerging Christology?

ii) What are we to be transformed from and what we are to be transformed for?

iii) How does the person and message of Jesus Christ become relevant today?

iv) What are the possible ways of the transformative presence of Jesus in the 21st century India?

These questions deal mainly with developing a Christology for a new social order as the groundwork for establishing justice and right in favour of the poor and the discriminated. That is to say, it is to bring about new hope and life to people who experience injustice, poverty, violence and all forms of oppression.

The Christological Approach

Our Christological approach begins with God's immense love for humanity in the Word who became flesh. From here stems the hope of us, Christians, who in our poverty know that we are loved, visited and accompanied by God; we look at the world and history as the place where we walk together with him and with each other, toward the new heaven and the new earth. Jesus' experience of God as *Abba* permeated his life. First, the Triune God decides that the Word be born as one among us. The mystery of God's choice to walk among humans ushers in a new and lasting expression of divine poverty and solidarity. Second, by the anointing with the Spirit at the Jordan river during his baptism, Jesus was equipped to carry out his prophetic mission. Third, Jesus is seen as the one who subverts the dominant structures of the time with a different vision of reality and human community.[110] He proclaims the kingdom of equality, justice and love through his word and deed. The values of the kingdom he preached were subversive in relation to the values of the society in which he lived. Fourth, he had to pay a heavy price by embracing the Cross, to let the Jews know, "the truth will set you free" (Jn 8:32b). The death of Jesus was inevitable for this-worldly transformative vision. Finally, in Jesus the Risen Lord is born a new promise, a new world, a new age of freedom and abundance of life, the outpouring of the Holy Spirit, and also a world that can always be renewed.

6.2 A Christology of Presence – Solidarity

Having focused on the landmark works of two prominent theologians, Rayan and Fiorenza, we have taken note of the areas where their perspectives diverge, converge and complement each other in varying dimensions of their theological vision. Now to respond to Jesus' question: 'Who do you say that I am?' is to depict various portraits of Jesus so as to propose a Christology of *Presence-Solidarity* for India of today. This hyphenated phrase is borrowed from Rayan.[111] This hyphenated phrase of Rayan aptly includes, in my opinion, the Christological thrust of Fiorenza also. The final section of this dissertation will deal with the implications of Jesus' *Presence-Solidarity* for today.

In the Gospel of Matthew, God's saving presence and solidarity is an all-encompassing experience, which is grounded in the reality of God-is-with-us in Jesus Christ. What permeates the entire gospel is the presence of Jesus within the community as *Immanuel*. "God's presence renews; his solidarity is transformative. His being with us already marks the dawn of a new age, and carries the promise of the day." The substance of the promise and grace enshrined in it reappears in Mt 28:20 as the crowning good news of the assurance of companionship of the Risen Jesus "to the end of time" (28:18-20).[112]

Presence-Solidarity can be defined as the very nature of God and is reflected in the communion of three persons in the Trinity impelled by love. The Trinitarian solidarity finds its human face in the activity of God starting from the creation account, moving through the Exodus event and culminating in the person of Jesus. The theological grounding of solidarity as both virtue and social principle is Christological at its core and Trinitarian in its approach:

> This communitarian character is perfected and fulfilled in the work of Jesus Christ, for the Word made flesh willed to share in human fellowship. He was present at the wedding feast at Cana, he visited the house of Zacchaeus, he sat down with the publicans and sinners. In revealing the Father's love and man's [and woman's] sublime calling he made use

of the most ordinary things of social life and illustrated his words with expressions and imagery from everyday life. He sanctified those human ties, above all family ties, which are the basis of social structures (GS 32).

Presence-Solidarity is the synthesis of God's presence here and now in today's context. The word Emmanuel means God-with –us; but it encompasses all and gives meaning to different kinds of people here and now. In Jesus Christ it is always possible to recognise the living sign of that measureless and transcendent love of God-with-us, who takes on the infirmities of his people, walks with them, saves them and makes them one. Jesus is the model of solidarity in his very person-hypostatic union.[113]

Thus the phrase *Presence-Solidarity* acquires a new meaning in the life and ministry of Jesus Christ. Realising his mission, "Jesus identifies Himself with the poor and the oppressed, in order to show them an active and effective concern."[114] "Jesus' identification with the poor, and his confrontation with the religiously and politically powerful of his time, led him inevitably to the conflict that culminated on the Cross."[115] "Thus Jesus' solidarity with the poor found its final and ultimate expression on the Cross."[116]

The path of God-in-Jesus begins on the margins: his concern goes for the poor and the outcasts, his action for a different social order sprung from his direct, first-hand knowledge of the people of his time, the conditions in which they lived.[117] In this sense the term 'presence' can be context specific, thereby all the individuals are empowered for an action that promotes solidarity. Rayan's and as well Fiorenza's concern for the poor and the marginalized stem from a simple hermeneutical principle that underlies their reading of the gospel.[118] This hermeneutics would emphasize over and above the ecclesial responsibility to enter into solidarity with the poor and undertake a mission of transformation from the shackles of poverty, exploitation, discrimination, casteism and violence.

The Christological language of Rayan and Fiorenza coincides with the teaching of *Evangelii Gaudium*.[119] Contemplating the mystery of God become human, Pope Francis' homily on Christmas midnight Mass, (Dec. 24, 2013) summarizes some of the images of Jesus that are reflected from the manger at St. Peter's Basilica:

> The grace which was revealed in our world is Jesus, born of the Virgin Mary, true man and true God. He has entered our history; he has shared our journey. He came to free us from darkness and to grant us light. In him was revealed the grace, the mercy, and the tender love of the Father: Jesus is Love incarnate. He is not simply a teacher of wisdom; he is not an ideal for which we strive while knowing that we are hopelessly distant from it. He is the meaning of life and history, who has pitched his tent in our midst.[120]

In Jesus Christ, the definitive encounter with the Word made flesh, with the God who has become the definitive revelation in Christ takes place in history. God's presence with us becomes explicit in Christic presence. George Soares-Prabhu says, "If it is the God-experience of Jesus that empowers him to identify with the poor and confront the rich, it is an act of solidarity with the poor that is the occasion for his experience of God."[121]

Christian thinking and the Christian message begin with the person, the message and the ministry of Jesus Christ. He is the beginning and the end, the *alpha* and the *omega*, everything that is Christian springs from him. We have culled out nine images that have emerged from the Christological insights of Rayan and Fiorenza and would describe it as a Christology of *Presence-Solidarity* for the socio-economic and cultural context of 21st century India.

Jesus: The Love Incarnate

Jesus is the 'Love incarnate' or the embodiment of God's love on earth, the *Immanuel*. "*Immanuel* or God-with-us is not a static presence among us of God-in-Jesus; rather an assurance of God's dynamic presence, active to save among us, and involves solidarity."[122] The incarnation is the very birth of Jesus as God's solidarity with humanity in Jesus.[123]

He commits himself to our liberation and salvation, risking life and laying it down in solidarity. God-in-Jesus shares with us his solidarity with humanity in Jesus. St Paul affirms that Jesus, who was in the form of God, emptied himself, and took the form of a slave (Phil 2:6-9). Soares-Prabhu rightly says that the incarnation is "the anticipation of Jesus' identification with the poor," expressed vividly and tangibly through his "consistent and progressive identification with the poor," and the Cross is "the ultimate expression"[124] of his *Presence-Solidarity* with the margins of society.

What John the evangelist announces is that in Jesus the enduring Word has become transient flesh and all humankind has been divinized in him (Jn 1:14). Soares-Prabhu says that "all humankind is divinized in Jesus." Therefore, what happens to ONE affects all. Humankind thus "becomes the locus of our encounter with God." We find it articulated in Matthew's language: "Truly I tell you, just as you did it to one of the least of these who are members of my family, you did it to me" (Mt 25:40). Therefore the mystery of incarnation – God's self-expression is a paradigm par *excellence* in the Indian context where the majority of the people are economically poor and socio-culturally oppressed. The mystery of God becoming human in Jesus is an expression of God's solidarity with the poor and their suffering. Therefore, the incarnation is always a call to follow Jesus in his solidarity with humankind, expressed concretely through his consistent and progressive identification with the poor.[125] The birth of Christ is the first sending which inaugurates the salvific action of God from the extreme periphery of rejection and displacement of the family of Nazareth.

Jesus: The Supreme Symbol of the Spirit

The Gospel of Luke tells us that after spending forty days in the wilderness "where he was tempted by the devil," Jesus returned "filled with the power of the Spirit, to Galilee" (Lk 4:1-2, 14). Luke implies that by the anointing with the Spirit at Jordan during his baptism, Jesus was equipped to carry out his prophetic mission, what he spells out in terms of the quotation from Isaiah: "The Spirit of the Lord is upon me, because he has anointed me to preach Good News to the poor…" (Lk 4:18-19). Since then the nature of Jesus' power was the Spirit who was upon him or the Wisdom teacher endowed with the Holy Spirit.[126] Where did Jesus get this inherent power? Luke 3:16 says that it was given to him by God through the Holy Spirit. Jesus' transformative presence is always in relation to the people of his time. Here the solidarity of Jesus is interrupted at the Jordan. Here we find a 'movement' on the part of Jesus who enters into the experience of the other (the crowd) to be present in solidarity, vulnerability, to be affected by the experience of the other and communion of experience.[127] The whole being of Jesus with his entire life is deeply rooted in and permeated by the Holy Spirit. His very conception was initiated by the Spirit's overshadowing of Mary. But it was at his baptism in the Jordan that the Spirit took charge of Jesus, of his life, and of his world.

Empowered and ennobled by the *Abba* experience, Jesus extends his horizons and sees beyond the fears and cares of the world. The world is full of icons of the Holy Spirit in the people who, like Jesus, love liberty and uphold human dignity.[128] Hence what he spoke thereafter was what God revealed to him in and through the Spirit. Likewise his deeds were regulated, determined, guided and made meaningful through the Spirit. Peter testifies to the Lord's ministry: "How God anointed Jesus of Nazareth with the Holy Spirit and with power; how he went about doing good and healing all who were oppressed by the devil, for God was with him" (Acts 10:38).

Thus Scripture makes it clear that the wonders he worked, the miracles he performed, all were done in and through the Spirit. Indeed Jesus is a great reservoir of the Spirit. Therefore he could claim: those who drink of the water that I will give them will never be thirsty (Jn 4:14). From his heart the Spirit was welling up and after his resurrection he shared his Spirit in different forms like in breaking the bread, in his appearances, and in his words and gestures: he breathed on the disciples and said to them, "Receive the Holy Spirit!" (Jn 20:19-22) and in the form of tongues of fire (Acts 2:14).

As a Spirit-filled person Jesus' life was focused on the total liberation of the human person, restoring wholeness to the sick and the deformed, hope to the desperate, recognition and honour to the despised, restoring freedom, dignity and equality to the enslaved and oppressed, siding with the poor and the powerless. The Holy Spirit was the way Jesus walked and lived his mission-existence.[129] In other words, the Spirit directed people's gaze to the *Reign of God* that was breaking in with Jesus' presence which is proactive and life enhancing.[130] The Holy Spirit gets associated with all the great and small beginnings.[131] The Spirit of God in Jesus is accessible to all, irrespective of who one is.

Jesus: The Inclusive House

The *Jordan-event* of Jesus holds within its embrace the fullness of God's all-inclusive love revealed to humankind, especially to the marginalized sections of his time. In Jesus God becomes fully involved in human existence even to the extent of identifying himself with the poor. In Jesus the eternal Word has become transient flesh and all humankind has been divinized. From now on, the human person is never an isolated individual but always part of a house that accommodates everyone, irrespective of caste, creed, gender or status.[132] The inclusive house is of great relevance for human inclusiveness. Jesus called and invited an everyday group of companions, left his home, and set out to tell people about a loving house in him. He was a healer, listener, teacher, reformer and more than a prophet. The inclusive Jesus offers love and forgiveness to all who reach, who need, and who search.[133] He transcends the barriers built on account of all discriminatory divisions in a tidal surge, dissolves the decisive walls of hatred, violence and discrimination, and religion. Therefore Jesus did not pay heed to social taboos or the restrictions of society and religion of his time, but he broke down barriers between God and sinners, tax collectors, Samaritans and women.

The remarkable inclusiveness and equality can be described as a discipleship of equals that was present in the *basileia* vision of the gospels, praxis of inclusive wholeness.[134] Matthew's gospel closes with a note of Jesus missioning his disciples: "Go therefore and make disciples of all nations" (Mt 28:19). It is in Luke's Gospel in particular that we see Jesus breaking down barriers; so all the references here will be to Luke unless otherwise indicated. He was inclusive, wanting all to enter the fullness of life. Jesus' table fellowship was a live-illustration of his all-inclusive attitude which was also a key feature of his new community/society. Jesus' movement was an inclusive movement transcending the boundaries, dividers and demarcations marked by any discriminatory structures. It included the lost, least and the last – the women, poor, voiceless, colourless, the peripheries, the excluded and as well "some people of stature who found his social vision attractive."[135]

God's liberative action is manifested in the bringing about of human liberation through Jesus, which resulted in the formation of a community of freedom, fellowship and justice. God's goodness brings about the *basileia* through Jesus. God's goodness establishes equality of all – righteous and sinner, rich and poor, men and women (Lk 13:34-35; Mt 23:37). The God whom Jesus proclaims is the Sophia-God of the poor, the outcasts, and those who suffer injustice. Fiorenza maintains that God in Jesus wills the wholeness of humanity and therefore enables the Jesus movement to become a discipleship of equals. As equal disciples they now bring the all-inclusive goodness of Sophia-God to all. This movement was egalitarian and inclusive of women's leadership as well. The role of women here was not peripheral or trivial, but is at the centre and thus of utmost importance to the praxis of solidarity from below.[136]

Jesus: The Initiator of a New Social Order

The Jordan event encompassed a new experience of God as self-revealing. The vision that compelled Jesus at the Jordan was the vision of the *basileia tou theou*, of God's different world of justice and love.[137] It was from there that his option for the poor gets manifested, moves him to take sides with the poor and victims of society; attracts him towards those who suffer the most, those who are abused by the exploitation of the powerful. Jesus was sensitive to the suffering of the innocent and to the humiliation of the marginalized. As a healer Jesus healed not only physically, but also in a social, psychological, and spiritual newness. As a preacher, Jesus was on the side of the voiceless and the victims of injustice and of evil social structures. As the Lord and Master, he emphasized the centrality of an intimate relationship with God.[138] Jesus enacted his vision at community meals with a list of wrong guests and tax collectors and sinners.

In his ministry, Jesus drew the map of his social world, expanded it to embrace all, irrespective of caste and color, status and gender.[139] The climax of the transforming presence of Jesus is the offering of his life on the Cross. The Cross of Jesus reveals that God suffers in love for humanity. Monica Hedwig rightly notes:

> Jesus stood his ground in the witness he personally had to give, as speaking the compassionate and loving word of God unto the human situation, and for this he was crucified. But he spoke the compassionate word of God into the world in all the truth of its non-violent respect for the free response of those who were not yet ready to respond, for it was only his death which set free in them the power to respond. Because of this God raised him from death, giving him a name above every name. It is this many-faceted compassion of Jesus that offers the key to the Resurrection.[140]

Jesus' obedience expressed in his death on the Cross was, a source of solidarity and empowerment for others. As Walter Kasper has pointed out, God in Jesus Christ is a God who suffers with humans: "Thus the omnipotence of God's love removes the weakness of suffering. Suffering is not thereby removed, but it is interiorly transformed, transformed into hope. In other words, God redeems human suffering."[141] The Cross is the ultimate expression of Jesus as the presence-solidarity with humans and the world.

Jesus: The Epitome of Freedom

The 'Nazareth *Manifesto*' of Jesus at the beginning of his public ministry (Lk 4:18-19) quoting Isaiah explains Jesus' consciousness of his mission of bringing wholeness and fullness to those who were dehumanized by various oppressive forces. Jesus thus defines his mission "as that of announcing good news to the poor."[142] Led by the Spirit, he proclaims the news of their liberation. The heart of the proclamation is as follows:

that the poor are to be freed from the oppression of their poverty; the prisoners are to be set free; the captives being released. This according to Luke the Evangelist is what sets the context for the mission of Jesus. A cursory glance at the various levels of the life of Jesus tell us that his mission in solidarity with the less privileged made a challenging paradigm shift. Right from the beginning till his death on the Cross we find him in solidarity with the marginalized of society leading them to the freedom of the children of God.

Jesus' birth ushered in a new and lasting expression of divine compassion and solidarity. The annunciation unfolds the mystery of compassion incarnate which symbolizes the identification of Jesus with the poor; the lowly shepherds - the outcasts of society despised by others become the beneficiaries of God's presence, the good news of Jesus' birth. Jesus' ministry ushers in an openness, inviting unto the promises of God everybody, especially those rendered outcasts, sinners, poor, and sick, etc., all who in a way lost their dignity in some measure. His table fellowship with tax collectors and sinners is his radical approach to the margins of society, and the climax of his solidarity is the offering of his life on the Cross. It becomes obvious that in essence, Jesus lives out his *manifesto*. This is the *Reign* that he came to inaugurate through his life, death and resurrection. Thus the resurrection of Jesus, the revelation of God-with us is realized, which becomes the key to enter with him into the sufferings and hope of his people.[143]

God's love is the force at the core of all Jesus' transformative activity. However, his love that set people free inevitably leads to conflict. The agape love of Jesus reaches out to all but it affects people in different ways. Because of his self-defining option, the life of Jesus is lived out in the twin dimensions of solidarity and conflict. These are but the complementary expressions of his God-experience.[144] For nothing offends God more than the unjust suffering and the indifference to his suffering daughters and sons.

What matters for Jesus was reaching out to save those far off, restoring to everyone the dignity which is inherent and inalienable. Though it was scandalous to some, Jesus was not afraid of those who are scandalized by his radical and revolutionary ways. As in the case of the woman with the flow of blood (Lk 8:43-48), the woman knew that she was ritually unclean and could not touch or approach Jesus.[145] The Gospel says that Jesus felt the power going out of himself and immediately she was healed. There was no exchange of words or looks, but Jesus responded to her cry. Adding to it, he could have let the incident pass by quietly. He brings it to the notice of the crowd around him. Why did he do that? He did it because he wanted to break through the taboos and discrimination of his milieu.[146]

What Jesus wanted was to reinstate the outcast, to save those outside the gate. In other words, Jesus upsets the prejudiced mentality of the Pharisees. He stands for truth and justice in freeing the burden of envy and the grumbling of the labourers who bore the burden of the day and the heat (Mt 20:1-16).[147] Living in a polarized society of the rich and poor, Jesus stood by the poor in a bid to transform society. It implied that he had to stand against the system which did not care for the poor. He took cognizance of the establishment which hampered the common well-being by not rendering justice and ushering in inequality. Thus real repentance implies the transformation of society. It would need courage, conviction and faith to acknowledge that such a commitment, though it may risk a lot of personal securities, is actually genuine and true to the call of being truly human and communitarian like Jesus.[148] Ultimately, everything was epitomized by Jesus in the episode of his own life. Although he being the Master washed his disciples' feet and thereby perpetuated the service commitment; he urged his disciples to follow his life style (Jn 13:14-15). The death of Jesus is a powerful act of affirmation and proclamation of his firm commitment and loyalty to the people. Jesus' ultimate expression on the Cross is the dance of the Spirit that brought about the birthing of a new age of freedom and fullness of life in the Spirit. Rayan descriptively says:

> The death of Jesus then is a powerful act of affirmation and proclamation of his firm commitment and loyalty to the people, to the fisher folk that followed him, to wineless and breadless crowds, to broken, crippled and

handicapped men and women, to the exploited working class, to the destroyed and fleeced wretched of the earth, to those held captive in tombs and prisons of poverty, ignorance and disease. The death of Jesus is an affirmation of human freedom and human dignity. His Cross is a symbol of fearless defiance of and resistance to evil.[149]

Therefore "the Cross of Jesus blossoming into the resurrection is the supreme affirmation of life, freedom and joy." Thus, the Cross epitomizes absolute assurance of the presence-solidarity of Jesus who in his freedom and love chooses to identify with the periphery of his time.[150] Perhaps, it is appropriate to say that the resurrection was Jesus' fullest and most decisive experience of the Spirit,[151] an experience that wholly transformed him to provide humanity with a decisive future. Also it is the resurrection that "gathers the cosmos into the profound harmony and unity of the Divine."[152]

Jesus: The Very Presence of God

The presence of Jesus is truly the revelation of God. Rayan affirms that it is in the humanity of Jesus that God is revealed rather than in what we call 'divine' in Christ's life. Divinity is best disclosed as the most human of his humanity. In Jesus, the humanity and divinity do not constitute two realities but one single mystery of faith.[153] Rayan states: "God-in-Jesus identifies with us and renounces privileges and riches in order to serve us; and immerses himself in the realities of our life including our sufferings and struggles. He commits himself to our liberation and salvation, risking life and laying it down in solidarity."[154] In Jesus, God became *Immanuel* in the liberative actions and events of history, in the all oppressed peoples and in all pursuit of justice and friendship. "Jesus means God-is-with-us. Jesus is the sacrament and guarantee of God's shielding presence." Jesus ensures the presence of God in his life.

Jesus broke all the rules of Jewish society when he extended his table fellowship to the social outcasts. Neusner's views go along with Rayan wherein he says that the outcasts in the Jewish society lived in a state of constant shame, "because they have violated the general cultural expectations of what it means to be whole, perfect, and 'in place,' they were classified as 'unclean.'"[155] For this reason, to have fellowship with the outcasts was considered morally contaminating. Moreover, table fellowship in the Jewish religious world-view also symbolized the eschatological community which is nothing but fellowship with God (Cf Isa 25:6; Mt 8:1; Lk 22:30). By sharing a meal with 'sinners,' God's love and solidarity is vividly painted as far more superior to any other action, for it reaches down even to the lowest level of human society. Jesus' table-fellowship can be best appreciated at the backdrop of the pharisaic understanding that viewed the tables on which they ate their meals as representations of God's altar in the Jerusalem Temple.[156] Fiorenza rightly states that the power of God's *basileia* is realized in Jesus' table community.[157] For Jesus, table-fellowship implied mercy that let everyone experience God's unconditional love. Jesus' presence with all is expressed in his parting commandment to love one another.

Jesus' unprejudiced openness saw him one with all sections of society. He radically expressed his solidarity with the poor by taking their sides. By going unto the poor, living with them, being like them, identifying himself with them, Jesus firmly stood against the system which let such polarization prevail.[158] The ultimate expression of the mystery of the transformative presence of Jesus is revealed in the humanness of Jesus. His death and resurrection unfolds the deepest truth of God become human.

Jesus: The Self-emptying of God

The word 'emptied' is a key concept in the divine *Kenosis* which describes 'the divine being and the divine action in Christ.'[159] The self-emptying love of God is revealed in Jesus' incarnation, life and ultimate death on the Cross. It is said in the Gospel Christ emptied himself and in humility stooped down to become human so as to save and reconcile all reality in God: "For God so loved the world that he gave his only Son, so that everyone who believes in him shall not perish but have eternal life" (Jn 3,16). The culmination of Christ's humility was on the Cross where the absolute manifestation of God's self-emptying love is revealed in a humiliating death. Christ emptied himself and shared human beings' destiny in suffering and death to pay the price of humans' sin. But one has to see the value of Christ's sacrifice as an expression of God's immense love than replacing the sinner who is under the wrath of God. Even at the point of terrible suffering and humiliation Christ's sacrifice on the Cross was his ultimate response in love of the Father on behalf of humankind that failed to respond to the Father's amazing love. This sacrifice of Christ becomes "His act of solidarity with humankind by embracing human suffering in order to transform this condition of human embodiment into the Trinitarian life of love."[160] Here he is one with all the marginalized and all the martyred victims of the earth. What was begun at incarnation now reaches its fulfilment.

For on the Cross Jesus is wholly poor and wholly outcast. Identification and confrontation have here reached their furthest possible limits. His Cross was the consequence of the kind of life he lived and yet a design of God. Jesus chose his way of life and was ready to pay the price. Given the historical context of Jesus' life, in which crucifixion was the mode of execution of the lowest of the low, his Cross becomes a testimony of God's *kenotic* way of identifying with the poor, and the oppressed. Thus the Cross exemplifies and vindicates with absolute assurance the essence and praxis of Jesus, who in his freedom and his love emptied himself in order to identify himself with the weak and the foolish and oppose the wise and the strong. As Pedro Arrupe says:

> We receive Christ hungering in the world. He comes to us not alone, but with the poor, the oppressed, the starving of the earth. Through him they are looking to us for help, for justice, for love expressed in action. Therefore we cannot properly receive the Bread of Life unless at the same time we give bread for life to those in need whenever and whoever they may be.[161]

The poor and the marginalized are the images of God who reveal to us the image of the Triune God. It summons us as followers of Jesus to assume the path of solidarity and struggle of *kenosis* and immersion with the *anawim* of God. Arrupe's theological reflections go well with Rayan's that can be summed up in one short expression: bread for all through a faith that does justice.[162] For him faith devoid of justice and concern for the poor and the marginalized was not a faith at all and this faith if it has to be Christian it must feed the hungry by making bread and sharing it which was for Rayan the living Eucharist.

Jesus: The Power of Empowerment

Jesus accepted women as his helpers, disciples and travel-companions in defiance of the patriarchal and androcentric culture of his time. Not only do women follow him to take care of his needs (Lk 8:2), but Mary who sits at his feet listening to what he teaches (and so assuming the role of a disciple) is commended for having chosen "what is best" (Lk 10:42).[163] His positive attitude to women enhanced their worth and dignity at different levels. In the New Testament, the first word uttered by the risen Christ, according to John (Jn 20:11-18) is: "Woman" addressed to Mary Magdalene. She was mandated to go and proclaim this great news to men including Peter. Though culturally women's testimony had no legal standing, Jesus acted counter-culturally when he made a woman as his first witness to his new life.

Jesus' empowering authority came not from the traditional institutions of his society – political, religious, structural or spiritual – but "from his own personal charism."[164] Jesus the empowering person, the liberative prophet became "an authorized transgressor."[165] Jesus challenged the powers of domination by taking the initiative to heal the woman who was bent over. "Jesus calls a woman bent went with a spinal disease for eighteen years out into the middle of the synagogue, lays his hands on her, and heals her from her "spirit of weakness."[166] He calls her a "daughter of Abraham" (v.16). By calling her a daughter of Abraham in those days, Jesus was recognizing her a "full-pledged member of the covenant and of equal standing before God with men (Lk 13:10-17)."[167]

> To heal her on a Sabbath was to liberate the Sabbath to be a jubilee of release and restoration. To touch her was to revoke the holiness code with its male scruples about menstrual uncleanness and sexual advances... To place her in the midst of Synagogue was to challenge the male monopoly on the means of grace and access to God. To assert that her illness was

not divine punishment for sin, but satanic oppression, was to declare war on the entire Domination System, whose driving spirit is Satan.[168]

The women in the life and ministry of Jesus are seen as channels of transformation by challenging the patriarchal structures and by retrieving their dignity.

Jesus: The Presence-Solidarity with Us

The phrase *Presence-Solidarity* is best revealed in the Gospel of Matthew as the good news of God's saving presence and solidarity with "us". It is on this note of divine *Presence-Solidarity* that the Gospel opens and closes (Mt 1:23 and 28:20). The question is, who can this "us" be? Some clarity concerning the identity of the 'us' is vital to the understanding of the Gospel since the *Immanuel* theme enfolds the work and acts as a term of hermeneutical reference.

> The affirmation God-is-with-us is more than a philosophical statement about the omnipresence of the Divine. It is more than the universal creative divine presence (Mt 5:45; Mt 6:26-30). It is the special, personal, saving Jesus-relationship gifted to 'us' by the Holy Spirit (Mt 1:20-21). It is God's presence in Mary's Child, in Jesus of Nazareth, of Capernaum, of the Galilean countryside, and of Bethany and the Supper Room; and of the resurrection place and the mountain of meeting and mission. An answer to the question concerning the identity of the 'us' may be sought from Isaiah 7 which is the original context of Immanuel; from Mt 1 which is its new context; from Mt 28 where the theme re-emerges; and indeed from the entire work, so thoroughly transfused with the consciousness of God's Presence-Solidarity in Christ Jesus.[169]

Matthew's narrative points to the dimension of Immanuel by identifying the sign of divine presence with Mary's Child, and by describing his birth and tracing his ancestry in the opening chapter, and by detailing the rest of the story Jesus as his total immersion in our human condition. God's presence with 'us' in Jesus is present for ages unending.

Let me explore some of the nuances of this "US" dimension illustrated in and through the *Presence-Solidarity* of the Immanuel: The dimensions of 'us' becomes clear, first, when one penetrates into Matthew's reference to Isaiah 7. God through the prophet Isaiah invites Ahaz the king to ask for a sign. Isaiah gives the king the *Immanuel* sign which seems to be both a promise and a threat.

> The 'us' in that historical context comprised not the whole world, not the entire Hebrew people, not at all those who planned aggression, but Ahaz and his realm, the threatened and frightened people of Judah, out of their wits for fear and powerless, and placed unjustly in the shadow of imminent invasion and destruction. Their resources are inadequate to cope with the situation. Therefore God takes their side. He does so not because their faith is anything wonderful, but because they were being victimized and oppressed. The sign means God is with the powerless to reassure, protect and save.[170]

Thus Jesus, the Word-made-flesh is the sacrament and guarantee of God's shielding and sheltering presence. A presence in solidarity, a totally immersive presence with "US", the powerless who stand in dire need of protection, liberation, reassurance and salvation. Pope Benedict XVI explains the depth of 'now-ness' in Jesus' incarnational solidarity: "Through Jesus' presence and action, God has here and now entered into history in a wholly new way. The reason why *now* is the fullness of time (Mk1:15), why now is in a unique sense the time of conversion and penance, as well as the time of joy, is that in Jesus it is God who draws near to us."[171]

Second, the character of Jesus' solidarity with the margins made explicit when we understand a little more about the apparent nature of the first century Christian society, the nature of Jesus' disputes with the Pharisees and of the threatened and persecuted little communities of Jesus' disciples. Jesus' identification with the poor and the marginalised was the hallmark of his life and mission. The early Christians, mostly poor, were harassed for announcing the love which Jesus had released into the world. They were persecuted for witnessing to Jesus as the crucified Messiah and the Saviour of the world.

Third, the four women, Thamar, Rahab, Ruth, Bathsheba whom Matthew the Evangelist includes in the ancestry of Jesus implicitly illustrate a nuanced dimension of "US" in God-is-with-us. By naming these women, he is saying that *Immanuel* is in solidarity with all those who are despised, abused and relegated to the outskirts of religion and society. He is saying that the blood of these women, the outsiders, the not chosen ones and the excluded, flows in the veins of the Saviour.[172]

Four, the "US" in God-is-with-us includes sincere and deep faith in unexpected zones, outside Israel. Jesus' act of extending the blessings of the Kingdom to the Canaanite woman (Mt 15:21-28; 21:28-32, 40-43) and the recognition of Jesus' presence by the Roman guard (Mt 27:54) are just a few incidents from the life of Jesus.

Fifth, the Immanuel was not with the powerful Herod but with the humble wise men. His presence was embodied not in the powerful but in the powerless who needed him. He was in complete solidarity with the unjustly killed or destroyed and the solidarity with them was total when Jesus himself was killed by the powers of evil.[173] Here God gives an assurance to people that God will be with them as the promise made to Moses asserts that God's presence will go with the chosen people (Exod 33:14). It is a dynamic process like yeast, which transforms everything and multiplies into plenty by emptying Himself in a *kenotic* way (Phil 2:5-11). It is a perfect model of 'walking together' like 'on the road to Emmaus', where the Risen Lord walks alongside by strengthening the disciples, who are saddened by the trauma of crucifixion, heavily burdened and aimless (Lk 25:13-15).

God's presence and solidarity with us in Jesus is present for ages unending and in every race and colour and gender. God is present in those who take sides with him for the cause of justice, and on behalf of the victims of every age. In the risen Christ, God is not only with the poor, the persecuted, the homeless and the powerless but with all those who stand with the poor and the oppressed. God's gifts are thus released from the grip of narrow ethnic and pharisaic claims and disclosed as free for the world. In Jesus' view, God is with the small people, the politically insignificant, those without power and with little learning, with no social status, no influence, but who are ready to work with God for the welfare of the world and risk one's life for the dawn of the reign of God.

In fact, Jesus launched his public ministry with his *Presence-Solidarity* declaration: "The Spirit of the Lord is upon me, because he has anointed me to bring good news to the poor. He has sent me to proclaim release to the captives and recovery of sight to the blind, to let the oppressed go free, to proclaim the year of the Lord's favour" (Lk 4:18-19). Therefore, his whole life was a *Presence-Solidarity* in self-emptying and self-giving. Jesus continues to summon us to opt for the poor and the marginalized and empowers us in our struggles to honour the dignity of the periphery. It's a call to hear the cry of the poor, for a *kenotic* mission.

Conclusion

The focus of this chapter was the area of convergences and divergences, leading to an assessment of the two contemporary theologians: Rayan and Fiorenza. Although there are several points that bring them together, we have limited ourselves to some of the theological elements that would enable us to perceive a Christological unity between the Indian theologian and the Western biblical scholar. In dealing with the theme of convergences and divergences, the focus in this chapter was twofold: first, to present what these two theologians have in common in terms of their theologizing approaches even though they come from different contexts, backgrounds and ecclesial settings; second, to identify the divergences likely to have arisen out of their specific cultural and religious experiences.

In our comparative study of these two theologians, our approach was not aimed at which one or who is better (which is a divisive question), but to focus on the commonalities shared within the social and theological construct of the corresponding milieus of Rayan and Fiorenza. Hence, it was an endeavour to gather the fruits of chapters two and three, with a view to draw up a Christology that would emerge from these proponents of theology.

Both the theologians base their theological reflections and insights and conclusions rightly on the 'divine Incarnation' model. That is to look at the world, its realities, peoples' struggles, its socio-economic-religious dynamics, from God's perspective, from the divine gaze, 'I have heard the cry of my people and I have seen their sufferings' (Exod 3:7-10). Simultaneously they show how God embarked upon his incarnational mission, by sending his Son, Jesus, into the messy realities of human suffering to eventually liberate God's people to true freedom, their true daughter-ship and sonship.

Our final observation is that a genuine Christology of *Presence-Solidarity* will have to centre on Jesus the God-with-us who is the primary lens for understanding divine and human partnership. The God-experience of Jesus and his identification with the poor and the marginalized of his time are thus joined together finding a powerful expression in three symbols all of which are basic to Christian life: the Incarnation, the Cross and the Resurrection. The Cross is therefore, the outcome of a life of solidarity with the poor and the outcast, and the resurrection of Jesus, is God's overwhelming response to our cry for life, and God's final approval of Jesus' absolute solidarity with humanity.

To put it succinctly, an aspect of God's justice and providence is that we in turn become providence to one another. Christian discipleship implies going to the poor, to the peripheries,[174] and to the margins where no one dares to go, and getting fully immersed in their life struggles. It was the dream and vision of Rayan and Fiorenza that the disciples of Jesus identify with the masses – the least, lost and the forgotten in the world. Associating with the rich and all powerful is easy but becoming one with the poor is a challenge and a Christian call. The task is not something that will give us instant glory but will make God present to the people by becoming the voice of the voiceless, the face of the faceless. This would be the significance of the Christology of *Presence-Solidarity* for India today. Therefore, the above discussion in five sections in this chapter, imply that our response should be comprehensive. It should touch the inside (*Ad Intra*) as well as the outside (*Ad Gentes*) in India today. What could be the way forward for a *kenotic* mission of the Indian Church today?

Endnotes

[1] Fiorenza, *In Memory of Her*, 184-189.

[2] The fact is that theology anywhere, any time is born of two interlacing experiences: of the faith and the realities of life. Rayan, "Doing Theology in India," in *Theologizing in Context*, 11.

[3] Fiorenza, *Burke Lecture*, https://youtu.be/dUDlV8B1aHw. It was in 1960s Fiorenza was there to witness the birthing of feminist thought that was emerging in the context of the then pervasive patriarchal system.

[4] Fiorenza, *Bread Not Stone*, xvi.

[5] Fiorenza, "The Will to Choose or to Reject,"126.

[6] Fiorenza, *In Memory of Her*, 92.

[7] John Paul II, "*Redemptoris Missio*: On the Permanent Validity of the Church's Missionary Mandate," *Encyclical Letter* 18 May, 1986 (Bangalore: Asian ding Corporation, 1986).

[8] Samuel Rayan, "Christian Participation in the Struggle for Social Justice," Some Theological Reflections." *Clergy Monthly* 38 (August, 1974): 288.

[9] Brezina, *Sojourner Truth's "Ain't I a Woman?*," 46, 50. Sojourner Truth like most of her female feminist counterparts judged herself alongside men and found herself fully equal on their terms.

[10] Hogan, *From Women's Experience to Feminist Theology*, 87-88.

[11] Fiorenza, *Discipleship of Equals*, 68.

[12] Rayan, "The March Has Begun," 180-181.

[13] Samuel Rayan, "The Challenge of the *Dalit* Issue: Some Theological Perspectives," in *Dalits and Women: Quest for Humanity*, ed. Devashayam (Madras: GLTCRI, 1992), 131.

[14] Rayan, "The Challenge of the *Dalit* Issue,"121.

[15] Rayan, "The Challenge of the *Dalit* Issue," 121, 132, 123, 122.

[16] Fiorenza, *Sharing Her Word*, 13-21, 28-36.

[17] Fiorenza, *In Memory of Her*, 184-189.

[18] Fiorenza, "We are Church.".

[19] Fiorenza, "We are Church-A Kingdom of Priests."

[20] Fiorenza, *In Memory of Her*, 56. Fiorenza frequently employs the word 'democratic' in reference to the discipleship of equals. In using this word, she means to underscore that this group of people is characterized by the equality of rights and privileges of all its members. I understand it as a synonym for 'egalitarian.'

[21] Especially, Rayan's articles, "Re-conceiving Theology in the Asian Context", "Theological Education in the Social Context", "The 'How' of Third World Theologies", and "The Irruption of the Third World – A Challenge to Theology."

[22] Elisabeth Schüssler Fiorenza, "For Women in a Men's World: A Critical Feminist Theology of Liberation," in *The Power of Naming: A Concilium-Reader in Feminist Liberation Theology*, ed. Elisabeth Schüssler Fiorenza (New York: Orbis Books, 1996), 6.

[23] Fiorenza, *Discipleship of Equals*, 62.

[24] Fiorenza, "Introduction," to *In Memory of Her*, xx.

[25] Elisabeth Schüssler Fiorenza, *Searching the Scriptures: A Feminist Introduction*, Vol.I (New York: Crossroad, 1993), 3

[26] Fiorenza affirms that the Bible is not only written in the words of men but also serves to legitimate patriarchal power and oppression insofar as it renders God male and determines ultimate reality in male terms, which make women invisible or marginal. Hence, there arises a need for a critical feminist hermeneutics of liberation that seeks to develop a critical dialectical mode of biblical interpretation. It can do justice to women's experiences of the Bible as a thoroughly patriarchal book written in androcentric language as well as to women's experience of the Bible as a source of empowerment and vision in our struggles for liberation. Fiorenza, *Bread Not Stone*, x-xi, xiii.

[27] Fiorenza, *Bread Not Stone*, xvii, 14-15.

[28] Fiorenza, *Sharing Her Word*, 41.

[29] Rayan, "Reconceiving Theology in the Asian Context," 139.

[30] Rayan, "Irruption of the Poor," 101-112, 106.

[31] Fiorenza, *In Memory of Her*, 130-131.

[32] Equality and inclusion are not only personal values but also key economic considerations in an analysis of the human good. Tatha Wiley, "Creation Restored: God's Basileia, the Social Economy, and the Human God," in *Earth, Wind, and Fire: Biblical and Theological Perspectives on Creation*, eds. Barbara Ellen Bowe, Carol J. Dempsey, Mary Margaret Pazdan (Collegeville, Minnesota: Liturgical Press, 2004). 78.

[33] Fiorenza, *Jesus*, 100.

[34] Fiorenza, *Discipleship of Equals*, 228.

[35] Joseph, "Trailblazers: Elisabeth Schüssler Fiorenza and George M. Soares-Prabhu," 53-68, 61. Fiorenza understands *ekklesia* as the people of Israel before God as understood from the First Testament. The Second Testament brings it into tangible expression through the agency of the Spirit when God's people, expressing their full citizenship as a community, gather around the table, eat together a meal, break the bread, and share the cup in memory of Christ's passion and resurrection.

[36] Fiorenza, *Discipleship of Equal*, 199, 197.

[37] Rayan, "Wrestling in the Night," in *Doing Theology*, 58.

[38] Fiorenza, *Bread not Stone*, xvi.

[39] Fiorenza, *Sharing Her Word*, 41.

[40] Fiorenza identifies a fourfold interpretative model that is constitutive of her critical feminist theology of liberation. These four elements are: hermeneutics of

suspicion, hermeneutics of proclamation, a hermeneutics of remembrance, and a hermeneutics of creative actualization. Although she is utilizing these hermeneutics in *In Memory of Her*, she does not distinguish them until *Bread Not Stone*. Fiorenza, *Bread Not Stone*, 15-22. (for more details see in section 4.2.4. "Inadequacy of the Hermeneutics of the Bible").

[41] Sexism is based on the belief that men are inherently superior to women and thus discrimination is justified. It encompasses economic, political, social, and institutional actions and beliefs that perpetuate an unequal distribution of privileges, resources, leadership and power between men and women. Sexism means discrimination based on sex or gender or the systematic oppression of women by men.

[42] Fiorenza, *In Memory of Her*, 119.

[43] Feminist theology emerges when women's faith seeks understanding in the matrix of the historical struggle for life in the face of oppressive and alienating forces. Johnson, *She Who Is*, 17.

[44] Fiorenza, *Bread Not Stone*, 45.

[45] For Critique, see section 4.4.4. "Critique of Fiorenza's Christology."

[46] Fiorenza, *Jesus*, 101.

[47] Fiorenza, *Jesus*, 106.

[48] For Critique, see section 4.4.4. "Critique of Fiorenza's Christology."

[49] Rayan, *Breath of Fire*, 129.

[50] Rayan, *Asia and Justice*, 360.

[51] Rayan, *Breath of Fire*, 128.

[52] It's a philosophical concept: God Suffers with People. Cf.

[53] Samuel Rayan, "Let the Rivers and the Trees Clap their Hands: Spirituality and ecological concern–A Christian View," in *Spiritual Traditions: Essential Visions for Living* ed. by David Emmanuel Singh (Bangalore/Delhi: UTC/ISPCK, 1998), 254-255.

[54] Rayan, "The March has begun," 180.

[55] In Christian interpretation, the empty tomb is only a secondary symbol, a negative but ambiguous!

[56] Fiorenza, *Jesus*, 123

[57] Fiorenza, *Jesus*, 123-137. For a detailed explanation see the section 3.3.1.5 "Jesus the Resurrected One".

[58] Rayan, *Breath of Fire*, 128.

[59] Rayan, *Breath of Fire*, 129, 128.

[60] Rayan, "Symbols of the Spirit,"125, 139.

[61] Hellwig, *Jesus*, 107.

[62] Hellwig, *Jesus*, 107-108.

[63] Samuel Rayan, "He is Our Peace," *The Bulletin*, 11/1 (1992): 94.

[64] Rayan, "Christian Participation in the Struggle for Social," 290-293.

[65] This is further taken up in section 4.4.4. "Critique of Fiorenza's Christology."

[66] Samuel Rayan, "The Significance of Women's Awakening in the Church," in *CWSR – I: Nature, Woman and the Church: Indian Christian Reflections on Ecology, Feminism and Ecclesiology* (New Delhi: ISPCK, 2013), 148. Originally published in *Birthing a New Way of Being a New Vision* (Pune: A Newsletter from Streevani, 2003), 7-11.

[67] Pushpa, "Trailblazers," 60.

[68] An articulation of such an experience of liberation is preserved in the form of a history of salvation recorded in the Bible. The experience of liberation can be personal or communal or both. It can be experienced in its fullness only in the context of a creative response on the part of the humans since freedom and creativity are two dimensions of God's own nature which we are called to share.

[69] Fiorenza, "Politics of Otherness," 314.

[70] Fiorenza, *Bread not Stone*, xiv. 5.

[71] Fiorenza's seven step-method consists of the hermeneutics of experience, of social location, of suspicion, of critical evaluation, of imagination, of re-membering and reconstruction and of transformation.

[72] Fiorenza, "The Will to Choose or to Reject," 126.

[73] Rayan, "Justice of God," 213.

[74] Samuel Rayan, "Mission after Vatican II: Problems and Positions," in *Selected Writings of Samuel Rayan,* ed. Kunnumpuram, 18. This article is part of a lecture given at the European Conference on Mission Studies, Oslo, 1970. Samuel Rayan, "Mission after Vatican II: Problems and Positions," *IRM* 59/236 (October, 1970): 414-426.

[75] Rayan, "The Justice of God," 211.

[76] Rayan, "Christian Participation in the Struggle for Social Justice," 283.

[77] Fiorenza, *In Memory of Her*, 123.

[78] Elisabeth Schüssler Fiorenza, "Jesus of Nazareth in Historical Tradition," in *Thinking of Christ: Proclamation, Explanation, Meaning*, ed. Tatha Wiley (New York London: Continuum, 2003), 43, 46.

[79] Samuel Rayan. "Jesus and the Struggles of the Masses in India," *TMILL* 11 (1999):18. Rayan's context is more that of Third World which India shares with the rest of the Third World (Asia, Africa and Latin America).

[80] Rayan, "Reconceiving Theology in the Asian Context," 139.

[81] Gustavo Gutiérrez, *A Theology of Liberation: History, Politics and Salvation*, trans. Caridad Inda & John Eagleson (New York: Orbis, 1988) 171.

[82] Michael Amaladoss, "The Kingdom of God as the Goal of Mission," *Vaiharai* 1 (1996) 277-292, 286-291.

[83] Johnson compliments: "Of all the doctrines of the Church, Christology is the one most used to suppress and exclude women." Cf. Elizabeth A. Johnson, *She Who Is:*

The Mystery of God in Feminist Theological Discourse (New York: Crossroad, 1992), 151, quoted in, Shalini Mulackal, "Who Is Jesus for Indian Women? A Feminist Critical Enquiry," *VJTR*, 8/6, (June 2016): 433-451, at 445. Therefore, feminists raise important questions related to the nature of the image of God in humanity, God's gender, the maleness of Jesus and their Christological reconstructions are extreme in response to traditional Christological claims.

84 Fiorenza, *Jesus: Miriam's Child*, 48.

85 Rayan, "Jesus and the Poor," 228.

86 Edward Schillebeeckx, trans. John Bowden, *Church, The Human Story of God* (London: SCM Press, 1990), 125.

87 Pope John Paul II, Address after the Way of the Cross," Good Friday (April 1, 1994).

88 Fiorenza, *Jesus*, 101, 104.

89 See. 3.3.1.3 Jesus the Wise Teacher.

90 Marie F. Fortune, "The Transformation of Suffering: A Biblical and Theological Perspective," in *Christianity, Patriarchy and Abuse: A Feminist Critique*, eds. Joanne Carlson Brown and Carole R Bohn, (Cleveland, Ohio: The Pilgrim Press, 1989), 145.

91 Mary Daly, *Beyond God the Father: Toward a Philosophy of Women's Liberation* (Boston: Beacon Press, 1973), 77.

92 Shalini Mulackal, "Who Is Jesus for Indian Women? A Feminist Critical Enquiry," *VJTR*, 8/6 (June 2016), 443.

93 Fiorenza, *Jesus*, 100.

94 Rayan, "Outside the Gate, Sharing Insults," 143.

95 Rayan, CWRS - II, "People's Theology," 98; *Journal of Dharma* 22 (1992): 175-202.

96 Pope Francis, Extraordinary blessing '*urbi et orbi*' Sagrato of St Peter's Basilica Friday, 27 March 2020, https://osvnews.com/2020/03/31/pope-francis-urbi-et-orbi-blessing/ (accessed 28, April 2020).

97 Elisabeth Schüssler Fiorenza, "Jesus of Nazareth in Historical Tradition," in *Thinking of Christ: Proclamation, Explanation, Meaning*, ed. Tatha Wiley (New York London: Continuum, 2003), 43, 46.

98 Fiorenza, *Jesus*, 123.

99 Walter Kasper, *Jesus the Christ* [new edition] (York Road, London: T&T Clark International, 2010), 119-120.

100 Cf. Donald Goergen, *The Death and Resurrection of Jesus* (Eugene, Oregon: Wipf and Stock Publishers, 2003), 154, https://books.google.co.in/books?id=6m2vCwAAQBAJ&source=gbs_na vli nks_s (accessed July 26, 2018).

101 Fiorenza, *Jesus, Miriam's Child, Sophia's Prophet*, 90.

102 Elizabeth Schüssler Fiorenza, "Wisdom Mythology in the Christological Hymns of the New Testament," in *Aspects of Wisdom in Judaism and Early Christianity*, ed. Robert L. Wilken (Notre Dame, IN: University of Notre Dame Press, 1975), 17.

[103] I am not the first Indian and Christian (woman religious) to ask the question: What does Jesus Christ mean to us in the 21st century? Who is Jesus for us today? Some prominent Hindu thinkers who were affected by the person and message of Jesus Christ both spiritually and existentially undertook serious Christological reflections since India's Independence in 1947. They include Raja Ram Mohan Roy, Keshab Chunder Sen and P.C. Muzoomdar and others. It is they who pioneered the christological discourses in the nineteenth century India. See, R.S. Sugirtharajah, *Asian Faces of Jesus* (Maryknoll, New York: Orbis Books, 1993), 3

[104] For Dupuis, Jesus Christ is the decisive revelation of God and the saving event of God's grace, on which the salvation of all depends. He, along with Vatican II's *LG*, affirms that "Jesus Christ is the sacrament of God. Through Jesus, God acts in history to bring about human salvation and reaches people in a variety of ways." Jesus is at the centre of God's plan of salvation for the world. Christopher McMahon, *Jesus Our Salvation: An Introduction to Christology* (Winona, MN: Saint Mary's Press, 2007), 222.

[105] Don Schweitzer, "Preface" to *Contemporary Christologies: A Fortress Introduction* (Minneapolis, Minnesota: Fortress Press, 2010), vii.

[106] J. P. Galvin, "Jesus Christ," in *Systematic Theology: Roman Catholic Perspectives*, eds. Francis Schüssler Fiorenza and John P. Galvin (Minneapolis: Fortress, 1991), 251.

[107] Obviously, the reference here is to Irenaeus and Hans Urs von Balthazar's view on the relationship of the Word and Spirit as two hands of God. "But in the incarnation, in the economic mission of the Son, the Spirit plays an active role to the extent that the mission of the Son appears to be the work of the Spirit." The incarnate Son in his obedience - enabled by the Holy Spirit was able to identify himself with sinners, experience the absence of God and even accept the abandonment by the Father out of his love for him. It is in his total self-offering (*kenosis*) that the economic and soteriological dimensions of the incarnation get merged. "The Spirit who accompanies the Son's entire mission as the trinitarian Spirit embodies in himself this double movements: the movement towards the Cross and the movement from the Cross to Resurrection." Cf. Hans Urs von Balthazar, *Theo-drama: Theological Dramatic Theory IV: The Action*, trans. Harrison from *Theodramatik: Bd III: Die Handling* (San Francisco: Ignatius Press, 1994), 325-327, as cited by Mohan Doss, *Christ in the Spirit: Contemporary Spirit Christologies* (Delhi: ISPCK, 2005), 196-197, 224.

[108] Karl Rahner, *Hearer of the Word* (Herder and Herder, 1969), 115.

[109] Doss, "Introduction" to *Christ in the Spirit*, xxi.

[110] Fiorenza, *In Memory of Her*, 142: Jesus' message subverts the structures of oppression by envisioning a different future.

[111] This emphasis does not attempt to pioneer a new concept called *Presence-Solidarity* but it is based on the Christological passage of Phil 2:5-11. It aims rather to renew the understanding of God's saving presence and solidarity with the oppressed masses of India today. In other words, *Presence-Solidarity* is an assurance of God's dynamic presence among His people in Jesus through the power of the Spirit, which involves solidarity-*Immanuel* or God-with-us. Samuel Rayan, "With Us-With Whom?-

Is God?" In *The Dharma of Jesus, Inter-disciplinary Essays in Memory of George M. Soares-Prabhu*, ed. Francis X D'Sa (Pune: Institute for the Study of Religion, Anand: Gujarat Sahitya Prakash, 1997), 37-83.

[112] In Mt 1 a genealogy and a birth narrative culminate in the naming of Mary's Son: Jesus and Immanuel. Both have references to the mission and meaning of the Child Jesus (Mt 1:21, 23). Rayan, "With Us-With Whom," 43, 38.

[113] Put differently, the person of Jesus Christ can never be divided from his work. There is a complete participation of his person in his work: he is his acts, and his acts are himself.

[114] Soares-Prabhu, "Jesus and the Poor," 176.

[115] Doss, *Led by the Spirit*, 146.

[116] Doss, *Christ in the Spirit*, 167.

[117] Samuel Rayan, "Jesus and the Poor in the Fourth Gospel," *BB* 4/3 (September 1978): 213-228. As discussed earlier in chapter three, the *ekklēsia* of wo/men is Schüssler's site of transformation which is structured around the notion of the democratic and egalitarian assembly of members. Further she creates a critical rhetorical place that operates as a transforming space within the tradition. Fiorenza, *Sharing Her Word*, 132.

[118] "Jesus articulates God's own concern, a concern that determines Jesus' own praxis for table community with sinners and outcasts." Fiorenza, *In Memory of Her*, 131. Hence, empowered by the Spirit, Jesus as God's ambassador proclaims the *basileia* (Mk 3:20).

[119] Pope Francis, *Evangelii Gaudium: The Joy of the Gospel*, published on 24 November 2013 to mark the conclusion of the Year of Faith proclaimed by Pope *Emeritus* Benedict XVI. Pope Francis teaches that the joy of the Gospel is such that it cannot be taken away from the Christians by anyone or anything (# 84). The heart of the Christian message is to share the Gospel, help the poor and work for social justice.

[120] Luanne D. Zurlo, "Christmas Eve Mass with Pope Francis," in *Fifteen Feet from the Pope: Dispatches from a Sabbatical in Rome* (Bloomington: Archway Publishing, 2014), Dispatch 12. https://books.google.co.in/books?isbn=1480811297 (accessed September 12, 2016).

[121] George M. Soares-Prabhu, "The Spirituality of Jesus as a Spirituality of Solidarity and Struggle," in *Liberative Struggles in a Violent Society: Proceedings of the Workshop on the "Dynamics of the Liberative Struggles of the Poor and the Oppressed,"* eds. Vattamattam et al., (Hyderabad: A Forum Publications, 1991), 152-153,

[122] Rayan, "With Us - With Whom? – Is God?", 43.

[123] The word 'incarnation' comes from the Latin *incarnatio*: being in flesh. Paul has adopted the Greek word *sarx* (= flesh) to indicate the entire human existence. God becomes fully involved in human existence. Hielke T. Wolters, *Theology of Prophetic Participation* (Delhi: ISPCK /UTC, 1996), 193.

[124] George M. Soares-Prabhu, "The Spirituality of Jesus" in *Biblical Spirituality of Liberative Action*, ed. Scaria Kuthirakkattel, 85-104 (Pune: Jnana-Deepa Vidyapeeth, Theology Series, 2003), 100, as cited in Mohan Doss, "Jesus; A Paradigm for a Spirituality of Solidarity," in *Led by the Spirit*, 146.

[125] Soares-Prabhu, "The Spirituality of Jesus," 99-100.

[126] Fiorenza, *Jesus*, 145.

[127] Rayan, "Jesus – A Flesh-Translation of Divine Compassion," 81.

[128] Samuel Rayan, "Symbols of the Spirit," *Ministerial Formation* 50 (July, 1990): 10.

[129] Doss, "The Spirit of Life: Rayan's Thoughts on the Holy Spirit," in *The Vision of a New Church and a New Society: A Scholarly Assessment of Dr Samuel Rayan's Contribution to Indian Christian Theology*, ed. Kurien Kunnumpuram (New Delhi: Christian World Prints, 2016), 44.

[130] Samuel Rayan, "Spirituality for Our Times," in *Life in Abundance: Indian Christian Reflections on Spirituality*, ed. Kurien Kunnumpuram (Mumbai: St Paul's, 2010), 232.

[131] Rayan, "The Basic Dilemma," Extract from "Development and Evangelization," in *The Church and the Development Dilemma*, ed. Tony Byrne (Eldoret, Kenya: Gaba Publications, 1971), 45.

[132] Therefore, Soares-Prabhu says that the incarnation is always a call to follow Jesus in his solidarity with humankind, expressed concretely through his consistent and progressive identification with the poor. Soares-Prabhu, *Biblical Spirituality of Liberative Action*, 99-100.

[133] For example, Mk 7:21-31 depicts the harshness of Jesus' reaction towards the Syrophoenician woman. She acts independently, without anyone to help on her behalf. Her trust in Jesus enables her to disregard the social boundaries between Jews and Gentiles to seek help from a Jewish man. She in fact challenges Jesus to ignore the barriers between Jews and Gentiles. In this she is similar to the woman with the flow of blood (5:24-34), who depicts the courage to act independently. Her story indicates that the mission of Jesus is for both Jews and Gentiles. Susan Miller, *Women in Mark's Gospel* (London, New York: T & T International A Continuum Imprint, 2004), 90-93.

[134] Fiorenza, *In Memory of Her*, 140-151. Fiorenza uses the idea of *basileia* of the Jesus movement, to reject oppression and to foster the process of transformation in the Church.

[135] Borg, *Meeting Jesus Again for the First Time*, 56.

[136] Fiorenza, *In Memory of Her*, 136, 152.

[137] Fiorenza, *Transforming Vision*, 197.

[138] Jacob Kavunkal, *Anthropophany: Mission as Making a New Humanity* (Delhi: ISPCK, 2008), 148-149.

[139] George M. Soares-Prabhu, "The Table Fellowship of Jesus: It's Significance for *Dalit* Christians in India Today," *JD* 22 (1999): 152-53.

[140] Hellwig, *Jesus: The Compassion of God*, 106-107.

[141] Kasper, *The God of Jesus Christ*, 196.

[142] Today's enhanced knowledge of the socio-economic and political conditions prevailing in Palestine at the time of Jesus helps us to understand better why his message and ministry in general were truly good news to the poor. From the large crowds of beggars, the sick, the crippled, the lame, and the 'possessed' that meet us in the Gospels it is clear that the poor made up a large part of the population of Palestine at the time of Jesus. George M. Soares-Prabhu, "Radical Beginnings: The Jesus Community as the Archetype of the Church," in *Theology of Liberation: An Indian Biblical Perspective, Collected Writings of George M. Soares-Prabhu*, vol. IV ed, Francis X. D'Sa (Pune: Jnana-Deepa Vidyapeeth Theology Series, 2001), 139.

[143] Surekha Lobo, *Compassion as Commitment to Christian Life: A Holistic Dimension of Theological Response to the Challenges Presented in Evangelii Gaudium*, A Research Paper Submitted to the Faculty of Theology in Partial Fulfilment of the Requirements for the Pre-doctoral Programme (Pune: Jnana-Deepa Vidyapeeth, 2015), 36-41.

[144] Therefore, an experience of God is not so much an insight into the ontological structure of reality but an insight into the meaning of life telling one what life is all about, offering a guide for living, showing us the way (*hodos, marga*). George M. Soares-Prabhu, "The Jesus of Faith: A Christological Contribution to an Ecumenical Third World Spirituality," in *The Dharma of Jesus*, ed. Francis Xavier D'Sa (Maryknoll, New York: Orbis Books, 2003), 93.

[145] What compelled the woman was her feminine genius and her faith propelled her to touch the hem of his garments in an unnoticeable way. The expression is taken from the *Letter to Women* which calls for attention, to become more visible so that society will be more humane, more respectful of the dignity and vocation of each person, and more to the measure of the human being. Adding to the idea of complementarity, the idea of feminine genius serves to highlight the specificity of women; the "feminine genius" can be a valuable category for conceptualizing the contributions that women as women make to the Church and society. Cf. Pope John Paul II, *Letter to Women* (1995), No.10.

[146] Virginia Saldanha says the women were an important group whom Jesus reached out to in breaking several taboos that oppressed them. E.g. Jesus talked to a Samaritan Woman, he asked for a drink of water and discussed theology with her (Jn 4:7-39); he allowed a woman to anoint his feet (Jn 12:1-8); he saved a woman from being stoned, (Jn 8:3-11). Cf. Virginia Saldanha, "Christian Discipleship: Women's Perspective" in *The Church in India in the Emerging Third Millennium*, ed. Thomas D'Sa (Bangalore: NBCLC, 2005), 462.

[147] Pope Francis urged the new cardinals "to serve Jesus crucified in every person who is marginated from society, for whatever reason; to see the Lord in every excluded person who is hungry, thirsty, naked; to see the Lord present even in those who have lost their faith, or turned away from the practice of their faith; to see the Lord who is imprisoned, sick, unemployed, persecuted; to see the Lord in the leper

– whether in body or soul - who encounters discrimination!" Gerard O'Connell, "Pope Francis: 'The Gospel of the Marginalized Is Where Our Credibility Is Found and Revealed,'" *America Jesuit Review*, February 2015, http://www.america magazine. org/content/dispatches/pope-francis-gospel-marginalized-where-our-credibility-found- and-revealed (accessed August 23, 2017).

[148] Soares-Prabhu, "The Spirituality of Jesus," 93.

[149] Rayan, "Jesus and the Poor," 228.

[150] Soares-Prabhu, "The Spirituality of Jesus," 101.

[151] Rayan, *Breath of Fire*, 35-36, 75, 128.

[152] Samuel Rayan, "Symbols of the Spirit," in *CWSR – III*, 138, as cited in Doss, "*The Spirit of Life*,"44-45.

[153] Samuel Rayan, "This Man is Jesus," *JD* 16/92 (March 1986), 155.

[154] Samuel Rayan, "With Us – With Whom – Is God?" in *Jesus: The Relevance of His Person and Message for our Times: Selected Writings of Samuel Rayan*, Vol I, ed. Kurien Kunnumpuram (Mumbai: St. Pauls, 2011) 162.

[155] Jacob Neusner, *From Politics to Piety* (Englewood Cliffs, NJ: Prentice Hall, 1973), 83-90.

[156] Jacob Neusner, "Two Pictures of the Pharisees: Philosophical Circle or Eating Club," *Anglican Theological Review* 64 (1982): 525-538.

[157] Fiorenza, *In Memory of Her*, 121.

[158] Soares-Prabhu, "The Spirituality of Jesus," 93.

[159] Dawe, Donald G. *The Form of a Servant* (WIPF & STOCK: Oregon, 2011), 17.

[160] Christopher Steck, "In Union with the Paschal Mystery: the Eucharist and Suffering in the Thought of John Paul II" in *Pope John Paul II on the Body: Human, Eucharistic, Ecclesial*, eds. John M. McDermott & John Gavin (Philadelphia: St. Joseph's University Press, 2007), 317-321.

[161] Pedro Arrupe, *Address delivered at the International Eucharistic Congress* (Philadelphia, August, 1976).

[162] T.K. John, ed. *Bread and Breath: Essays in Honour of Samuel Rayan SJ. Jesuit Theological Forum Reflections* 5 (Anand, Gujarat: Gujarat Sahitya Prakash, 1991), xii

[163] Soares-Prabhu, *Biblical Spirituality of Liberative Action*, 6-7.

[164] Soares-Prabhu, *Dharma of Jesus*, 32.

[165] Max Weber, *The Theory of Social and Economic Organization* ed. Talcott Parsons (New York: Free press, 1964), 328, as cited in George M. Soares-Prabhu, "The Liberative Pedagogy of Jesus: Lessons for an Indian Theology of Liberation," in *Leave the Temple: Indian Paths to Human Liberation*, ed. Felix Wilfred (Maryknoll, NY: Orbis, 1992), 106

[166] Walter Wink, *Engaging the Powers: Discernment and Resistance in a World of Domination* (Minneapolis: Fortress Press, 1992), 129.

[167] Wink, Engaging the Powers, 129

[168] Wink, *Engaging the Powers*, 129

[169] Rayan, "With Us-With Whom? –Is God?"44.

[170] Rayan, "With Us-With Whom? –Is God?" 45.

[171] Pope Benedict XVI, *Jesus of Nazareth* (New York: Doubleday, 2007), 60.

[172] Rayan, "With Us-With Whom?-Is God?" 46.

[173] Parappally, "Meaning of Jesus Christ in the Indian Context: The Christological Vision of Samuel Rayan," 13.

Chapter 5

Presence-Solidarity: A Paradigm for a *Kenotic* Mission

Introduction

The analysis of the situation and the challenges that emerge from a globalized era in the 21st century India (Chapter I) provides the context for the Church in India to make a decisive choice and an appropriate Christian response. The purpose of this chapter is to bring out the correlation between the Christology of *Presence-Solidarity* and the polarized Indian society of today – the *locus theologicus* of Christian theological reflection.[1] This is the crux of the reign of God which Jesus preached, practised and for which he died. Theology is authentic when it is at the service of life, when concerns of life are related to it, and when it has praxis. In addition, this chapter will respond to the concerns related to the socio-economic and cultural context in the light of the Christology of *Presence-Solidarity*.

In the context of socio-economic and cultural context of India this chapter proposes a renewed vision for the Church that is shaped by the *kenotic* mission of Jesus.[2] This chapter consists of three sections: 1) the vocation of the Church; 2) Presence-Solidarity as a paradigm for mission today; and 3) vision ahead for a *kenotic* mission today.

1. The Vocation of the Church

The Christology of *Presence-Solidarity* invites the Christians for an appropriate response in the Indian context. What follows next is an assessment of the commitment of the Church safeguarding the centrality of the human person and the sublimity of the Gospel values in all her projects and vision of solidarity. The effort here is to deepen insights based on the rich heritage of the Church's teachings founded on Gospel values.

1.1 *Imago Dei* Based Approach

The source of the Church's understanding of the intrinsic worth of every human being is human dignity. From the Christian perspective the source of human dignity is rooted in the concept of *imago Dei* (Gen 1:26-27), in Christ's redemption and in humans' ultimate destiny of union with God. Human dignity, therefore, transcends any social order as the basis for rights; it is neither granted by society nor can it be legitimately violated by society. In this way, human dignity as God given in alienate gift is the theological basis for human rights.[3] The Church is called upon and challenged to recognize the inherent worth and dignity of each person, and then take up the challenges faced today. Without such a perspective and focus, lasting and sustaining effects can only be a dream and not a reality.

In the liberative mission, the Church assumes the role of being a servant as Jesus was. She imitates his work in mutual service as brothers, sisters, and friends to one another. Thereby Christ continues to be present in history through the Spirit "as the true image of God in God's basic attitude towards humankind" (Jn 1:14, 13:1).[4] Such a practice of faith responds to God's will and favours life and not a 'culture of death'. The Church therefore has to challenge the fundamental division between the rich and the poor, and stand in solidarity with the poor. What impels the Church to solidarity with the poor is Christ the Incarnate and the Crucified One. The suffering of Christ continues in the lives of the poor. This is our faith and our assumption.

The Catholic Church, down the ages, has not only identified the sanctity of human life as a precious gift of God, but the Church is always prompt to address any threats to human dignity and contribute her share to enhance the quality of life.[5] The emphasis on the sanctity of human life is defined in the *Catechism of the Catholic Church*: God has imprinted his own image and likeness on humans (cf. Gen 1:26), conferring upon them an incomparable dignity:

> Human life is sacred because from its beginning it involves the creative action of God and it remains forever in a special relationship with the Creator, who is its sole end. God alone is the Lord of life from its beginning until its end: no one can under any circumstance claim for himself the right directly to destroy an innocent human being (CCC 2258).

Pope John Paul II in his encyclical *Centesimus Annus* states: Human persons are willed by God; they "are imprinted" with God's image and likeness (cf. Gen 1:26). Their dignity does not come from the work they do, "but which flow from his essential dignity as a person" (*CA* 11). The Church while highlighting the inherent dignity and prolife approach to human life expresses her deep concern over human beings who are defined by their creation as the image of God. Therefore, human dignity is grounded in the biblical motif of humanity created in God's image and existing as *imago Dei* before God. Human persons are to be treated with equal dignity and respect after the example of Christ the promoter of life. Dehumanization is the greatest threat to humans today, which means taking the human persons for granted, taking away the human dignity in the name of freedom and development. The Church continues to take an approach proper to individuals and societies to live as a dignified person.

1.2 Preferential Option for the Poor

The preferential option for the poor derives from the biblical understanding of the *anawim*, the vulnerable ones, who have only Yahweh as their protector. God's love takes up human fragility at its breaking point and embraces it, not in a dream, but in the flesh of his only Son. Quoting Isaiah, Jesus too describes his mission in Luke 4:16-21 as one of Good News to the poor, liberty for captives, healing for the sick and freedom for the oppressed. Here in the Gospel the ministry of Jesus is basic, and the basic thrust of this ministry is to the poor, the *anawim*. The ministry of Jesus excludes no one, but the authenticating sign of this is that the Good news is preached to the poor.

Following the ministry of Jesus faithfully, the preferential option for the poor and the vulnerable has been the most consistent insistence by the Church.[6] In this way the Church continues to keep alive her faith in the God of Jesus Christ who is present in the poor and whose glory is the life of the poor. When the Church takes on a preferential identification with the poor, she affirms the universality that is proper to God, an affirmation which gradually enhances fellowship in the world; thereby the Church validates God's presence in human history.

The Church as we know stood as the spokesperson for humanity wherever there were elements of dehumanization and injustice. The outreach was to any section of humanity irrespective of religion, caste, creed or gender.[7] In 1961 Pope John XXIII in *Mater et Magistra*, an encyclical on Christianity and Social Progress, gave favourable support to the members of the Church working in solidarity with the poor and oppressed:

> The solidarity which binds all men [and women] together as members of a common family makes it impossible for wealthy nations to look with indifference upon the hunger, misery and poverty of other nations whose citizens are unable to enjoy even elementary human rights. The nations of the world are becoming more and more dependent on one another and it will not be possible to preserve a lasting peace so long as glaring economic and social imbalances persist (*MM* 114).

The old formula 'no salvation outside the Church' is now replaced by 'no salvation outside God's covenant with the poor'. The evangelically poor receive their mission through their solidarity with the socially poor.[8] The poor are not just objects of charity. They are agents of social change as well. As for all human beings, their dignity comes from being the image of God, being co-responsible for creation. Therefore, the efforts for the empowerment of the poor are the manifestation of the option for the poor. Accordingly, when God in Jesus reigns in justice and mercy, no child on earth will go hungry, no one will be pushed into the state of frustration and self-hatred, and poverty will become history. The women will be helped to generate regard and respect, equity and equality. The labourers and farmers will receive their rightful reward.

1.3 A Church of the Poor

In all epochs the Church has made efforts to resolve the problems of the poor and has considered it as part of her mission of sharing in the great mission of God. God in Jesus Christ has participated in human life. The divine-human interaction in Jesus Christ is of a substantial meaning to humanity. The phrase "Church of the Poor" was first used by Pope John XXIII in his radio message to the world on 11th September, 1962.[9]

Fifty seven years ago, on the eve of the Second Vatican Council, Pope John XXIII called on the faithful to be the "Church of the poor." He proclaimed that the Church is a "Church of all and in particular the Church of the poor."[10] It was later picked up by Asian Bishops at their historic first meeting in Manila in 1970. Finally, it became the core message of the Second Plenary Council of the Philippines (PCP II) in 1991.[11] Since the Vatican II, notably the Document *Gaudium et Spes*, the Church has addressed issues of concern to everyone without limiting its reach to Christian believers alone. Thus the document clearly stated that whatever the joy and hope, grief and anguish are experienced by the women and men of our age would be embraced by the Christians everywhere as their own joy and hope, grief and anguish, thereby believing and living their role in ushering in God's salvation for every woman and man.[12]

A theological basis for solidarity with the poor has to be founded on human dignity. *Sollicitudo Rei Socialis* (SRS 40) views solidarity as a unique Christian virtue, which, coupled with Christian charity or love, ought to inspire us more than what it does in a secular ambience. (cf. Jn 13:35). Therefore, solidarity as a moral virtue and spiritual value has to begin with a personal conversion of one's interior attitude and eventually lead to commitment and service. Well aware the obstacles humans face in their integral growth, the Pontiff particularly encourages and invites people to reflect and change their spiritual attitudes. (*SRS*, 38).

The vision of a Church of the poor has been the defining factor in Pope Francis's papacy. We have already witnessed the impact of his unique and amazing approach. Pope Francis's conception of poverty and the poor goes far beyond conventional secular understandings of these subjects. Pope Francis further affirmed it strongly when he gave a blueprint of his understanding of the Church as the Church of the poor and for the poor; a Church that is bruised and broken, one with the poor on the streets: "I prefer a Church which is bruised, hurting, and dirty because it has been out on the streets, rather than a Church which is unhealthy from being confined, and from clinging to its own security. I do not want a Church concerned with being at the centre, and then ends by being caught up in a web of obsessions and procedures. Instead a Church which goes forth is a Church whose doors are open" (*EG* 49).

A theology of solidarity is a theology of empowerment and transformation that fully recognizes the worth of the human person and supports the initiatives of the oppressed in working out their own salvation. The Church, by her active involvement and participation in the struggles of the poor, "can become a real symbol of the poor".[13] According to Jon Sobrino, "A Church that arises in solidarity with the poor, protests against their material poverty as being an expression of the world's sin, engages in a struggle against this poverty as a form of liberation, and allows itself to be affected by this poverty and its consequences as an expression of its own *kenosis*."[14] If the Church has to continually incarnate herself in the footsteps of her master, she has to be the Church of the poor.

The Church continues to stand as the spokesperson for humanity whenever there are elements of injustice and inhumanity is marked out. However, a culture of *Presence-Solidarity* is the need of the hour over our culture of indifference. The Church has emphasized this several times, but the system continues as before, because the market economy is dominated by a dynamics that lacks ethics.

1.4 Dignity of Labour and of the Labourer

When human persons are cared for, when there is equal distribution of wealth and opportunities, poverty can be eradicated, and human dignity can be ensured. But the operating value system of the corporate culture seems to be: you are what you have, and the society is ruled by the tendency to accumulate material wealth and consider it equal to growth and prosperity. The Church however upholds the dignity of both labour and the labourer. *Pacem in Terris* (Peace on Earth, John XXIII, 1963, henceforth referred as *PT*) was a key document that picked up and embraced fully the language of human rights. The "rights" language provided an important framework to promote and defend human dignity. *PT* asserted a need for social and economic rights, not just political and legal rights. Life in community is the context in which human dignity can be protected and expanded.[15] Indian society and in fact any human society, if it is to be well-ordered and productive, must lay down as a foundation the principle: 'Every human being is a person.' Indeed, precisely because one is a person one has rights and obligations (*PT* 9).

Catholic Social Teaching holds that work is dignified and an intrinsic good and workers must always be respected and valued. John Paul II observed in *Laborem Exercens*: On Human Work: "Christianity brought about a fundamental change of ideas in this field [the nature of work], taking the whole content of the Gospel message as its point of departure, especially the fact that the one who, while being God, became like us in all things [and] devoted most of the years of His life on earth to manual work at the carpenter's bench."[16]

Expounding on the dignity of work, Pope Francis said: "We do not get dignity from power or money or culture. We get dignity from work. Work is fundamental to the dignity of the person. Work, to use an image, 'anoints' with dignity, fills us with dignity, makes us similar to God who has worked and still works, who always acts."[17]

1.5 Inclusive Approach to Humanity

The Pastoral Constitution of the Church in the Modern World (*Gaudium et Spes*)[18] was path-breaking in broadening the Church's viewpoint from a closed approach to openness to the well-being of the "whole of humanity" (*GS* 2). The document marks a historical and radical development in the Catholic Church's openness to, and commitment to dialogue with the modern world. Human dignity is presented positively as the right to share in the decisions that structure political, social, and economic life. Since the Second Vatican Council, notably the document *Gaudium et Spes*, the Church has addressed issues of concern to the whole human family without limiting its reach to Christian believers alone:

> The joy and the hope, the grief and the anguish of the men [women] of this age, especially of those who are poor or in any way afflicted, these are the joy and hope, the grief and anguish of the followers of Christ. Nothing that is genuinely human fails to raise an echo in their hearts. For theirs is a community composed of men [women]. United in Christ, they are led by the Holy Spirit in their journey to Kingdom [the reign of God] of their Father and they have welcomed the news of salvation which is meant for every man [woman]. [19]

This is a dramatic link between the lives of the people – all people, but especially the poor and the suffering – with the lives of those who confess to be Christian. This document, is considered as, "the most authoritative and significant document of catholic social teaching issued in the twentieth century."[20] The focal point of this document is the person, who is the crown and centre of all creation in the universe. In its concern for equal opportunity for women, its positive appreciation of culture, its sense for what is now called globalization, it's pointing to social and economic inequalities as threats to peace, and calling for a multilateral approach to justice issues, *GS* was clearly prophetic.[21]

The Second Vatican Council's call to the Church to be inclusive speaks of the passionate desire of the Fathers of the Council to embrace everyone - women and men, and the people of all cultures, creeds and classes, and particularly the ones on the margins and peripheries.

1.6 Communion of Communities

In *Ecclesia in Asia*, Pope John Paul II interpreted the saving work of Christ in terms of a twofold communion or relationship offered to the believers: first a communion with Trinity and secondly a communion among themselves (*EA* 12). To effect this twofold communion and initiate in the believers the process of the saving mission, Jesus enters human history to reconcile humanity with the God and makes it possible for people to live as brothers and sisters (Mt 23:9) (*EA* 13).

Christian *Presence-Solidarity* is more radical: even the enemy must be loved "with the same love with which the Lord loves him or her, which ultimately means a willingness to lay down our lives for him or her" (*SRS* 40). The clarion call of the teachings of the Church, as articulated very remarkably in *Sollicitudo Rei Socialis* is to see the neighbour not only as an autonomous human being with rights and fundamental equality but as the living image of God the Father, redeemed by the blood of Jesus Christ and placed under the permanent action of the Holy Spirit.

In this context John Paul II brings an apt line of thought which he had developed in Catholic Social Teaching through the twentieth century: *Opus Solidaritatis Pax* – that peace will come only through solidarity – or (to put it negatively) without solidarity we shall never have peace (*SRS* 39). [22]

In the task of building communion of communities the Church can contribute significantly through her social ministries. George Pattery's reflections are pertinent here:

> A principal weapon to fight against communalism in India is our Constitution that places equality, fraternity and community as central tenets in contrast to the divisive agenda of the communalists. We should highlight the values of our Constitution in all our ministries. Our social ministries should collaborate with local government and law enforcing agencies to promote peace and reconciliation among communities at the grassroots. We should work for harmony, mutual understanding and

anticipate communal tensions and also work for peace and reconciliation of the protagonists after incidents of communal violence occur …[we shall] join all people of goodwill to defeat the forces of hate and violence by promoting a politics of pluralism and inclusion that ensures justice, equality, liberty and fraternity.[23]

The various themes based on the conciliar documents discussed above reflect the consistency of the Church in reaching out to the periphery, upholding human dignity after the model of Jesus Christ in a spirit of solidarity.

Vatican II insists in its documents Church's role in encouraging Ecumenism *Unitatis Redintegratio (UR)* and also on Church's interest in relation to non-Christian religions *Nostra Aetate (NA)*. The Catholic Church is invited to enter into dialogue and collaboration with all Christians, all faith communities and with all people of good will.[24] Hence Vatican II speaks of the Church as a "sacrament-a sign and instrument, that is, of communion with God and of unity among all people"[25] Pope Francis in *EG* reemphasises, the importance of the dialogue and collaboration with all religions with a view to further the cause of the common good.[26] Pope Francis declares that "Interreligious dialogue is a necessary condition for peace in the world. And so it is a duty for Christians as well as other religious communities."[27] All the religions are but journeying towards the reign of God and are therefore called to collaborate in the task of building communion of communities for the promotion of freedom, fellowship and justice. What follows is a "Gender Sensitive approach."

1.7 Gender Sensitive Approach

The description of women as portrayed in the ecclesial documents reveals the place given to women by the official Church. Catholic Social Teaching and the documents contain a solid roadmap for opening doors to women because God has given a lead, by choosing Mary, a woman to collaborate with the plan of Salvation.[28] The *Catechism of the Catholic Church* leaves no room for doubt: "Man and woman have the same dignity and are of equal value" (CCC 369). This is not merely a truth to be acknowledged but a statement that needs continuous and active promotion. In 1963, *Pacem in Terris* Pope John XXIII approved of women becoming increasingly confident of their natural dignity, and of their 'demanding both in domestic and in public life the rights and duties which belong to them as human persons' (PT 41).

Second Vatican Council emphasized the need for greater recognition of the equality of all, and for the eradication, as contrary to God's intent', of every kind of discrimination, including that based on sex.[29] Further, the Apostolic Letter, *Mulieris Dignitatem*, declares:

> The Church gives thanks *for all the manifestations of the feminine "genius"* which have appeared in the course of history, in the midst of all peoples and nations; she gives thanks for all the charisms which the Holy Spirit distributes to women in the history of the People of God, for all the victories which she owes to their faith, hope and charity: she gives thanks for all *the fruits of feminine holiness.*[30]

The CBCI has been interested in women's empowerment for many years now. In 1979 during the General Assembly held in Ranchi, the Bishops acknowledged that the "women are still considered in many ways inferior to man."[31] In 1988, the General Body Meeting of the CBCI, Nagpur.[32] In 1996 General Assembly of Bishops, the Women's Desk was raised to the status of a Commission "because of the specific problems related to women in our social, economic, cultural and political realities."[33] The 28th Plenary Assembly of the CBCI, held in Jamshedpur in February 2008, deliberated on the theme – Empowerment of Women in the Church and Society. On 8th December 2009, the Catholic Bishops' Conference of India issued a document titled - *Gender Policy of the Catholic Church of India.*

The Church down the centuries has failed to uphold the place Jesus gave to women. Women still feel controlled under a patriarchal and androcentric ideology. Pope Francis is in fact taking forward the spirit of gospel and of the Second Vatican II and he calls for an inclusion of women in the life of the Church at all levels namely pastoral, formation of youth, accompaniment of people, families, as well as in the theological reflection.[34] Pontiff's approach reflects a sense of urgency in creating equal space for women in the Church.

Although the Church officially has advanced in successive ages of her history, in making a dialogue with the modern context, no one can negate that the Church down the centuries was dominated by patriarchy and struggles to uphold the place Jesus gave to women. The question whether the contents of the official texts are sensitive to the emerging consciousness of women, is a matter of some concern.

The various themes based on the conciliar and post conciliar documents discussed above reflect the consistency of the Church in reaching out to the periphery, upholding dignity after the model of Jesus Christ in a spirit of solidarity. The following section focuses on the relevance of *Presence-Solidarity* as a paradigm for a *kenotic* mission.

2. Presence–Solidarity as a Paradigm for Mission Today

The book began with a question: Does Jesus have an appeal for India today or what relevance has his message and person for the liberation of our masses? The significance of Jesus' *Presence-Solidarity* as a paradigm for a *kenotic* mission from the perspective of the dehumanized women and men is the nucleus of this book . Brief explanations of the key concepts would enable us to decipher the relevance of the *Presence-Solidarity* of God in Jesus. *Presence Solidarity* is not limited to Christianity but it goes beyond the boundaries of caste, creed and gender.[35]

This subsection attempts to reflect on the three interrelated aspects of the paradigm *Presence-Solidarity* and its relevance for India today, namely: 1) key challenges; 2) Presence-Solidarity; 3) *kenotic* mission today.

2.1 Review of Today's Key Challenges

The challenges of today's milieu (Chapter 1) beckon the Church to adopt a new approach, a new perspective and a new vision for mission today. The challenges of today impel us to take note of the growing interculturality of society, and the continuing dehumanized situation of millions of our brothers and sisters. The present Indian scenario is witnessing the awakening of the marginalized groups such as the *Dalits*, Tribals, and women. They seek their identity and rights in the socio-economic and cultural process, though they still struggle to liberate themselves to grow to full humanity. However, the socio-economic systems still hold them captive and insignificant due to centuries of patriarchy that is embedded in their psyche.

Discrimination and inequalities of gender, caste, and class are very much interlinked to the traditional, socio-cultural, religious and economic roots. Caste system is becoming virulent day by day. The reality of women who, on the one hand, are beginning to find their space in knowledge making, political leadership and economic productivity, while on the other, are being constrained by the persistence of the different expressions of gender discrimination and are subject to in their particular socio-economic and multi-religio-cultural contexts in society. Can we simply bypass the systematic denial of human dignity in India today? Communalism uses religion as a political tool to branding of the other as enemy. There are political parties which are using religion to promote their economic and political interests.

The *kenotic* model of Jesus' mission brings hope to the socio-economic and multi-religio-cultural society of India, where relationship with God and others and even unto one's self gradually losing its essence and value. The need of the hour is to conscientise the people, both the victims and the oppressors – of the value and sacredness of human dignity. Accordingly, the mission of the Church is to understand the challenges of today's milieu and our responsibility to discern the movement of God's continuing but invisible presence of Jesus Christ today.[36] The Statement XXXIII Biennial Plenary of CBCI states: "Our Christian faith gives us hope to move ahead to continue our work for unity in diversity so as to establish peace and harmony and make our country live up to its exalted calling."[37]

The Indian Church, "in the five decades after Vatican II, has never stopped its explorative search for different ways to serve the nation, while engaging itself in the evangelization mission, which is the very purpose of its existence."[38] However, it must also be candidly accepted that the Indian Church has fallen prey to unjust systems like the caste system, and distanced herself from the poor through her institutions that cater to the needs of the rich. In the present struggles the Church has "to join hands with our fellow citizens to ensure the authentic human development" and to transcend every kind of divisiveness "in order to establish a truly secular, socialist and democratic nation as is enshrined in the Constitution of India". The Church should leave no stones unturned "to respect the equal dignity of women and to promote the role of the laity in the life and mission of the Church."[39]

2.2 Presence-Solidarity

The hyphenated phrase *Presence-Solidarity* is a theological expression which speaks of God's saving presence and solidarity with us in Jesus Christ. It refers to God's dynamic presence among us, which involves solidarity - *Immanuel* or God with us. This theological expression *Presence-Solidarity* should be understood as a DYNAMIC process of God's *kenotic* mission in Jesus. It is like the yeast in the dough. Yeast is apparently quiet or silent or invisible, but actually it is dynamic, churning, fermenting, and transforming the dough. *Presence-Solidarity* after the model of Jesus should be seen as a dynamic way of being present in the mission. For example, the presence of Mother Mary at Cana is an effective presence, dynamic presence, and a timely presence, or Veronica, who was being moved internally, went forward in a daring way to wipe the face of Jesus carrying the Cross. Simon of Cyrene's presence towards Jesus to carry the Cross is another example. From an unwilling passer-by, he became a generous helper to Jesus in his redemptive path. Every good done to the needy becomes an experience of the *Presence-Solidarity*. The pioneering works of all the founders/ foundresses of various Religious Congregations are in reality a pedagogy for *Presence-Solidarity*.[40]

Amidst the changes and progress, there arises in us an earnest desire to find a place for Jesus Christ and his message: How to present Jesus and make his message relevant in India today? The 'presence solidarity' of the Word made Flesh demands the destruction of the unjust structures that exploit and disrupt the very fabric of human relationship.

2.3 Partners of Mission Today

Etymologically the word *mission* derives from the Latin word *mittere*, "to send," and *missio*, "sending." The term mission entered common usage in the seventh century. Previously one spoke more of 'apostolate', or 'apostolic office'.[41] However, mission takes many forms and meanings. In all cases it implies a person or an agency which sends someone to somebody else with a message that implies an action. In theological and pastoral language the primary sender of the mission is God. There is *missio Dei* underlying all missions.[42] Therefore, Rayan says:

> Mission consists in doing God's will and in helping, persuading, challenging more and more people to do ever more fully God's will in everything, in ensuring God's rule and sway over our hearts and lives, and histories in terms of justice, love and forgiveness, in terms of bread for all and fair access for all to all divine provisions; in terms of mutual support and collaboration as becomes the children of the one Creator Father who has loved all of us into existence and cares for all without ceasing.[43]

The mission of the Church is a participation in the mission of God in Jesus. Within this context, the researcher looks from the viewpoint of the dehumanized with a view to enhance the life of the peripheries of India today. In order to swim against the current tides of today, the Church is called upon to rediscover her nature so as to be dynamic and achieve her God given mandate for India today.

Nature of *Kenotic* Mission

To paraphrase the questions Rayan posed: Could the Christic *Presence-Solidarity* be a blueprint for a *kenotic* mission? Could it serve as a plan to make this planet free from war, torture and destruction of life, and devoid of greed and domination and distortion of visions and values?[44] Jesus' way is one of *KENOSIS*,[45] a way of self-emptying through self-immersion. The example of the historical Jesus - "in his solidarity with the marginalized of society, his crucifixion and resurrection as signs of his solidarity in suffering and hope…the incarnation as a solidarity of the human and the divine,"[46] is an appropriate paradigm for *kenotic* mission.

The questions then arise: Why this paradigm? Is the concept *kenosis* an appropriate paradigm for women? Wouldn't this paradigm be in conflict with the goal of women's liberation that advocates the empowerment and equality of women? Well, the proposed Christology of *Presence-Solidarity* as a paradigm for a *kenotic* mission for today underscores "a transcending dimension to human suffering" that gives significance to the Christ-event today.[47] *Kenosis* is a way of describing the divine being and the divine action in Jesus Christ. Thus, the nature of a *kenotic* mission would assume visibility when it manifests in love, justice, truth, freedom, equality and peace. It will manifest itself fully when "leading to the emergence of a community of brothers and sisters, changing, therefore, the unjust situations into just ones, oppressive ones to liberative ones, and divisive ones into communitarian ones."[48] In other words, it is an action that describes not only who God is in Jesus Christ but also who the believer must be. It is a call to follow him who came down and emptied himself fully on the Cross. The *Kenotic* model of involvement or leadership is to become a servant leader among the people as one who seeks to serve. It is not a lording over leadership.

Partners of the Mission

The partners of the Radical mission are the poor who are economically exploited, politically oppressed, socially marginalized, culturally dominated and religiously alienated by legalism and ritualism; the marginalized who are the victims of economic self-centeredness, of cultural alienation and of political and religion's domination; the Dalits who are broken, driven asunder, downtrodden, crushed, destroyed, and are displayed; women who are socially unequal, racially discriminated against, sexually harassed; the laity who are marginalized; women who are deprived of their rightful role in the Church; and, all those who are denied communion and participation in the life of human community and hence their rightful place in the Church and society. On the whole, they are those who suffer from injustice and oppression, those who are marginalized and pushed to the peripheries of human society.

The privileged partners of the *Kenotic* mission are obviously the poor in all their nuances as explained above. But the process of reconciliation or transformation of an oppressive structure necessarily calls to the table of or dialogue of reconciliation the oppressors also. The historical Jesus' preaching began inviting people to respect (Mk 1:15). Hence, a *kenotic* mission has to consider also the oppressors, exploiters and the authorities of the power structures to be partners, to make the reign of God a tangible reality here and now. The promoters of the patriarchal institutional Church would also inevitably be partners in this *kenotic* mission.

Pope Francis articulated in one of his homilies his vision: "To be human means to care for one another!"[49] Eventually, forgiveness has to be the liberation of both the oppressor and the oppressed in a new social order. For, hatred begets violence and dies; while love begets peace and dies to live for a new humanity. Hence, according to *de* Lubac, humanity is organically and structurally made one by its divine nature, and the mission of the Church is to help and lead women and men to that pristine unity that they have lost by sinning.[50]

3. The Implications of the Presence–Solidarity for Mission Today

After having read the signs of the times and identifying the concerns and challenges, we reflect on the horizons of hope and harmony that emerge from the *Presence-Solidarity* of Jesus for a *kenotic* mission. Christ is the centre and is at the periphery. The model for the mission of the Church is the Jesus Paradigm, the Christ Event.

Rayan and Fiorenza emphasis on the gospel values for the transformation of the individuals and society. Both of them centre their emphasis on the centrality of the person and message of Jesus for furthering their cause of holistic dimension of Christian vocation.

Presence-Solidarity, therefore, obliges the disciples of Jesus to immerse in the life of the poor, to share in their suffering and restore their dignity. The experience of Jesus as the person-in-solidarity with us provides us not only with hope to transcend the violent social order but also enables the re-birthing of a new social order, a new humanity with peace, freedom, justice and life. It is a call for the Church in India to be on the side of the periphery today. God did not create a finished world, but wants us to join in the task of transformation.

The following section will respond to the concerns initially identified in this book. The new vision for a *kenotic* mission for India today as envisioned by the author is explained in three broad categories: 1) *Presence-Solidarity* that responds to *intra*-Church concerns, 2) *Presence-Solidarity* for a mission of the Church to Indian society, and 3) *Presence-Solidarity* for a multi-religio-cultural society. The focus of the following section is to instill hope and confidence by proposing a horizon for a *kenotic* mission. God's presence in Jesus for the vulnerable will bring freedom, justice and dignity, in spite of numerous hurdles, and in the process will pave the way to build a new humanity. The Church needs to concretize its missionary vocation in the light of the liberative role played by Christ to the point of laying down his life for others.

3.1 Presence-Solidarity that Responds to Intra-Church Concerns

A Christology of *Presence-Solidarity* responds to *Intra*-Church concerns, calls for a new orientation, a new focus, renewed mission, and new values that contrast with today's milieu and with the values promoted by political power. The Church in India is in need of a radical paradigm shift as per Vatican II. This Council made it possible for a new form of Church to emerge in India. The changed perspective will lead to a new emphasis on the existence of the Church in India today.

Partnership – A Challenge to Clericalism

Partnership is a challenge to clericalism. An inclusive integration of laity and women in the ministries of the Church flow from the concept of Church as the People of God. There is fear and anxiety in the hierarchical Church to place an equal emphasis on the role of laity and women in particular in the decision making process and in the exercise of ministries. This emphasis on partnership emerges from the book of Genesis: "God created humankind in his image, in the image of God he created them; male and female he created them" (1:27). There is a dire need to look at this image as one of equals in partnership, sharing goodness and greatness of God himself made visible in the human persons as children of God, man and woman, husband and wife who share the fullness and wholeness of creation. They complete the work of God in a most sublime manner as partners in creation, communication and consecration in the mission of the Lord here on earth. What is needed today is a prophetic witnessing *via* exercise of prophetic ministry – a passionate love for God and humanity. This sort of passion will bring forth something new and radical in keeping with the signs of the times and in accordance with the will of God.

The Church has to recognize the unique role and the immense contribution of women in general and the religious in particular in the field of theology, spirituality, and community. Empowering the powerless is meant to make for an equitable distribution of power in the Church and society. The powerless are those who are silenced by the powerful through domination, violence, injustice, and discrimination. Their voice echoes from the margins, calling the powerful to true freedom and justice. Therefore, giving voice to the voiceless is to give all a chance to participate in and contribute to the common good. Moreover, the prophetic critique keeps the Church faithful to her original mission of witness and service.

Affirming the necessity of an inclusive approach in the Church, Fiorenza recalls the character of the earliest Christian Churches. According to her, Christianity was not originally patriarchal, because the Jesus movement and the early Christian missionary movement were countercultural, radically egalitarian, and inclusive.[51] She further affirms: "Only an egalitarian model for the reconstruction of early Christian history can do justice to both the egalitarian traditions of women's leadership in the Church as well as to the gradual process of adaption and theological justification of the dominant patriarchal Greco-Roman culture and society."[52] According to the gospel narratives/traditions Jesus radically rejected all sorts of dominance and dependence. There is no doubt that women had an affirming atmosphere and a significant role to play in the ministry of Jesus and in the early history of the Church.

The inclusive structures in the Jesus movement provide the theological basis for participatory decision-making and shared responsibility. Women were not marginal figures in the ethos of the Jesus movement, but they exercised leadership as missionaries, founders of Christian communities, apostles, prophets and leaders of the Churches.[53] Although the Church's essential vocation is to be a community without dividing boundaries, in reality the Church in India too is "impoverished and incomplete because it follows only one mode of being Church that is the patriarchal mode which is the unquestionable and accepted mode."[54]

Do women encounter an affirming atmosphere in the Church when a sense of dignity as persons is denied to them in society? Is the Church providing women the much-needed space for participation in the Church? As Joan Chittister observes, "Jesus born of a woman without the agency of a man defies in that very generation all the dualism, hierarchy, domination, and inequality practiced in his name."[55] "From the fact that the Church is a communion, there follow the consequences such as equality, personal dignity, fraternity, solidarity, disciplined obedience and collaboration."[56] Even if women are excluded from the ordained ministry and/or are not included in formal religious hierarchies, women as the recipients of the gifts of the Holy Spirit have a prophetic role to play in the Church and society.

Vatican II categorically affirms that all forms of discrimination are contrary to God's plan, and teaches that all persons are co-equal sharers in the mission and life of the Church. The teaching of the Church respects the dignity of women and calls for women's active participation in almost all spheres. Vatican II emphasized the dignity of women and their unique role in society: "It is fitting that women are able to assume their proper role in accordance with their own nature. It will belong to all to acknowledge and favour the proper and necessary participation of women in the cultural life" (*GS* 60). A call for partnership in the mission and life of the Church, demands collaboration and co-operation for growing in wholeness and becoming aware of fullness of the life in Christ here on earth with a sense of unity and communion.

Positive steps have been taken by the Church in India to make it a reality for men and women to collaborate in the mission of the Church as equal partners. For example, in 1996, the Meeting of the General Body of the CBCI acknowledged: "We reiterate our sincere desire to improve and to perfect the movement towards a truly participatory Church where all sections of the People of God revitalizing their baptismal grace fulfil their vocation and mission. In this context we resolve to emphasize the importance of involving all sections of the Church, especially the laity, and reposing greater confidence in them."[57] The *Gender Policy of the Catholic Church* prepared and promulgated by the CBCI in 2010 lists many objectives.[58] The CBCI has taken a bold step forward by articulating the guiding principles of the *Gender Policy*, which include statements like: i) "equality and dignity of all human persons form the basis of a just and humane society"; ii) "women's empowerment is central to achieving gender equality"; iii) "gender equality is a cross-cutting issue that needs to be integrated in all the commissions, church bodies, institutions, policies and programs of the Church"; and iv) gender equality can be achieved through equal partnership among and between women and men. It is commendable that the document has short-listed eight important areas of concern, policies and strategies for implementation.[59] Therefore, a need arises to set up structures and organs of participation in order to implement such ecclesiological idioms and all-inclusive policy statements and make them a reality in the Church.

What will uphold the dignity of women in the Church is an alternative understanding of authority. An alternative understanding of authority embraces the following: one, an understanding of authority that nurtures life through a life system of partnership and interdependence; two, an attitude that makes the other as vital agent of dialogue and collaboration; three, an ability to recognize creative power and reaffirm it by entering into relationships of partnership; and four, a horizon in which all discriminatory exercise of power games disappears, prejudices are shed, and one is free to hold dialogue with women as equal partners. In addition to an alternative mode of authority, an adequate biblical and theological formation will invest women with power/scope to play their apt role in the Church. Further, an appropriate strategy of constructive dialogue in view of challenging and changing the gender stereotypes in the Church and society will help in handling these concerns.

Therefore, there arises a need for greater mutuality in mission, which implies working out new structures of collaboration at the parochial and diocesan levels as well as at the national level. More women are to be seen and heard in the fields of theological formation, spiritual direction and leadership. "Partnership is a concept that needs to delve into a greater depth so that women's place and role in the Church becomes clearer."[60] What is required is to break down the wall of patriarchy by "the deconstructing myths and stereotypes that discriminate and marginalize women", and "by re-writing his-story that is inclusive of her-story." To put it succinctly, "a levelling of hierarchical grades will bring about a constructive change in the balance" of status and position between women and men, and clerics and laity.[61]

Obviously the question would be: "who will roll the stone away?" It is the task of both men and women in the Church to give a new understanding of where women stand and how women and men together can make of the Church a sacrament of the *Presence-Solidarity* of God with humanity. The foundation for the Church's praxis of a partnership or shared responsibility is the Holy Trinity. The equality that prevails in the mystery of the Trinity is to be regained in ways that shape the life and praxis of the Church in India into a participatory Church that is inclusive and respects diversity.

Engendering Emancipation of Women

The term "emancipate" implies the presence of oppressive historical factors that have shaped assumptions, values, attitudes, and behaviours in both tradition and people.[62] Jesus was committed to the structural changes in society and to justice, which is amply clear from his vision of a new society inferred from his proclamation of the reign of God. One of the most conspicuous and controversial aspects of the renewal movement founded by him was his table fellowship. It is an expression of a radically new theological vision, rooted in a new experience of God, and calling for a new kind of society.[63] Jesus emerged as a prophet of counter culture, undoubtedly it was out of his experience and that of his community's experience of brokenness, enslavement and oppression. Jesus was victimised for his stand in favour of a society that manifests the reign of God.

In addition to all our discussions, Mary's *Magnificat* highlights the grandeur dimensions of God's universal salvific plan transcending the boundaries of time, space and class. God's mercy is for all who fear God (Lk 1:50); God reaches out to the poor, the lowly and the destitute (Lk 1:52-53). Mary as the representative of the new Israel, the new people of God, speaks of God's work of liberation, justice and fullness of life for all and forever. Hence, "developing freedom of thought about the worth of women with their individuality would lead to transformation of women's perception of themselves."[64] The empowerment of women would reinforce women to recognize their worth and value their share in the wider context of the Church and society.

Evolving woman theology has to be brought to light and highlighted in manifesting the unique theological interpretation of the life and mission of the Lord as he recognized and respected the role of women in his public ministry. This is beautifully and powerfully reflected in the gospels in the person of Mary our Blessed Mother. The role of our Blessed Mother in the life of her Son from womb to tomb is so unique and special in realizing the plan of God in a sublime manner. For example, Mary at Cana. Her instrumentality in the messianic plan of God in Jesus revealing his own glory signifies women's contribution in daily life and in the significant events in the Church's life (Jn 2:1-11). Mary at the foot of the Cross, sharing in the suffering and agony of her only Son at crucifixion (Jn 19:25-29).

Considering the oppression of women on the basis of gender, caste and their struggle for freedom and human dignity, our effort is to make the emancipation of women possible. This would imply creating an alertness, which would involve developing a counter culture in India today, in affirming first of all the dignity of the human person and promoting life enhancing protection. For the dream to come true the Church together with all the religions – whose basic message is to value human life – has to strive assiduously. As a result, the dignity of women is recognized, thereby, they get involved in the decision-making processes. Thus, more women in leadership ascertain that the progress of women includes the progress of the Church and society and ultimately of the nation.

The Church in India will flourish only when it recognizes the full potential of women's role and status in the Church and society. Pope Francis calls for more widespread and "incisive" female presence in the leadership of the Catholic Church. Further, Pope expresses his desire to see "many women involved in pastoral responsibilities, in the accompaniment of persons, families and groups, as well as in theological reflection."[65]

The 33rd Plenary Body Meeting of the CBCI held in 2018 reaffirmed the inclusive mode in the life of the Church. To live in unity in the midst of diversity, both within the Church and in the country, CBCI proposes certain measures: to ensure adequate representation of women in all Church bodies; to respect the equal dignity of women; and, to promote the role of the laity in the life and mission of the Church.[66]

We will describe below some of the ways through which the vision of the CBCI Statement concerning the life of women in the Church and in society can be realized:

i)   A continued dialogue with women in the Church as well as in society is imperative; dialoguing with women would create a platform for healthy reconciliation, mutual reciprocity, which would result in greater collaboration, and "cooperation among women and men at all levels – family, work place, Church and society."[67]

ii) Women on their part need to speak aloud their concerns, and carry on their search till all their untapped resources are explored and utilized for the mission of Christ with greater relevance. Moreover, a discourse on ministry, taking into consideration the updated biblical expertise, to read the Scripture in the light of people's struggles, pain and problems, is very essential. Kochurani Abraham asserts that in today's society dialogue with women and equal space for women in the society is as essential as dialogue with other religions, cultures and ideologies.[68] This sort of text-context dialogical dynamic will enable and enhance the liberative praxis. Therefore, the changing reality of women in India today is crucial.

iii) The Church has to recognize and encourage women to interpret theological and spiritual truths hidden in the scriptures with a sense of respect, reverence and admiration. There is a greater need in the Church that the clergy has to reach out to women with a greater sense of wonder and gratitude.

It is necessary that the Church as the people of God aim at an effective complementarity, so that women and men bring their riches and dynamism into making India a better place to live in today. For as long as one half of humanity is discriminated against, humankind cannot blossom fully. Fiorenza in her article "Wo/men, Mission and the Catholicity," has a focus to respond theologically to the concerns of women today:

> A critical feminist understanding of universality and catholicity can foster socio-religious plurality and global connectedness linking radically

different local churches and variegated cultures. It is engendered by radical democratic spirituality that envisions an all-embracing and inclusive reality in which all people are truly equal but not the same; an ekklesial culture where differences are respected and people are truly free, where social-religious responsibility rather than individualistic self-absorption prevails; a society and world-Church which is truly just and in which status and power inequalities are recognized for what they are.[69]

Catholicity entails the ability to appreciate that unity is not uniformity but solidarity in diversity. In today's world of globalization, sharing across boundaries, openness to cultural and religious diversities is itself a paradigm on how to live in diversity, tolerance and respect.[70] This form of *Presence-Solidarity* is deeply embedded in Scripture.

Accordingly, the Trinity is the basis for a Church praxis of a presence-in-solidarity. "Growing in understanding from a hierarchical view of the Trinity to one of equal relationships" is a task to be engendered for the Church in India. The Trinity presents an egalitarian vision of equal partnership that i) "the God of Jesus is not a hierarchical, dominating power but rather God in solidarity with the poor, the marginalized and the outcasts"; ii) the Holy Trinity is "a mystery of relations and these relations model a social order that is open to the poor" and that it resists oppression. [71]

Therefore, theologically women and men are grounded in the fact that "every one of us is made in God's very own image because God, who created people in the divine image, has gifted and called every individual differently. The divine image is neither male nor female, white or black, rich or poor, neither Christian, nor Muslim, nor Hindu or Buddhist but multi-coloured, multi-gendered, multi-religious, and more."[72] We, the Church, the people of God, cannot opt out of today's situation but wake up and rise to meet the challenges and opportunities and thus represent the person of Jesus Christ for India today.

Renewed Passion for Missionary Outreach

The universality of the Gospel is the reason for missionary outreach. Preaching the good news in today's India means, first of all, to be in solidarity with all those who suffer due to injustice, discrimination, exploitation, oppression and violence. According to Schillebeeckx, "God conceals his superior power over evil and expresses it at the time of his defencelessness, in order to give us room to become ourselves in solidarity with the oppressed men and women. However, in this defencelessness at the same time he uses his superior power so that his defencelessness is the consequence of his fight against evil in an evil world."[73] Moreover, the prophetic critique keeps the Church faithful to her original mission of witness and service. The prophetic voice of the Church has to be addressed precisely to the oppressors, the rich and the powerful rather than to the ordinary.

The Church is to be the channel through which people experience the steadfast love and presence of God. It is the responsibility of the Church to minister to those in need, to bring the healing and comforting touch of Christ without partiality. Christians become united with Christ when they translate the message of Jesus of Nazareth into good news to the marginalized.[74] In this regard, the role of a Christian is to liberate and empower everyone so as to learn to become a creative contributor to the building up of a new humanity.[75] What is implied here is not only the sensitivity to and vulnerability to be affected by the experience of the other, but also the courage to take remedial action against suffering and oppression by getting involved in the situation.

According to Mohan Doss that by moving out to the periphery, we feel privileged to honor the dignity of the poor, the marginalized and the exploited and recognize the dynamic presence and operation of the life giving Spirit of God.[76] Through "this we bring healing into the lives of the people of the margins and in the process we ourselves become healed".[77] Felix Wilfred highlights the following:

> The aspects of Jesus as God in the poor and the lowly, and as the suffering
> one – symbolised by the Cross – have been most appealing to the millions
> of Hindus in the country. It is this identification with themselves and
> their sufferings the poor and the lowly expect from the Church. So
> that the Indian Church may go all the way where this solidarity leads

it, following Jesus outside the gate to Calvary, it is important that the Church constantly look at the world through the eyes of the poor, the suffering and the humiliated.[78]

The vision for the Church springs from Jesus whose identification with the powerless and of confrontation with the religiously and politically powerful of his time, led him inevitably to the conflict that culminated on the Cross. Jesus' solidarity with the poor found its final and ultimate expression on the Cross.[79] His Father's approval of his solidarity with the poor in his resurrection constantly reminds the Church to go out of herself passionately to share God's love to all particularly with the poor.

The Church's authentic identity is realized when she stands with and for the marginalized. It implies her responsibility to uphold their three most important rights: the *right to life*, which is the source of human dignity, the *right to freedom*, which derives from the close relationship between dignity and autonomy, and the *right to equality*, which is based on the equal dignity of all people and closely resembles justice.[80] Each individual Christian and every community is called to be an instrument of God for the liberation and promotion of the poor, and to enable them to be fully part of society (*EG* 187).

In *Evangelii Gaudium* Pope Francis calls for the Church to go out firstly to the poor and sick, those who are despised and overlooked, and says that "if something should rightly disturb us and trouble our consciences, it is the fact that so many of our sisters and brothers are living without the strength, light and consolation born of friendship with Jesus Christ" (*EG* 49). In Cardinal Tagle's words:

The *kenosis* of Christ means first and foremost emptying oneself of prerogatives. Although it is a minority in Asia, the Church still has so much of which to divest itself in terms of privileges and wealth, whether real or claimed. As Christ emptied himself taking the form of a humble hidden human existence, the Church in Asia must learn to choose it because it is the way of the Spirit-filled Jesus. It just cannot wait for circumstances and place to dictate it. It is edifying to see discipleship lived in the humblest of ways among the poor of Asia. When priests and religious are content to have as little food as the nearest neighbours

> even when they could use their influence to collect more, dialogue in self-emptying happens....When the leaders of the Church declare that the poor are the centre of gravity of the Church's life and live by it, dialogue of self-emptying happens. The nobility of self-emptying love simply radiates through these heroic Christians of Asia.[81]

The Federation of Asian Bishop's Conferences (FABC) in Vietnam, 2012 also recognized a pressing demand on the Church to live out and follow the Spirit of Jesus, identify herself by being actively involved with the poor and the oppressed. The demanding mission of the Church in India/Asia requires a radical emptying of herself as Christ emptied himself (Phil 2:5-8). In other words, through exercising solidarity with the poor the lives of Christians become Christic presence.

3.2 Presence-Solidarity that Renews a Mission to Indian Society

A Christology of *Presence-Solidarity* appeals for a renewed vision of the Church to Indian Society, to walk with the oppressed, to exercise a liberative leadership, promote participative women's empowerment, and a call for conversion of heart toward God, others and nature.

Church that Walks on the Periphery

The phrase "Walking on the Periphery" is from Pope Francis and it is a concept of paramount significance to his pontificate.[82] The direction of Francis' pontificate is periphery-bound, moving the Church from security to risk-taking, "from inward looking to outward looking," from the center to society's edges.

After the example of Jesus who not only walks with us or we walk with him, but "in his company we become companions to one another". The mission of the Church cannot be reduced to a merely spiritual proclamation for individual conversion with no social impact on the world. Therefore, "to walk with Jesus in the company of others describes the very essence of the Church."[83] The imperative for the Church in India today is to walk with Jesus and "preach the Gospel to all: to all places, on all occasions, without hesitation, reluctance or fear. The joy of the Gospel is for all people: no one can be excluded." (*EG* 23).

The Decree *Ad Gentes* affirms that in order to be effective "the Church must walk the same road which Christ walked: a road of poverty and obedience, of service and self-sacrifice to death" (*AG* 5). This is the compelling mission for a counter-cultural approach. The two options before the Church for our times are: "one who walks this earth as Jesus did and takes the path less trod so as to make a difference; and one who sets his sail against the wind and braves the stormy sea."[84] One is motivated to see things as Jesus himself sees them, eventually it becomes a participation in his way of seeing (*LF* 19).

'Walking with' is the approach of Jesus Christ by which he personally enters into another's brokenness. By entering into a person's life, Christ calls for faith and discipleship. Hence, the need to promote a new avenue that enables the Church to break out of her isolation and to build bridges, to reach out to others in need is emphasized by Pope Francis in his September (2017) prayer intention. He says:

> Parishes must be in contact with homes, with people's lives, with the life of society. They have to be houses where the door is always open so as to go forth toward others. And it is important that this going-forth follows a clear proposal of faith. The doors must be opened so that Jesus can go out with all of the joy of his message.[85]

The call is to walk with the people on the peripheries with a word of consolation. It is primarily an attitude, an outlook, a way of viewing the situation. It is an outlook motivated by the quest for the common good, an outlook that is realistic, hard-edged, and unromantic, an outlook which engages directly with injustice and wrong-doing, seeing it for what it is and actively opposing it.

Walking alongside the people is the very core of being human, for it is: "a commitment to the good of one's neighbour with readiness, in the Gospel sense, to 'lose oneself' for the sake of the other instead of exploiting him, and to 'serve him' instead of oppressing him for one's own advantage" (Lk 22:25-27) (SRS 38). Hence the need for the missionary to "go forth" on the periphery as places of destiny is compelling.

> Going out to others in order to reach the fringes of humanity does not mean rushing out aimlessly into the world. Often it is better simply to slow down, to put aside our eagerness in order to see and listen to others, to stop rushing from one thing to another and to remain with someone who has faltered along the way. At times we have to be like the father of the prodigal son, who always keeps his door open so that when the son returns, he can readily pass through it (*EG* 46).

Incarnation is the key to understand what it means "to go forth" to the peripheries. The self-emptying love of the Trinity is behind the "going forth of God" in "taking the form of a servant, being made in the likeness of men" (Phil 2: 6-7). Therefore, this vision begets a form of life that runs out to the periphery, embraces the vulnerable, and touches the suffering. It is the form of life conformed to the mystery of the Incarnation, the form of life that offers oneself in the very act of mercy. It is in drawing "near to new forms of poverty and vulnerability." In it we embrace human life and touch the "suffering flesh of Christ in others," and by which we both render present and encounter "the fragrance of Christ's closeness and his personal gaze" (*EG* 169).

Actions of compassion and solidarity are part of the realisation of the divine plan and become sacraments of salvation, along the way. This way of walking with is to imbibe the spirituality of solidarity of Jesus of Nazareth. It is "to hear the cry of the poor as he heard it on the roadside, amidst the crowd, and by the side of a bier at the gate of Nain (Lk 7:12), having the indomitable courage to accompany the poor and the suffering in their struggle for justice, dignity and life, and the conviction of the need to transform" oneself and the unjust structures. In the process of walking the way one discovers that one is called "to lead not from over but from among, not from certainty but by exploration, cooperation and faith, not from power but from a powerlessness that depends on the power of God, not out of any compulsion but from an inner freedom, and not from the centre but from the margins."[86]

Rooted and grounded in Christ's *Presence-Solidarity*, allowing hope to work through all initiatives, both individual and collective, we need to build a new social order of freedom, justice and peace, a world in which no one is exploited, oppressed and excluded from the right to live in dignity, freedom and solidarity.[87] The Church has to be on the periphery so that the dignity of every person and the sacredness of every human life are not arbitrarily denied and determined by whims and fancies of power-crazy individuals. Respect for human life and freedom are essential for building up a humane, just and peaceful society for a holistic living. Consequently, every initiative and movement of people and communities towards liberation, life, dignity, justice, and solidarity are to be upheld for a new social order. A joint venture consisting of the Church and others together will contribute to the ushering in of the new social order.

To stand up for human rights, to promote the integral human liberation, especially of the poor and the oppressed and the marginalized as well as to foster spiritual values are the prerequisites for building a new social order. It is by working among the poor and getting involved in their pain and suffering, that one begins to appreciate one's own dignity, develops new insights towards the ultimate truth of things, finds new meaning in life, and seeks new ways and energy to reach out to them. All these generate a "co-responsibility and make co-responsibility an imperious ethical demand and make the experience of co-responsibility something good, fulfilling and salvific."[88]

A Christology of *Presence-Solidarity* calls for a radical response to the construction of a new society leavened by the values of freedom, fellowship, truth, love and justice.[89] Walking on the periphery is important to be acquainted with the life-experiences of people.[90] As in Jesus' resurrection God has taken sides with the crucified of history, so too the execution shall not triumph over God's victims. Jesus is the ultimate and the definitive presence of God's solidarity with us. "Jesus' death on the Cross was an act of defiance of all the principalities and powers which humiliated people and held them in bondage. Through his ceaseless struggle to death, he realized the new humanity of freedom and dignity right within the oppressive tangles of history and took a stand against oppression. A new day was dawning when he died."[91]

The Church in India is to be present and active in the changing patterns of Indian society. Hence, the awareness of different cultures, religions, traditions, social systems, and the polarized society call for a creative think-tank Christian leadership which responds effectively to promote life.

A Liberative Leadership

Christian leadership is a response to a divine call to be in the service of God's love and justice. It focuses on a pattern of God's calling leaders to a mission, to be at the service and restoration of God's image in everyone and in everything. In the Old Testament God's creation has been identified as the first act of leadership. It reveals the importance of servant leadership in the divine operation of creation (Gen 1:26-27).

In the New Testament the story of God's leadership is seen in the event of Incarnation. The Word left heaven to live among the sinful humanity and minister to the needs of people. Since the source of Christian leadership is Christ himself, one needs to be constantly inspired and strengthened by Christ himself. An authentic leadership begins with a vision that is led by a mission. "Jesus was a leader by his very nature and by his mission."[92] Above all Jesus' leadership was fundamentally context specific. Jesus is *Presence-Solidarity – Immanuel*-God-with-us. As *Immanuel* he pitched his tent among the marginalized of his times. Therefore the dynamic of the leadership of Jesus is "comprehensively context sensitive." It means that today's leadership in the Church ought to become "context sensitive"[93] He came to seek and to save the lost, to serve others rather than to be served. These traits of service, love, and compassion are to likewise mark those who seek to be effective Christian leaders. That is to say, Christian leadership in India needs to be effective after Jesus, the leader *par excellence*.[94] How one is to be a Christian leader and what does it mean to be a leader today? The teachings and life of Jesus offer an important answer to this question.

The Church must respond to the burning issues in the Indian scenario today when defining her vision for a *kenotic* mission. Cardinal

Telesphore Toppo said: "the challenge of the leadership of the Indian Church is to take off the sandals, stand on the holy ground and listen to the voice heard in the burning bush. Is it a call to go to Pharaoh from whom we are running away?"[95] This means that liberative leadership is a constitutive element of the Church's fundamental mission for the totality of the human person.

The core issues and challenges of today's milieu are to be encountered by drawing inspiration from Jesus whose self-emptying leadership is dialogical, inclusive and liberative. Obviously, Jesus' leadership was not by himself and for himself, but he also imparted leadership to others with a special mission, and he taught how to build organization (Mt 16: 18-20), how to promote teamwork (Lk 10:1), and how to care for one another (Mk 12:31). If Jesus' main concern was saving people from alienation, marginalization and negation, and to restore them to life in its fullness (Jn 10:10), and if Jesus is the way to be human, then it can be said that this is the project that he has bequeathed to the community of his disciples in the world.

For Jesus, and so for the Church, the poor and the oppressed come first, irrespective of race, gender, and creed. In this way they can really become a liberative force of humankind.[96] From this perspective, the Church's concern for the peripheries of society and her availability to side with the oppressed are certainly essential dimensions of leadership in the Church in India today.

Participative Presence-Solidarity

The cry of the people in the Old Testament initiated a history. When that cry was heard by Yahweh, who decided to enter into their history, and participate in their life of struggle and slavery, the very same history was transformed into a history of liberation.

> I have observed the misery of my people who are in Egypt; I have heard their cry on account of their taskmasters. Indeed, I know their sufferings, and I have come down to deliver them from the Egyptians, and to bring them up out of that land to a good and broad land, a land flowing with milk and honey... The cry of the Israelites has now come to me; I have

> also seen how the Egyptians oppress them. So come, I will send you to
> Pharaoh to bring my people, the Israelites, out of Egypt (Ex 3:7-10).

Neuner underscores the same thrust while saying, "The prophets in the OT are more than a message of God's word and their work and life are woven into the life of the people as part of God's saving design."[97] But it is in Jesus that God's liberating intervention in human history reaches its climax.

Jesus affirmed that loving one's fellow being is the best response to the love received from God. The Gospels affirm the truth that Jesus was found always in the midst of the poor. As followers of the self-emptying Christ, one must be drawn into his self-surrender, into his *Presence-Solidarity* with the lost and into his self-emptying. Moltmann rightly says:

The fellowship called into life by Christ's surrender serve to reconcile the world through solidarity with the suffering of the people through participation in the representative work of Christ in the Spirit. The Christian, "being-for-others' cannot be separated from 'being-with-others' in solidarity; and being-with-others cannot be separated from being-for-others.[98]

The implications would be to discover Christ outside the box of traditional Christology, as ONE who stands with us in our human struggles, who is at home and incarnated in the lives of the marginalized and who is experienced as the Cosmic Christ, beyond religions and even anthropocentric Christian categories. It is to affirm him as One who opted for justice that involved challenging the religious authorities of his time and initiating a counter culture. It is an invitation to share in Jesus' own ministry and to work in collaboration with different members of the community. It is to walk with all the oppressed and oppressors towards the fullness of life and love for which the Incarnate Word was born to usher in to all humans. In other words, the participative aspect of the *Presence-Solidarity* would be visible in Church's capacity to build, sustain and make home with those who are without homes and affirm the worth of those deprived of their dignity and worth as God's children.

The impelling message of *Presence-Solidarity* is to see the suffering of our brothers and sisters around us with the heart of God. It is to learn from Jesus' egalitarian attitude that gave every woman, no matter her background, the respect due to a human person. Jesus' refusal to treat women as sex objects or shun them as insignificant or ritually "impure," is a serious challenge to the consumeristic society today.

Jesus' *Presence-Solidarity* of God is that which made him break the traditional barriers upheld by the Jews and include in his reign children and women, publicans, prostitutes and sinners, the sick and the maimed, and the impure, and which provokes us to consider new ways of being Church. Finally Jesus' suffering and crucifixion were a consequence of this choice. This Jesus stands as an inspiration to women who have been taught to "suffer in silence", and urges them to demolish the social, political and religious structures of their oppression.[99] That is to say that every area of life that is still not sufficiently transformed by the values of the reign of God – our politics, social relationships, trade relations, economic structures – everything has become concerns of the mission of the Church.[100]

Hence, an in-depth look into Jesus, the *Presence-Solidarity* of God, from the perspective of the periphery, can impel us to witness to God's saving power by making the type of options that he made, options which can uphold the dignity of everyone who is created in the image and likeness of God.

Pope John Paul II exhorted that "those who are more influential, because they have a greater share of goods and common services, should feel responsible for the weaker and be ready to share with them all they possess" (*SRS* 39). This applies both within societies and between societies, both locally and nationally. It means the Church has to enter into new ministries where the need is most. It means challenging people to change casteist and patriarchal attitudes and mind-sets, creating awareness about the sacredness of sexuality and about the need to recognize and affirm the dignity of all people irrespective of their economic status, caste and religious affiliations; these are all new areas where one can try to resolve conflict or bridge the gap between a just and unjust society. It calls everyone to participate and work together, collaboratively, to end injustice and to provide grounds for hope. Therefore, social cohesion can only be achieved through participation and solidarity, and by achieving a shared vision, not by threat or coercion.

Conversion of Minds for a Societal Transformation

God's liberative action is manifested in bringing about human liberation through Jesus, which resulted in the formation of a community of freedom, fellowship, and justice. Ever since Jesus went into Galilee, proclaiming the good news, conversion has been fundamental to Christian life.[101] The Christian understanding of conversion as a moral-religious reality finds it roots in the Old Testament: the history of Israel is the story of a people repeatedly being called to conversion. They were called to return to its covenant with God that it abandoned (Mk 1:15). John the Baptist continues the prophet's call to conversion in the New Testament. After John's arrest, it is said that Jesus takes up the call and begins his ministry by announcing the arrival of the reign of God: "The time is fulfilled, and the kingdom of God has come near; repent, and believe in the good news" (Mk 1:15).

For Jesus, human holiness must express human wholeness. The oppressive and dehumanizing power structures are the evil spirits and demons that kept people in bondage. Jesus cast these evil powers out. Jesus not only stood against injustices done to the people, but also took his stand among them. His vision and mission were fashioned by his *Abba* experience.

The time has come for a conversion of heart toward God and humanity rather than movement from one particular belief system into another without caring to elevate humanity into a higher level of authentic consciousness. It's a call for a change of mindset of men and women which is of paramount need to bring about a societal change. The existing imbalance must be remedied through our commitment to the deprived and by challenging the favoured section of the society.

Therefore, the awareness of the suffering caused by the caste-cultural-conflict is the starting point of the way to transformative and liberative process for all members of caste-ridden society. Conflict and violence destroy the means of livelihood of individuals and society. Violence has adversely affected every tenor of life in a large number of countries including the developed ones, causing unprecedented loss of human life and degradation of the environmental and ecological systems sof the planet.

In the face of signs of such death and pessimism, the Christ's *Presence-Solidarity* assures us that the forces of darkness and evil do not and cannot have the last word. Jean Vanier presents a radical way to get in touch with others individually as well as collectively, when he says: "Each one is carrying the capacity to be, to become, to love and to be loved."[102] Therefore, building societies based on values so as to transform those dehumanising ambiences and pain is important. This will pave a way to all to grow toward authentic humanity in all its fullness of life.[103] This is even vital in the evangelizing mission of the Church.

The Christology of *Presence-Solidarity* invites the disciples to transform the structures in India today by a wide-ranging restructuring of the existing order. This is a challenge and an invitation to the Church in India and to share in Christ's mission of solidarity. Vision for a new social order encompasses a commitment to an onward journey towards a God-oriented and *basileia*-centred approach of Jesus to the situation which is marred by suffering, dissension, hatred and violence, through a counter-culture of peace, harmony, respect and dignity.

3.3 Presence-Solidarity that Renews a Multi-Religio-Cultural Society

The multi-religio-cultural context is a challenge and an opportunity for the mission of the Church in India. It is a challenge and an opportunity because it provides space for Christians (though the Christians constitute just above two percent of the total population) to collaborate with others in the building up of a humane society. The Church along with other religions is on a pilgrimage towards the Ultimate destiny of human life, which is God. Our quest for God, therefore, calls us to collaborate with the believers of other religions and all people of good will. One positive, constructive step towards promoting harmony among all religious communities is a collaborative approach. It is to combat the many unjust social systems and practices widespread across communities in the pluri-cultural Indian context.

All religions and religious leaders jointly and mutually plan and implement programs and projects to promote Indian women's status, dignity and empowerment, since all religions are committed towards the welfare of women and men. The Golden Rule of the Gospel, - "Do to others as you would have them do to you" (Lk 6:13) – can serve as a critique as well as a solid edifice on which justice, reconciliation and peace could be established. This section will discuss integral unity in diversity, raising God-consciousness, and *Presence-Solidarity* as *Shalom*. The goal is to build a collaborative society, in which every religious community is recognized, accepted and respected and has an opportunity to collaborate with others in the building up of a humane society.

Integral Unity in Diversity
Our lives as human beings is a search for 'being' and 'becoming', transforming one's way of seeing and living, discovering of one's real self, and returning to the Ultimate. The dynamic vision of human beings and society is to live, move and act as authentic humans taking an integral approach in analysing and devising ways towards fullness. Viewed from a multi-religio-cultural perspective, India is now faced with two different ideologies. On the one hand, the secularists, who seek to privatize religion and to build up a community that will be based on modern, scientific principles and secular values. On the other, the proponents of the Hindutva, who seek to build the unity of the country based on the motto, 'one nation, one religion and one culture,' and by asking everyone to identify with an Indian national culture, which is interpreted as rooted in Hinduism. What could be the path possible for unity in diversity?

The only path possible for integral unity in diversity is to share spiritual riches, for, religion touches the depths of human reality. Moreover, it's our conviction that "beyond the barriers of belief and practice lies the stark and simple reality of relating to God: the practice of the presence of God."[104] Therefore, the multi-religio-cultural society of India today poses challenges to revitalize the understanding of spirituality. This is imperative for at least three reasons. One, a spirituality that creates a sense of responsibility in every citizen to uphold each other's religions; two, a spirituality that appreciates and respects other's cultures and faiths; three, a spirituality that is rooted in the encounter with reality, to resist the forces that ravage and destroy life, in order to draw from the wells of the spirituality of the oppressed. It is a spirituality in which we "let reality come and invade, enter, affect, disturb, challenge, and move us to action."[105]

Integral Unity in diversity has its foundation in the Word-Incarnate in the *Presence-Solidarity* of God in Jesus. The language of the Chalcedonian Christology, hypostatic union refers to this dimension. The divine and human natures are united in Jesus. He is ONE person in two natures. Seen from this perspective the very integrity of the Church and the credibility of her mission demand the following: i) a spirituality that does not divide but unites people irrespective of creed, ethnicity, religion, gender, and race. Everyone is equal and in a relationship of mutuality with each other; God-with-us permeating the entire reality; ii) a spirituality that shows concern for the humanity and the cosmos. Hence it has to be communitarian, spiritual togetherness, oneness, etc. Or else there is a danger of falling into individualism; iii) a liberative spirituality that brings transformation in society, for dialogue with other religions, cultures and ideologies. Spirituality of liberation as explained by Rayan is a spirituality of interdependence and interconnectedness where everyone discovers he/she is also a strand in the web of life.[106] In other words, the Church affirms that genuine and authentic spirituality is the discovery of the sacred in the various dimensions of life under the guidance of the Spirit and the discovery of the divine presence.

Therefore, integral unity can be seen in terms of a genuine spirituality that sustains life and subverts the forces of evil. Further, spirituality is openness to reality and a humanizing response to the same. Reality could be negative or positive.[107] Obviously, no spirituality is without a context, for every human being lives in society and is influenced by it. In biblical and Christian tradition, spirituality is not assumed as a weak, pallid thing but it is the life-force which acts in us and in the whole creation as we accept to live it each day.[108]

Can we not therefore say that integral unity is very much connected to transformation - a platform for implementation? Here we need to ask: what are we to be transformed from and transformed for? In response, we explore a kind of wholeness that offers harmony and hope. We are to be transformed from our narrowness into full awareness, from our social divisions into community. Ultimately it promotes an integral unity that does justice – justice to oneself, justice to the other, justice to the world and to the environment. Therefore integral wholeness is a spirituality that tries "to integrate the opposites in one harmonious whole: the interplay of light and darkness, conscious and unconscious, body and soul, the masculine and feminine, are all part of one reality."[109] The central point is that male and female, Hindu, or Christian or Muslim or Sikh or Jain or Buddhist are like the two sides of the same creative principle: unique ways of being human and all are called to develop their full humanhood. Everybody is equal yet each is different. All are called "to reciprocity and mutuality and work together as partners."[110] The need of the hour is "to evolve a new kind of democratic order ... [that] will be respectful of diversity and participative, allowing each group to contribute its riches to the good of all."[111] Individuals committed to the values of a new kind of democratic order become catalyst for change in the society.

Mediating God-Consciousness

In the context of the Church in India, there is an urgent need to be rooted in God for "without a committed pursuit of God in contemplation, all kinds of good activities lose all purpose and relevance."[112] The source of Jesus' approach was his intimate relation with his *Abba* [Amma] which denotes God's unconditional love.[113] Jesus' *Abba* experience finds expression in his struggle for liberation to the captives (Lk 4:18). Jesus goes up the mountain, a symbol of the place of encountering God (Mk 3:13) to be with God his *Abba*. His own life of communion in the Spirit with his Father evoked in his disciples an intense desire to pray. So they asked him to teach them to pray (Lk 11:2). His profound experience of God and of humankind empowered him to identify himself with the poor and the outcast and to confront the powerful and the rich. As it is well illustrated and documented in the life of Jesus, the idea of an all-pervading and all-powerful God is fundamental to most of the religions. God consciousness is the ethos of all Indian religions and more so of Christianity. Hence one of the main opportunities that the Church in India today has is to mediate God experience and God-consciousness. God is more to be experienced than to be intellectually known.

Holiness is to walk "in the presence of God and being perfect"; it means to live in "constant encounter with Jesus Christ" which involves a call; "the call may be a great one or a small one, but it is always there" (Mt 4:18-19; 9:9; 10:1-4).[114] For this, one has to encounter God who transcends human-made petty divisions of caste, creed, clan and gender. In that divine-human encounter arises the discovery of the fruits of holiness which one is able to appreciate in the other believers too. "The divine human encounter is immediate, is available to everyone through their conscience; what we call 'salvation' is nothing but the sharing in divine life which is the fruit of divine-human encounter."[115]

Therefore, the Church is called to step outside her comfort zone "to bear witness to God who sets people free, who lets His sun shine on the good and the evil, and who gives life and promotes the community of life."[116] Thus the contemplation of the Divine gives rise to a new sense of belonging, a new way of recognizing God in the cry of the poor, the oppressed and even in the cry of all creation. This profound merging of one's being with God is contemplation. Contemplation of God seeks to discern God's ways. Listening is to hasten to stand by God and become God's channels, instruments, co-partners in the salvific\liberative struggle. Finally, "the same mystery points to our common origin, our shared substance, our universal breathing with the immense diversity that surrounds each and every one of us, each a unique and original creation, a path along the road of life."[117] The Christian experience of God as communion of persons invites people to be in communion with one another, in equality, existing together in harmony, and respecting each other with their differences. It is a call to the disciples of Christ to be instruments of the life-giving Spirit and co-workers in Christ and thus be in communion with the Triune God.

Therefore, the implications of the God-experience are radically new. God-experience is an invitation: i) to abide in God's all-inclusive love and to participate in Jesus' presence solidarity and struggle for transformation. Solidarity with the oppressed implies also respecting their religio-cultural heritage, which has been violated for centuries. ii) to join hands with the new awakening of the peoples and their expression of power in demanding genuine participation in decision making, in opposition to structural or systematic violence. iii) to an involvement for the liberation of women and the call for reunification of the divided society and the Church; and iv) to live in harmony and to enter into dialogue with people of other faiths and cultures. Thus, in God experience one should be awakened to the invitation of the reign of God to go beyond the confines of our religious institutions, from our ghetto and enter into the struggles of people, in order to respond more effectively to the cause of the poor and the oppressed. Thus the God of contemplation should come alive in the midst of the struggles of the oppressed. For the human situations are the places of God-encounter.

Presence-Solidarity as *Shalom*

Shalom is the Hebrew word inadequately translated as wellbeing, justice prosperity and peace. The word *shalom* is used in the Old Testament and refers both to secular and religious wholeness, secular in its individual and communal spheres and religious which is the result of righteousness, covenant, blessing and salvation. Whereas *Shalom* in the New Testament is the gift of God in Jesus Christ which can be understood in various contexts and aspects: i) social peace refers to economic prosperity which results from the absence of corruption and injustice; ii) political security which results from the absence of war, or secular which is the cessation of war or strife; and iii) religious which is a "restored relationship – which is the 'indwelling presence of the risen Lord.'" Jesus' proclamation of the Reign of God is the same as that of *Shalom* in the Old Testament.[118]

Jesus' manifesto (Lk 4:16-21), Beatitudes (Lk 6:20-22) and credentials (Mt 11:2-5) revealed his perspective of looking at society. His values, he expressed through his reaction to cult (Mt 5:23-24), law (Mk 2:27) and ritual (Mk 7:15), are the values of the Reign of God. Jesus' solidarity with the marginalized made him the enemy of the powerful who were blind to his values and took him to the Cross. Conflict was very much part of Jesus' ministry of *Shalom*. Jesus handled the conflicting situation not by retreating himself into a spirituality that is preoccupied with his own security (Gethsemane), but by committing himself to God who is present in the midst of his people for their liberation.[119] Therefore, the goal of *Shalom* is the humanization of life and thus it is a component of social change.

Down the centuries, it has been the aspiration of humankind to build a harmonious society where every individual can bloom and thrive. This means that peace is not possible while human beings are despised and discriminated against on account of caste, creed and gender. Peace is not possible while women are deprived of equality with men. The threats of the evil effects of globalization and consumerism beckon us to unite and stand up for the values of the reign of God. In short, peace has become a distant dream. But when justice rules, peace is not far from realization. Social structural changes are an integral part of transforming towards peace, as well as addressing the injustice that may have fuelled conflict in the first place. Indeed, peace building must involve systemic change that helps create and sustain a new social reality.[120]

Influenced by the social reality, the Church in India today is called once again for a shift in orientation.[121] In this context, value education is essential to build young men and women of character and ability, committed to national service and development. An integral part of minimizing violent conflict is transforming those structures and dynamics that govern social and political relations, as well as access to power and resources.[122] The primary task of conflict transformation is not to find quick solutions to immediate problems, but rather to generate creative platforms that can simultaneously address surface issues and change underlying social structures and relationship patterns.

As Jesus was a man for others, the central challenge of Christianity is living for others. The hallmark of Christianity is a movement from self-centeredness to other-centeredness. Counter-cultural attitudes and movements[123] are not against culture as such but against a perversion of culture that creates oppressive structures and systems, dehumanizes humans and alienates humans from their authentic selves.[124] Along these lines Fiorenza explains: "resistance has two phases or moments that are interdependent: the abolition of relations of domination and the struggle for autonomy. The possibility of genuine human respect, love and equality can be achieved only when relations of domination are resisted and transformed into relations of equality."[126] Counter-culture and resistance will produce an amazing effect. Therefore, this change or counter-culture from the perspective of the periphery aims at the re-birthing of a new humanity and a new serenity.

All the baptized faithful have a mission to raise their voices against the structures and systems that dehumanize the poor. They are called to oppose the misuse of power and positions that hinder authentic human relationship. Peace is not a state of inaction which we live passively as absence of conflict, but the fruit of intense action in building the communities empowered by the Word and Spirit. It is a gift that we achieve by collaborating with God-with-us who is operative in us personally and in community.[127] The Church's mission is to speak a new language that expresses her responsibility to find ways and means of promoting peace. Moreover, the network of institutions and contacts are a wonderful instrument to sow seeds of peace and harmony in the minds of the young learners. "Give peace a chance" needs to be our constant refrain.

Conclusion

The main thrust of this final chapter was to bring into focus the correlation between the Christology of *Presence-Solidarity* and the polarized Indian society of today. The thrust of this book is the significance of Jesus Christ for India today. First and foremost, God in Jesus Christ has participated in human life. The human person is the clearest reflection of God's presence in the world. This chapter began by highlighting the various documents of the Church which underscore the life-promoting and life-enhancing work of the Church in pursuit of both justice and peace. The Church's immense contribution envisions God's presence in Jesus for the vulnerable and in the pursuit of human solidarity. On a personal note, I am enlightened by the relentless and persevering efforts made by the Universal Church down the ages in promoting and safeguarding the principles of human dignity and human solidarity.

The chapter described how the Church in India, down the centuries has never stopped her explorative search for different ways to carry on the person and message of Jesus, which is the very purpose of her existence. The quote that describes the Church in India today is: "Much remains to be done ...." (*CA* 58). These words contain an implicit reminder that there is a call to respond to the diversity of cultures, religions, ideologies and approaches to confront life's realities. Thus the Church in India is called to have the spirit of openness, to strive, to affirm and uphold always the eternal principles of human dignity and human solidarity and usher in a humane society.

Premising upon the preceding analysis, this chapter explored the relevance of Christology of the *Presence-Solidarity* for India today. In the light of the above discussion, we see that one of the most essential steps for a renewed *kenotic* mission is the need for an effective and fruitful kenotic mission of the Church in India. This chapter has responded to the concerns related to the socio-economic and cultural context (as dealt with extensively in the first chapter) in the light of the Christology of *Presence-Solidarity*. Faith in Jesus Christ who is God's *Presence-Solidarity* with humanity becomes the point of departure to make India our Motherland, a better place to live in. Jesus holds greater relevance for the transformation of Indian society into a more just, humane, inclusive and women affirming and participatory society.

Resurrection gives hope in the midst of rising hopelessness of society, gives meaning to the struggles for justice. The one who is resurrected is the one who has suffered and is suffering till the coming of the new heaven and the new earth.[128] In the reconstruction, Christ's *Presence-Solidarity* becomes a source of hope. It challenges us to restore the world view of comradeship and co-existence with a sense of equality rather than of a mastery and absolute hierarchy in relation to our fellow beings as well as the environment. Therefore, it is not only the empty tomb that proves the resurrection but also the living presence of Jesus Christ experienced by the past and present generations.

The *kenosis* of God in Jesus will be experienced only within a *kenotic* community. It is imperative that the Church imbibes Jesus' vision and life style. However, the motifs like self-emptying and self-sacrifice are appropriate only when what is given up is proportionate to the price of the ultimate end. In this respect, the liberative principles of the person and message of Jesus Christ replace anti-human values. Thereby the value of sharing will replace exploitation, justice will replace powerlessness. Domination, inequality and discrimination in policy making processes will give place to equality, respect and participation. The Church in India as the visible face of the invisible *Presence-Solidarity* of Christic presence on earth has the mandate and responsibility to build up a just and humane society to live in.

Endnotes

[1] The end of every search to develop a relevant Christology is to facilitate the encounter with the person of Christ which would transform individuals and societies. Parappally, *Emerging Trends in Indian Christology*, 249.

[2] Christ's way is one of *kenosis,* one of self-emptying. It is Jesus' way of serving through self-emptying and self-effacing and self-sacrificing ultimately. But this is not a masochistic approach of experiencing pleasure through pain on oneself. Rather, the goal is to remove poverty and suffering and pain of the people, through one's selfless service and self-emptying life style. Phil 2:5-11 implies that *kenosis* is the event in which God in Jesus makes room for human action.

[3] Nilanjana Sanyal, *Peace Loving Nations* (Delhi: Gyan Publishing House, 2010), 169-170.

[4] Jon Sobrino and Juan Hernandez Pico, *Theology of Christian Solidarity* (New York: Orbis Books, 1985), 59.

[5] For example the latest response of the Catholic Church to the Supreme Court's (on 9 March, 2018) ruling allowing individuals the right to die with dignity and reject any proposal concerning active euthanasia as well as passive euthanasia, stating that it is immoral in accordance with the teachings of the Church. Stephen Fernandes, National Secretary, *Catholic Bishops' Conference of India* (CBCI) *Office for Justice Peace and Development*, http://www.cbci.in/detail_Slide.aspx? id=441&type=1; Express Web Desk, "Passive Euthanasia: Church says 'taking of innocent life is never a moral act,'" 12 March, 2018, http://indianexpress.com/article/ india/ passive-euthanasia-church-says-taking-of-innocent-life-is-never-a-moral-act5094906/ (accessed April 2, 2018).

[6] The *Catechism of the Catholic Church* in numbers 2030 to 2051 extensively elaborates varied aspects of the Church under the title 'The Church, Mother and Teacher.' In 1961 Pope John XXIII wrote an encyclical called *Mater et Magistra* (Mother and Teacher). It described the Church's role as a mother of the faithful, and also about her ever vigilant duty as teacher of humankind. Reading through such documents would provide deeper insights into the above mentioned characteristics of the Catholic Church.

[7] To reminisce how Pope Pius XI in *Quadragesimo Anno* (1931), taking into account the economic situation of the time, asserted the need to work for the poor in solidarity. *Quadragesimo Anno* is an encyclical written forty years after Pope Leo XIII's *Rerum Novarum* on the condition of workers.

[8] Aloysius Pieris, *God's Reign for God's Poor: A Return to the Jesus' Formula* (Kelaniya: Tulana Research Centre, 1999), 60.

[9] Confronted by the under-developed countries, the Church presented herself the Church of all, and in particular the 'Church of the poor'. Adrian Hastings, *A Concise Guide to the Documents of the Second Vatican Council Volume Two* (London: Darton, Longman & Todd, 1969), 212.

[10] This statement, from a radio address one month before the opening of Vatican II, was further developed in a number of council documents that articulated the

nature and mission of the Church as responsible for, and accountable to, the poor and afflicted (*Ad Gentes* nos. 5 and 12). Cf. Marcus Mescher, "Fifty Years Later, Are We Still the Church of the Poor?" *Millennial Journal.com*, September 11, 2012, https:// millennialjournal.com/2012/09/11/fifty-years-later-are-we-still-the-church-of-the-poor/ (accessed October 2, 2019).

[11] Bishop Julio Xavier Labayen, *Revolution and the Church of the Poor* (Manila: Socio-Pastoral Institute and Claretian Publication, 1995), 2, quoted in Ferdinand M. Mangibin, "Church Of The Poor: Revisiting the Catholic Social Teachings of the Church," *LUMINA*, Vol 20/2, https://www. researchgate.net/publication/49600924_Church_Of_The_Poor_Revisiting_The_Catholic_Social_Teachings_Of_The_Church (accessed September 29, 2019).

[12] *GS* 1

[13] Sobrino and Pico, *Theology of Christian Solidarity*, 11.

[14] Jon Sobrino, *The True Church and the Poor*, translated by Mathew J. O'Connell (New York: Orbis Books, 1984), 95.

[15] Kenneth Himes, *Modern Catholic Social Teachings* (Washington, DC: Georgetown University Press, 2005).

[16] *Laborem Exercens*, 6.

[17] John A. Coleman, Pope Francis on the Dignity of Labor, November 20, 2013, https://www.americama gazine. org /faith/2013/11/20/pope-francis-dignity-labor (accessed23, April 2020).

[18] The Pastoral Constitution on the Church in the Modern World *(hereafter referred to as GS)* was one of the four Apostolic Constitutions resulting from Vatican II. The document is an overview of the Catholic Church's teachings about humanity's relationship to society, especially in reference to economics, poverty, social justice, culture, science, technology and ecumenism.

[19] *GS*, 1.

[20] David Hollenbach, "Commentary on *Gaudium et Spes*: Pastoral Constitution on the Church in the Modern World," in *Modern Catholic Social Teaching: Commentaries and Interpretations*, 2nd *Edition*, ed. Kenneth R. Himes (Washington DC: Georgetown University Press, 2017), chapter 11.

[21] Thomas P. Rausch, *Towards a Truly Catholic Church: An Ecclesiology for the Third Millennium* (Minnesota: Liturgical Press, 2005), 43-44.

[22] A period during which war was in progress Pope Pius XII had urged that *Opus Iustitiae Pax* – that peace could only be founded on justice; and while Paul VI said, in *Populorum Progressio*, that "development is the new name for peace," (PP 87).

[23] George Pattery "Contesting Hindu Rashtra: An Alternative Narrative and Strategies for Reconciliation in the New India," *Statement of the Jesuit Conference of South Asia*, South Asian Assistancy, India, 2017, sjweb.info/documents/sjs/docs/JCSA_Statement.pdf (accessed February 12, 2018).

[24] LG, 14-17; GS, 22, 92

[25] LG 1

[26] EG 238-258.

[27] *EG 250.*

[28] Jesus' approach to women was "personal, equal, free human beings, as people worthy of respect as someone called and named by God." Samuel Rayan, In Christ: The Power of Women," in *Collected Writings of Samuel Rayan: Nature, Woman and the Church Indian Christian Reflections on Ecology, Feminism and Ecclesiology*, ed. Kurien Kunnumpuram, Vol I (Delhi: ISPCK, 2013), 128.

[29] *Gaudium et Spes, 29.*

[30] *Mulieris Dignitatem*, 31.

[31] Donald D'Souza, ed. *Final statements of the General Body Meetings of CBCI-1966-2002* (New Delhi: CBCI, 1979), 56-61.

[32] Report of the General Meeting of the CBCI held in Nagpur (New Delhi: CBCI, 1984), 79.

[33] Report of the CBCI General Body Meeting. Trivandrum 13-21 February 1996. 73, cited in CBCI, Commission for Women. Gender Policy of the Catholic Church of India, 8-9.

[34] Astrid Lobo, "Women," in *A Pope Francis Lexicon* ed. Cindy Wooden, Joshua J McElwee (Collegeville Minnesota: Liturgical Press, 2018), 191.

[35] The theme of the 33rd General Body meeting of CBCI, "Unity in Diversity for a Mission of Mercy and Witness" is timely in inviting the Church and all the believers for exploring new ways of building a human society today. cf. Catholic Bishops Conference of India, "Final Statements," *XXXIII Biennial Plenary of the Catholic Bishops' Conference of India* (Bangalore: St John's, 2018).

[36] The community in India is in need of a solidarity-presence like that of Jesus who became an 'insider', God-with-us, of Moses for the people of Israel, of Mahatma Gandhi, the Father of our nation for Ram Rajya, of Archbishop Oscar Romero for the people of El Salvador, of Nelson Mandela for the South Africans, Fr A.T. Thomas, Fr. Christudas, Mother Teresa of Kolkata, Sr Rani Maria, Sr Mary Sujita, Graham Staines for the Church in India. Such a *presence-solidarity* could help India realize a societal transformation, a movement which would bring us from the brink of poverty, discrimination and violence to an economic conversion, and a deeper love and service toward a suffering humanity.

[37] Catholic Bishops Conference of India, "Final Statements" *XXXIII*, 4.

[38] Poulose Mangai, "Editorial: To Be A Responsive Church in India Today," *VJTR*, 82/3 (March 2018): 3. Francis Gonsalves, "Interview with His Grace Archbishop Anil Couto," *AJRS* 65/4 (July-August, 2018): 21.

[39] Team ICM, "India Needs Church and Church Needs India: Indian Catholic Bishops," February 9, 2018, *Indian Catholic Matters: A New Home for the Community*. https://indiancatholic matters.org/india-needs-church-and-church-needs-india-indian-catholic-bishops/ (accessed March 12, 2018).

[40] I, a member of the Congregation of the Sisters of the Little Flower of Bethany, Mangalore, take delight in mentioning one such person, my revered founder, Msgr Raymond Mascarenhas, who a century ago has shown us the way.

[41] The word *mission* was first used in 1544 by the Jesuits, Ignatius Loyola and Jacob Loyner to describe the spread of the Christian faith. In 1588 Ignatius Loyola wrote, "By mission I mean journeys and undertakings carried on from town to town for the sake of the Word of God." Craig Ott, Stephen J. Strauss, Timothy C. Tennent, "Introduction," in Encountering *Theology of Mission*: Biblical Foundations, Historical Developments and Contemporary Issues (Grand Rapids: Baker Books, 2010), xiv, as cited in Karl Müller, *Mission Theology: An Introduction* (Nettal: Steyler Verlag 1987), 30.

[42] Surekha Lobo, "The Emerging Challenges to Christian Mission Today," in *The Emerging Challenges to Christian Mission Today: Revisioning Mission from Religious, Cultural, Historical & Women Perspectives*, eds. S.M. Michael & Jose Joseph (Pune: Ishvani Kendra, 2016), 55.

[43] Samuel Rayan, "A Vision of Mission for the New Millennium: *Dalit* Perspective," in *A Vision of Mission*, eds. Thomas Mallipurathu and Lazar Stanislaus (Mumbai: St Pauls, 200), 117.

[44] Samuel Rayan, "The Kingdom of God – A Blueprint for a New Society?" *Kristu Jyoti* 1/3 (May 1985): 24.

[45] In this section *kenosis* is an essential theological category for understanding the nature of *Presence-Solidarity*. The traditional understanding of *kenosis*, comes from the Greek verb *kenoō*, "to empty." The foundational text for this theory is Phil 2:6-8; of which verse 7 says that Christ "emptied himself, taking the form of a slave" (*NRSV*). Moreover, the emphasis does not attempt to pioneer a new term called "*Kenotic*". It aims rather to renew the understanding of the concept that it picks up a way to carry out any mission, which is quite different. Further the concept will be explained in the subsequent sections.

[46] Anselm Kyongsuk Min, *The Solidarity of Others in a Divided World: A Postmodern Theology After Postmodernism* (York Road, London: T & T Clark International, 2004), 1.

[47] Lucian J. Richard, *A Kenotic Christology: In the Humanity of Jesus the Christ, the Compassion of our God* (Vancouver, British Columbia: Regent College Publishing, 2010), 12.

[48] Joseph A Samarakone, "A Response to the Case-Study," in *Liberative Struggles in a Violent Society: Proceedings of the Workshop on the "Dynamics of the Liberative Struggles of the Poor and the Oppressed*, eds. John Vattamattam, Varghese Theckanath, S. Arokiasamy and Thoonunkaparambil K. John (Hyderabad: A Forum Publications, 1991), 19.

[49] Pope Francis, "Vigil of Prayer for Peace," 7 September 2013, https://w2.vatican.va/conten t/francesc0/en/homilies/2013/documents/papa-francesco_20130907_veglia-pace.html(accessed October 21, 2017).

[50] Henri de Lubac, *Catholicism: Christ and the Common Destiny of Man* (San Francisco: Ignatius Press, 1988), 53, 297.

[51] Fiorenza, *In Memory of Her*, 97-323.

[52] Elisabeth Schüssler Fiorenza, "You Are Not to Be Called Father," *Cross Currents* 29 (1979): 318.

[53] This is evident in the following accounts: "Mary, Mother of Jesus of Acts 2 in the midst of dejected apostles, Mary of Magdala… for the proclamation of the resurrection *kerygma* to the disciples, the woman of Samaria who was sent on a witnessing mission, the Syrophoenician, the boundary-breaker and hailed as the apostolic foremother of world Catholicism, Martha and Mary, trusting disciples and friends of Jesus, support the leadership functions of women in the Jesus movement." Monteiro, "Towards Partnership in a Participatory Church," 118.

[54] Evelyn Monteiro, "Who will Break down the Wall?" in *Dreams and Visions: New Horizons for an Indian Church: Essays in Honour of Professor Kurien Kunnumpuram* eds. Rosario Rocha and Kuruvilla Pandikattu (Pune: Jnana-Deepa Vidyapeeth, 2002), 245.

[55] Joan Chittister, Heart of Flesh: A Feminist Spirituality for Women and Men (Michigan: W. B. Erdmans, 1998), 25.

[56] Nelson Falcao, A Church of the Laity (Bangalore: KJC, 1991), 21.

[57] CBCI, Evaluation Report: Response of the General Body (Trivandrum: 1996), no.4-5 as cited in The Indian Church of the Future, ed. Kurien Kunnumpuram (Mumbai: St Pauls, 2007), 27.

[58] The Objectives: one, to facilitate change in the mind-sets of women and men so that they relate to each other with respect and dignity; two, to ensure fulfillment of the human rights of women especially of the marginalized groups; three, to ensure that all Church ministries, policies, structures, procedures and programs are gender sensitive and gender balanced; and four, to make provisions for adequate human and material resources to achieve the objectives. CBCI, Commission for Women, Gender Policy, 11.

[59] The areas include women and family; women and education; women and health; women and social involvement; special areas of concern such as rights of the girl child, Tribal and Dalit women, violence against women, women in difficult circumstances, and trafficking and sexual abuse; women's life in the Church women and CBCI; women and diocesan social service societies; women's representation and participation in Church bodies; formation of consecrated women and seminarians; research, documentation and dissemination of information; and networking. CBCI, Commission for Women, Gender Policy, 14-37.

[60] Kochurani Abraham, "The Place and Role of Women in the Catholic Church," JPJRS 7/1 (January 2004): 86.

[61] Monteiro, "Who will Break down the Wall?", 252.

[62] Nestor C. Rilloma, "The Challenges of Emancipatory Theological Education for Churches in the Third World," JATS 13/2 (autumn 2002): 121.

[63] Marcus Borg, Conflict, Holiness and Politics in the Teachings of Jesus (New York: Million, 1984), as cited in Soares-Prabhu, in Biblical Themes for a Contextual Theology Today, vol I eds. Francis X. D'Sa and Scaria Kuthirakkattel (Pune: Jnana-Deepa Vidyapeeth, 1999), 223, 227.

[64] Rita Sanctis, A Quest for Life and Transformative Resistance: An Explorative Study on Religious and Philosophical Resources of Resistance to Female Foeticide and Infanticide in India (Nijmegen: Ipskamp Drukkers, 2014), 248.

[65] Joshua J. McElwee, "Pope Francis, calls again for 'incisive' women's presence in church, offers no specifics," National Catholic Reporter February 7, 2015, https://www.ncronline.Org /news/vatican/pope-calls-again-incisive-womens-presence-church-offers-no-specifics (accessed March 8, 2019).

[66] Catholic Bishops Conference of India, "Final Statements," *XXXIII*, 3.

[67] Karl Rahner, "The Position of Women in the New Situation in which the Church Finds Herself," in *Theological Investigations*, Vol 8, trans., by David Bourke (New York: Herder & Herder, 1971): 75-93, as cited in *Concerns of Women*, eds. Monteiro and Abraham, 123.

[68] Kochurani Abraham, "The Place and Role of Women in the Catholic Church," in *Towards the Full Flowering of the Human*, eds. Kunnumpuram and Monteiro, 66.

[69] Fiorenza, "Wo/men, Mission and the Catholicity," in *The Church In Mission*, eds. Malipurathu and Stanislaus, 153.

[70] The theological field should show one is not boundary limited but open to reading the signs of the times in other cultures too and to discern the movement of the Spirit among other people.

[71] Antoinette Gutzler, "Coming Out of the Shadows: A Feminist Vision of a Participatory Church," in *Towards the Full Flowering of the Human* eds. Kunnumpuram and Monteiro, 175.

[72] Fiorenza, "Wo/men, Mission and the Catholicity," 172.

[73] Edward Schillebeeckx, *For the Sake of the Gospel*, trans. John Bowden (London: SGM Press, 1989), 96-97.

[74] Jacob Kavunkal, "Vatican II and the Mission of the Church in India," in *Quest for an Indian Church: An Exploration of the Possibilities Opened up by Vatican II*, eds. Kurien Kunnumpuram, and Lorenzo Fernando (Anand, Gujarat, India: Gujarat Sahitya Prakash, 1993), 43.

[75] Michael Amaladoss, *Beyond Inculturation: Can the Many be One?* (Delhi: ISPCK, 1998), 73.

[76] Doss, *Led By the Spirit*, 149.

[77] Jacob Kavunkal, "The Eucharist and Mission," *JPJRS 8/2* (July 2005): 85.

[78] Felix Wilfred, "Liberation in India and the Church's Participation," in *Leave the Temple: Indian Paths to Human Liberation*, ed. Felix Wilfred (Maryknoll, NY: Orbis, 1992), 183. The Church needs to concern itself for every one without exception. However, the solidarity of the Church today needs to be with the India of the peripheries precisely because they are poor, discriminated against, weak and powerless. Through this choice and commitment the Church will be able to bear witness to the necessity of the whole society to be in solidarity with the poor and marginalized. By its choice to be with the poor the Church will contribute powerfully to the creation of a general culture of solidarity. Felix Wilfred, "Church's Commitment to the Poor in the Age of Globalization," *VJTR 62* (1998): 87.

[79] Doss, *Christ in the Spirit*, as cited in *Led By the Spirit,* 146-147.

[80] Equality addresses systematic injustice and emphasizes the dignity of all people regardless of status, gender and class, whereas freedom ensures that each individual can realize one's potential by safeguarding self-determination under equal circumstances. Nico Vorster, "A theological perspective on human dignity, equality and freedom" *Verbum et Ecclesia* 33/1, 2012, http://dx.doi.org/10.4102/ ve.v33i1.719 (accessed 17 November, 2014): 1-6.

[81] Antonio Luis Tagle, "The Mission of the Church in Asia: Living the Incarnation in Poverty and Plurality" in *Reaping a Harvest from the Asian Soil*, ed.Vimal Tirimanna (Bangalore: Asian Trading Corporation, 2011), 128-129, as cited in Vimal Tirimanna, "Some Salient Contributions of the FABC to the Asian Churches during the Past 40 Years," *Asian Horizons* 6/4 (December 2012): 597-615.

[82] Periphery is not only geographical but also existential: where there is injustice, inequality, ignorance and indifference, where there is human misery.

[83] Blase J Cupich, "Foreword" to Pope Francis, *Walking with Jesus: A Way Forward for the Church* (Chicago: Loyola Press, 2015), x, https://www.amazon.com/Walking-Jesus-Way-Forward-Church/dp/08294425 (accessed February 12, 2018).

[84] Heredia, "A Church That is Poor and For the Poor," 22.

[85] Pope's Worldwide Prayer Network "Parishes at the service of the mission," September, 2017, *News And Update*, http://cbcpnews.com/yearoftheparish/?p=312 (accessed September 18, 201 7).

[86] Doss, *Led by the Spirit,* 150-151.

[87] Editorial, "Easter, Freedom, Woman," *VJTR* 72/3 (March 2008): 161.

[88] Sobrino and Pico, *Theology of Christian Solidarity*, 11.

[89] George M. Soares-Prabhu, "The Miracles" in *Jesus Today* ed. Sebastian Kappen (Madras: AICUF 1985), 5.

[90] Philip Jenkins. "A Peripheral Vision." February 2017, http://www.patheos.com/ blogs/ anxiousbench/2014/02/a-peripheral-vision/ (accessed January 10, 2015).

[91] Samuel Rayan, "He Walks with Us" in *Jesus Today,* ed. Kappen, 151.

[92] Jacob Parappally, "Christian Leadership and the Praxis of Jesus," in *Christian Leadership: The Shifting Focus in Theological Education*, ed. Antony Kalliath (Bangalore: Dharmaram Publications, 2001), 69.

[93] Kalliath, "Preface," in *Christian Leadership,* xii.

[94] Mohan Doss, "Jesus' Culture of Leadership," *AJRS* 57/5 (Sept 2012): 6-18.

[95] Telesphore P. Cardinal Toppo, "Indian Church-Leadership of Tomorrow," *JD* 44/259 (January 2014): 5-12. A keynote address delivered at an Ecumenical Consultation organized jointly by the Asian Centre for Cross-Cultural Studies (ACCS) and the Board of 'Theological Education of the Singapore College (BTESSC), from 18th to 19th November 2013 at the Asian Centre for Cross-Cultural Studies, Panayur, Chennai; Mohan Doss, "Jesus the Listener," *AJRS* 57/3 (May 2012):10-21.

[96] Gali Bali, "Asian Synod and Concerns of the Local Church," *JD*, 28/166 (July 1998): 319.

[97] Joseph Neuner, *The Prophetic Role of the Laity* (Pune: National Vocation Service Centre, 1981), 2-5.

[98] Jürgen Moltmann, *The Church in the Power of the Spirit* (New York: Harper & Row, 1975), 97 as cited in Lucian J. Richard, *A Kenotic Christology: In the Humanity of Jesus The Christ, The Compassion of Our God* (Washington, DC: University Press of America. Inc., 1982), 314; The word 'be with' has varied connotations and nuances. One, the word 'be with' is a Latin word: *Convivium*. It means "being or living together." *Con* means with and *vivere* is live. The Eucharist is called '*sacrum convivium*'; two, The Spanish term for *convivium* is *convivir* which is a twofold notion: to *live* and *with*. "It means to create a communal space, which is inaugurated by a gesture of hospitality that offers nourishment to the other. Angel F. Mendez Montoya, *The Theology of Food. Eating and the Eucharist* (Oxford: Wiley-Blackwell, 2009), 160.

[99] Statement of the IWTF, "'Liberating Christ' in the Indian Context: A Feminist Theological Search," *Annual Meeting*, 24th-26th April, 2016, Bangalore, *VJTR* 80/6 (June, 2016): 476-478.

[100] Joseph Mattam, "Formation of Evangelizers for the Church's Mission and Ministry in the 3rd Millennium," *Paper Presented in the National Mission Seminar* (Rajkot, 2010).

[101] The key biblical words for conversion are *nacham* and *shub* in Hebrew, and *metanoia* and *epistophe* in Greek. If conversion means a radical turning, or a redirection of one's life, the first word in each pair emphasizing repentance, specifies a turning from sin, while the second indicates a turning toward God. Christoph Barth "Notes on 'Return' in the Old Testament," *Ecumenical Review* 19/3 (July 1967): 310-312; William Barclay, "Conversion in the New Testament," in *Turning to God* (London: Epworth, 1963), 11-25.

[102] Jean Vanier, *Encounter the 'Other'* (New Jersey Mahwah: Paulist Press, 2006), 29.

[103] Mercy Oduyoye, *Hearing and Knowing* (Maryknoll: Orbis, 1986), 98.

[104] Jenifer Kavanagh, *The World Is Our Cloister: A Guide to the Modern Religious Life* (Christian Alternative (Christian Alternative: John Hunt Publishing, 2007), https://www.jennifer kavanagh.co.uk/books/world-cloister/ (accessed October 12, 2019).

[105] Samuel Rayan, "The Search for an Asian Spirituality of Liberation," in *Asian Christian Spirituality*, eds. Virginia Fabella, Peter K.H. Lee, and David Kwang-sun Suh (Maryknoll, NY: Orbis Books, 1992), 22.

[106] Rayan, "The Search for an Asian Spirituality of Liberation," 25.

[107] By negative reality is meant dispositions, situations, traditions, structures, policies, relationships, events, actions which are dehumanizing, oppressive and enslaving, decisive and conflictual. By positive reality is meant, experiences which are liberating and integrating, promotive creativity, solidarity and hope, promises and possibilities. Samuel Rayan, "Spirituality for Our Times," *JPJRS*, 8/1 (January 2005): 127-128.

[108] Rayan, "Let the Rivers and the Trees Clap their Hands: Spirituality and Ecological Concern–A Christian View", 256.

[109] Philomena D'Souza, "Weaving an Empowering Spirituality for Women," *JPJRS* 7/2 (July 2004): 91.

[110] M. Amaladoss complements saying: "Our task in India will focus on our service for the liberation of *Dalits*, Tribals, women and nature. Being a small minority (just 2.3 per cent), we Christians cannot bring about any social transformation unless we collaborate with people of good will of all religions and ideologies. As a matter of fact, our contemporary experience is one of inter-religious conflict. Religious fundamentalism and communalism are vitiating relations between people and leading to violence. For this reason, even before promoting justice, we will have to engage in conflict resolution and reconciliation." Cf. Michael Amaladoss, "Faith and Justice in a Postmodern World," *Promotio Iustitiae* 100 (2008/3): 34, as cited in Veluswamy Jeyaraj, "Our Jesuit Faith Today: An Indian Perspective," *Promotio Iustitiae* 104 (2010/1), 86-92. Therefore, inter-religious dialogue becomes a constitutive part of the process of social transformation.

[111] Michael Amaladoss, "Religious Pluralism and Mission," in *A Vision of Mission in the New Millennium*, eds. Thomas Mallipurathu and Lazar Stanislaus (Mumbai: St Pauls, 2001), 77.

[112] George Kaitholil, *Consecrated Life: Challenges and Opportunities* (Bandra, Mumbai: St Paul's, 2014), 173.

[113] Jesus' God experience allowed him to address God as *Abba*–loving parent–a name which, like all the names of God, is an invocation rather than a description. *Abba* is the usual invocation Jesus used to address God in prayer. God is never directly addressed as 'Father' in the Hebrew Bible; God is addressed as 'Father' with a qualification ('Our Father in heaven' or 'our Father our King') in rabbinic texts of the time of Jesus. The language of Jesus, then, is unique and points to a unique personal experience of God. Mt 11:25; Mk 14:36; Jn. 11:41. *Abba*. Soares-Prabhu, *Biblical Spirituality of Liberative Action*, 3.

[114] Pope Francis, Jorge Mario Bergoglio, *Open Mind, Faithful Heart: Reflections on Following Jesus, ed. Gustavo Larrazábal* (Bangalore: Claretian Publications, 2013), 8-9. Vivekananda says, only a soul can quicken the spirit of awakening in another soul. Swami Vivekananda, *The Complete Works of Swami Vivekananda*, vol. 4 (Kolkata: Advaita Ashrama, 1979), 45.

[115] Michael Amaladoss, "The Multi-Religious Experience and Indian Experience," in *Society and Church: Challenges Theologizing in India Today*, ed. Victor Machado (Bangalore: Dharmaram Publications, 2004), 166-167.

[116] Kunnumpuram, *Towards a New Humanity*, 45.

[117] Siji Noorokariyil, *Children of the Rainbow: An Integral Vision and Spirituality for Our Wounded Planet* (Delhi: Media House, 2007), 32.

[118] Selva Rathinam, "Biblical Understanding of Peace," *JPJRS* 21/1 (January 2017): 11-14. *Shalom* occurs in the Old Testament 250 times! *Eirene* is the Greek word for 'peace,' which occurs 100 times in the NT. Shalom also designates innocence from moral wrongdoing (Gen 44:17; 2 Kgs 5:19).

[119] Rathinam, "Biblical Understanding of Peace," 20.

[120] John Paul Lederach, *Building Peace: Sustainable Reconciliation in Divided Societies* (Washington: United States Institute of Peace, 1997), 118.

[121] Influenced by the social reality, the Catholic Church has gone through a transition from a 'mission age' in the 19th century to an increasingly "institution building" or consolidation phase in the 20th century. The mission age coincided with the colonialism and the primary focus was on evangelization interpreted as conversion. Though at that time there was a network of institutions for education, health and social welfare services, they were perceived to have an instrumental function in supporting the primary orientation to evangelization. Walter Fernandes, *The Indian Catholic Community: Its Peoples and Institutions in Interaction with the Indian Situation Today* (Brussels: Pro Mundi Vita, 1980) as quoted in Alfred De Souza, "The Relevance of Christianity in India Today," *VJTR*, 47 (January to December, 1984): 4-25.

[122] Patricia Ardon, *Post-War Reconstruction in Central America: Lessons from El Salvador, Guatemala and Nicaragua* (Oxford, Great Britain: Oxfam, 1999), 10.

[123] Counter-culture and resistance are context specific words. They can be understood in positive or negative ways. In positive sense they can produce a new hierarchy of values or a new world order and *vice versa*.

[124] For example, the Bhakti movement was a protest movement against Brahmanical Hinduism and ritualistic religion. This movement originated in Tamil Nadu and spread to other states like Karnataka and Maharashtra and eventually to the whole of North India during the late medieval ages. Krishna Sharma, *Bhakti and the Bhakti Movement: A New Perspective* (New Delhi: Munshiram Manoharlal Publishers, 1987) 296-299.

[125] Fiorenza, *Wisdom Ways,* 88.

[126] Michael Amaladoss, *Peace on Earth* (Bandra, Mumbai: St Pauls, 2003), 12-13.

[127] Abraham Oommen, "Editorial: The Mystery of the Life Restored," *NCCR* 116/4 (April 1996): 226.

Conclusion

Our present study has tried to establish that the Christological writings of Samuel Rayan and Elisabeth Schüssler Fiorenza make a significant contribution towards understanding the person and message of Jesus Christ. Although belonging to different milieus, Rayan and Fiorenza revitalize Christological insights for the 21st century Indian context. The question stated in the general introduction was: How to present Jesus Christ and make his message relevant in 21st century India, especially for the liberative process of those who are on the periphery of today's India?

Indian society today is in a process of change which can be described in various ways: it is a pluralistic, multi-cultural, multi-religious, post-modern, digital, and globalized society equipped with market economy, modern information and communication technology. Paradoxically there still remains a big chasm between the haves and have-nots, the rich and the poor, the centre and the periphery, the mainstream and the marginalized. Obviously there are many factors leading to such a situation. The Indian situation can be described through certain polarizations. The analysis shows that these issues are interrelated and have to be addressed together. These are but some of the present-day problems that become the *locus* for theologizing and create a new society. In an empowered era, women of today are influenced by the contemporary society in which they live. The 21st century women are still claiming their rightful space and place in the Church as well.

This divide poses a great challenge to the Church as she seeks to affirm equal dignity of all persons.

The human person struggling for dignity and wholeness is at the centre of Rayan's theological enterprise. It offers an avenue to examine how those who are downtrodden and marginalized today can work towards living out the socio-political reality of the vision of the new social order. Two elements characterize Fiorenza's vision: one is an egalitarian vision of the Church that affirms the equality of all and the full discipleship of women; and the other is a critical feminist biblical interpretation that is evident in her feminist hermeneutics and rhetorical analysis. For Fiorenza, the critical issue for interpretation is that of securing justice and freedom for all.

Our reading of Rayan and Fiorenza found that the Christian faith is the backbone that runs through their theological vision. We see it, for example, in their pro-life approach to the Gospel and the person of Jesus for inspiration and insights. They lay emphasis on the gospel-oriented radical changes and transformation in the individuals and in society as a whole. The goal both of them have is of social relevance. Remaining faithful to their fundamental vision, they propose a more radical way of interpreting the scripture and a new way of theologising. While responding to the socio-religio-economic contexts of their specific milieu, Rayan and Fiorenza have offered an alternative and comprehensive approach towards human dignity and solidarity oriented towards emancipation.

The basis for Fiorenza's all-inclusive approach is the *basileia* vision of the Jesus movement and the early Christian community where she finds inclusiveness, participation, wholeness and well-being. For her the *basileia* was the prophetic-liberative central message of Jesus. She looks forward to an all-inclusive transforming vision of the oppressed subjects and stands in solidarity with all those subjects of struggles. For Fiorenza, the resurrection of Jesus means that He is not just a memory, rather he is the Living One who is "going ahead" as a "path finder" in the emancipatory struggle for a society of justice, liberation and freedom from *kyriarchal* oppression. He is "going ahead" in wo/men's struggle to mend their ways.[1] In other words, her perception of the Jesus movement as the emancipatory *basileia* of God's movement is the "envisioned" world that is already anticipated in the inclusive table-sharing, in the healing and liberating practices, as well as in the domination-free-kinship community which is a vision of God's alternative world of justice and salvation. She offers a Christology that seeks to discover the true historical Jesus – A Christology that is very much experiential and based on the pluralistic subjective feminine experience of Jesus by women in real life contexts. It is that which empowers women and liberates all the oppressed masses irrespective of race, class, colour or gender. In other words, she maps a Christology that excludes none from the *Reign of God*.

An analysis of the Christological insights of Rayan reveals that he considers the dignity of the human person as a gift of God. Motivated by the historical Jesus he gets involved in the task of liberating the poor and establishing their rights and their human dignity. For him, Jesus is a man of freedom who was able to identify himself freely and authentically with the poor, their longing and struggles. Rayan defines the invisible presence of Jesus in all the struggles of people to live in dignity as humans created in the image and likeness of God. Rayan's personal commitment to Jesus and his faith-experience of God in Jesus is the basis and foundation of his theological pursuit. In this process the person and event of Jesus Christ are his norm. Hence, theologizing in India, the interpretation of the mystery of Jesus Christ and the self-understanding of his community take place in a multi-religious context and in a situation of massive poverty and oppression. The context of the untold suffering of the peripheries of society with their entire existential crisis becomes the *locus theologicus*. The poor are to be perceived as a 'privileged locus' of God's incarnation in history. For Rayan, Jesus brings salvation, realises it historically and becomes its perfect exemplar. Jesus is unique as a normative manifestation of God; Jesus is decisive and absolute for Christians. God's history is our history; God is with us (*Immanuel*). Rayan has passionately opted for a

Christology from below: a Christology that partakes in human suffering and continues to suffer wherever there is suffering and injustice and exploitation and violence, a Christology to be at the service of life and to human wholeness, a Christology that is at the service of those who work, suffer, and hope, those who struggle for justice and human dignity for all men and women.

Moreover, attempts were made to take note of the areas where Rayan and Fiorenza's perspectives converge, diverge, and complement each other in varying dimensions of theological vision. This was done with a view of proposing a Christology for India today that emerged primarily from the study of their theological pursuit. In order to envisage a Christology, a synthesis of their theological vision was done. Three important aspects were taken for our ongoing consideration:

Firstly, as complementary horizons the aim was to focus on the commonalities shared with their social and theological constructs of their corresponding milieus. They both lay emphasis on the gospel oriented radical changes and transformation. Both use different approaches to interpret the Bible. For Rayan, the Bible and the context are the main basis for Christological reflections. For Fiorenza, the Christian traditions, history of the Israelites and the early Christian communities are the reference points for her approach.

Secondly, the differing perspectives in their theological pursuits were brought into focus. Fiorenza's interest lies in institutional transformation, as a consequence her analysis emphasizes structural forms of oppression. Rayan starts with an analysis of the context and tries to respond to the cries of the poor.

Thirdly, their Christological unity was considered to evolve a Christology for India today. Fiorenza understands the Jesus movement as an egalitarian Jewish movement of wo/men, a prophetic movement of Divine-Sophia wisdom and eventually as the *basileia* movement in which Jesus is *primus inter pares* that is first among equals in whom is the envisioned world that is already anticipated in inclusive table-sharing. Rayan's Christology is from below: a God who became a despised human being in Jesus, a suffering and oppressed God. We find Christ as the giver of the Spirit who liberates one from bondage, the one who liberates the poor and the oppressed. From this discussion the study interprets Jesus' *Presence-Solidarity* as a paradigm for a *kenotic* mission today.

Presence-Solidarity is defined as the very nature of God and is reflected in the communion of three persons in the Trinity impelled by love. The Trinitarian solidarity finds its human face in the activity of God starting from the creation and moving towards the Exodus event and culminating in the person of Jesus, the living sign of that measureless and transcendent love of God-with-us. God's presence with us becomes explicit in Christic presence, who walks with his people, saves them and makes them one. Thus the phrase *Presence-Solidarity,* unearthed from the writings of Rayan, acquires a new meaning in the life and ministry of Jesus Christ.

In order to envision a Christology, nine images were culled out from the Christological insights of Rayan and Fiorenza: one, Jesus the love incarnate or the embodiment of God's love on earth, the *Immanuel.* The mystery of God becoming human in Jesus is an expression of God's solidarity with the poor and their suffering, his confrontation with all those who were responsible for the oppression of the poor of his time. Jesus' solidarity with them led him eventually to its final and ultimate expression on the Cross.

Two, Jesus as the supreme symbol of the Spirit was equipped to carry out his prophetic mission. As a Spirit filled person his life was focused on the total liberation of the human person. The wonders he worked, the miracles he performed, all were done in and through the Spirit. He shared his Spirit in different ways and he breathed his Spirit on the disciples. In other words, the Spirit directed people's gaze to the *Reign of God* that was breaking in with Jesus' presence which is proactive and enhancing.

The next two images of Jesus culled out from the writings of Rayan and Fiorenza are the following. Third, Jesus as the inclusive house offers love, forgiveness and mercy to all who reach, who need and who search for him in their hearts. He breaks down the barriers built on account of all discriminations and divisions, and initiates building communities through table fellowship and formation of a community of freedom, fellowship and justice. Four, Jesus as the initiator of a new social order, enacts his vision at community meals with the list of wrong guests and tax collectors and sinners. As a preacher he is on the side of the voiceless, of the victims of injustice and of evil social structures. As the Lord and Master he emphasizes the centrality of an intimate relationship with God who suffers with humans. Likewise Jesus redraws the map of his contemporary social world, expanding it to embrace all, irrespective of caste, creed, colour and gender. The Cross is the ultimate expression of Jesus as the transforming presence in solidarity with humans and the world.

Five, Jesus as the epitome of freedom, proclaims wholeness and fullness to those who were dehumanized by the oppressive system of his time. Led by the Spirit, he lives out his proclamation. He preaches good news to the poor and frees those in captivity and releases the oppressed. Jesus stood by the poor in a bid to transform society. He stood against the system which did not care for the margins. Ultimately, everything was epitomized by Jesus in the episode of his own life on the Cross which is the dance of the Spirit that brought about the birthing of a new age of freedom and fullness of life in the Spirit.

Six, Jesus the very presence of God is revealed not as two realties but as One who is divine and human as one single mystery of faith. Jesus' table-fellowship can be best appreciated against the backdrop of the pharisaic understanding that viewed the tables on which they ate their meals as representatives of God's altar in the Jerusalem Temple.

The next two images that emerge in the Christological writings of Rayan and Fiorenza are the following. Seven, Jesus as the source of empowerment, emptied himself and shared the destiny of humans in suffering and death. His Cross as the consequence of the kind of life he lived summons us, his followers, to assume the path of solidarity and struggle. Eight, Jesus as the self-emptying of God stooped down to become human so as to save and reconcile all reality in God: "For God so loved the world that he gave his only Son, so that everyone who believes in Him shall not perish but have eternal life" (Jn. 3,16). He beckons his followers to assume the path of solidarity and struggle of *kenosis* and immersion with the anawim of God

Finally, God's saving presence is best revealed in Jesus as the 'presence-solidarity' with us. It is the special, personal, saving Jesus-relationship gifted to us humans by the Spirit. Our final observation is that the mission of Jesus to empower humanity and usher in human solidarity continues after his death and resurrection through his followers and through the ministry and the teachings of the Church. It is the presence of God with us in Jesus, a personal presence present for ages unending in every race, colour and gender. Jesus is with those who are ready to work with God for the welfare of his brothers and sisters and risk their lives. Therefore, Jesus continues to summon us to opt for the poor and the marginalized and empowers us in our struggles to honour the dignity of the periphery. It is a call to hear the cry of the poor, for a *kenotic* mission.

The book also centres on the correlation between the Christology of *Presence-Solidarity* and the polarized Indian society of today which is the *locus theologicus* of Christian theological reflection. The call of the study is to renew our Christian commitment towards bringing transformation and liberation to society and humanity after the example of Jesus the *Presence-Solidarity* par excellence. The thrust being the significance of Jesus Christ for India today, and efforts to assess the role of the Catholic Church down the ages. The Church in fidelity to Jesus Christ has responded on behalf of the people of the periphery. The Catholic social teachings tell us that our dignity does not come from the work we do, from our social positions, or from what we have, but from the fact that we are all children of God, beloved by our Creator.

Therefore, it is imperative that the Church continues Jesus' vision and life style, because the liberative principles of the person and message of Jesus Christ would replace anti-human values.

Premising upon the preceding analysis, it explores the relevance of the Christology of *Presence-Solidarity* as a paradigm for a *kenotic* mission for India today. One of the most essential steps for a *kenotic* mission is the need for a renewed understanding of the nature and mission of the Church in India. The novelty of this book lies in self- emptiness and self-sacrifice of Jesus. Thereby it hopes, the value of sharing will replace exploitation, cooperation will take the place of competition; and freedom, brotherhood and sisterhood of people will replace hate and suppression; justice will replace powerlessness. Domination, inequality and discrimination in decision making processes will give place to equality, respect and participation. Christ is the centre and is at the periphery, that is to say, the presence of Christ is present in the joys and sorrows, pain and gain as the main life-giving source. This opens up the problem of theodicy. The Cross is the ultimate expression of Jesus' *Presence-Solidarity* in action. Undeniably, the delight of the empty tomb lies behind the Cross of Calvary. It is the *kenosis* of God in Jesus experienced within a *kenotic* community that could become a source of hope in bringing about views of comradeship and co-existence with a sense of equality, justice and freedom. It's only in dying that a grain of wheat reaps fruit in plenty. In other words, it's a movement from emptiness (personal and dynamic) to fullness. The Christian tradition provides abundant resources for theological reflection: the incarnation as a display of solidarity of the human and the divine in their radical difference, the historical Jesus in his solidarity with the marginalized of society, his crucifixion and resurrection as signs of his solidarity in suffering and hope, and the whole biblical trajectory of liberation and reconciliation.

A Christology of *Presence-Solidarity* an interpretation of the Christ-event, could enable the Christian community to be present and active in a dynamic way in the mission. For instance, the role of Mother Mary at

Cana, an effective presence, dynamic presence, and timely intervention, or Veronica, who was being moved internally, went forward in a daring way to wipe the face of Jesus carrying the Cross. Simon of Cyrene's helping Jesus to carry the Cross had a profound impact. The pioneering works of all the founders/foundresses of various Congregations are in reality a pedagogy for presence-solidarity. As a member of the Congregation of the Sisters of the Little Flower of Bethany, Mangalore, I take delight in mentioning one such person, our revered founder, Msgr Raymond Mascarenhas, who a century ago has shown us the way.[2] He would say that every good cause in the Church after the example of the Divine Founder, Jesus Christ, experiences the same - *"Per Crucem Ad Lucem."* It means through the Cross to the Light. Every good done to the needy becomes an experience of the Presence-Solidarity.

The *Presence-Solidarity* of the Word made Flesh demands the destruction of the unjust structures that exploit and disrupt the very fabric of human relationship. Instead, it calls for a radical commitment for a transformation that is fashioned by the values of justice, love, compassion, truth and freedom. The significance of the person and message of Jesus Christ for the liberative process of the masses on the periphery of India today, being the subject of this book, is to be proclaimed and realized through a personal, dynamic and transformative way of being present in the mission. It is like the yeast in the dough, apparently quiet or invisible, but actually dynamic, churning, fermenting, and transforming the dough. Resurrection gives hope in the midst of the rising hopelessness of society, and gives meaning to the struggles for justice. The one who is resurrected is the one who has suffered and is suffering till the coming of the new heaven and the new earth. This ensures transformation of the existing peripheral structures.

Various Church documents were highlighted, as it was necessary to briefly sketch the life promoting and life enhancing work of the Church in pursuit of both justice and peace. The Church's immense contribution envisions God's presence in Jesus for the vulnerable and in the pursuit of human solidarity. Chapter five described that the Indian

Church, down the centuries has never stopped her explorative search for different ways to share the person and message of Jesus, which is the very purpose of her existence.

We, the Church, the People of God, cannot opt out of the situation, we are called upon to wake up and rise up to meet the challenges of today as an opportunity to represent Jesus the *Presence-Solidarity par excellence*. Down the centuries, it has been the aspiration of humankind to build a harmonious society where everyone can bloom and thrive. It means that peace is not possible while human beings are despised and discriminated against on account of caste, creed and gender. Peace is not possible while women are deprived of equality with men. As long as justice rules peace is not far from realization. The possibility of genuine human respect, love and equality can be achieved only when relations of domination are resisted and transformed into relations of equality. Counter-culture and resistance will produce an amazing effect. For example, any resistance against injustice will reject the dehumanizing realities and strive for adopting a new order of justice and liberation and *vice versa*. Hence this change or counter-culture from the perspectives of the periphery aims at the re-birthing of a new humanity and new social order.

Finally, it proposes possibilities for the Church to concretize her missionary vocation in the light of the liberative role played by Christ to the point of laying down his life for others. The paradigm of Christological *Presence-Solidarity* for a mission of the Church to Indian society, a multi-religio-cultural society, envisioned and explained in this book, is the renewed vision for a *kenotic* mission for India today. *Kenotic* mission was forgotten in the middle ages and has found revival in the modern times. Some of the thrust of this study, partnership is a challenge to clericalism, engendering emancipation of women, and renewed passion for missionary outreach are responses to *intra*-Church concerns to re-orient the vision and mission of the Church in India as Vatican II intended.

A Church that walks with the oppressed, a leadership that is liberative, participative, *Presence-Solidarity*, and a conversion of heart toward God and humanity require vision coupled with courage, foresight coupled with confidence, appraisal of the reality coupled with commitment to action in order to bring freedom and dignity to the oppressed masses. Integral unity in diversity, mediating God-consciousness, and *Presence-Solidarity* as *shalom* are indicated and reflected as factors that facilitate building up an inter-cultural and multi-religious society, in which every community of believers is recognized, accepted and respected with their differences, has an opportunity to collaborate with others in the building up of a humane society. Such an understanding stands in line with the 'presence-solidarity' which emphasizes personal integrity, social and cosmic harmony, an experience of unity, communion and harmony that result out of an authentic awareness of the self.

Therefore, the paradigm of Christological *Presence-Solidarity* integrates the opposites in one harmonious whole: the interplay of light and darkness, conscious and unconscious, body and soul, the masculine and the feminine; they are all part of one reality. The central point is that male and female, Hindu, or Christian or Muslim or Sikh or Jain or Buddhist are like the two sides of the same creative principle. Everybody is equal yet each is different. All are called to reciprocity and mutuality and work together as partners. In truth, an authentic culture would express the presence of Christ and bring people to live in harmony, peace and communion. The quote that describes the Church in India today is: "much remains to be done" (*CA* 58). These words contain an implicit reminder that there is a call unto action amidst the diversity of cultures, religions, ideologies and approaches to confront life's realities.

The Church in India, together with other religious and secular institutions is called to imbibe the spirit of openness, to strive to affirm and uphold the eternal principles of human dignity and human solidarity and usher in a humane society. This integral wholeness is very much connected to transformation. Msgr Raymond Mascarenhas, the revered founder of my Congregation, is one among the many examples of women and men who faced the challenges of their times - a tribute to the Servant of God who showed us the way a century ago. Alert as he was to his context, nothing escaped his attention as he dialogued and interacted with it. What is required of the Church in India today is to put our shoulders to the wheel and our hands to the plough. We are to collaborate with all people of good will, including adherents of other faiths to break down all gender and racial barriers so as to bring about the full flowering of both women and men – images of God.

Endnotes

[1] Fiorenza, "Jesus of Nazareth in Historical Tradition," 43, 46.

[2] Msgr Raymond Mascarenhas' faith in God led him to question the way society was functioning, sidelining the poor on one side and pushing women - the one half of humanity - to the margins on the other, without paying attention to their dreams and aspirations. This gave birth to the Congregation of the Sisters of the Little Flower of Bethany in the Church.

Glossary

Ahimsā	non-violence
Anawim	a Hebrew word; the vulnerable ones, who have only Yahweh as their protector *Anubhava* experience, inner experience
Arkhēs	ruler.
Avarnas	casteless
Basileia	A Greek word inclines toward a more inclusive language, a better image of the reign of the Messiah, a reminder of the 'nearness of the liberator.' where the Reign of God is realized through the values of love, equality justice, freedom and well-being, where all are treated with dignity.
Basileia tou theou	the Reign of God
Brahmins	are the members of the highest caste or *varna* in Hinduism.
Dalit	is derived from a Sanskrit word *dal* meaningcrack, split and open. The *Dalit* endures the most inhumane forms of oppression and exploitation within a lifelong imprisonment of the caste hierarchical society
Dama	self-control
Dana	charity
Daya	kindness
Decus	meaning ornament, distinction, honour, glory.
Dignitas	worth

Dignus	worthy
Ekklēsia	a Greek word that is understood by Fiorenza as assembly, gathering or congress of full citizens.
Ekklesia of wo/men	That is the full democratic assembly of women, attempts to conceptualize a feminist space.
G*d	Fiorenza uses this incomplete form of the word to highlight the fact that God is not fully representable or describable in our limited language. This is similar to Jewish usage of not fully spelling out the name God.
Harijan	Children of Hari the supreme absolute in Vedas. Hari is often used interchangeably with Visnu in Hindu tradition, that is God, a name given by Gandhi to the so called casteless group in Indian Caste system.
Jnana	Knowledge.
Karma	Action, work
Kath'holou	Catholic means universal, entire, and complete.
Kenosis	Comes from the Greek verb *kenoō*, to empty. It's way of serving through self-emptying and self-effacing and self-sacrificing ultimately
Kristallnacht	Night of Crystal - often referred to as the night of broken glass. The name refers to the wave of violent anti-Jewish pogroms which took place on November 9, 1938.
Kshama	patience
Kshatriyas	a member of the second of the four Hindu castes, the military / warrior caste.
Kyriarchy	the rule of the emperor/master/ lord/father/husband over his subordinates - coined by Fiorenza as an elaborationof patriarchy to express the interconnectedness of oppressions such as racism, classism, sexism and homophobia.
Locus theologicus	the point where God acts and speaks in history here and now.

Manusmṛiti	Laws of Manu
Nishkama Karma	selfless action, desireless action
Opus Iustitiae Pax	peace could only be founded on justice - Pius XII
Opus Solidaritatis Pax	peace will come only through solidarity - John Paul II
Panchamas	the fifth caste in the Indian Caste means family or clan
Patriarchy	designates the structure of male dominance over women, both in the family and in society
Per Crucem ad Lucem	through the Cross to the Light
Plerosis	fullness
Shudras	it is the fourth *varna*, or one of the four social categories found in the texts of Hinduism, and in Indian Caste system
Soucha	Cleanliness
Sui juris	Churches "of one's own right/law," or "of a particular nature." This means that the churches have their own particular liturgy, theology, spirituality, and code of law that set them apart. Example, Latin, Syro-Malabar and Syro-Malankara churches
Tapas	penance
Vaisyas	members of the third of the four Hindu castes, comprising the merchants and farmers
Wo/men	means "people" in a broad sense, including men, women, feminists of any gender, and non-feminists and it is meant to convey diversity

Bibliography

PRIMARY SOURCES: SAMUEL RAYAN

BOOKS

Rayan, Samuel. *In Christ: The Power of Women*. *Stree Reflect Series*, 4. Madras: All India Council of Women Publications, 1986.

__________. *The Anger of God*. Bombay: Bombay Urban Industrial League for Development, 1982.

__________. *Breath of Fire: The Holy Spirit: Heart of the Christian Gospel*. New York: Orbis Books, 1979.

__________. *Development and Evangelization: A Theological Sketch*. Cochin: Lumen Institute, 1971.

ARTICLES IN EDITED BOOKS

Rayan, Samuel. "New Efforts in Pneumatology." In *God's Hope Becoming Visible: Indian Christian Reflections on some Relevant Issues of our Times: Collected Writings of Samuel Rayan*, Vol. III. Edited by Kurien Kunnumpuram, 77-112. Delhi: ISPCK: 2013.

__________. "Symbols of the Spirit." In *God's Hope Becoming Visible: Indian Christian Reflections on Some Relevant Issues of our Times: Collected Writings of Samuel Rayan*, Vol. III. Edited by Kurien Kunnumpuram, 113-140. Delhi: ISPCK: 2013.

__________. "Spirituality for Our Times." In *Life in Abundance: Indian Christian Reflections on Spirituality*. Edited by Kurien Kunnumpuram, 219-235. Mumbai: St Pauls, 2010.

__________. "Decolonization of Theology." In *Quotations on Terrorism*. Edited by Harry Kawilarang, 426-427. Victoria, British Columbia: Trafford, 2004.

__________. "Doing Theology in India." In *Theologizing in Context: Statements of the Indian Theological Association*. Edited by Jacob Parappally, 11-22. Bangalore: Dharmaram Publications, 2002.

__________. "A Vision of Mission for the New Millennium: Dalit Perspective." In *A Vision of Mission in the New Millennium*. Edited by Thomas Malipurathu and Lazar Stanislaus 115-122. Madras: St. Pauls Publications, 2001.

__________. "Decolonizing Theology." In *Dictionary of Third World Theologies*. Edited by Virginia Fabella and R.S. Sugirtharajah, 65-66. Maryknoll, New York: Orbis Books, 2000.

__________. "Hierarchy-Religious Relationship in the Context." In *It Shall Not Be So Among You*. Edited by Forum of Religious for Justice and Peace, 87-96. Hyderabad: A Forum Publication, 1999.

__________. "Let the Rivers and the Trees Clap their Hands: Spirituality and Ecological Concern - A Christian View." In *Spiritual Traditions: Essential Visions for Living*. Edited by David Emmanuel Singh, 254-255. Bangalore/Delhi: UTC/ISPCK, 1998.

__________. "With Us-With Whom?-Is God?" In *The Dharma of Jesus, Interdisciplinary Essays in Memory of George M. Soares-Prabhu*. Edited by Francis X D'Sa, 37-83. Pune: Institute for the Study of Religion, Anand: Gujarat Sahitya Prakash, 1997.

__________. "The Earth is the Lord's." In *Ecotheology: Voices from South and North*. Edited by David C Hallman, 130-148. Maryknoll: Orbis Books, 1994.

__________. "Outside the Gate, Sharing the Insult." In *Leave the Temple: Indian Paths to Human Liberation*. Edited by Felix Wilfred, 125-139. Maryknoll, New York: Orbis Books, 1992.

__________. "The Search for an Asian Spirituality of Liberation." In *Asian Christian Spirituality: Reclaiming Traditions*. Edited by Virginia Fabella, Peter K.H. Lee and David Kwang-sun Suh, 11-30. Maryknoll, New york: Orbis Books, 1992.

__________. "The Challenge of Dalit Issue: Some Theological Perspectives." In *Dalits and Women: Quest for Humanity*. Edited by V. Devashayam, 117-140. Madras: Lutheran Theological College and Institute, 1992.

__________. "The 'How' of Third World Theologies." In *The Third World Theologies in Dialogue: Essays in Memory of D.S. Amalorpavadass*. Edited by J.R. Chandran, 42-66. Bangalore: EATWOT, 1991.

__________. "Commonalities, Divergences, and Cross Fertilization among Third World Theologies." In *Third World Theologies: Commonalities and Divergences*. Edited by Abraham K.C. 195-213. Maryknoll: Orbis Books, 1990.

__________. "Religions, Salvation, Mission." In *Christian Mission and Interreligious Dialogue*. Edited by Paul Mozjes & Leonard Swidler, 126-139. Lewiston, New York: Edwin Mellen Press, 1990.

__________. "Spirituality for Inter-Faith Social Action." In *Liberation and Dialogue*. Edited by Xavier Irudayaraj, 64-73. Bangalore: Claretian Publications, 1989.

__________. "Wrestling in the Night." In *The Future of Liberation Theology: The Essays in Honour of Gustavo Gutierrez*. Edited by M.H. Ellis & O. Maduro, 450-469. Maryknoll: Orbis Books, 1989.

__________. "Analysis of Society and Indian Theology." In *Socio-Cultural Analysis*. Edited by Kuncheria Pathil, 139-148. Bangalore: Indian Theological Association, 1987.

__________. "Asia and Justice." In *Liberation in Asia: Theological Perspectives*. Edited by S. Arokiasamy & G. Gispert-Sauch, 1-15. Anand, Gujarat: Gujarat Sahitya Prakash, 1987.

__________. "Baptism and Conversion: The Lima Text in the Indian Context." In *A Call to Discipleship*. Edited by Godwin Singh, 166-187. Delhi: ISPCK, 1985.

__________. "Re-conceiving Theology in the Asian Context." In *Doing Theology in a Divided World*. Edited by Virginia Fabella and Sergio Torres, 124-143. Maryknoll, New York: Orbis Books, 1985.

__________. "Theological Education in the Social Context of India Today." In *Theological Education in India*. Edited by Felix Wilfred, 12-32. Bangalore: ATC, 1985.

__________. "Prophet and Poet in One." In *Jesus Today*. Edited by Sebastian Kappen, 167- 173. Madras: AICUF, 1985.

__________. "The Ecclesiology at Work in the Indian Church Today." In *Searching For an Indian Ecclesiology: The Statement, Papers and the Proceedings of the Seventh Annual Meeting of the Indian Theological Association*. Edited by Gerwin van Leeuwen, 191-212. Bangalore: ATC, 1984.

__________. "Theological Priorities in India Today." In *Irruption of the Third World: Challenge to Theology: Papers from the Fifth International Conference of Ecumenical Association of Third World Theologians*. Edited by Virginia Fabella and Sergios Torres, 30-41. Maryknoll: Orbis Books, 1983.

__________. "The Justice of God." In *Living Theology in Asia*. Edited by John C. England, 211-220. London: SCM Press, 1981.

__________. "Reflections on a Live-in-Experience 'Slum Dwellers.'" In *Asia's Struggle, for Full Humanity Towards a Relevant Theology*. Edited by Virginia Fabella, 50-56. Maryknoll: Orbis Books, 1980.

__________.. "The Justice of God." In *Third World Liberation Theologies: A Reader*.

Edited by Deane William Ferme, 348-355. Maryknoll, New York: Orbis Books, 1979.

__________. "The Basic Dilemma." Extract from "Development and Evangelization." In *The Church and Development Dilemma*. Edited by Tony Byrne, 41-46. Spearhead No. 5, Eldoret, Kenya: Gaba Publications, 1971.

ARTICLES IN JOURNALS

Rayan, Samuel "Spirituality for Our Times," *Jnanadeepa: Pune Journal of Religious Studies* 8/1 (January 2005): 127-128.

__________. "Jesus and the Struggles of the Masses in India," *Third Millennium* 11 (1999):18.

__________. "Decolonization of Theology." *Jnanadeepa: Pune Journal of Religious Studies* 1/2 (July 1998): 140-155.

__________. "Give Us This Day Our Daily Bread." *Basic Community Library Service* 7 (1997-1998): 1-7.

__________. "A Spirituality of Mission in an Asian Context." *SEDOS Bulletin* 29/6&7 (June & July, 1997): 194-206.

__________. "Inculturation and Peoples' Struggles." *Indian Missiological Review* 19 (1997): 35-45.

__________. "Local Cultures: Instruments of Incarnated Christian Spirituality." *SEDOS Bulletin* 29/6&7 (1997): 207-213.

__________. "Jesus: A Flesh-Translation of Divine Compassion." *Jeevadhara: A Journal of Christian Interpretation* 26/153 (1996): 212-229.

__________. "The *Kairos* of the Galilaioi: An Indian Liberationist Reading of John 1-7." *Jeevadhara: A Journal of Christian Interpretation* 25/146 (1995): 149-160.

__________. "Five Girls Ask, Why? and a Woman Says, No!: The Revolution of Mahlah, Hoah, Hoglah, Milcah and Tirzah, and of Queen Vashti." *Vidyajyoti Journal of Theological Reflection* 57/5 (1993) 306-313.

__________. "People's Theology," *Jeevadhara: A Journal of Christian Interpretation* 22/129 (1992): 175-202.

__________. "He is our Peace," *The Bulletin* 11/1 (1992): 94.

__________. "Editorial," *Jeevadhara: A Journal of Christian Interpretation* 21 (1991): 184.

__________. "Communalism or Commonalism: A Study of Matthew's Account of Jesus' Baptism (3:13-17)." *Indian Theological Studies* 25/4 (1988): 334-347.

__________. "The Johannine Perspective on Mission in Christ's Praxis." *Bangalore Theological Forum* 20/3 (1988): 3-16.

__________. "Third World Theologies: Where Do We Go From Here?" *Concilium* 199/5 (1988): 127-140.

__________. "Neither on This Mountain nor in Jerusalem: The Johannine Understanding of Worship." *Bangalore Theological Forum* 19/2 (1987): 121-29.

__________. "Spirituality." *Voices from the Third World* 10/3 (September, 1987): 62-63.

__________. "Editorial." *Jeevadhara: A Journal of Christian Interpretation* 17/99 (1987): 181-186.

__________. "Asia and Justice" *Vidyajyoti Journal of Theological Reflection* 50/7 (1986): 352-364.

__________. "Meditation: Worship Him with Bread and Rice." *Vidyajyoti Journal of Theological Reflection* 50/6 (July, 1986): 312-316.

__________. "Irruption of the Poor: Challenge to Theology." *Concilium*, 197/5 (1986): 101-112.

__________. "The Kingdom of God – A Blueprint for a New Society?" *Kristu Jyoti* 1/3 (May 1985): 24.

__________. "Editorial." *Jeevadhara: A Journal of Christian Interpretation* 14/81 (May, 1984).): 255-258.

__________. "The Truth that sets us Free." *Jeevadhara: A Journal of Christian Interpretation* 14/81 (May, 1984): 206-230.

__________. "The Irruption of the Third World – A Challenge to Theology." *Vidyajyoti Journal of Theological Reflection* 46/3 (1982): 106-127;

__________. "Outside the Gate: Sharing the Insult." *Jeevadhara: A Journal of Christian Interpretation* 11/63 (1981): 203-231.

__________. "The March Has Begun." *Jeevadhara: A Journal of Christian Interpretation* 9/51 (1979): 161-188.

__________. "Asian Theological Conference: A Reflex of its Dynamics." *Vidyajyoti Journal of Theological Reflection* 43/6 (July 1979): 246-260.

__________. "Jesus and the Poor in the Fourth Gospel." *Bible Bhashyam* 4/3 (1978): 213-228.

__________. "The Churches and Justice to Christians of Scheduled Caste Origin." *Word and Worship* 11 (1978): 236-245.

__________. "Sociological Factors and the Local Church as Eucharistic Community." *Vidyajyoti Journal of Theological Reflection* 40 (1976): 307-314.

__________. "The Underlying Philosophy of Jesus Christ." *The Rally* (Dec. 1974-Jan. 1975): 5.

__________. "Interpreting Christ to India: Contributions of Roman Catholic Theological Seminaries." *Indian Journal of Theology* 23/4 (1974): 223-231.

__________. "Christian Participation in the Struggle for Social Justice: Some Theological Reflections." *Clergy Monthly* 38 (August, 1974): 282-296.

__________. "Editorial." *Jeevadhara: A Journal of Christian Interpretation* 6 (1976): 255-258.

__________. "Flesh of India's Flesh." *Jeevadhara: A Journal of Christian Interpretation* 6/33 (1976): 259-267.

__________. "Human Well-Being on Earth and the Gospel of Jesus." *Jeevadhara: A Journal of Christian Interpretation* 5/7 (Jan-Feb 1972): 35-46.

__________. "An Indian Christology: A Discussion of Methods." *Jeevadhara: A Journal of Christian Interpretation* 1/3 (1971): 212-227.

__________. "Mission after Vatican II: Problems and Positions." *Indian Missiological Review* 59 (October 1970): 414-426.

SECONDARY SOURCES

BOOKS

De La Torre, Miguel A. ed. *Introducing Liberative Theologies*. Maryknoll, New York: Orbis Books, 2015.

Ferm, Deane William. *Profiles in Liberation: 36 Portraits of Third World Theologians*. Eugene, Oregon: Wipf & Stock Publishers, 2004.

Fitzmyer, Joseph A. *The Pontifical Biblical Commission: "The Interpretation of the Bible in the Church": Text and Commentary*. Rome: Gregorian Biblical Bookshop, 1995.

Fabella Virginia and Torres, Sergio. eds. *Doing Theology in a Divided World*. Maryknoll, New York: Orbis Books, 1985.

John, T.K. ed. *Bread and Breath: Essays in Honour of Samuel Rayan SJ on the occasion of his Seventieth Birth Anniversary, Jesuit Theological Forum Reflections*. Anand, Gujarat: Gujarat Sahitya Prakash, 1990.

John, P R. *Indian Faces of Jesus*. Anand: Gujarat Sahitya Prakash, 2012.

Kunnumpuram, Kurien ed. *The Vision of a New Church and a New Society: A Scholarly Assessment of Dr Samuel Rayan's Contribution to Indian Christian Theology*. New Delhi: Christian World Imprints, 2016.

__________. ed. *Jesus: The Relevance of His Person and Message for Our Times: Selected Writings of Samuel Rayan*. Vol I. Mumbai: St Paul's, 2013.

__________. ed. *Mission of the Church: Selected Writings of Samuel Rayan*. Vol II. Mumbai: St Pauls, 2013.

__________. ed. *In Spirit and Truth: Indian Christian Reflection on Spirituality and Worship: Selected Writings of Samuel Rayan*. Vol III. Mumbai: St Pauls, 2013.

__________. ed. *Nature, Woman and the Church: Indian Christian Reflections on Ecology, Feminism and Ecclesiology: Collected Writings of Samuel Rayan*. Vol. 1. Delhi: ISPCK: 2011.

__________. ed. *Doing theology: Indian Christian Reflections on Theologizing in India Today: Collected Writings of Samuel Rayan*. Vol. II. Delhi: ISPCK: 2011.

__________. ed. *God's Hope Becoming Visible: Indian Christian Reflections on some Relevant Issues of our Times: Collected Writings of Samuel Rayan*. Vol. III. Delhi: ISPCK: 2011.

Keene, Michael. *St Mark's Gospel and the Christian Faith*. Cheltenham: Nelson Thornes, 2002.

Kim, Kirsteen, *The Spirit in the World: A Global Conversation*. Maryknoll, New York: Orbis Books, 2007

__________. *Mission in the Spirit: The Holy Spirit in Indian Christian Theologies*. Delhi: ISPCK, 2003.

Lobo, Joseph. *Encountering Jesus Christ in India: An Alternative Way of Doing Christology in a Cry-for-life Situation*. Bangalore: Asian Trading Corporation, 2004.

Pinto, Cynthia. *Encountering Christ in the Suffering Humanity (Mt 25:31-46): Christological Contributions of Samuel Rayan and Raimon Panikkar and the Significance of the Suffering of the Battered Women of Maher from Christian and Hindu Perspective*, Wien & Berlin: LIT Verlag, 2009.

Rajendran, G. *Ezhava Community and Kerala Politics*. Trivandrum: The Kerala Academy of Political Science, 1974.

Scott, David Carlyle and David Emmanuel Singh. *Spiritual Traditions: Essential Visions for Living: A Book in Honour of David C. Scott*. Bangalore: United Theological College, 1998.

Tharsiuse, Nicholas. *Christian Faith: A Liberative Praxis: Theology of Samuel Rayan*. Delhi: ISPCK, 2015.

Wilfred, Felix. *Beyond Settled Foundations: The Journey of Indian Theology*. Madras: Department of Christian Studies, 1993.

ARTICLES IN EDITED BOOKS

Bartchy, S. Scott. 'Table Fellowship." In *Dictionary of Jesus and the Gospels*. Edited by Joel B. Green and Scot McKnight, 796-800. InterVarsity Press: Downers Grove, IL, 1992.

Doss, Mohan. "The Spirit of Life: Rayan's Thoughts on the Holy Spirit." In *The Vision of a New Church and a New Society/: A Scholarly Assessment of Dr Samuel Rayan's Contribution to Indian Christian Theology. Christian*

Heritage Rediscovered-26. Edited by Kurien Kunnumpuram, 39-65. New Delhi: Christian World Imprints, 2016.

George, Geomon Kizhakkemalayil. "The Immediacy of Presence in the Experience of God: An Indian Christian Perspective." In *World Christianity in Local Context: Essays in Memory of David A. Kerr*, Vol.1. Edited by Stephen R. Goodwin, 168-177. London: Continuum, 2009.

George, M.K. "Samuel, the Teacher." In *Bread and Breath: Essays in Honour of Samuel Rayan SJ. Jesuit Theological Forum Reflections* 5. Edited by T.K. John, 22-24. Anand, Gujarat: Gujarat Sahitya Prakash, 1990.

Gispert-Sauch, George. "Asian Theology." In *The Modern Theologians: An Introduction to Christian Theology in the Twentieth Century*, 2nd Edition. Edited by David F. Ford, 455-476. Oxford: Blackwell Publishers, 1997.

Gutiérrez, Gustavo. "Theology as Wisdom," in *Bread and Breath Bread and Breath: Essays in Honour of Samuel Rayan, on the Occasion of his Seventieth Birth Anniversary*. Edited by T. K. John, 3-5. Anand: Gujarat Sahitya Prakash, 1991.

__________. "Liberation Praxis and Christian Faith." In *Frontiers of Theology in Latin America*. Edited by Rosino Gibellini and trans. John Drury. 1-33. Maryknoll, New York: Orbis Books, 1979.

Hendricks, Barbara. "Life, Work and Word: The Contribution of Samuel Rayan SJ to the Renewal of US Missionaries." In *Bread and Breath: Essays in Honour of Samuel Rayan SJ. Jesuit Theological Forum Reflections* 5. Edited by T.K. John, 6-17. Anand, Gujarat: Gujarat Sahitya Prakash, 1990.

John, P. R. "The Divine in the Writings of Samuel Rayan." In *The Vision of a New Church and a New Society: A Scholarly Assessment of Dr Samuel Rayan's Contribution to Indian Christian Theology. Christian Heritage Rediscovered-26*. Edited by Kurien Kunnumpuram, 20-37. New Delhi: Christian World Imprints, 2015.

John, T.K. "Forward" to *Bread and Breath: Essays in Honour of Samuel Rayan, on the Occasion of his Seventieth Birth Anniversary*, x-xi. Anand: Gujarat Sahitya Prakash, 1991.

Kim, Kirsteen. "Indian Contribution to Contemporary Mission Pneumatology." In *Ancient World: Reader*, 5th edition. Edited by Robert Winter, Stephen D. Morad and Beth Snodderly, 289-295. California, Institute of International Studies, 2004.

Kunnumpuram, Kurien. ed. "Introduction." In *Jesus: The Relevance of His Person and Message for our Times: Selected Writings of Samuel Rayan*, Vol. 1, 7-12. Mumbai: St. Pauls, 2013.

__________. "Samuel Rayan – A Great Indian Theologian." In *Bread and Breath:*

Essays in Honour of Samuel Rayan SJ. Jesuit Theological Forum Reflections 5. Edited by T.K. John, 18-21. Anand, Gujarat: Gujarat Sahitya Prakash, 1991.

Mathew, P.T. "Exploring the Realm of Implicit Theologies: Reflections on Samuel Rayan's Method of Theologizing." In *The Vision of a New Church and a New Society: A Scholarly Assessment of Dr Samuel Rayan's Contribution to Indian Christian Theology. Christian Heritage Rediscovered-26.* Edited by Kurien Kunnumpuram, 309-329. New Delhi: Christian World Imprints, 2015.

Parappally, Jacob. "Meaning of Jesus Christ in the Indian Context: The Christological Vision of Samuel Rayan." In *The Vision of a New Church and a New Society: A Scholarly Assessment of Dr Samuel Rayan's Contribution to Indian Christian Theology. Christian Heritage Rediscovered-26.* Edited by Kurien Kunnumpuram, 3-19. New Delhi: Christian World Imprints, 2015.

Reghu, J. "'Community' as de-imagining nation: Relocating the Ezhava Movement in Kerala." In *Development, Democracy and the State: Critiquing the Kerala Model of Development.* Edited by K. Ravi Sharma, 40-53. New York: Routledge Taylor & Francis Group, 2010.

Tharsiuse, Nicholas. "The Social and Liberative Consequences of Samuel Rayan's Theology." In *The Vision of a New Church and a New Society: A Scholarly Assessment of Dr Samuel Rayan's Contribution to Indian Christian Theology. Christian Heritage Rediscovered-26.* Edited by Kurien Kunnumpuram, 198-210. New Delhi: Christian World Imprints, 2015.

Wilfred, Felix. "Liberation in India and the Church's Participation." In *Leave the Temple: Indian Paths to Human Liberation*, 175-195. Maryknoll, NY: Orbis, 1992.

ARTICLES IN JOURNALS

John, P.R. "Catholic Christology and the Challenge of Religious Pluralism." *Vidyajyoti Journal of Theological Reflection* 76/9 (2012): 942.

__________. "Images of Jesus Christ in India: in the Writings of Samuel Rayan." *Vidyajyoti Journal of Theological Reflection* 68/7 (2004): 499-500.

Jose, Ben. "A New Light to Enlighten the Indian Church: The Significance of Samuel Rayan SJ." *Asian Journal of Religious Studies* 60/2 (March 2015): 5-8.

Kim, Kirsteen "The Holy Spirit in Mission. Where and How is the Spirit Working in Religions, Cultures and Movements for liberation?" *Connections* 2/10 (Spring, 2001): 25

Sahi, Jyoti. "Indian Symbols of the Holy Spirit." *Jeevadhara: A Journal of Christian Interpretation* 45 (May-June 1978): 245-246.

INTERNET SOURCES

Gomes, Janina. "Theologian finds gospel in life of the people." National Catholic Reporter. May 12, 2000. http://www.natcath.org/NCR_Online/archives2/2000b/051200/051200o.html (accessed June 14, 2016).

Fernando, Leonard. "Indian Christian Theology." *Class Notes.*11 November 2011. http://leocpps.blogspot.in/2011/11/class-note-on-indian-christian-theology.html (accessed Au-gust 28, 2017).

PRIMARY SOURCE: ELISABETH SCHÜSSLER FIORENZA

BOOKS

Fiorenza, Elisabeth Schüssler. *Wisdom Ways: Introducing Feminist Biblical Interpretation.* Maryknoll, NY: Orbis Books, 2015.

__________. *Feminist Biblical Studies in the Twentieth Century: Scholarship and Movement.* Atlanta: Society of Biblical Literature, 2014.

__________. *Changing Horizons: Explorations in Feminist Interpretation.* Minneapolis: Fortress Press, 2013.

__________. *The Transforming Vision: Explorations in Feminist Theology.* Minneapolis, MN: Fortress Press, 2011.

__________. *Democratizing Biblical Studies: Toward an Emancipatory Educational Space.* Louisville: Westminster John Knox Press, 2009.

__________. The *Power of the Word: Scripture and the Rhetoric of Empire.* Minneapolis: Fortress Press, 2007.

__________. *Jesus and the Politics of Interpretation.* New York: Continuum, 2000.

__________. *Rhetoric and Ethic: The Politics of Biblical Studies.* Minneapolis: Fortress Press, 1999.

__________. *Jesus: Miriam's Child, Sophia's Prophet: Critical Issues in Feminist Christology.* New York: Continuum, 1995.

__________. *Discipleship of Equals: A Critical Feminist Ekklesia-logy of Liberation.* London: SCM Press, 1993.

__________. *Searching the Scriptures: A Feminist Introduction.* Vol.I. New York: Crossroad, 1993.

__________. *But She Said: Feminist Practices of Biblical Interpretation.* Boston: Beacon Press, 1992.

__________. *The Book of Revelation: Justice and Judgment.* Philadelphia: Fortress Press, 1985.

__________. *Bread Not Stone: The Challenge of Feminist Biblical Interpretation.* Beacon Press: Boston, 1984.

__________. *In Memory of Her: A Feminist Theological Reconstruction of Christian Origins*. London: SCM Press, 1983.

ARTICLES IN EDITED BOOKS

Fiorenza, Elisabeth Schüssler. "Between Movement and Academy: Feminist Biblical Studies in the Twentieth Century." In *The Bible and Woman: The Contemporary Period*. Vol. 9.1: *Feminist Biblical Studies in the Twentieth Century*, 1-17. Atlanta: Society of Biblical Literature, 2014.

__________. "Jesus of Nazareth in Historical Tradition," In *Thinking of Christ: Proclamation, Explanation, Meaning*. Edited by Tatha Wiley, 29-48. New York London: Continuum, 2003.

__________. "Women, Mission and the Catholicity of Theology." in *The Church in Mission: Universal Mandate and Local Concerns*. Edited by Thomas Malipurathu and Lazar. Stanislaus, 147-180. Anand: Gujarat Sahitya Prakash, 2002.

__________. "To Follow the Vision: the Jesus Movement as *Basileia* Movement." In *Liberating Eschatology: Essays in Honor of Letty M. Russell*. Edited by Letty M Russell, Margaret A Farley, Serene Jones, 123-155. Louisville, Kentucky: Westminster John Knox Press, 1999.

__________. "Discipleship of Equals: Reality and Vision." In *In Search of a Round Table: Gender, Theology and Church Leadership*. Edited by Musimbi R.A. Kanyoro, 1-11. Geneva: WCC Publications, 1997.

__________. "For Women in a Men's World: A Critical Feminist Theology of Liberation." In *The Power of Naming: A Concilium- Reader in Feminist Liberation Theology*, 3-15. New York: Orbis Books, 1996.

__________. "Introduction: Feminist Liberation Theology as Critical Sophialogy." In *The Power of Naming*, xiii-xxxix. Maryknoll, New York: Orbis Books, 1996.

__________. "The Bible the Global Context and the Discipleship of Equals." In *Reconstructing Christian Theology*. Edited by Rebecca S. Chopp & Mark Lewis Taylor, 79-99. Minneapolis: Fortress Press, 1994.

__________. "Women in the Early Christian Movement." In *Woman Spirit Rising: A Feminist Reader in Religio*. Edited by Carol P. Christ and Judith Plaskow, 84-92. San Francisco: HarperCollins, 1992.

__________. "Politics of Otherness: Biblical Interpretation as a Critical Praxis for Liberation." In *The Future of Liberation Theology: Essays in Honour of Gustavo Gutierrez*. Edited by Mark Ellis and Otto Maduro, 311-325. Maryknoll: Orbis, 1989.

__________. "The Will to Choose or to Reject: Continuing our Critical Work." In *Feminist Interpretation of the Bible*. Edited by Letty Russell, 125-136. Oxford: Basil Blackwell, 1985.

ARTICLES IN JOURNALS

Fiorenza, Elisabeth Schüssler. "Reaffirming Feminist/Womanist Biblical Scholarship." *Encounter* 67/4 (Fall 2006): 361-373.

__________. "Speaking About G*d." *Living Pulpit* 6/1 (Jan-Mar 1997): 20-21.

__________. "G*d at Work in Our Midst: From a Politics of Identity to a Politics of Struggle." *Feminist Theology* 13 (1996): 47-72.

__________. "Wartime as Formative." *The Christian Century* (August 16–23, 1995): 778-779.

__________. "Changing the Paradigms." *Christian Century* 107/25 (September 5-12, 1990): 797-798.

__________. "Changing the Paradigms." *Christian Century* 107/25 (September 5-12, 1990): 797-798.

__________. "Biblical Interpretation and Critical Commitment." *Theological Studies* 43/1 (1989): 5-18.

__________. "You Are Not to Be Called Father." *Cross Currents.* 29 (1979): 318.

__________. "Feminist Theology as a Critical Theology of Liberation." *Theological Studies,* 36/4 (1975): 605-625.

__________. "Roundtable Discussion on Feminist Methodology." *Journal of Feminist Studies in Religion* 1/2 (Fall 1985): 73-88.

SECONDARY SOURCES

BOOKS

Brezina, Corona. *Sojourner Truth's "Ain't I a Woman?" Speech: A Primary Source Investigation.* New York: Rosen Central Primary Source, 2005.

Cone, James H. *God of the Oppressed.* New York: Seabury Press, 1975.

Enander, Glenn. *Spiritual Leaders: Elisabeth Schüssler Fiorenza: Biography-Discussion of Work.* Philadelphia: Chelsea House, 2005.

Hogan, Linda. *From Women's Experience to Feminist Theology.* England: Sheffield Academic Press, 1995.

Isherwood, Lisa. *Introducing Feminist Christologies.* Cleveland, Ohio: Pilgrim Press, 2002.

Hopkins Julie M. *Towards A Feminist Christology: Jesus Of Nazareth, European Women and the Christological Crisis.* Grand Rapids, Michigan: William B. Eerdmans publishing Company, 1995.

J'annine, Jobling. *Feminist Biblical Interpretation in Theological Context.* Burlington: Ashgate, 2002.

Ji-Sum Kim, Grace. *The Grace of Sophia: A Korean North American women's Christology*. Cleveland: The Pilgrim Press, 2002.

Johannes Kristiansen, Staale and Rise, Svein. eds. *Key Theological Thinkers: From Modern to Post Modern*, Ashgate: England/USA, 2013.

Matthews, Shelly. Kittredge, Cynthia Briggs and Johnson-Debaufre, Melanie. eds. *Walk in the Ways of Wisdom: Essays in Honor of Schüssler Fiorenza*. Maryknoll, NY: Orbis Books, 2003.

O'Boyle, Aidan. *Towards Contemporary Wisdom Christology: Some Catholic Christologies in German, English and French, 1965-1995*. Roma: Editrice Pontificia Università Gregoriana, 2003.

Peacore, Linda D. *The Role of Women's Experience in Feminist Theologies of Atonement*. Eugene, Oregon: Pickwick Publications, 2010.

Ruether, Rosemary Radford. *Sexism and God-Talk: Toward a Feminist Theology – With a New Introduction*. Boston: Beacon Press, 1983.

Ricoeur, Paul. *Freud and Philosophy*: An Essay on Interpretation. New Haven: Yale University Press, 1970

Schaberg, Jane. Bach, Alice and Fuchs, Esther. eds. *On the Cutting Edge: The Study of Women in Biblical Worlds: Essays in Honor of Elisabeth Schüssler Fiorenza*. New York, London: Continuum, 2003.

Segovia, Fernando F. ed. *Toward a New Heaven and a New Earth. Essays in Honor of Schüssler Fiorenza*. Maryknoll: Orbis Books, 2003.

Segundo, Juan Luis. *Liberation of Theology*. Maryknoll, New York: Orbis Books, 1976.

Stephenson, Lisa. *Dismantling the Dualisms for American Pentecostal Women in Ministry: A Pneumatological Approach*. Leiden: brill, 2012.

Stevens, Maryanne. ed. *Reconstructing the Christ Symbol*. New York: Paulist, 1993.

West, Cornel. *The Cornel West Reader*. New York: Basic Civitas Books, 1999.

White, Hayden. *Tropics of Discourse*. Baltimore: John Hopkins University Press, 1978.

Wiley, Tatha. *Thinking of Christ: Proclamation, Explanation, Meaning*. New York, London: Continuum, 2003.

ARTICLES EDITED IN BOOKS

Ann Voipe, Medi. "Elisabeth Schüssler Fiorenza." In *The Student's Companion to the Theologians*. Edited by Ian S. Markham. West Sussex, UK: A John Wiley & Sons, Ltd., 2013.

Boff, Clodovis. "Methodology of the Theology of Liberation." In *Systematic Theology: Perspectives from Liberation Theology*. Edited by John Sobrino and Ignacio Ellacuria, 1-21. New York: Orbis, 1998.

Borg, Marcus J. "Portraits of Jesus in Contemporary North American Scholarship." In *Jesus in Contemporary Scholarship*, 18-46. Harrisburg, Pennsylvania, Trinity Press International, 1994.

Chabot, Rebecca and Neeley, Sarah. "Feminist Liberative Theologies." In *Introducing Liberative Theologies*. Edited by Miguel A. De La Torre, 172-186. Maryknoll, New York: Orbis Books, 2015.

Fiorenza, Francis Schüssler. "From Interpretation to Rhetoric: The Feminist Challenge to Systematic Theology." In *Walk in the Ways of Wisdom: Essays in Honor of Schüssler Fiorenza*. Edited by Shelly Matthews, Cynthia Briggs Kittredge, and Melanie Johnson-Debaufre, 17-45. Maryknoll, NY: Orbis Books, 2003.

Joseph, Pushpa. "Trailblazers: Elisabeth Schüssler Fiorenza and George M. Soares-Prabhu." In *On the Cutting Edge: The Study of Women in Biblical Worlds*. Edited by Jane Schaberg, Alice Bach, and Esther Fuchs, 53-68. New York, London: Continuum, 2004.

Metz, Baptist Johannes and Jürgen Moltmann,. "Theology in the Struggle." In *Faith and the Future: Essays on Theology, Solidarity, and Modernity*, 49-56. New York: Orbis Books, 1995.

Moesor, Annelies. "Elisabeth Schüssler Fiorenza." In *Key Theological Thinkers: From Modern to Post Modern*. Edited by Kristiansen Staale Johannes and Svein Rise, 327-337. Ashgate: England/USA, 2013.

Ruether, Rosemary Radford. "Can Christology Be Liberated from Patriarchy?" In *Reconstructing the Christ Symbol*. Edited by Maryanne Stevens, 7-29. New York: Paulist, 1993.

Segovia, Fernando F. "Looking Back, Looking Around, Looking Ahead: An Interview with Schüssler Fiorenza." In *Toward a New Heaven and a New earth: Essays in Honour of Elisabeth Schüssler Fiorenza*, 5-13. Maryknoll: Orbis Books, 2003.

ARTICLES IN JOURNALS

Aarde, Andries van. "Methods and models in the quest for the historical Jesus: Historical criticism and/or social scientific criticism," Department of New Testament Studies, University of Pretoria, *Theological Studies* 58/2 (2002): 423.

Johnson, Elizabeth. A. "Jesus the Wisdom of God: A Biblical Basis for Non-Androcentric Christology." *Ephemerides Theologicae Lovanienses: Louvain Journal of Theology and Canon Law* 61 (1985): 261-294.

West, Cornel. "Review of Elisabeth Schüssler Fiorenza, 'In Memory of Her.'" *Religious Studies Review* 11/1 (1985): 1-5.

INTERNET SOURCES

Aarde, Van Andries. "Methods and models in the quest for the historical Jesus: Historical criticism and/or social scientific criticism." June 12-15, 2001. Department of New Testament Studies, University of Pretoria, *HTS Theological Studies*, 58/2 (2002): 423. http://www.hts.org.za/ index.php/ HTS/article/viewFile/562/461 (accessed January 12, 2016).

Abrahams, Lutasha Ann-Louise. "A Critical Comparison of Elizabeth Schüssler Fiorenza's Notion of Christian ministry as a 'Discipleship of Equals' and Mercy Amba Oduyoye's notion as a 'Partnership of both Men and Women.'" University of the Western Cape, 2005. http://hdl.handle.net/11394/1446 (accessed September 5, 2015).

Chapman, Amy. "Suffering Our Way to Salvation: Ivone Gebara, Elisabeth Schüssler Fiorenza, and the Adequacy of the Cross as a Symbol for Women." Boston College School of Theology and Ministry, *Lumen et Vita*. June 2011. https:// ejournals.bc.edu/ojs/index.php/lumenetvita/article/download/1698/1555 (accessed November 4, 2015).

Beasley, Jonathan G. "Divinity School faculty recognized for scholarship, teaching." *Harvardgazette News*. May 16, 2011. http://news.harvard.edu/gazette/ story/ newsplus/divinity-school-faculty-recognized-for-scholarship-teaching/ (accessed September 15, 2015).

Cone, James H. "The Marty Forum: Elisabeth Schüssler Fiorenza." *American Academy of Religion Annual Meeting*, Chicago, Illinois. Panellists: Elisabeth Schüssler Fiorenza. Harvard University and Judith Plaskow, Manhattan College. Sunday, November 18, 2012. https:/ /www.youtube .com/watch=8 YAwm M52wjw (accessed July 12, 2015).

Education, E-Collaborative for Civic. "The 1960s-70s American Feminist Movement: Breaking Down Barriers for Women." https://tavaana.org/ en/ content/1960s-70s-american-feminist-movement-breaking-down-barriers-women (accessed on April 27, 2014).

Elliott, Megan. "A Critical Reflection on the "Debate." Between Elisabeth Schüssler Fiorenza and Musa Dube.", Masters of Arts in Theology: Department of Theology: University of St. Michael's College, 2012. http://hdl.handle.net/ 1807/34879 (accessed October 29, 2015).

Fiorenza, Elisabeth Schüssler. "Public Discourse, Religion, and Wo/men's Struggles for Justice, 51 *DePaul Law. Review* 1077, (2002)." http://via.library.depaul. edu/law-review/vol51/iss4/6 (accessed December 30, 2015).

__________. "Between Movement and Academy: Feminist Biblical Studies in the Twentieth Century." In *Feminist Biblical Studies in the Twentieth Century: Scholarship and Movement*, edited by Fiorenza Elisabeth Schüssler 1-18.

Society of Biblical Literature, 2014. http:// www.jstor.org/stable/j.ctt1287 n2p.5 (accessed March January 21, 2016).

__________. "Burke Lectureship on Religion & Society." *University of California Television.* January 31. Burke Lecture Series: 2008. https://youtu.be/ dUDlV8B1aHw (accessed July 21, 2015).

__________. "We are Church-A Kingdom of Priests." *Keynote Address for Women's Ordination Worldwide* (WOW) *Second International Conference Breaking Silence, Breaking Bread: Christ Calls Women to Lead.* Ottawa, Canada. July 22-24, 2005. http://womensordinationworldwide.org/ottawa-2005/2014/2/2/ elizabeth-schussler-fiorenza-we-are-a-church-a-kingdom-of-priests (accessed June17, 2015).

__________.The Power of the Word: Scripture and the Rhetoric of Empire." *Burke Lecture Leadership on Religion and Society.* March 3, 2007. https://youtu. be/ dUDlV8B1aHw (accessed July 21, 2015).

__________. "Changing the Paradigms." *Christian Century* September 1990. http:// www. religion-online.org/showarticle.asp?title=439 (accessed February 28, 2017).

Funk, Robert W. "Milestones in the Quest for the Historical Jesus." *The Fourth R,* 14: 4. July /August, 2001. https://www.westarinstitute.org/resources/ the-fourth-r/milestones-in-the-quest-for-the-historical-jesus/ (accessed July 2, 2016).

Kim, Min Hee. Elizabeth. The voice of the voiceless: reading Luke 1:46-55 in the context of HIV/AIDS in response to Elisabeth Schüssler Fiorenza's feminist theology. Thesis MTh. Stellenbosch University, 2013. http://hdl.handle.net/ 10019.1 /85677 (accessed October 5, 2015).

McKim, Donald K., ed. *Dictionary of Major Biblical Interpreters.* Downers Grove, Illinois: Intervarsity Press, 2007. Exported from Logos Bible Software (accessed October 21, 2016).

Museum, United States Holocaust Memorial. "KRISTALLNACHT: A Nationwide Program." *Holocaust Encyclopedia.* www.ushmm.org/wlc/en/article.php? ModuleId=10005143 (accessed October 3, 2015).

Trible, Phyllis. "The Creation of a Feminist Theology." *The New York Times.* 1 May 1983. http://www.nytimes.com/1983/05/01/books/the-creation-of-a-feminist-theology.html (accessed November 23, 2015).

Robert, Lawson. Fiorenza, Elisabeth Schüssler. "Jesus: Miriam's child, Sophia's Prophet." *Book Review.* February 25, 2013. http://robertlawson.weebly.com/ uploads/1/5/4/9/ 15493052/jesus_-_miriams_child_sophias_prophet.pdf (accessed November 2, 2015).

Tuohy, Anne Patricia. "Rhetoric and Transformation: The Feminist Theology of Elisabeth Schüssler Fiorenza." *Australian e-Journal of Theology.* Vol 5/1 (August 2005): 1-8. http://aejt.com.au/data/assets/pdf_file/0009/395514/AEJT_5.12_Tuohy.pdf (accessed January 3, 2016).

Tuohy, Anne Patricia. "Transforming the categories of western theology: a critical comparison between the political theology of Johannes Baptist Metz and the feminist theological hermeneutics of Elisabeth Schüssler Fiorenza." Australian Catholic University, 1999. http://researchbank.acu.edu.au/theses/16 (accessed September 4, 2015).

Voipe, Medi Ann. "Elisabeth Schüssler Fiorenza." *The Student's Companion to the Theologians*, edited by Ian S. Markham, 515-517. West Sussex, UK: A John Wiley & Sons, Ltd., 2013. DOI: 10.1002/9781118427170.ch73 (accessed august 2017).

Wood, Maureen Maeve. "A Dialogue on Feminist Biblical Hermeneutics: Elisabeth Schüssler Fiorenza, Musa Dube, and John Paul II on Mark 5 and John 4." University of Dayton. 2013. http://rave.ohiolink.edu/etdc/view?acc_num=dayton1375116095 (accessed September 10, 2015.

OTHER SOURCES

CHURCH DOCUMENTS

Catholic Bishops Conference of India. *Evaluation Report: Response of the General Body*. Trivandrum: 1996.

__________. "Final Statements." *XXXIII Biennial Plenary of the Catholic Bishops' Conference of India*. Bangalore: St John's, 2018.

CBCI. *Report of the General Meeting of the CBCI held in Nagpur*. New Delhi: CBCI, 1984.

CBCI, Commission for Women. *Gender Policy of the Catholic Church of India*. Delhi: CBCI Centre, 2010.

CBCI. *Report of the CBCI General Body Meeting. Trivandrum 13-21 February, 1996*. Cited in CBCI, Commission for Women. *Gender Policy of the Catholic Church of India*. Delhi: CBCI Centre, 2010.

Flannery, Austin. ed. *Vatican Council II: The Conciliar and Post-Conciliar Documents*, Vol. I&II. Bombay: St. Paul Publications, 1998.

Francis, Pope. *Evangelii Gaudium: Apostolic Exhortation on the Proclamation of the Gospel in Today's World*. 24 November 2013. Trivandrum: Carmel International Publishing House, 2013.

__________. *Misericoridiae Vultus: Bull of Indiction of the Extraordinary Jubilee of Mercy*. 11 April 2015. Vatican: Libreria Editrice Vaticana, 2015.

__________. *Laudato Si: Encyclical on Praise be to You: Our Care for Our Common Home*. 24 May, 2015. Kerala: Carmel International Publishing House, 2015.

John Paul II. *Catechism of the Catholic Church*. 15 August 1997. Libreria Vaticana: Liguori Publications, 1994.

John, Paul II. *Redemptoris Missio: Encyclical Letter on the Permanent Validity of the Church's Missionary Mandate*. 7 December 1990. Bangalore: Asian Trading Corporation, 1986.

__________. *Mulieris Dignitatem: Apostolic Letter on the Dignity of Women*. 15 August 1988. Bombay: St Paul Publications, 1988.

__________. *Sollicitudo Rei Socialis: Encyclical on Social Concern*. 30 December 1988. Mumbai: St Paul Publications, 1988.

__________. *Lumen Gentium*: Dogmatic Constitution on the Church." In *Vatican Council II: The Conciliar and Post-Conciliar Documents, Vol I*. Edited by Austin Flanner, 320-385. Mumbai: St. Paul Publications, 1998.

__________. "*Unitatis Redintegratio*: Decree on Ecumenism." In *Vatican Council II: The Conciliar and Post-Conciliar Documents, Vol I*. Edited by Austin Flanner, 408-496. Mumbai: St. Paul Publications, 1998.

__________. "*Nostra Aetate*: Declaration on the Relation of the Church to Non-Christian Religions." In *Vatican Council II: The Conciliar and Post-Conciliar Documents, Vol I*. Edited by Austin Flanner, 653-675. Mumbai: St. Paul Publications, 1998.

__________. "*Dignitatis humanae*: Declaration on Religious Freedom." *In Vatican Council II: The Conciliar and Post- Conciliar Documents,Vol I*. Edited by Austin Flanner, 703-714. Mumbai: St. Paul's, 1998.

__________. "*Gaudium et Spes*: Pastoral Constitution on the Church in the Modern World. *In Vatican Council II: The Conciliar and Post- Conciliar Documents, Vol I*. Edited by Austin Flanner, 794-879. Mumbai: St. Paul's, 1998.

__________. *Ecclesia in Asia: Post-Synodal Apostolic Exhortation on Mission in Asia*. 6 November 1999. Bangalore: NBCLC, 1999.

__________. *Novo Millennio Ineunte*: Apostolic Letter to the Bishops, Clergy and Lay Faithful at the Close of the Great Jubilee of the Year 2000.

__________. *Tertio Millennio Ineunte: Apostolic Letter with a Pastoral Plan for the Church in the New Millennium*. 6 January 2001.

__________. *Centesimus Annus*: Encyclical Commemorating the Hundredth year of *Rerum Novarum*. 1 May 1991. Trivandrum: Carmel International; Publishing House, 2005.

John XXIII, *Mater et Magistra: Encyclical on the role of the Church as Mother and Teacher in the light of Social Progress*. 15 May 1961.

__________. *Pacem in Terris: Encyclical on Peace on Earth.* 11 April 1963. Paulist Press, 1963.

Leo XIII. *Rerum Novarum:* Encyclical on the Rights and Duties of Capital and Labour.15 May1891.

Paul VI. "*Populorum Progressio*: Encyclical on Catholic Social Teaching on the Development of Peoples." 26 March 1967. In *Proclaiming Justice and Peace. Documents from John XXIII to John Paul II.* Edited by Michael Walsh & Brian Davis. Bangalore: Theological Publications in India, 1985.

__________. "*Humane Vitae*: Encyclical on the Regulation of Birth." In *Vatican Council II: The Conciliar and Post-Conciliar Documents,Vol II.* Edited by Austin Flanner, 397-416. Mumbai: St. Paul's, 1998.

__________. *Evangelii Nuntiandi,* Apostolic Exhortation on the Renewal of the Religious Life. In *Vatican Council II: The Conciliar and Post-Conciliar Documents. Vol II,* edited by Austin Flanner, 711-761. Mumbai: St. Paul's, 1998.

Pius XI. *Quadragesimo Anno: Encyclical on the 40th Year of Rerum Novarum.* 15 May 1931.

Pontifical Council for Justice and Peace. *The Compendium of the Social Doctrine of the Church.* London, New York: Burns & Oates A Continuum Imprint, 2004.

BOOKS

Abraham, K.C. ed. *Third World Theologies: Commonalities & Divergences.* New York: Orbis Books, 1990.

Abram, Anna. Peter Gallagher, and Michael, Kirwan. eds. *Philosophy, Theology and the Jesuit Tradition: 'The Eye of Love'.* Oxford: Bloomsbury T&T Clark, 2017.

Agrawal, Meenu. *Economic Reforms, Unemployment and Poverty: The Indian Experience.* New Delhi: New Century Publications, 2008.

Amaladoss, Michael. *Beyond Inculturation: Can the Many be One?* Delhi: ISPCK, 1998.

__________. *Peace on Earth.* Bandra, Mumbai: St Pauls, 2003.

__________. *The Asian Jesus.* Delhi: ISPCK & Chennai: IDCR, 2005.

Ardon, Patricia. *Post-War Reconstruction in Central America: Lessons from El Salvador, Guatemala, and Nicaragua.* Oxford: Oxfam GB, 1999.

Arrupe, Pedro. *Address delivered at the International Eucharistic Congress.* Philadelphia, August, 1976.

Balthazar, Hans Urs von. *Theo-drama: Theological Dramatic Theory IV: The Action,* trans. Harrison from *Theodramatik: Bd III: Die Handling.* San Francisco: Ignatius Press, 1994.

Barry, A. William. *Who Do You Say I Am? Meeting The Historical Jesus In Prayer.* Notre Dame IN: Ave Maria Press, 1996.

Beal, John P. James A. Coriden, and Thomas J. Green. eds. *New Commentary on the Code of Canon Law.* New York: Paulist Press, 2000.

Benedict XVI. *Jesus of Nazareth.* New York: Doubleday, 2007.

Boff, Leonardo. *The Lord's Prayer: The Prayer of Integral Liberation.* Maryknoll: Orbis Books, 1983.

Borden, Margot Esther. *Psychology in the Light of the East.* Lanham. Maryland: Rowman & Littlefield, 2017.

Borg, J. Marcus. *Conflict, Holiness and Politics in the Teachings of Jesus.* New York: Million, 1984.

Borg, J. Marcus. *Meeting Jesus Again for the First Time.* San Francisco: Harper San Francisco, 1994.

Botha, Eugene. Willem S. Vorster, *Speaking of Jesus: Essays on Biblical Language, Gospel Narrative, and the Historical Jesus.* Leiden, Netherlands: Brill Publishers, 1999.

Bowe, Barbara Ellen, Carol J. Dempsey, and Mary Margaret Pazdan. *Earth, Wind, and Fire: Biblical and Theological Perspectives on Creation.* Collegeville, Minn: Liturgical Press, 2004.

Braude, Ann. *Transforming the Faiths of Our Fathers.* New York: Palgrave Macmillan, 2004.

Chakkalakal, Pauline. *Discipleship a Space for Women's Leadership: A Feminist Theological Critique.* Mumbai: Pauline Publications, 2004.

Chandrababu, B. S. and L. Thilagavathi, *Woman: Her History and Her Struggle for Emancipation.* Chennai: Bharathi Puthakalayam, 2009.

Cheethan, David. Pratt Douglas, and Thomas, David. eds. *Understanding Interreligious Relations.* Oxford: Oxford University Press, 2013.

Chittister, Joan. *Heart of Flesh: A Feminist Spirituality for Women and Men.* Michigan: W. B. Erdmans, 1998.

Comblin, Joseph. *Holy Spirit and Liberation.* New York: Orbis Books, 1989.

Coontz, Stephanie. *A Strange Stirring: The Feminine Mystique and American Women at the Dawn of the 1960s.* New York: Basic Books, 2011.

Crossan, John Dominic. *Jesus: A Revolutionary Biography.* San Francisco: Harper, 1994.

Cush, Denise Robinson, Catherine York, Michael. eds. *Encyclopedia of Hinduism* London: Routledge, 2008.

D'Sa, Francis. ed. *The Dharma of Jesus, Interdisciplinary Essays in Memory of George M. Soares-Prabhu*. Pune: Institute for the Study of Religion, Anand: Gujarat Sahitya Prakash, 1997.

__________. ed. *Collected Writings of George M. Soares-Prabhu. Vol. 4: Theology of Liberation: An Indian Biblical Perspective*. Pune: Jnana Deepa Vidyapeeth, 2001.

D'Sa, Thomas. ed. *The Church in India in the Emerging Third Millenium*. Bangalore: N.B.C.L.C. 2005.

D'Souza, Dinesh. *What's So Great about Christianity?* Mumbai: Jaico Publishing House, 2008.

D'Souza, Donald. ed. *Final statements of the General Body Meetings of CBCI- 1966-2002*. New Delhi: CBCI, 1979.

Das, Somen. *Christian Ethics and Indian Ethos*. Delhi: ISPCK, 2001.

De Lubac, Henri. *Catholicism: Christ and the Common Destiny of Man*. San Francisco: Ignatius Press, 1988.

Deshpande, Ashwini. *The Grammar of Caste: Economic Discrimination in Contemporary India*. New Delhi: Oxford University Press, 2011.

Devashayam, V. ed. *Dalits and Women: Quest for Humanity*, Madras: Lutheran Theological College and Institute, 1992.

Doss, Mohan. *Christ in the Spirit: Contemporary Spirit Christologies*. Delhi: ISPCK, 2005

__________. ed. *Led By the Spirit: Mission, Spirituality and Formation*. Delhi: ISPCK, 2008

__________. Andreas Vonach and Jose, Thayil. eds. *Cross-Cultural Encounter, Experience and Expression of the Divine*. Innsbruck: Innsbruck University Press, 2009.

Dupuis, Jacques. *Who Do You Say I Am? Introduction to Christology*. Maryknoll, New York: Orbis Books, 1994.

Engineer, Asghar Ali, ed. *Problems of Muslim Women in India*. Hyderabad: Orient Longman Limited, 1995.

Espín, Orlando O. James, B. Nickoloff. eds. *An Introductory Dictionary of Theology and Religious Studies* Collegeville: Liturgical Press, 2007.

Fabella, Virginia, ed. *Asia's Struggle for Full Humanity Towards a Relevant Theology*. Maryknoll: Orbis Books, 1980.

__________. and Sergios, Torres. eds. *Irruption of the Third World: Challenge to Theology: Papers from the Fifth International Conference of Ecumenical Association of Third World Theologians*. Maryknoll: Orbis Books, 1983.

__________. and Sun Ai Lee Park. *We Dare to Dream, Doing Theology as Asian Women.* Maryknoll, New York: Orbis, 1989..

__________. Lee, Peter K.H. Suh Kwang-sun David. *Asian Christian Spirituality: Reclaiming Traditions.* Maryknoll, New York: Orbis Books, 1992.

__________. and Quirico, Pedregosa. eds. *Religious Life: A Service to Life in Asia Today: FABC Papers: Sixth Plenary Assembly of the Federation of Asia Bishops' Conference,* Manila, Philippines, 1995.

Falcao, Nelson. *A Church of the Laity.* Bangalore: KJC, 1991.

Fernandes, Walter. *The Indian Catholic Community: Its Peoples and Institutions in Interaction with the Indian Situation Today.* Brussels: Pro Mundi Vita, 1980.

Fiorenza, Francis Schüssler and John P. Galvin. eds. *Systematic Theology: Roman Catholic Perspectives.* Minneapolis: Fortress, 1991.

Fitzmyer, A. Joseph. *A Christological Catechism: New Testament Answers.* New York: Paulist Press, 1991.

Forum of Religious for Justice and Peace. eds. *It Shall Not Be So Among You.* Hyderabad: A Forum Publication, 1999.

Francis, Pope. Bergoglio, Jorge Mario. *Open Mind, Faithful Heart: Reflections on Following Jesus, Reflections on the scriptures and pastoral experiences of Pope Francis.* ed. Gustavo Larrazábal. Bangalore: Claretian Publications, 2013.

Fuellenbach, John. *The Kingdom of God: The Central Message of Jesus' Teachings in the Light of the Modern World.* Indore: Satprakashan Sanchar Kendra, 1994.

Gajiwala, Astrid Lobo. Theckanath, Varghese and Passanha, Raynah Braganza. eds. *Gender Relations in the Church: A Call to Wholeness and Equal Discipleship.* Delhi: Media House, 2012.

Gateley, Edwina. *A Warm, Moist Salty God: Woman Journeying Towards Wisdom.* Trabuco Canyon, CA: Source Books, 1993.

Gatwood, Lynne. *Devi and the Spouse Goddess: Women, Sexuality and Marriage in India.* New Delhi: Manohar Publications, 1991.

Geetha, V. *Patriarchy, Theorizing Feminism.* Calcutta: STREE, 2007.

Ghadially, Rehana. *Women in Indian Society: A Reader.* New Delhi: Sage Publications India Pvt. Ltd., 1998.

Ghodke, N. B. *Encyclopaedic Dictionary of* Economics. Delhi: Mittal Publications, 1985.

Griffith, Ralph T.H. Trans. *The Hymns of the Rigveda,* 3rd edition, Vol. II. Benares: E.J. Lazarus & Co., 1926.

Gutiérrez, Gustavo. *A Theology of Liberation: History, Politics and Salvation,* trans. Caridad Inda & John Eagleson. New York: Orbis, 1988.

Harvey, David. *A Brief History of Neoliberalism*. New York: Oxford University, 2005.

Hedlund, E. Roger. ed. *Christianity is Indian: The Emergence of an Indigenous Community*. Delhi: ISPCK, 2000.

Hellwig K., Monica. *Jesus: The Compassion of God*. Wilmington, Delaware: Michael Glazier, 1983.

Heredia, C. Rudolf. *A Church That is Poor and for the Poor*. Pune: Jnana-Deepa Vidyapeeth, 2013.

Ilaiah, Kancha. *The State and Repressive Culture- the Andhra Experience*. Hyderabad: Swecha Prachurenalu, 1989.

Iyengar, BKS. *The Illustrated Light on Yoga: An easy-to-follow Version of the Classic Introduction to Yoga*. New Delhi: Harper Collins, 2005.

Neusner, Jacob. *From Politics to Piety*. Englewood Cliffs, NJ: Prentice Hall, 1973.

Jogdand, Prahlad Gangaram and S. M. Michael. eds. *Globalization and Social Movements: Struggle for a Humane Society*. Jaipur: Rawat Publications, 2003.

Johnson, Elizabeth A. *She Who Is: The Mystery of God in Feminist Theological Discourse*. New York: Crossroad, 1993.

Joseph, M. P. ed. *Confronting Life: Theology Out of the Context*. Delhi: ISPCK, 1995.

Kaitholil, George. *Consecrated Life: Challenges and Opportunities*. Bandra, Mumbai: St Pauls, 2014..

Kalliath, Antony and Thomas, D'Sa. eds. *Retelling the Story of Jesus Through the Stories of People*. Bangalore: Sugranth Subodhana Publications & NBCLC, 2011.

Kärkkäinen, Veli-Matti. *Christology A Global Introduction*. Grand Rapids, Michigan: Baker Academic, 2013.

Karotemporel, Bishop Gregory. Jacob, Marangattu and Paul, Vithayathil. eds. *Church in India Tomorrow: A Roadmap for her Mission and Ministry in the Third Millennium*. Rajkot: Deepti Publications, 2011.

Kasper, Walter. *Jesus the Christ*. London: Burns and Oates, 1976.

Kasper, Walter. *The God of Jesus Christ: New Edition*. T &T Clark International, 2012.

Kavunkal, Jacob. *Anthropophany: Mission as Making a New Humanity*. Delhi: ISPCK, 2008.

Keene, Michael. *St Mark's Gospel and the Christian Faith*. Cheltenham: Nelson Thornes, 2002.

Himes, Kenneth. *Modern Catholic Social Teachings*. Washington, DC: Georgetown University Press, 2005.

Ketkar, Shridhar V. *The History of Caste in India*. Vol. 1. New York: Taylor & Carpenter, 1909.

Kim, Grace Ji-Sum. *The Grace of Sophia: A Korean North American women's Christology*. Cleveland: The Pilgrim Press, 2002.

Kulasrestha, Mahendra, ed. *Culture India: Philosophy, Religion, Arts, Literature and Society*. Delhi: Lotus Press, 2006.

Kunnumpuram, Kurien and Evelyn Monteiro, eds. *Towards a New Humanity: Reflections on the Church's Mission in India Today*. Bombay: St Pauls, 2005

__________. *Towards the Full Flowering of the Human: Interdisciplinary Studies on the Empowerment of* Women. Bandra, Mumbai: St Pauls, 2011.

Küster, Volker. *The Many Faces of Jesus Christ: Intercultural Christology*. Maryknoll, N.Y.: Orbis, 2001.

Lambert, Willi. *Directions for Communication: Discoveries with Ignatius. Loyola*. Bangalore: Claretian Publications, 2001.

Lankapalli, Prasad. *Hindutva Challenge: Christian Response as a Call to Community*. Delhi: ISPCK, 2014.

Lederach, John Paul. *Building Peace: Sustainable Reconciliation in Divided Societies*. Washington: United States Institute of Peace, 1997.

Leeuwen, Gerwin Van, ed. *Searchings for an Indian Ecclesiology*. Bangalore: ATC, 1984

Lockyer, Herbert. *All the Women of the Bible*. Grand Rapids: Zondervan, 1967.

Lonergan, Bernard. *Method in Theology* Toronto: University of Toronto, 1999.

MacArthur, John. *Twelve Extraordinary Women: How God Shaped Women of the Bible, and What He Wants to Do with You*. Nashville: Thomas Nelson, 2008.

MacArthur, John. *Twelve Extraordinary Women: How God Shaped Women of the Bible, and What He Wants to Do with You*. Nashville: Thomas Nelson, 2008.

Manohar, Christina. *Spirit Christology: An Indian Christian Perspective*. Delhi: ISPCK, 2009.

Marger, Martin. *Social Inequality, Patterns and Processes*. 5th edition. New York: MacGrow–Hill, 2011.

Marty, Martin E. and R. Scott, Appleby. eds. Fundamentalism *and the State: Remaking Politics, Economies, and Militance*. Chicago: University of Chicago Press, 1993.

Massey, James. *Indigenous People: Historical Roots*. Delhi: ISPCK, 1998.

McKim, Donald K. *Historical Handbook of Major Biblical Interpreter*. Downers Grove, Ill: InterVarsity Press, 1998.

McLean, Iain and Alistair, McMillan. *Oxford Concise Dictionary of Politics*. New York: Oxford University Press, 2009.

McLuhan, Marshall. *The Gutenberg Galaxy: The Making of Typographic Man*, London: Routledge and Kegan Paul, 1962.

McMahon, Christopher. *Jesus Our Salvation: An Introduction to Christology*. Winona, MN: Saint Mary's Press, 2007.

Michael, S.M. and Jose, Joseph. eds. *The Emerging Challenges to Christian Mission Today: Revisioning Mission from Religious, Cultural, Historical and Women Perspectives*. Pune, Ishvani Kendra, 2016.

Mikula, Maja. *Key Concepts in Cultural Studies*. Basingstoke: Palgrave Macmillan, 2008.

Miller, Susan. *Women in Mark's Gospel*. London, New York: T & T International A Continuum Imprint, 2004.

Min, Anselm Kyongsuk. *The Solidarity of Others in a Divided World: A Postmodern Theology After Postmodernism*. York Road, London: T & T Clark International, 2004.

Moltmann, Jürgen. *The Crucified God: The Cross of Christ as the Foundation and Criticism of Christian Theology*. London: SCM Press, 1974.

__________. *The Church in the Power of the Spirit*. New York: Harper & Row, 1975.

__________. *Creating a Just Future*. London: SCM. Press, 1989.

Monteiro, Evelyn and Kochurani, Abraham. eds. *Concerns of Women: An Indian Theological Response*. Bangalore: Dharmaram Publications, 2005.

Müller, Karl. *Mission Theology: An Introduction*. Nettal: Steyler Verlag 1987.

Nair, V. Balakrishnan. *Social Development and Demographic Changes in South India: Focus on Kerala*. New Delhi: M.D. Publications, 1994.

Narayan, D., R. Patel, K. Schafft, A. Rademacher, and S. Koch-Schulte, *Voices of the Poor: Can Anyone Hear Us?* New York: Oxford University Press, 2000.

Neuner, Joseph. *The Prophetic Role of the Laity*. Pune: National Vocation Service Centre, 1981.

Nolan, Albert. *Jesus Before Christianity*. New York: Orbis Books, 1976.

Noorokariyil, Siji. *Children of the Rainbow: An Integral Vision and Spirituality for Our Wounded Planet*. Delhi: Media House, 2007.

Nouwen, Henri J. Donald P. McNeill and Douglas A. Morrison. *Compassion: A Reflection on the Christian Life*. New York: Doubleday Image Books, 1982.

O'Collins, Gerald. *Christology: A Biblical, Historical, and Systematic Study of Jesus*. New York: Oxford University Press, 1995.

O'Boyle, Aidan. *Towards a Contemporary Wisdom Christology: Some Catholic Christologies in German, English and French, 1965-1995*. Roma: Editrice Pontificia Universita, Gregoriana, 2003.

Oduyoye, Mercy. *Hearing and Knowing*. Maryknoll: Orbis, 1986.

Ortega, Ofelia. *Women's Vision: Theological Reflection, Celebration, Action*. Geneva: WCC Publication, 1995.

Padinjarekuttu, Isaac, ed. *Biblical Themes for a Contextual Theology Today*. Vol. 1. Pune: Jnana Deepa Vidyapeeth, 1999.

Padinjarekuttu, Isaac, ed. *Biblical Themes for a Contextual Theology Today: The Collected Work of George Soares Prabhu*. Pune: JDV Theological Series, 1999.

Parappally, Jacob. *The Meaning of Jesus Christ: An Introduction to Christology*. Bangalore: Theological Publications in India, 2016.

Patel, Narayan, D., RK. Rademacher, Schafft, A. and Schulte, S. Koch. *Voices of the Poor: Can Anyone Hear Us?* .New York: Oxford University Press and the World Bank, 2000.

Pathil, Kuncheria. ed *Socio-Cultural Analysis*. Bangalore: Indian Theological Association, 1987.

Pieris, Aloysius. *An Asian Theology of Liberation*. Maryknoll, New York: Orbis Books, 1988.

Pieris, Aloysius. *God's Reign for God's Poor: A Return to the Jesus Formula*. Kelaniya: Tulana Research Centre, 1999.

Pinto, Joseph Prasad. *Journey to Wholeness: Reflections for Life in Abundance*. Bombay: St. Pauls, 2006.

Ponnumuthan, Selvister. Aerath, Chacko and Menachery, George, eds. *Christian Contribution to Nation Building: A Third Millennium Enquiry*. Cochin: Documentary Committee of CBCI-KCBC National Celebration of the Jubilee of St. Thomas and St. Francis Xavier: Distributors, Fr Zacharias Memorial Book Centre, 2004.

Pulickal, Jose A. *Dynamics of Jesus Community: Towards the Discipleship in Lucan Theology*. Bangalore: Asian trading corporation, 2007.

Quartiroli, Ivo. *The Digitally Divided Self: Relinquishing Our Awareness to the Internet*. USA: SIlens-Global Book Publishing, 2011.

Radford Ruether, Rosemary. *Women Healing Earth*. London: SCM, 1996.

Rahner, Karl. *Hearer of the Word*. Herder and Herder, 1969.

Raja, Arul M.R. *Jesus The Dalit*. Hyderabad: Volunteer Centre, 1996.

Rajkumar, Peniel. *Dalit Theology and Dalit Liberation: Problems, Paradigms and Possibilities*. Surrey, England: Ashgate, 2010.

Richard, J. Lucian. *A Kenotic Christology: In the Humanity of Jesus The Christ, The Compassion of Our God*. Washington, DC: University Press of America. Inc., 1982.

Rothermund, Dietmar. *India: The Rise of an Asian Giant*. New Haven and London: Yale University Press, 2008.

Rowland, Christopher. *The Cambridge Companion to Liberation Theology*. Cambridge: Cambridge University Press, 1999.

Ruether, Rosemary Radford. *To Change the World. Christology and Cultural Criticism*. London: SCM, 1981.

Ruether, Rosemary Radford. *Women Healing Earth*. London: SCM, 1996.

Saldanha, Virginia. ed. *Discipleship of Asian Women at the Service of Life*. Vol. II. Bangalore: Claretian Publications, 2011.

Saldanha, Virginia. Varghese, Theckanath and Julie, George. eds. *Women as Equal Disciples*. Delhi: Media House, 2016.

Sanctis, Rita. *A Quest for Life and Transformative Resistance: An Explorative Study on Religious and Philosophical Resources of Resistance to Female Foeticide and Infanticide in India*. Nijmegen, Netherlands: Radboud University, 2014.

Sanyal, Nilanjana. *Peace Loving Nations*. Delhi: Gyan Publishing House, 2010.

Sarkar, Sukhdeo Thorat and Katherine, Newman. eds. *Blocked by Caste: Economic Discrimination in Modern India*. New Delhi: Oxford University Press, 2010.

Sarkar, N. K. *Social Structure and Development Strategy in Asia*. Delhi: People Publishing House, 1978.

Sawyer, F. A. John. "The Blackwell Companion to the Bible and Culture." Oxford, UK: Blackwell Publishing Ltd., 2012.

Scheuerer, Franz Xavier. *Interculturality: A Challenge for Mission of the Church*. Bangalore: Asian Trading Corporation, 2001.

Schillebeeckx, Edward. *For the Sake of the Gospel*, trans. John Bowden. London: SGM Press, 1989.

Schneiders, Sandra Marie. *Women and the Word: The Gender of God in the New Testament and the Spirituality of Women*. New York: Paulist Press, 1986.

__________. *The Revelatory Text: Interpreting the New Testament as Sacred Scripture*. New York: Harper Collins, 1991.

Sharma, Krishna. *Bhakti and the Bhakti Movement: A New Perspective*. New Delhi: Munshiram Manoharlal Publishers, 1987.

Sheen, Fulton J. *Religion without God*. New York: Longmans, Green and Co., 1936.

Sheen, Fulton J. *Peace of Soul*. New York: Garden City Books, 1951.

Smith, Susan E. *Women in Mission: From the New Testament to Today*. New York: Orbis Books, 2015.

Sobrino, Jon. *The True Church and the Poor*, Translated by Mathew J. O'Connell. New York: Orbis Books, 1984.

__________. and Pico, Juan Hernandez. *Theology of Christian Solidarity*. New York: Orbis Books, 1985.

Srinivasan, Bina. *Negotiating Complexities: A Collection of Feminist Essays*. New Delhi: Promilla & CO Publishers in association with Bibliophile South Asia, 2007.

Steck, Christopher. *In union with the paschal mystery: the Eucharist and suffering in the thought of John Paul II, 317-321*. Philadelphia: St. Joseph's University Press, 2007.

Sugirtharajah, R.S. ed. *Asian Faces of Jesus*. New York: Orbis Books, 1993.

Theckaanth, Varghese and Julie, George. eds. *Living Nirbhaya: Pathways to Violence Free Church and Society*. Bangalore: Claretian publications, 2014.

Thottakara, Augustine. ed. *Religion and Politics in Asia Today*, Bangalore: Dharmaram, 2001.

Tripathy, P.C. *Contemporary Social problems and the Law*. New Delhi: A.P.H. Publishing Corporation, 2000.

Vanier, Jean. *Encounter the 'Other'*. New Jersey Mahwah: Paulist Press, 2006.

Vivekananda, Swami. *The Complete Works of Swami Vivekananda*, Vol. VI. Kolkata: Advaita Ashrama, 1979.

Vorster, Willem S. Botha, J. Eugene. *Speaking of Jesus: Essays on Biblical Language, Gospel Narrative, and the Historical Jesus*. Leiden, Netherlands: Brill Publishers, 1999.

Weber, Max. *The Theory of Social and Economic Organization*. Trans, by A. M. Henderson and Talcott Parsons. Edited by Talcott Parsons. New York: Free Press, 1964.

Webster, John C. B. *The Dalit Christians: A History*. Delhi: ISPCK, 1994. .

Wooden, Cindy. Joshua J McElwee. *A Pope Francis Lexicon*. Collegeville Minnesota: Liturgical Press, 2018.

Wolters, T. Hielke. *Theology of Prophetic Participation*. Delhi: ISPCK /UTC, 1996.

ARTICLES IN EDITED BOOKS

Abraham, Kochurani. "The Place and Role of Women in the Catholic Church." In *Towards the Full Flowering of the Human: Interdisciplinary Studies on the Empowerment of* Women. Edited by. Kurien Kunnumpuram and Evelyn Monteiro, 50-72. Bandra, Mumbai: St Pauls, 2011.

Amaladoss, Michael. "Religious Pluralism and Mission." In *A Vision of Mission in the New Millennium*. Edited by Thomas Malipurathu and Lazar Stanislaus, 63-82. Madras: St. Pauls Publications, 2001

__________. "The Multi-Religious Experience and Indian Experience." in *Society and Church: Challenges Theologizing in India Today*. Edited by. Victor Machado, 165-184. Bangalore: Dharmaram Publications, 2004.

Arokiasamy, Soosai. "Doing Theology with Asian Resources in the Context of FABC." In *Reaping a Harvest from the Asian Soil*. Edited by Vimal Tirimanna, 1-20. Bangalore: Asian Trading Corporation, 2011.

Boff, Clodovis. "Methodology of the Theology of Liberation." In *Systematic Theology: Perspectives from Liberation Theology*. Edited by John Sobrino and Ignacio Ellacuria, 1-19. New York: Orbis, 1993.

Doss, Mohan. "Jesus: A Paradigm for a Spirituality of Solidarity." In *Led By the Spirit: Mission, Spirituality and Formation*, 140-156. Delhi: ISPCK, 2008.

Galvin, J. P. "Jesus Christ." In *Systematic Theology: Roman Catholic Perspectives*. Edited by Francis Schüssler Fiorenza and John P. Galvin, 297-314. Minneapolis: Fortress, 1991.

Gnanadason, Aruna. "Feminist Methodology: Indian Women's Experience." In *Confronting Life: Theology Out of the Context*. Edited by. M. P. Joseph, 174-193. Delhi: ISPCK, 1995.

Groenhout, Ruth. "*Kenosis* and Feminist Theory." in *Exploring Kenotic Christology: The Self-Emptying of God. Edited by* C. Stephen Evans, 291-312. New York: Oxford University Press, 2006.

Gutzler, Antoinette "Coming Out of the Shadows: A Feminist Vision of a Participatory Church." In *Towards the Full Flowering of the Human. Edited* by Kunnumpuram and Monteiro, 163- 177. Mumbai: St Paul's, 2011.

Hollenbach, David. "Commentary on *Gaudium et Spes*: Pastoral Constitution on the Church in Modern World." In *Modern Catholic Social Teaching: Commentaries and Interpretations*, Second Edition. Edited by Kenneth R. Himes, 266-291. Washington DC: Georgetown University Press, 2017.

Kavunkal, Jacob. "Vatican II and the Mission of the Church in India." In *Quest for an Indian Church: An Exploration of the Possibilities Opened up by Vatican II*. Edited by Kurien Kunnumpuram, and Lorenzo Fernando, 31-45. Anand, Gujarat, India: Gujarat Sahitya Prakash, 1993.

Kavunkal, Jacob. "Church's Service to the World." In *Vatican II: A Gift & A Task. International Colloquium to Mark the 40th Anniversary of Vatican Council II*. Edited by Jacob Kavunkal, Errol D'Lima and Evelyn Monteiro, 116-130. Mumbai: St. Pauls, 2006.

Lobo, Astrid. "Women." In *A Pope Francis Lexicon*. Edited by. Cindy Wooden, Joshua J McElwee. 190-195. Collegeville Minnesota: Liturgical Press, 2018.

Lobo, Surekha. "The Emerging Challenges to Christian Mission Today." In *The Emerging Challenges to Christian Mission Today: Revisioning Mission from Religious, Cultural, Historical & Women Perspectives*. Edited by S.M. Michael & Jose Joseph, 51-60. Pune: Ishvani Kendra, 2016.

Mattam, Joseph. "Formation of Evangelizers for the Church's Mission and Ministry in the 3rd Millennium." *Paper Presented in the National Mission Seminar*. Rajkot, 2010.

Michael, S. M. "Inculturation in the Context of India." In *In His Foot Steps: Together Towards the New Millennium. Divine Word Missionaries 1875-2000*. Edited by Scrampical Clarence, 167-173. Indore: Divine Word Missionaries, 2000.

Monteiro, Evelyn. "Who will Break down the Wall?" In *Dreams and Visions: New Horizons for an Indian Church: Essays in Honour of Professor Kurien Kunnumpuram*. Edited by. Rosario Rocha and Kuruvilla Pandikattu, 233-254. Pune: Jnana-Deepa Vidyapeeth, 2002.

__________. "Towards Partnership in a Participatory Church: A Feminist Dream and Vision." In *Concerns of Women: An Indian Theological Response*, eds. Evelyn Monteiro & Kochurani Abraham, 103-129. Bangalore: Dharmaram Publications, 2005.

Muricken, Ajit. "Foreword" to *Secular Challenge to Communal Politics – A Reader*, ed. P. R. Ram, iii-xi. Mumbai: Vikas Adhyayan Kendra, 1999.

Ott, Craig. Stephen J. Strauss and Timothy C. Tennent. "Introduction." In Encountering *Theology of Mission*: Biblical Foundations, Historical Developments and Contemporary Issues, xi-xxx. Grand Rapids: Baker Books, 2010.

Parappally, Jacob. "Christian Leadership and the Praxis of Jesus." In *Christian Leadership: The Shifting Focus in Theological Education*. Edited by Antony Kalliath. Bangalore: Dharmaram Publications, 2001.

Rahner, Karl. "The Position of Women in the New Situation in which the Church Finds Herself." In *Theological Investigations*, Vol 8, trans., by David Bourke, 75-93. New York: Herder & Herder, 1971.

Saldanha, Virginia. "Christian Discipleship: Women's' Perspective." In *The Church in India in the Emerging Third Millennium*. Edited by Thomas D'Sa, 454-474. Bangalore: NBCLC, 2005.

Samarakone, A Joseph. "A Response to the Case-Study," in *Liberative Struggles in a Violent Society: Proceedings of the Workshop on the "Dynamics of the Liberative Struggles of the Poor and the Oppressed."* Edited by John Vattamattam, Varghese Theckanath, S. Arokiasamy and Thoonunkaparambil K. John, 19-32. Hyderabad: Forum Publications, 1991.

Schweitzer, Don. "Preface" to *Contemporary Christologies: A Fortress Introduction*, vii-viii. Minneapolis, Minnesota: Fortress Press, 2010.

Soares-Prabhu, George M "The Miracles: Subversion of a Power Structure?" In *Jesus Today*. Edited by Sebastian Kappen, 21-29. Madras: AICUF, 1985.

__________. "The Spirituality of Jesus as a Spirituality of Solidarity and Struggle." In *Liberative Struggles in a Violent Society*. Edited by John Vattamattam, Varghese Theckanath, S. Arokiasamy and Thoonunkaparambil K. John, 136-161. Hyderabad: A Forum Publication, 1991.

__________. "From Alienation to Inculturation: Some Reflections on Doing Theology in India Today." In *Biblical Themes for a Contextual Theology Today: Collected Writings of George M. Soares-Prabhu, Vol.1*. Edited by Isaac Padinjarekuttu, 79-112. Pune: JDV, 1999.

__________. "Radical Beginnings: The Jesus Community as the Archetype of the Church." In *Collected Writings of George M. Soares Prabhu, Vol IV: Theology of Liberation: An Indian Biblical Perspective*. Edited by Francis X. D'Sa, 136-149. Pune: Jnana-Deepa Vidyapeeth Theology Series, 2001

__________."Jesus and the Poor." In *Collected Writings of George M. Soares Prabhu. Vol. IV: Theology of Liberation: An Indian Biblical Perspectiv*e. Edited by Francis X. D'Sa, 173-197. Pune: JDV Theological Series, 2001.

__________. "The Spirituality of Jesus." In *Collected Writings of George M. Soares Prabhu, Vol III: Biblical Spirituality of Liberative Action*. Edited by Scaria Kuthirakkattel, 85-104. Pune: Jnana-Deepa Vidyapeeth, Theology Series, 2003.

__________. "The Jesus of Faith: A Christological Contribution to an Ecumenical Third World Spirituality." In *The Dharma of Jesus*. Edited by. Francis Xavier D'Sa., 267-295. Maryknoll, New York: Orbis Books, 2003.

Tagle, Antonio Luis. "The Mission of the Church in Asia: Living the Incarnation in Poverty and Plurality." In *Reaping a Harvest from the Asian Soil*. Edited by Vimal Tirimanna, 128-129. Bangalore: Asian Trading Corporation, 2011.

Tharakan, T.D John and Mani, CST. "Liberative Struggles in a Violent Society." In *Liberative Struggles in a Violent Society: Proceedings of the Workshop on the "Dynamics of the Liberative Struggles of the Poor and the Oppressed."* Edited by John Vattamattam, Varghese Theckanath, S. Arokiasamy and Thoonunkaparambil K. John, 97-110. .Hyderabad: A Forum Publications, 1991

Vithayathil, Varkey Cardinal. "Foreword" to *Gender Policy of the Catholic Church of India* Delhi: CBCI Centre, 2010.

Wiley, Tatha. "Creation Restored: God's Basileia, the Social Economy, and the Human God." in *Earth, Wind, and Fire: Biblical and Theological Perspectives on Creation*. Edited by Barbara Ellen Bowe, Carol J. Dempsey, Mary Margaret Pazdan, 77-102. Collegeville, Minnesota: Liturgical Press, 2004.

Wilfred, Felix. "A Vision for the New Century: Role of Religious and Approaches to Christian Mission." In *A Vision of Mission in the New Millennium*. Edited by Thomas Malipurathu and Lazar Stanislaus, 83-114. Mumbai: St Paul's Publications, 2001.

ARTICLES IN JOURNALS

Abraham, Kochurani. "The Place and Role of Women in the Catholic Church." *Jnanadeepa: Pune Journal of Religious Studies* 7/1 (January 2004):51-68.

Michael Amaladoss, "Faith and Justice in a Postmodern World," *Promotio Iustitiae* 100 (2008/3): 34-40.

Amaladoss, Michael. "The Kingdom of God as the Goal of Mission." *Vaiharai* 1 (1996) 277-292.

Bali, Gali. "Asian Synod and Concerns of the Local Church." *Jeevadhara: A Journal of Christian Interpretation* 28/166 (July 1998): 319.

Barth, Christoph. "Notes on 'Return' in the Old Testament." *Ecumenical Review* 19/3 (July 1967): 310-312.

Catholic Bishops Conference of India (CBCI). "'The Church in Dialogue.' The Final Statement of 25th General Body Meeting of the CBCI. Jalandhar 1-8 March, 2002." *Indian Theological Studies* 39/3&4 (2002): 375-378.

D'Souza, Philomena. "Weaving an Empowering Spirituality for Women." *Jnanadeepa: Pune Journal of Religious Studies* 7/2 (July 2004): 91

Dabre, Bishop Thomas. "Christian Influence in the Transformation of Indian Society. II. Towards an Indian Christology." *Vidyajyoti Journal of Theological Reflection* 67 (2003): 109.

De Souza, Alfred. "The Relevance of Christianity in India Today." *Vidyajyoti Journal of Theological Reflection* 47 (January to December, 1984): 4-25.

Editorial. "Easter, Freedom, Woman." *Vidyajyoti Journal of Theological Reflections* 72/3 (March 2008): 161-164.

Guha, Ramachandra. "Ten Years of Change: Politics and Play." *The Telegraph* 36/30 (August 2017).

Gonsalves, Francis. "Interview with His Grace Archbishop Anil Couto." *Asian Journal of Religious Studies* 65/4 (July-August, 2018): 20-23.

Irudayadason, Nishant A. "The Role of Religion in Indian Secularism." *Smart Companion India*, 8/2 (February, 2017): 12-13.

Jayanth, Matthew. "Body Spirituality: Incarnation as an Invitation to an Embodied Spirituality." *Jnanadeepa: Pune Journal of Religious Studies* 7/2 (July 2004): 112-135.

Jose, Dennis. "A Contemporary Biblical Perspective on the Vow of Poverty." *Indian Journal of Christian Spirituality* 30/1 (January-March, 2017): 44.

Kalliath, Antony. "Revisiting Liberation Theology in a Neo-Liberal World." *Vidyajyoti Journal of Theological Reflections* 72/3 (March, 2008): 174.

Kavunkal, Jacob. "The Eucharist and Mission," *Jnanadeepa: Pune Journal of Religious Studies* 8/2 (July 2005): 85.

Kumar, Dr Pawan. "Religious Pluralism in Globalized India: A Constitutional Perspective" IOSR *Journal of Humanities and Social Science* 3/3 (Sep-Oct. 2012): 05-10.

Mangai, Poulose. "Editorial: To Be A Responsive Church in India Today." *Vidyajyoti Journal of Theological Reflections* 82/3 (March 2018): 3.

Neusner, Jacob. 'Two Pictures of the Pharisees: Philosophical Circle or Eating Club?' *Anglican Theological Review* 64 (1982): 525-538.

Oommen, Abraham. "Editorial: The Mystery of the Life Restored." *National Council of Churches Review* Vol. 116/4 (April 1996): 226.

Pattery, George. "Gandhian Social Vision for the Twenty-First Century." *Jnanadeepa: Pune Journal of Religious Studies* 2/1 (1999): 42-43.

Rathinam, Selva. "Biblical Understanding of Peace." *Jnanadeepa: Pune Journal of Religious Studies* 21/1 (January 2017): 11-14.

Rilloma, C. Nestor. "The Challenges of Emancipatory Theological Education for Churches in the Third World." *Journal Article Tag Suite* 13/2 (autumn 2002): 121.

Ruether, Rosemary Radford. "The Liberation of Christology from Patriarchy." *Religion and Intellectual Life* 2 (1985): 116-128.

Stanislaus, Lazar. "Challenges to Mission and Characteristics of a Missionary," *Word & Worship* 34/1&2 (January 2001): 1-2.

Soares-Prabhu, George M. "The Table Fellowship of Jesus: It's Significance for *Dalit* Christians in India Today." *Jeevadhara: A Journal of Christian Interpretation* 22, (1999): 152-53.

Sobrino Jon and Wilfred, Felix. "Introduction: The Reasons for Returning to This Theme." *Concilium* 5 (2001): 14-15.

Team Herald, "Inter-religious conference sends message of peace and unity." *Herald: The Voice of Goa* 6 (April 2018): 5.

Telesphore P. Cardinal Toppo, "Indian Church-Leadership of Tomorrow." *Jeevadhara: A Journal of Christian Interpretation* 44/259 (January 2014): 5-12.

Tirimanna, Vimal. "Some Salient Contributions of the FABC to the Asian Churches During the Past 40 Years." *Asian Horizons* 6/4 (December 2012): 597-615.

Veluswamy, Jeyaraj. "Our Jesuit Faith Today: An Indian Perspective." *Promotio Iustitiae* 104 (2010/1): 86-92.

Wilfred, Felix. "Church's Commitment to the Poor in the Age of Globalization." *Vidyajyoti Journal of Theological Reflections* 62 (1998): 87.

Wilfred, Felix. "Temptation of the Church in India Today." *Vidyajyoti Journal of Theological Reflection* 47 (1983): 320-333.

UNPUBLISHED RESEARCH PAPER

Lobo, Surekha. "Compassion as Commitment to Christian Life: A Holistic Dimension of Theological Response to the Challenges Presented in Evangelii Gaudium." *A Research Paper Submitted to the Faculty of Theology in Partial Fulfilment of the Requirements for the Pre-doctoral Programme.* Pune: Jnana-Deepa Vidyapeeth, 2015.

INTERNET SOURCES

Brueggemann, Walter. "The Alternative Community of Moses." In *The Prophetic Imagination*, 1978. http://teacherrenewal.wiki.westga.edu/file/vicw/Prophetic Imag-ination.pdf (accessed September 10, 2014).

CBCI Commission for Education and Culture, "The Contribution of the Indian Catholic Church in the Field of Education" http://www.cbcieducation.com/contribution.aspx (accessed July25, 2018).

Chaudhary, Prabhat. "Impact of Economic Liberalization on Employment Generation in India" *PhD Thesis* on Commerce, C.C.S. University, Meerut, March 10, 2010. URI: http://hdl.handle.net/10603/24233 (accessed August 19, 2017).

CNA/EWTN News, "Spiritual Generosity is form of Solidarity, Pope States" Rome, Italy, May 30, 2013, as cited in Mary Sujita, "Solidarity for Life on The Periphery," *UISG PLENARY ASSEMBLY*, ROME: May,2016, http://www.internationalunionsuperiorsgeneral.org/wp-content/uploads/2016/ 04/Pl-2016_ -Sujita_ENG.pdf (accessed May, 2014)

Cupich, Blase J. "Foreword" to Pope Francis, *Walking with Jesus: A Way Forward for the Church.* Chicago: Loyola Press, 2015. https://www.amazon.com/ Walking-Jesus-Way-Forward-Church/dp/08294425 (accessed February 12, 2018).

Desk, Express Web. "Passive Euthanasia: Church says 'taking of innocent life is never a moral act.'" 12 March, 2018. http://indianexpress.com/article/ india/ passive-euthanasia-church-says-taking-of-innocent-life-is-never-a-moral-act5094906/(acessed April 2, 2018).

Fernandes, Stephen. National Secretary, *Catholic Bishops' Conference of India* (CBCI) *Office for Justice Peace and Development.* http://www.cbci.in/ detail_Slide.\